A THOUSAND SHIPS

Volume 1

A THOUSAND SHIPS

by Eric Shanower

Age of Bronze
Volume 1
A Thousand Ships

ISBN 1-58240-200-0

Published by
Image Comics, Inc.
Office of Publication: 1942 University Ave. Suite 305
Berkeley, CA 94704

Erik Larsen *Publisher*
Todd McFarlane *President*
Marc Silvestri *CEO*
Jim Valentino *Vice President*

Eric Stephenson *Executive Director*
Brett Evans *Production Manager*
Jim Demonakos *PR & Marketing Coordinator*
Allen Hui *Production Artist*
Joe Keatinge *Traffic Manager*
Mia MacHatton *Administrative Assistant*
Jonathan Chan *Production Assistant*

The story of
A Thousand Ships
was originally serialized in
the comic book series
Age of Bronze,
issues 1 though 9.

First printing July 2001
Second printing November 2003
Third printing November 2005

Visit the *Age of Bronze* website at
www.age-of-bronze.com

Printed in Canada.

For Mom.

Contents

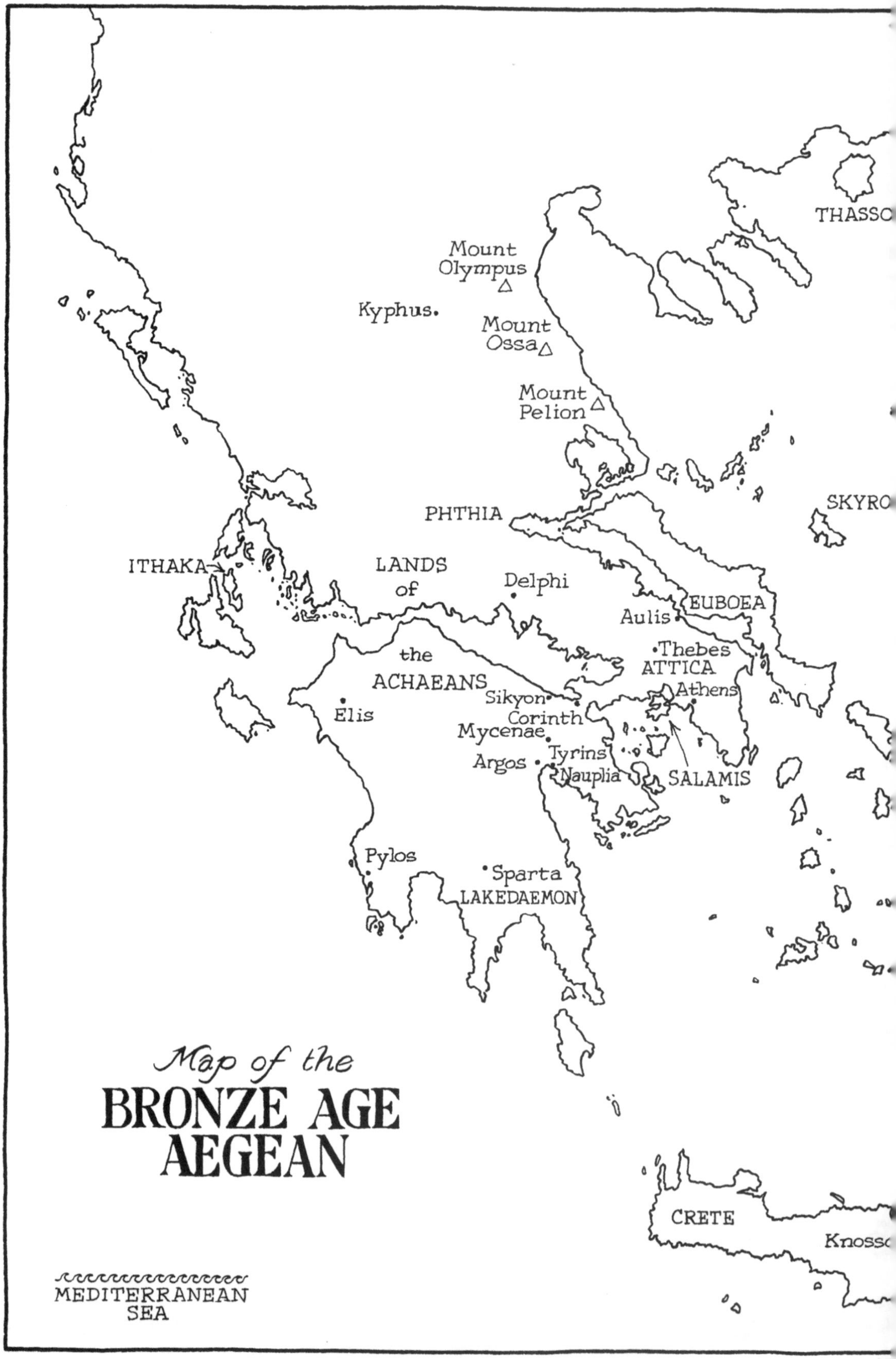
Map of the
BRONZE AGE
AEGEAN
Mount
Olympus
Kyphus.
Mount
Ossa
Mount
Pelion
THASSO
SKYRO
PHTHIA
ITHAKA
LANDS
of
the
ACHAEANS
Delphi
Aulis
EUBOEA
Thebes
ATTICA
Athens
Sikyon
Corinth
Mycenae
Elis
Tyrins
Argos
Nauplia
SALAMIS
Pylos
Sparta
LAKEDAEMON
CRETE
Knosso
MEDITERRANEAN
SEA

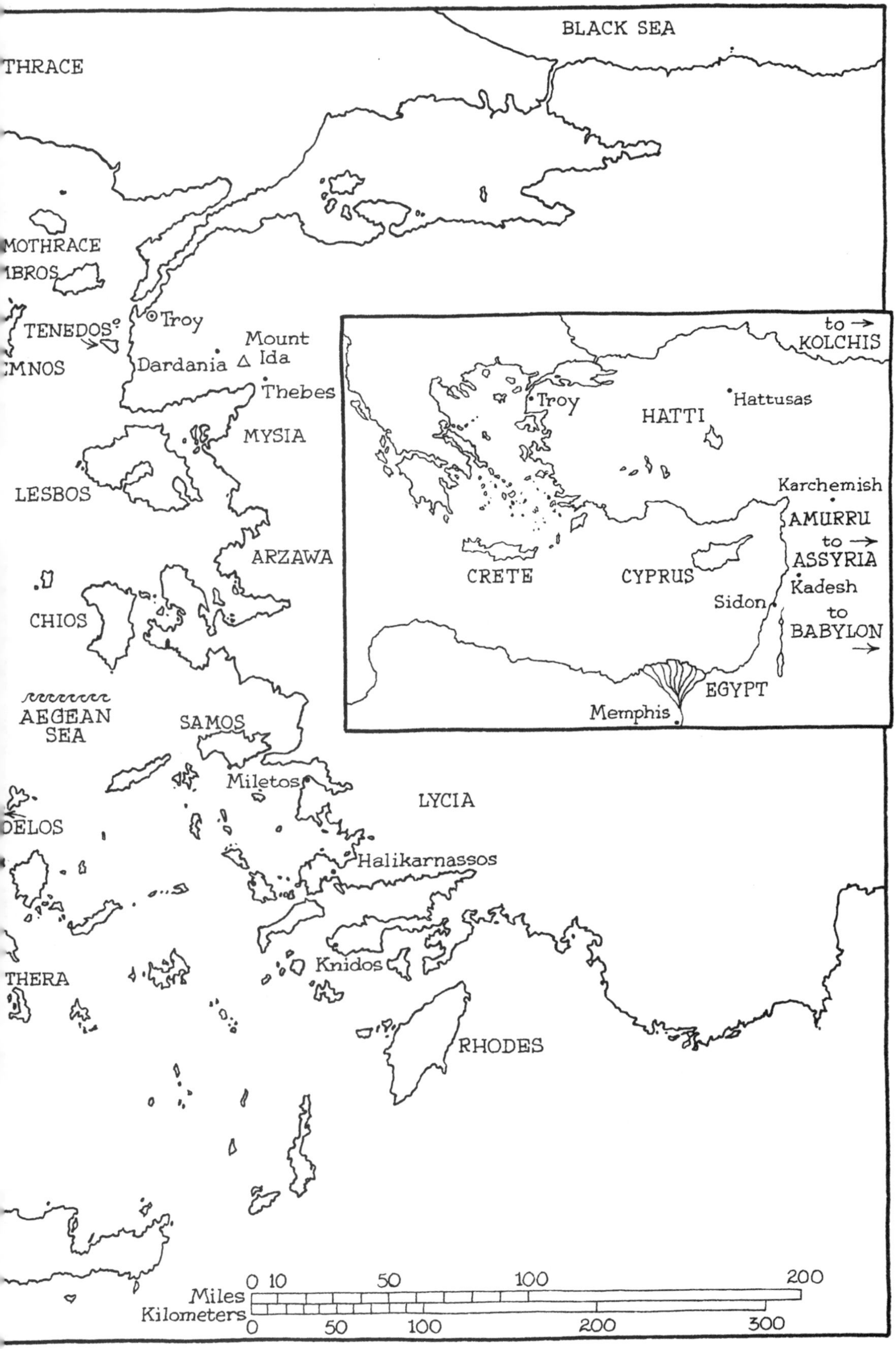
BLACK SEA
THRACE
MOTHRACE
IBROS
TENEDOS
Troy
Mount Ida
Dardania
MNOS
Thebes
MYSIA
LESBOS
ARZAWA
CHIOS
AEGEAN SEA
SAMOS
Miletos
LYCIA
DELOS
Halikarnassos
THERA
Knidos
RHODES
to KOLCHIS
Troy
Hattusas
HATTI
Karchemish
AMURRU
to ASSYRIA
CRETE
CYPRUS
Kadesh
Sidon
to BABYLON
EGYPT
Memphis
0 10 50 100 200
Miles
Kilometers
0 50 100 200 300

FAUSTUS: One thing, good servant, let me crave of thee
To glut the longing of my heart's desire:
That I might have unto my paramour
That heavenly Helen which I saw of late. . . .

Enter HELEN

Was this the face that launched a thousand ships
And burnt the topless towers of Ilium?
Sweet Helen, make me immortal with a kiss.
Her lips suck forth my soul—see where it flies!
Come, Helen, come, give me my soul again.
Here will I dwell, for heaven is in these lips
And all is dross that is not Helena.

Doctor Faustus, Scene XIII
Christopher Marlowe, circa 1588

A THOUSAND SHIPS

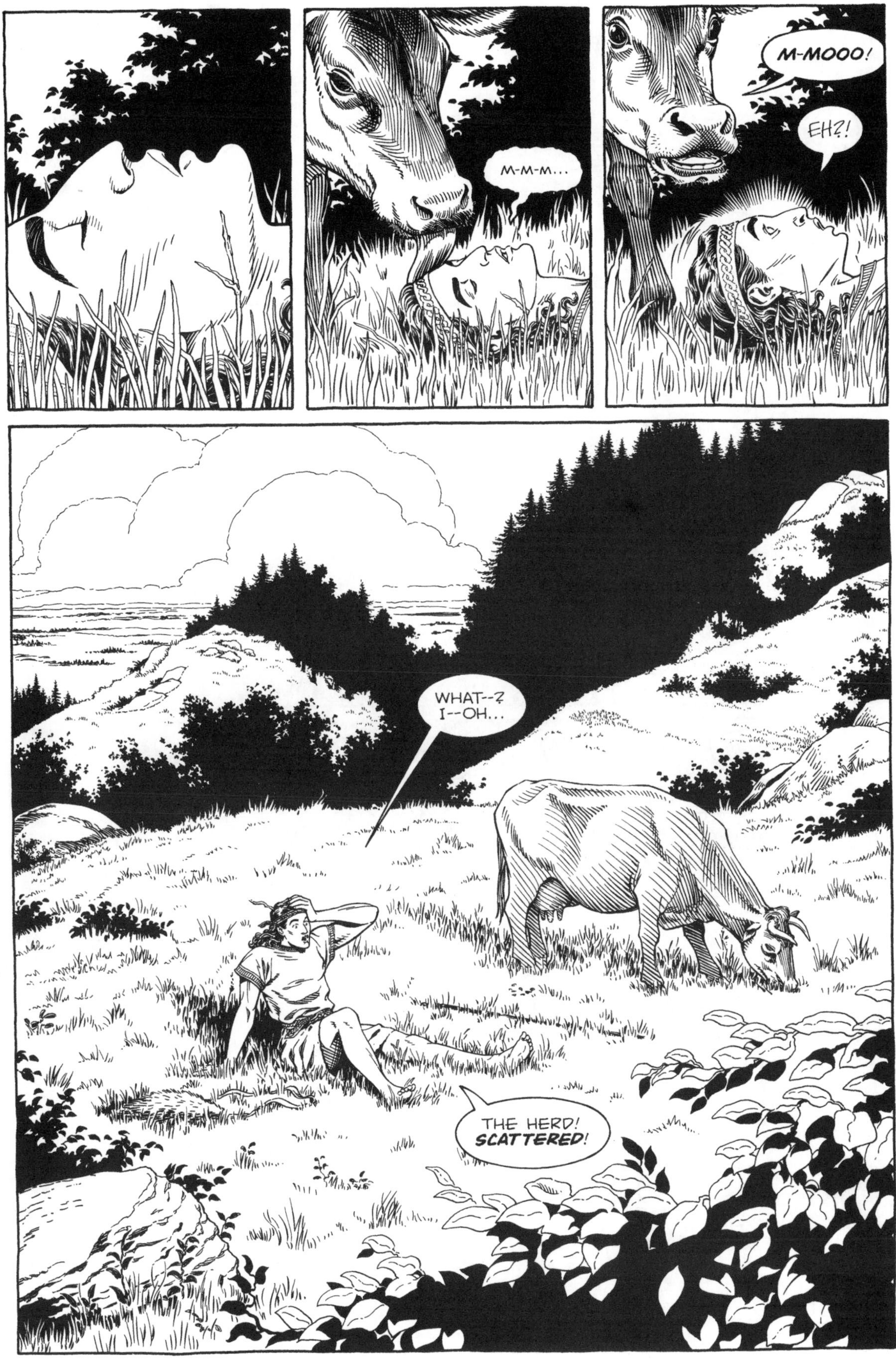
M-M-M...
M-MOOO!
EH?!
WHAT--?
I--OH...
THE HERD!
SCATTERED!

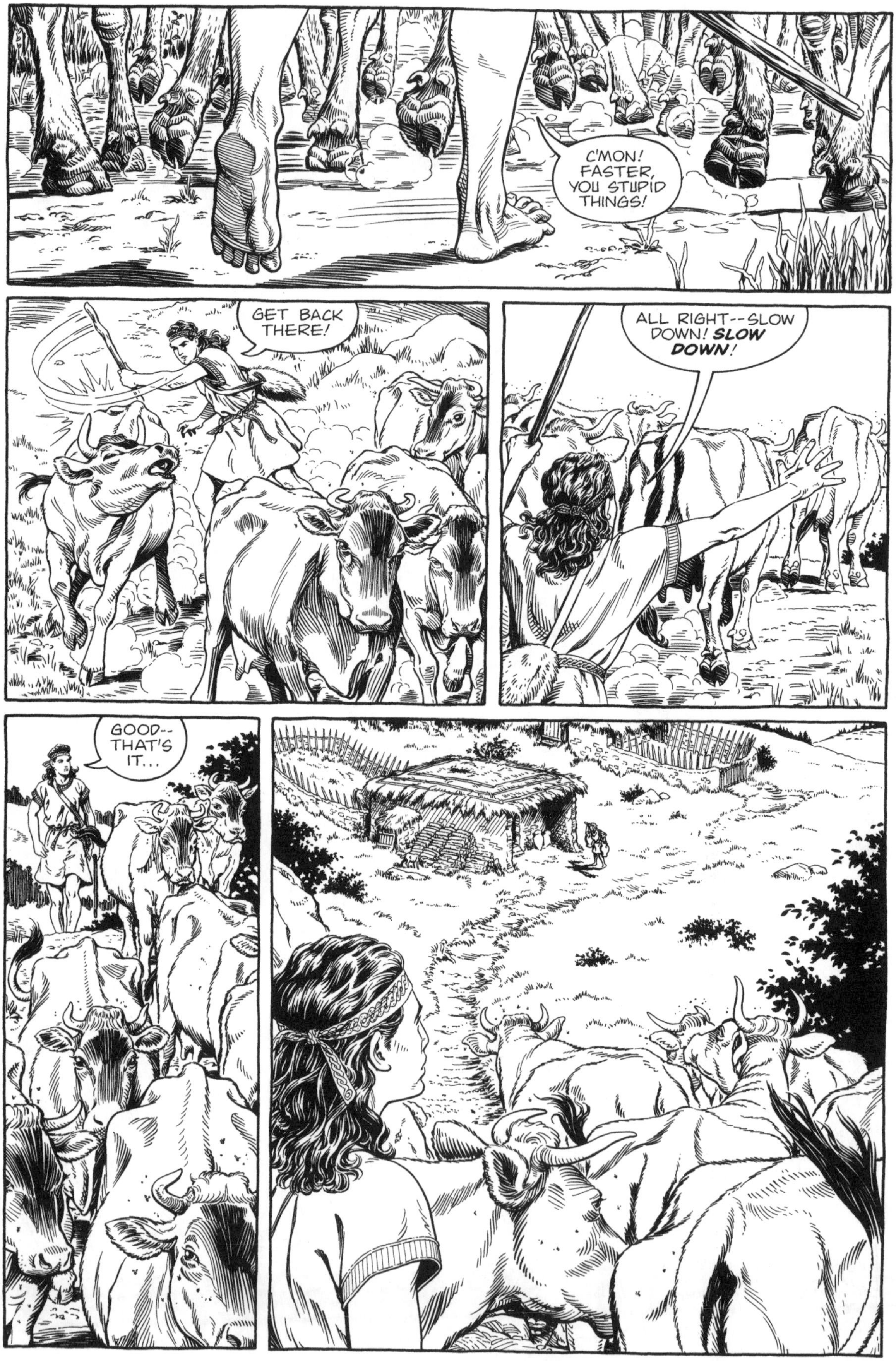
C'MON! FASTER, YOU STUPID THINGS!
GET BACK THERE!
ALL RIGHT--SLOW DOWN! **SLOW DOWN**!
GOOD--THAT'S IT...

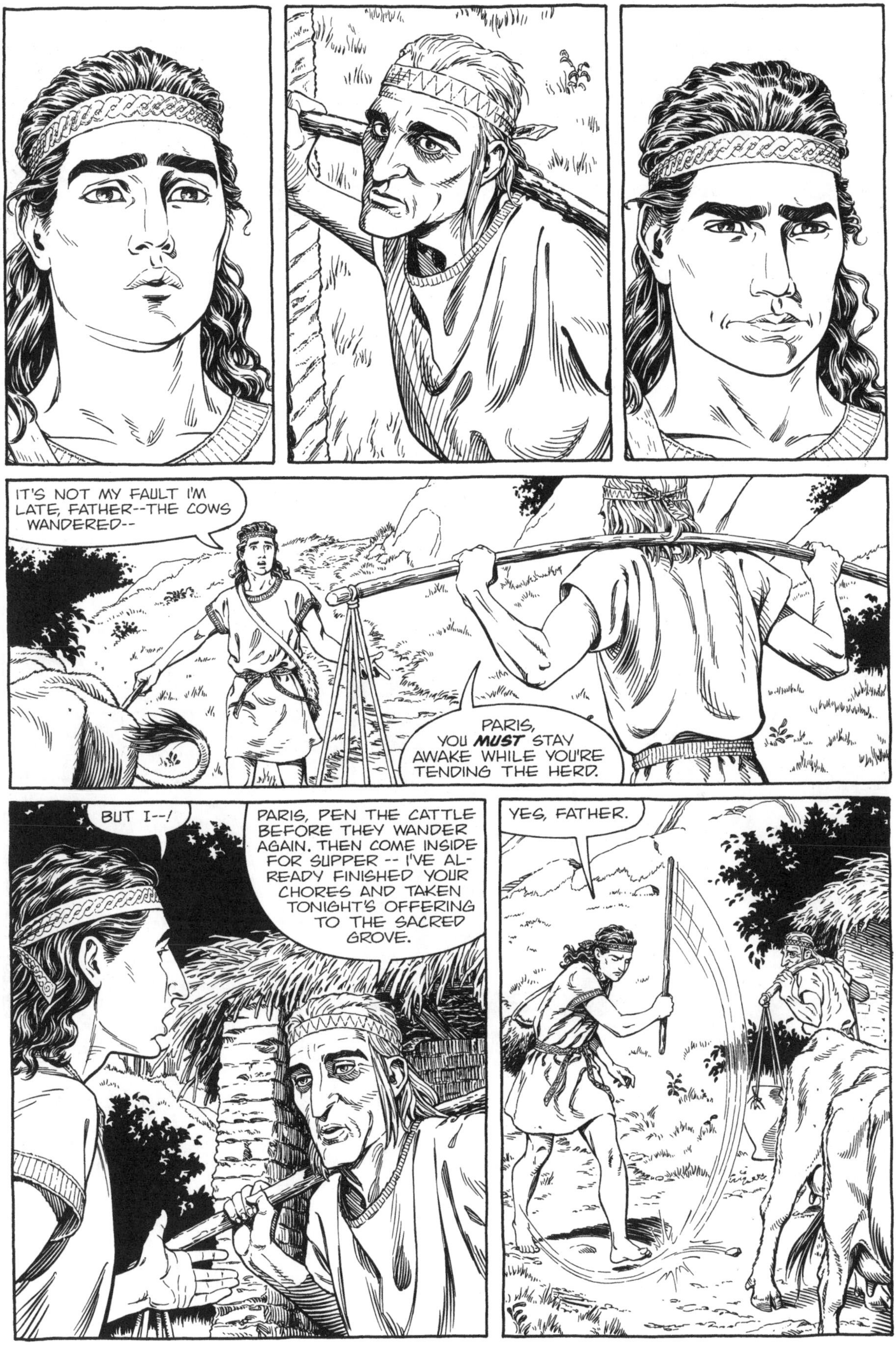
IT'S NOT MY FAULT I'M LATE, FATHER--THE COWS WANDERED--
PARIS, YOU MUST STAY AWAKE WHILE YOU'RE TENDING THE HERD.
BUT I--!
PARIS, PEN THE CATTLE BEFORE THEY WANDER AGAIN. THEN COME INSIDE FOR SUPPER -- I'VE ALREADY FINISHED YOUR CHORES AND TAKEN TONIGHT'S OFFERING TO THE SACRED GROVE.
YES, FATHER.

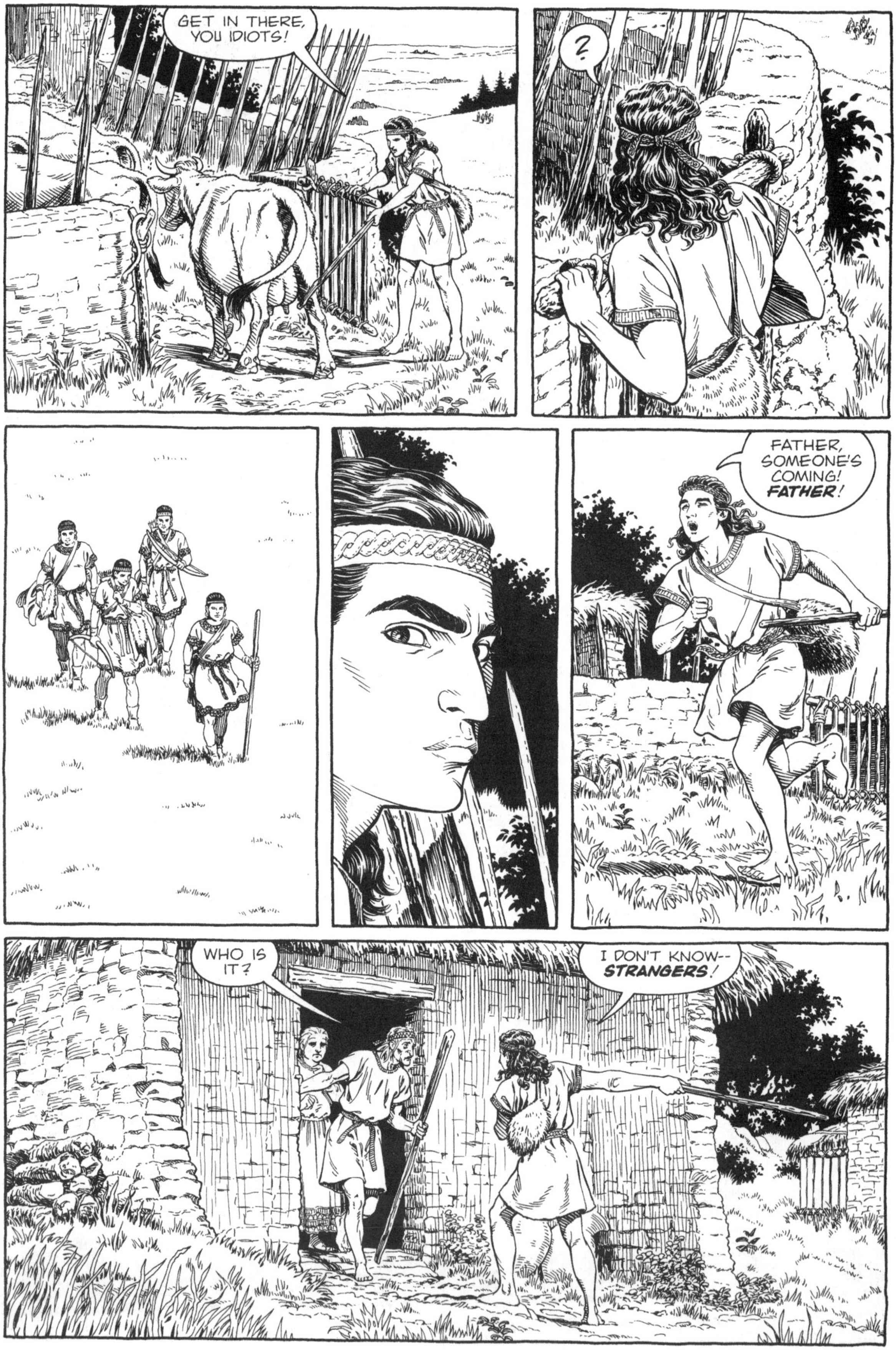
GET IN THERE, YOU IDIOTS!
?
FATHER, SOMEONE'S COMING! FATHER!
WHO IS IT?
I DON'T KNOW-- STRANGERS!

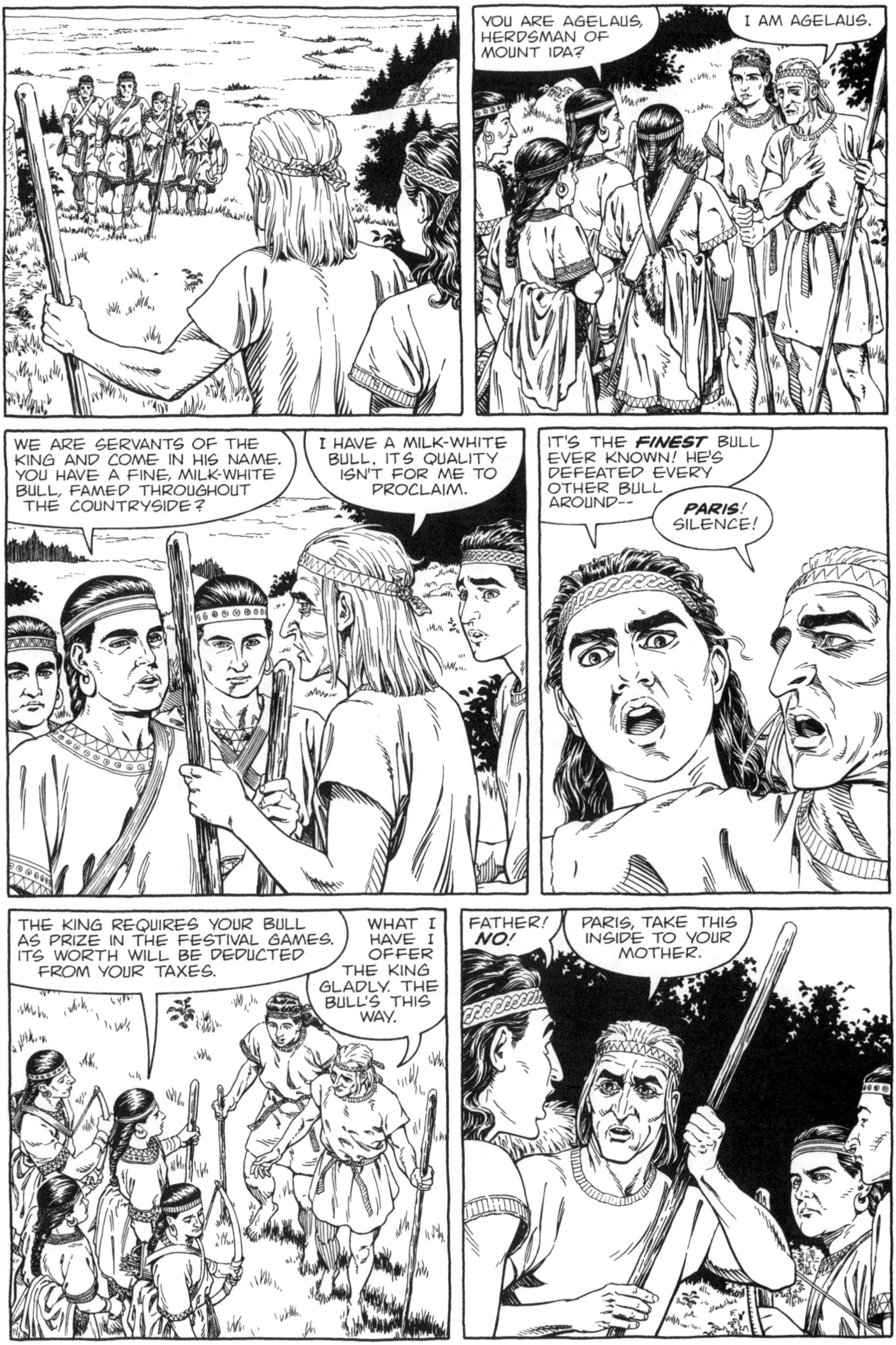

YOU ARE AGELAUS, HERDSMAN OF MOUNT IDA?
I AM AGELAUS.
WE ARE SERVANTS OF THE KING AND COME IN HIS NAME. YOU HAVE A FINE, MILK-WHITE BULL, FAMED THROUGHOUT THE COUNTRYSIDE?
I HAVE A MILK-WHITE BULL. ITS QUALITY ISN'T FOR ME TO PROCLAIM.
IT'S THE ***FINEST*** BULL EVER KNOWN! HE'S DEFEATED EVERY OTHER BULL AROUND--
PARIS! SILENCE!
THE KING REQUIRES YOUR BULL AS PRIZE IN THE FESTIVAL GAMES. ITS WORTH WILL BE DEDUCTED FROM YOUR TAXES.
WHAT I HAVE I OFFER THE KING GLADLY. THE BULL'S THIS WAY.
FATHER! ***NO!***
PARIS, TAKE THIS INSIDE TO YOUR MOTHER.

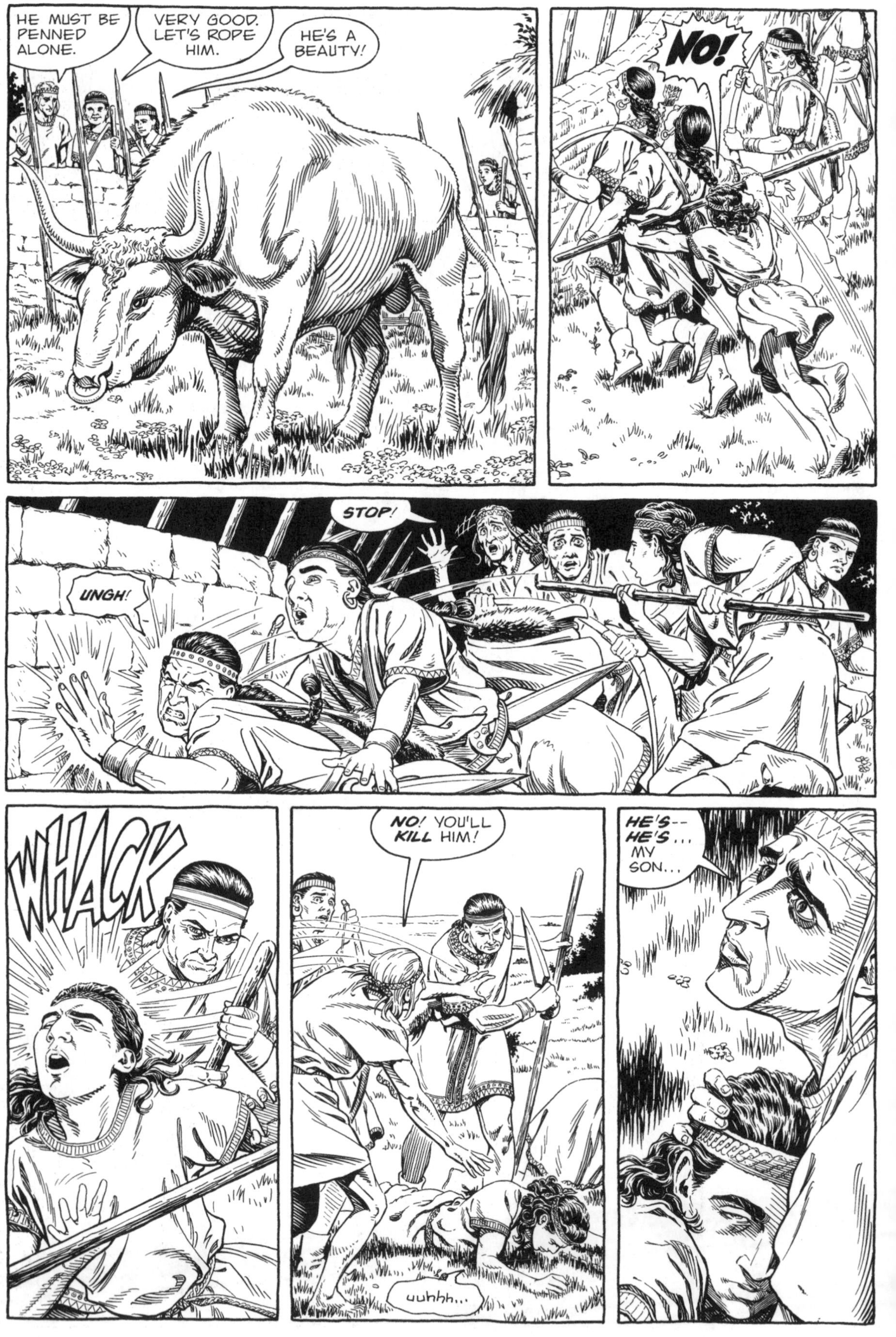
HE MUST BE PENNED ALONE.
VERY GOOD. LET'S ROPE HIM.
HE'S A BEAUTY!
NO!
STOP!
UNGH!
WHACK
NO! YOU'LL KILL HIM!
uuhhh...
HE'S-- HE'S... MY SON...

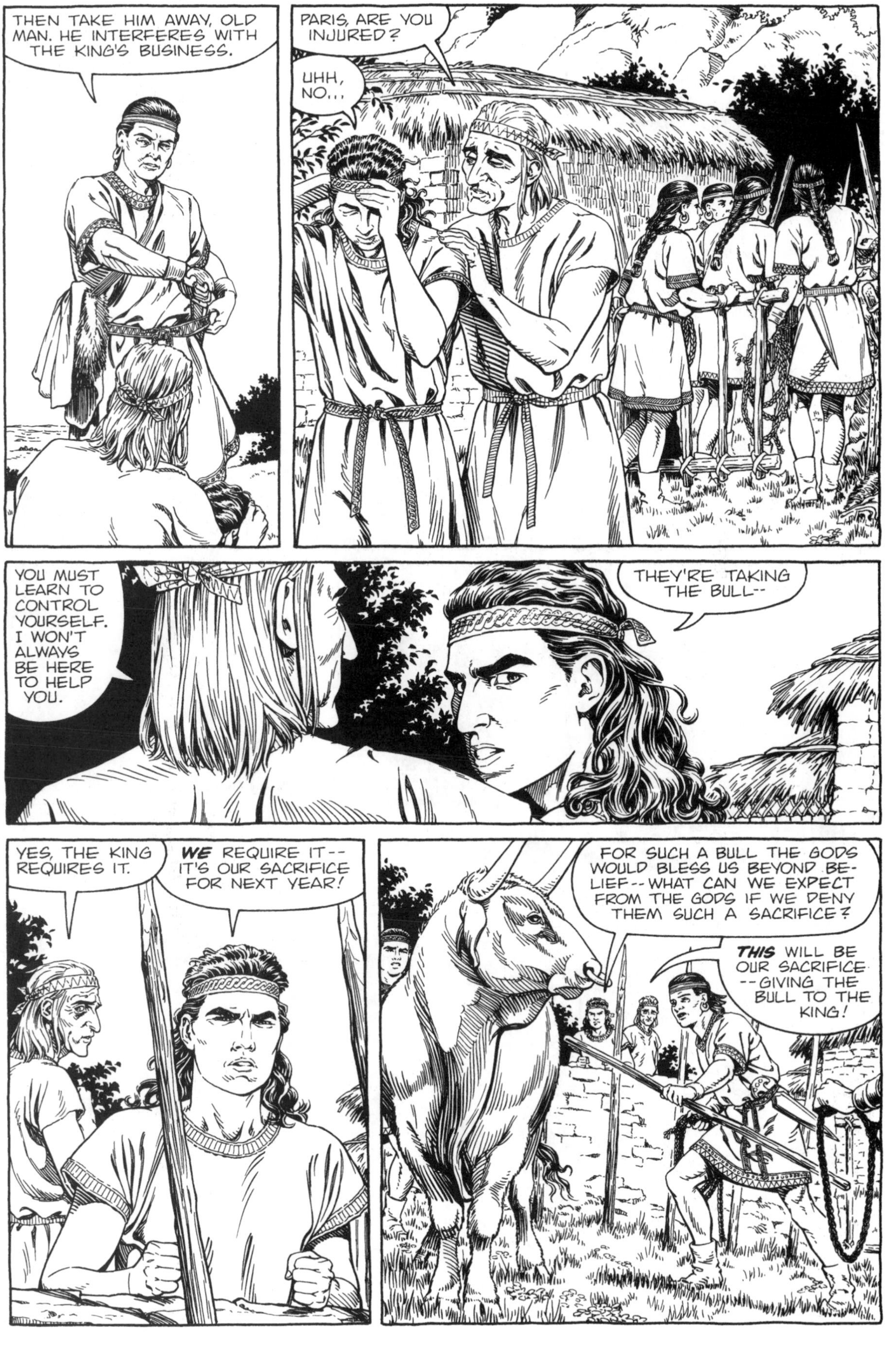
THEN TAKE HIM AWAY, OLD MAN. HE INTERFERES WITH THE KING'S BUSINESS.
PARIS, ARE YOU INJURED?
UHH, NO...
YOU MUST LEARN TO CONTROL YOURSELF. I WON'T ALWAYS BE HERE TO HELP YOU.
THEY'RE TAKING THE BULL--
YES, THE KING REQUIRES IT.
WE REQUIRE IT-- IT'S OUR SACRIFICE FOR NEXT YEAR!
FOR SUCH A BULL THE GODS WOULD BLESS US BEYOND BELIEF-- WHAT CAN WE EXPECT FROM THE GODS IF WE DENY THEM SUCH A SACRIFICE?
THIS WILL BE OUR SACRIFICE --GIVING THE BULL TO THE KING!

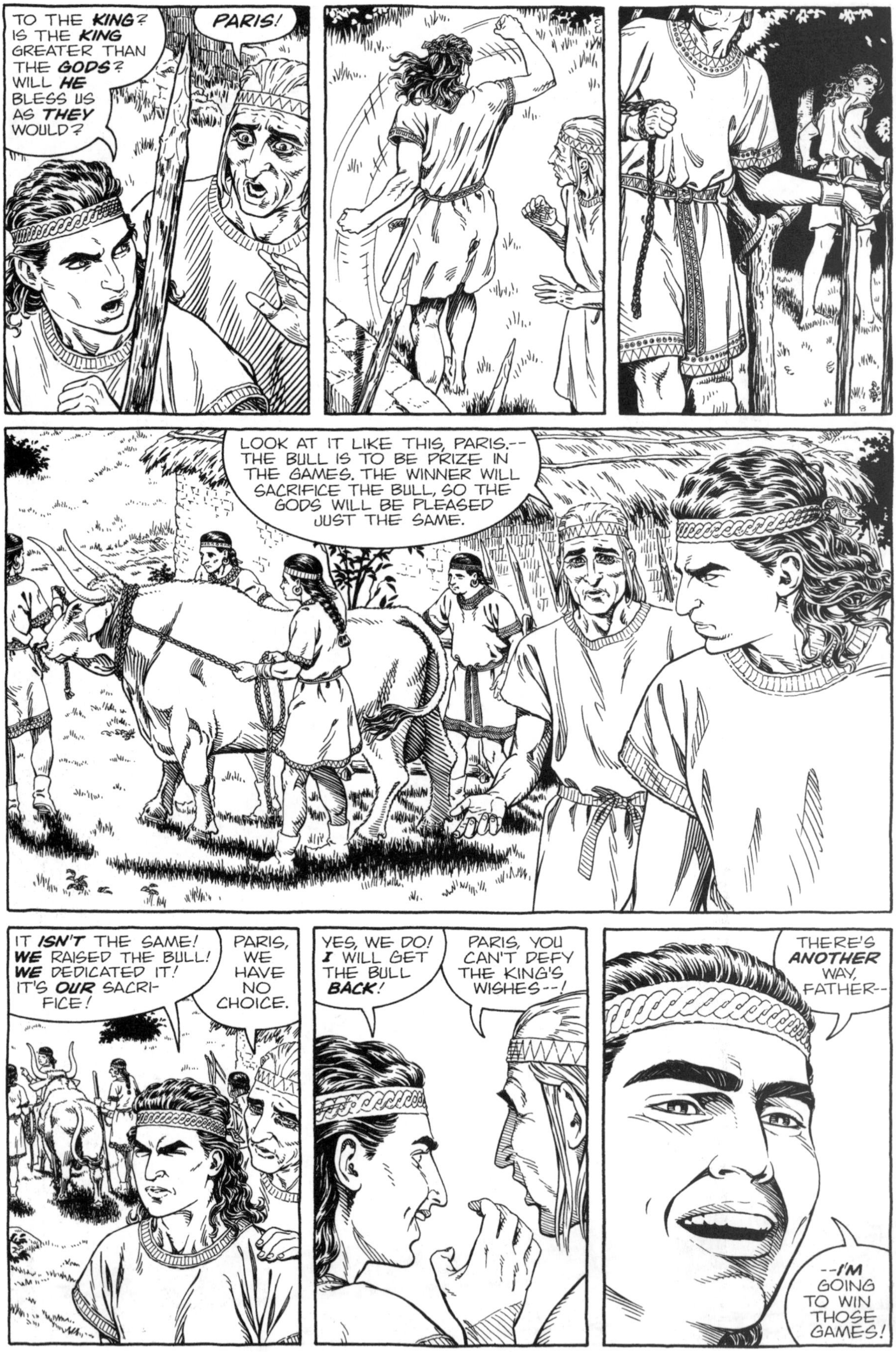
TO THE KING? IS THE KING GREATER THAN THE GODS? WILL HE BLESS US AS THEY WOULD?
PARIS!
LOOK AT IT LIKE THIS, PARIS.-- THE BULL IS TO BE PRIZE IN THE GAMES. THE WINNER WILL SACRIFICE THE BULL, SO THE GODS WILL BE PLEASED JUST THE SAME.
IT ISN'T THE SAME! WE RAISED THE BULL! WE DEDICATED IT! IT'S OUR SACRIFICE!
PARIS, WE HAVE NO CHOICE.
YES, WE DO! I WILL GET THE BULL BACK!
PARIS, YOU CAN'T DEFY THE KING'S WISHES--!
THERE'S ANOTHER WAY, FATHER--
--I'M GOING TO WIN THOSE GAMES!

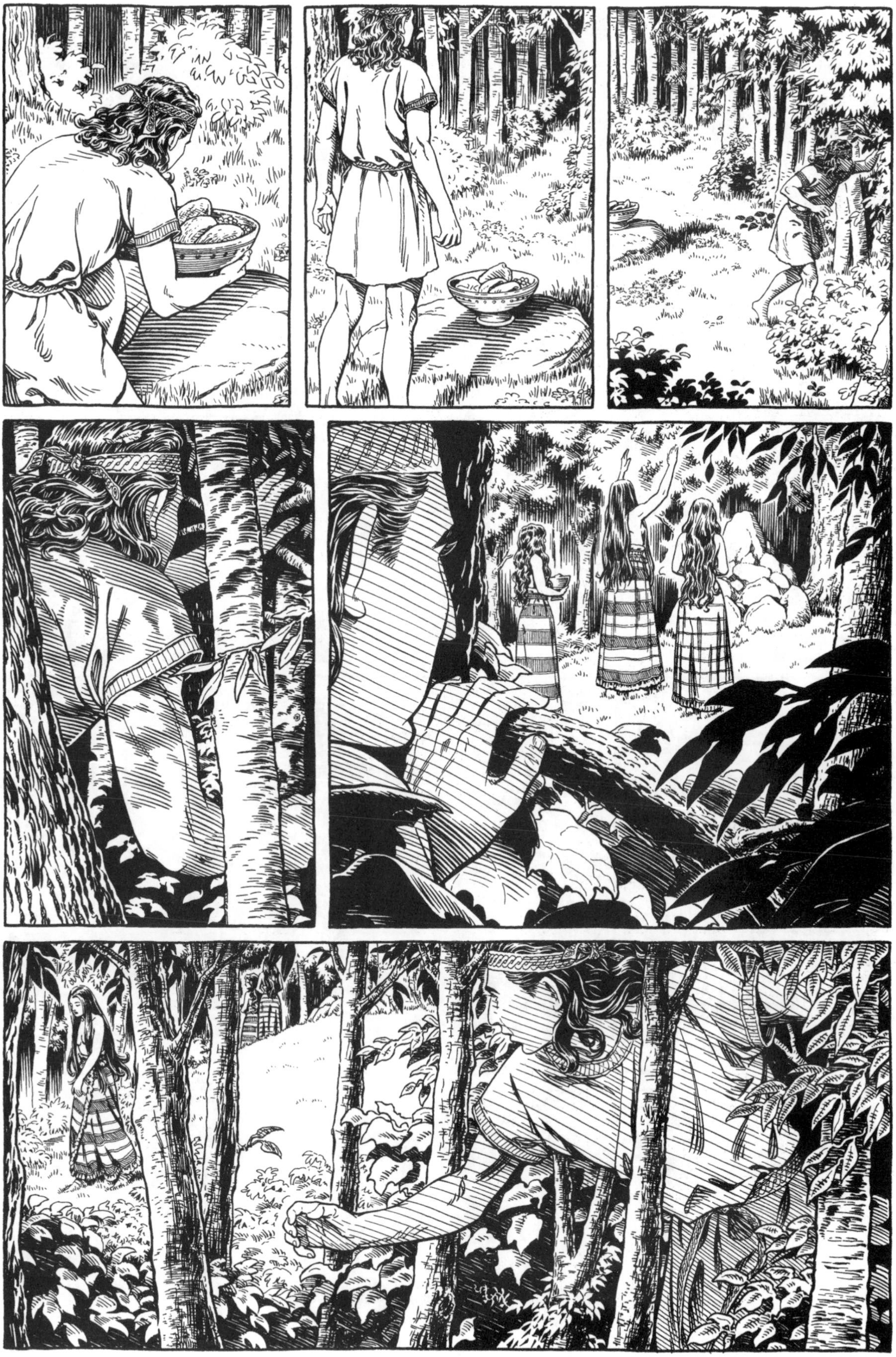

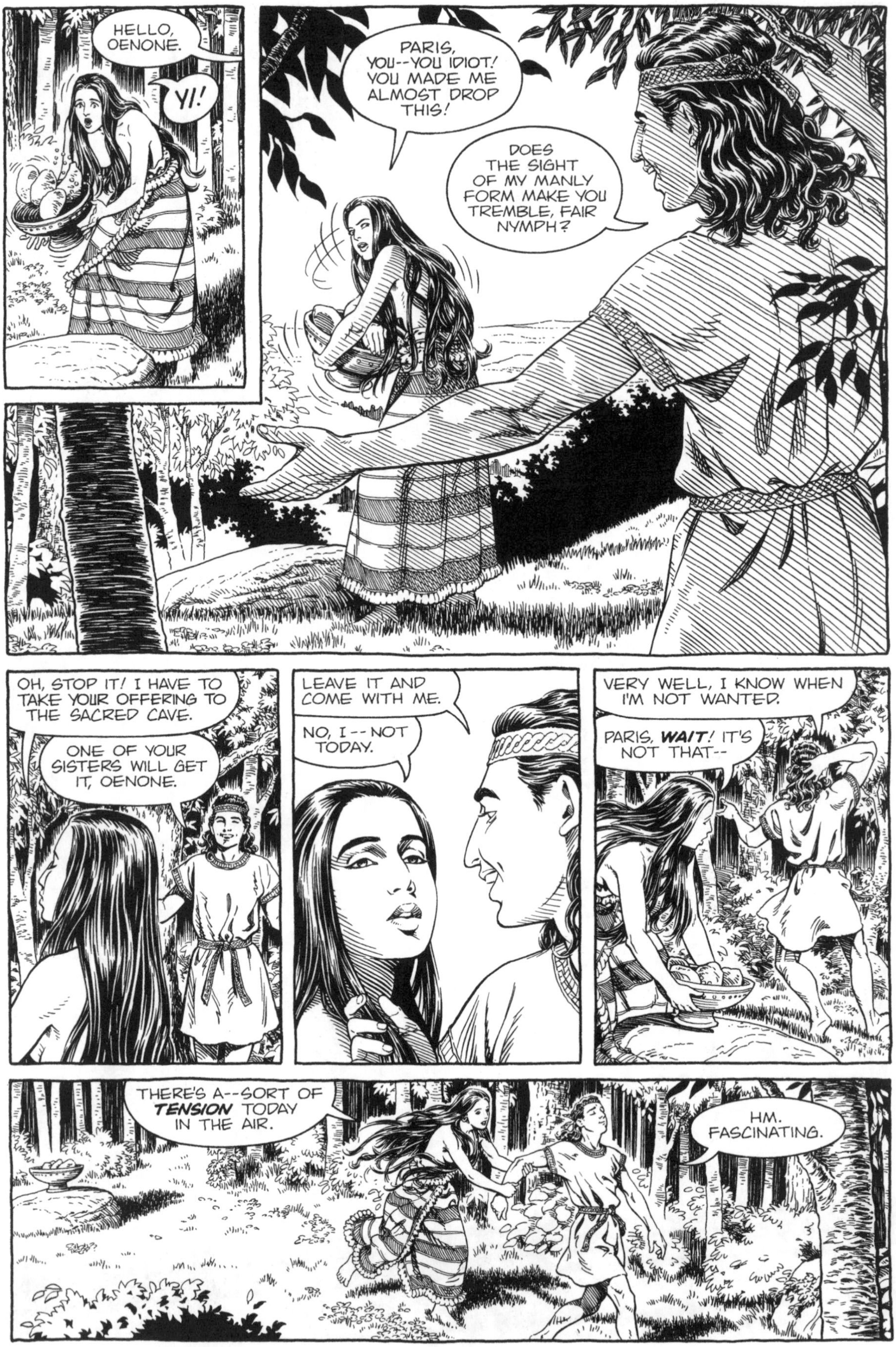
HELLO, OENONE.
YI!
PARIS, YOU--YOU IDIOT! YOU MADE ME ALMOST DROP THIS!
DOES THE SIGHT OF MY MANLY FORM MAKE YOU TREMBLE, FAIR NYMPH?
OH, STOP IT! I HAVE TO TAKE YOUR OFFERING TO THE SACRED CAVE.
ONE OF YOUR SISTERS WILL GET IT, OENONE.
LEAVE IT AND COME WITH ME.
NO, I--NOT TODAY.
VERY WELL, I KNOW WHEN I'M NOT WANTED.
PARIS, WAIT! IT'S NOT THAT--
THERE'S A--SORT OF TENSION TODAY IN THE AIR.
HM. FASCINATING.

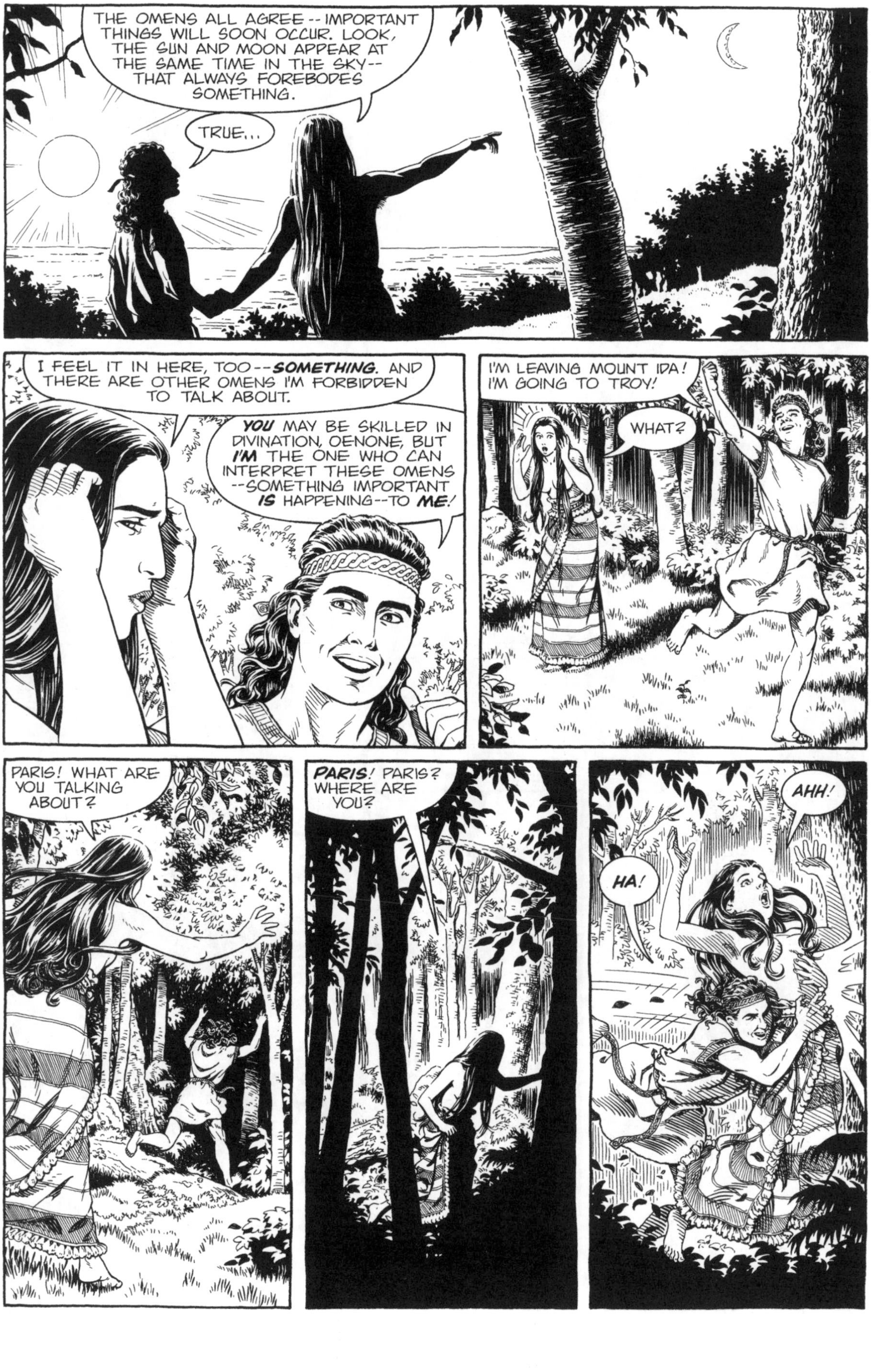
THE OMENS ALL AGREE--IMPORTANT THINGS WILL SOON OCCUR. LOOK, THE SUN AND MOON APPEAR AT THE SAME TIME IN THE SKY--THAT ALWAYS FOREBODES SOMETHING.
TRUE...
I FEEL IT IN HERE, TOO--SOMETHING. AND THERE ARE OTHER OMENS I'M FORBIDDEN TO TALK ABOUT.
YOU MAY BE SKILLED IN DIVINATION, OENONE, BUT I'M THE ONE WHO CAN INTERPRET THESE OMENS--SOMETHING IMPORTANT IS HAPPENING--TO ME!
I'M LEAVING MOUNT IDA! I'M GOING TO TROY!
WHAT?
PARIS! WHAT ARE YOU TALKING ABOUT?
PARIS! PARIS? WHERE ARE YOU?
AHH!
HA!

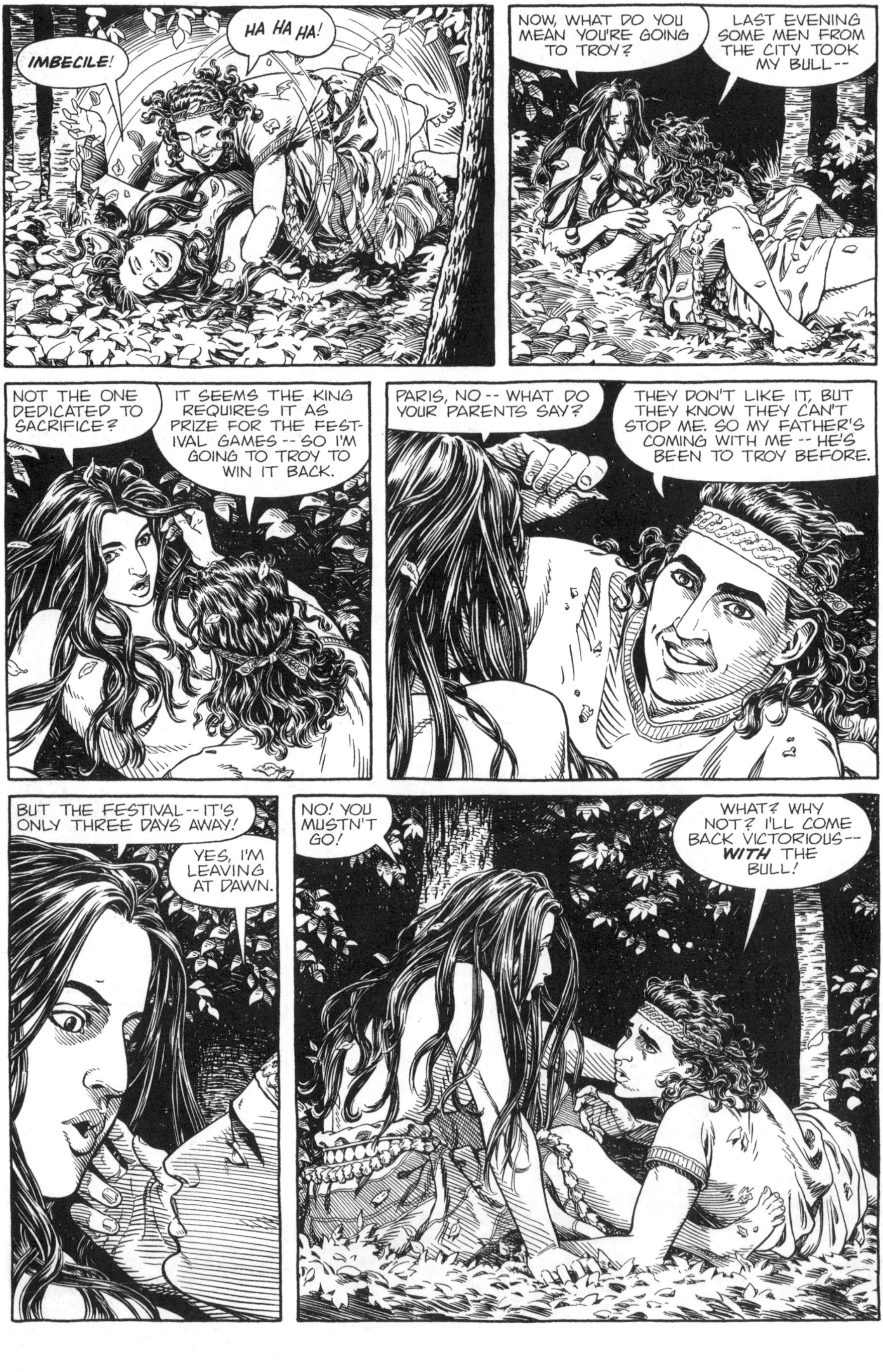
IMBECILE!
HA HA HA!
NOW, WHAT DO YOU MEAN YOU'RE GOING TO TROY?
LAST EVENING SOME MEN FROM THE CITY TOOK MY BULL--
NOT THE ONE DEDICATED TO SACRIFICE?
IT SEEMS THE KING REQUIRES IT AS PRIZE FOR THE FESTIVAL GAMES -- SO I'M GOING TO TROY TO WIN IT BACK.
PARIS, NO -- WHAT DO YOUR PARENTS SAY?
THEY DON'T LIKE IT, BUT THEY KNOW THEY CAN'T STOP ME. SO MY FATHER'S COMING WITH ME -- HE'S BEEN TO TROY BEFORE.
BUT THE FESTIVAL -- IT'S ONLY THREE DAYS AWAY!
YES, I'M LEAVING AT DAWN.
NO! YOU MUSTN'T GO!
WHAT? WHY NOT? I'LL COME BACK VICTORIOUS -- WITH THE BULL!

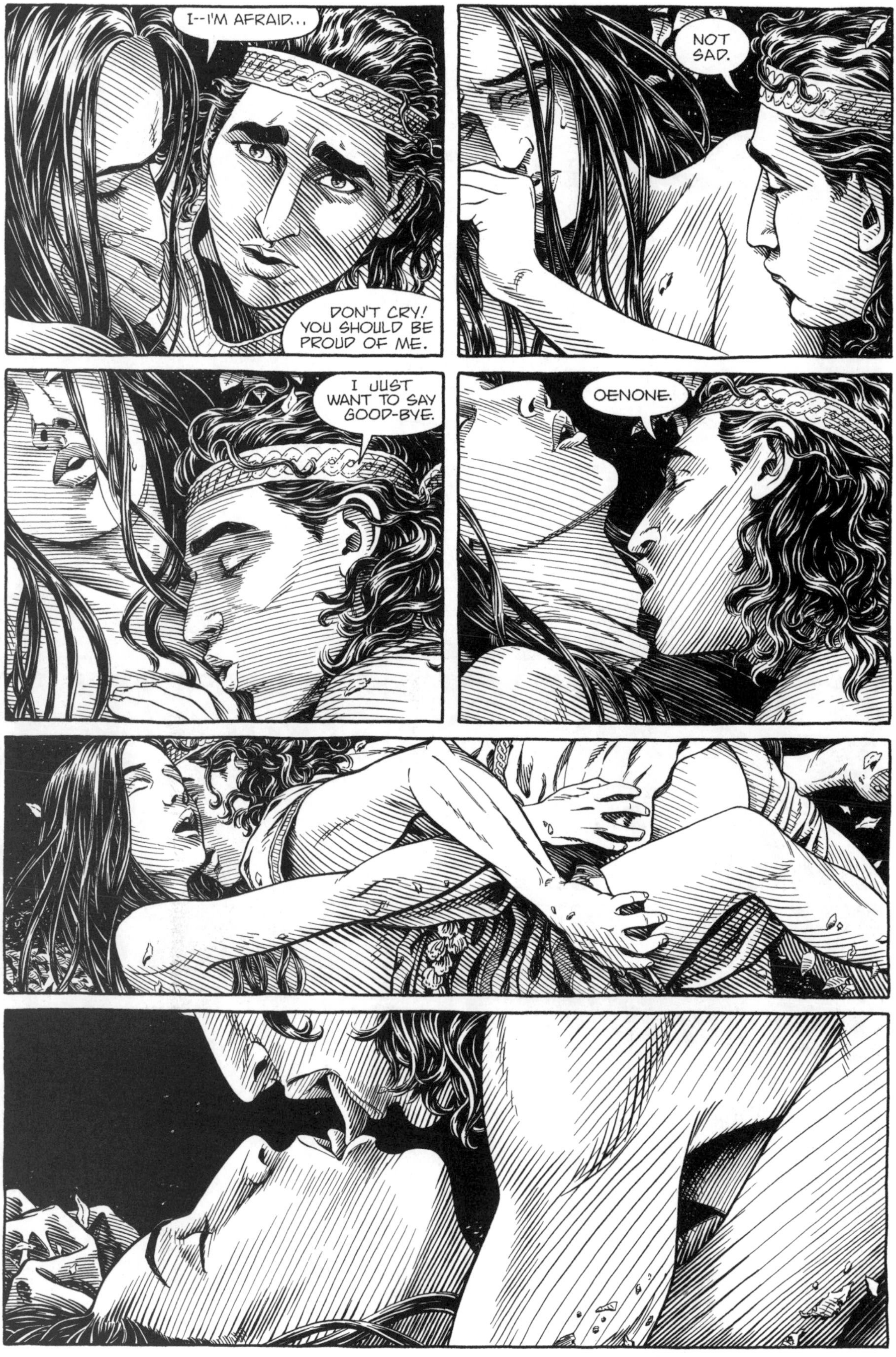
I--I'M AFRAID...
DON'T CRY! YOU SHOULD BE PROUD OF ME.
NOT SAD.
I JUST WANT TO SAY GOOD-BYE.
OENONE.

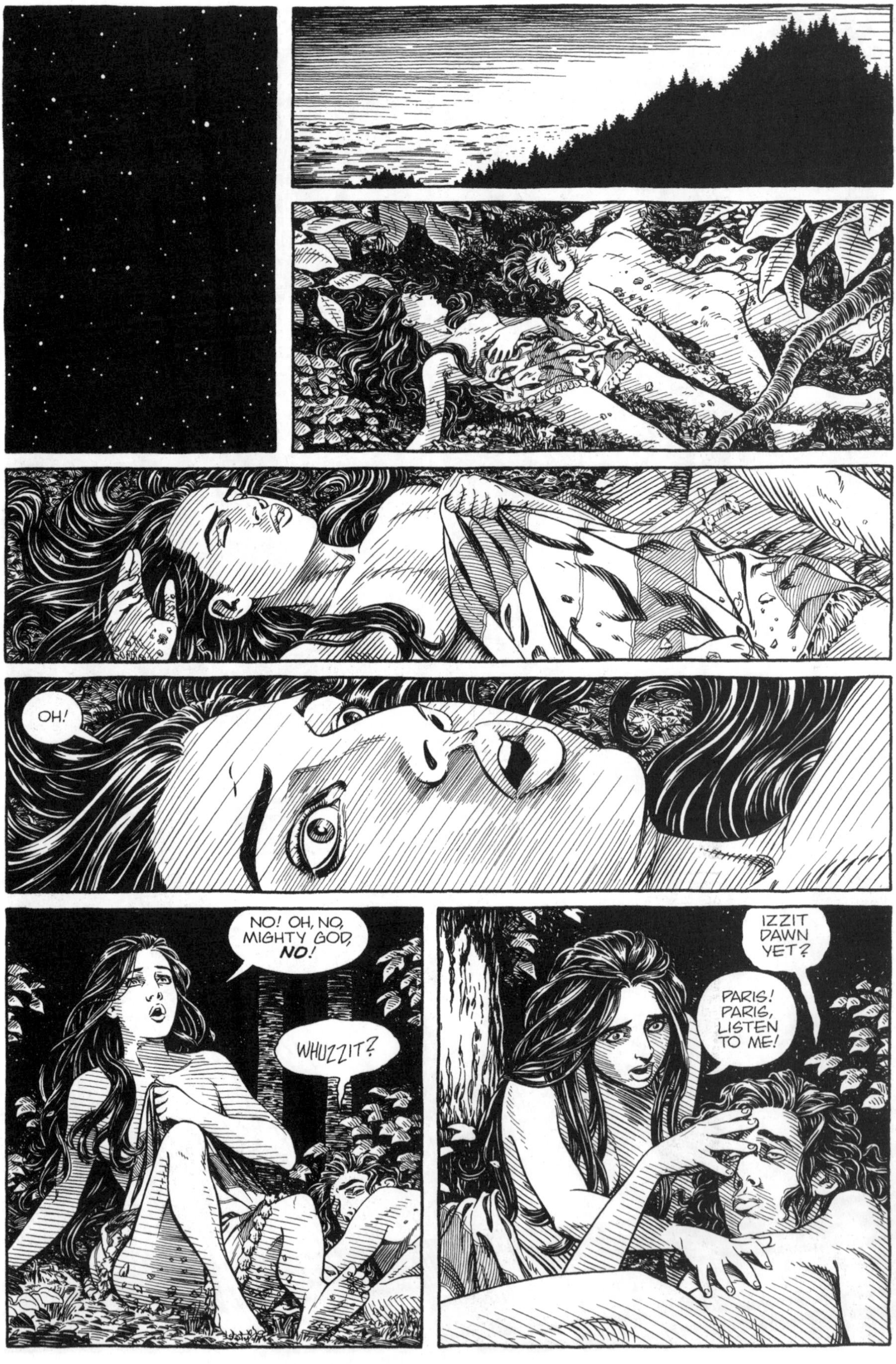
OH!
NO! OH, NO, MIGHTY GOD, NO!
WHUZZIT?
IZZIT DAWN YET?
PARIS! PARIS, LISTEN TO ME!

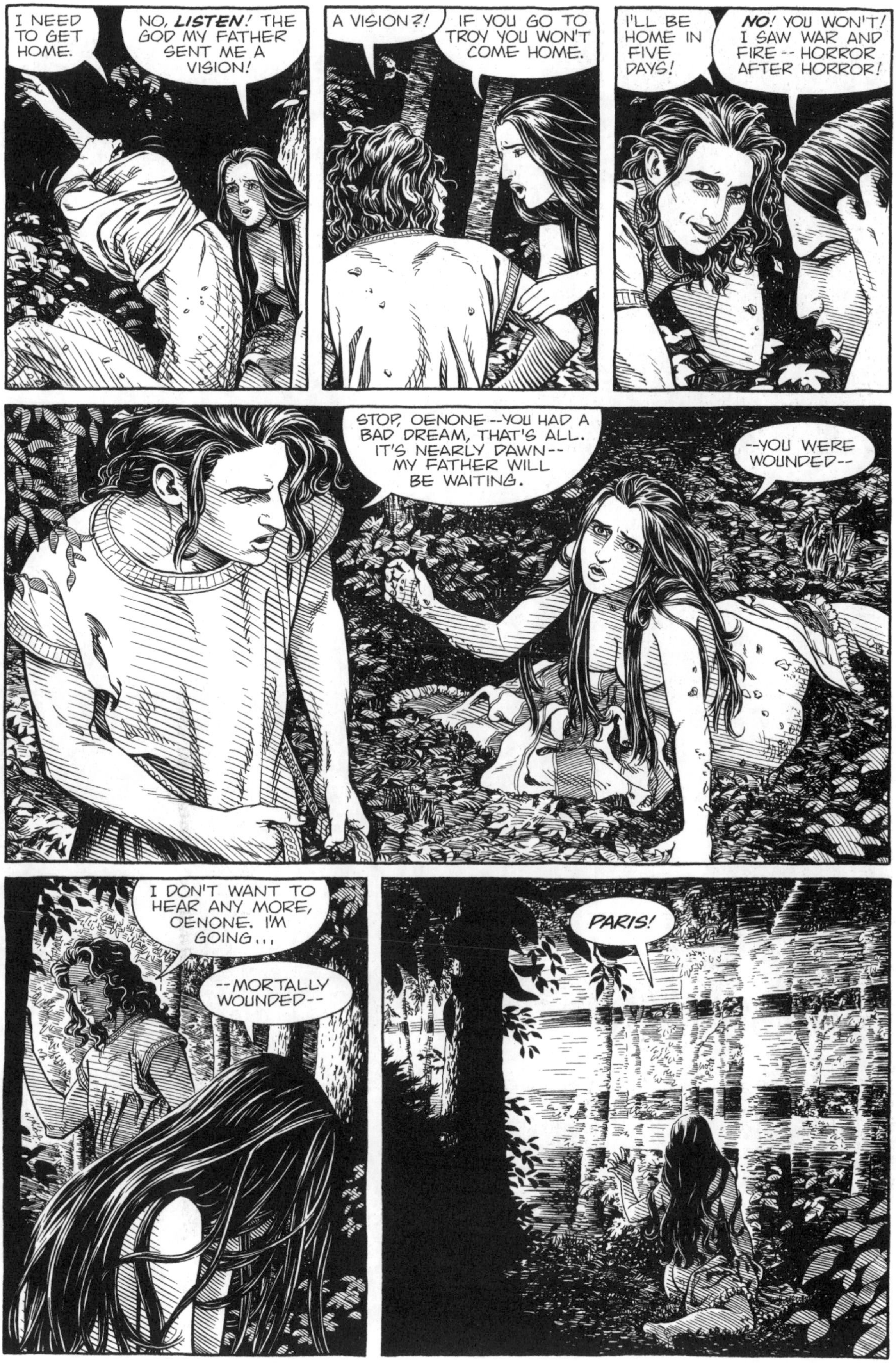
I NEED TO GET HOME.
NO, LISTEN! THE GOD MY FATHER SENT ME A VISION!
A VISION?!
IF YOU GO TO TROY YOU WON'T COME HOME.
I'LL BE HOME IN FIVE DAYS!
NO! YOU WON'T! I SAW WAR AND FIRE -- HORROR AFTER HORROR!
STOP, OENONE -- YOU HAD A BAD DREAM, THAT'S ALL. IT'S NEARLY DAWN -- MY FATHER WILL BE WAITING.
-- YOU WERE WOUNDED --
I DON'T WANT TO HEAR ANY MORE, OENONE. I'M GOING...
-- MORTALLY WOUNDED --
PARIS!

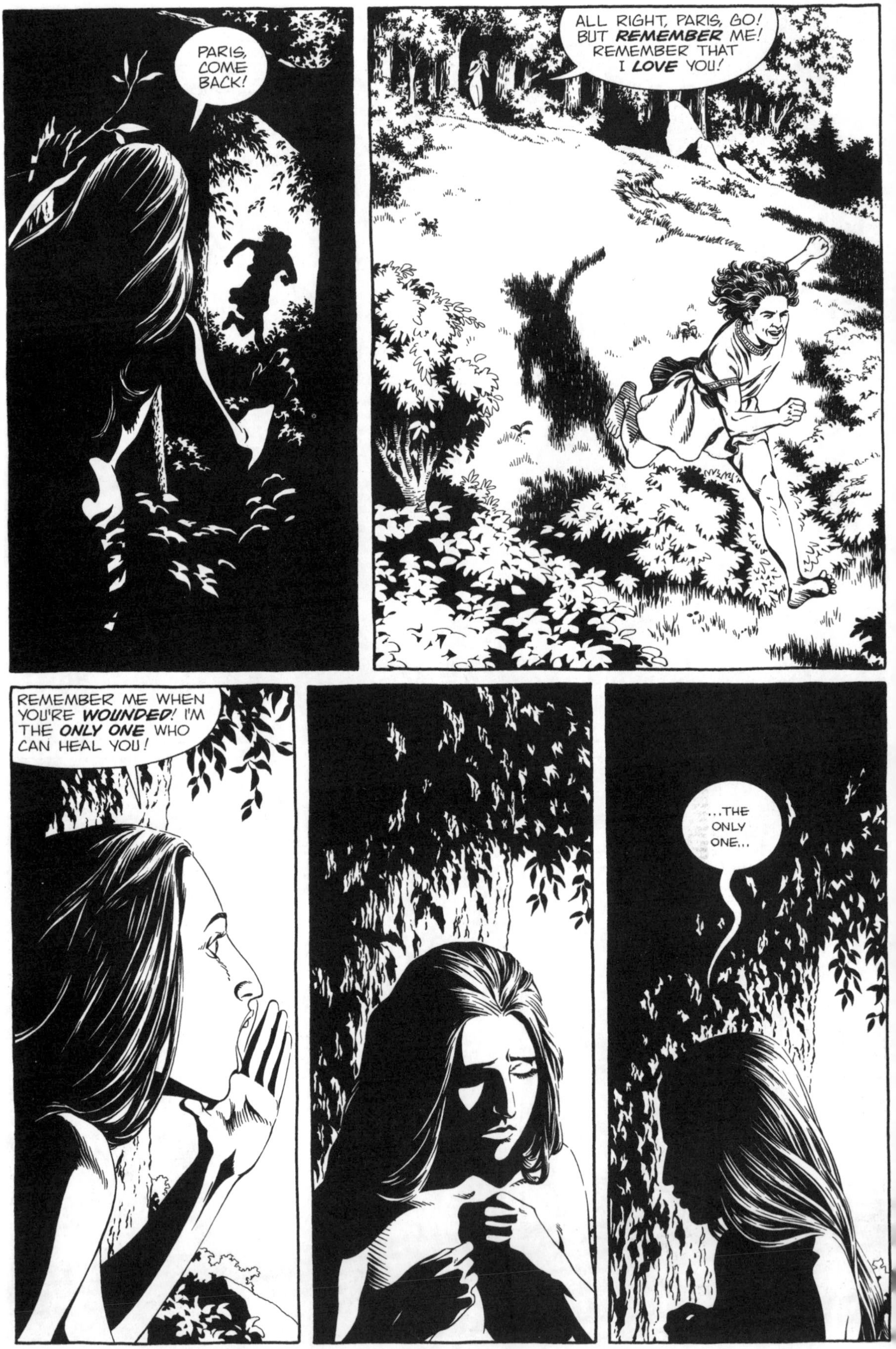
PARIS, COME BACK!
ALL RIGHT, PARIS, GO! BUT REMEMBER ME! REMEMBER THAT I LOVE YOU!
REMEMBER ME WHEN YOU'RE WOUNDED! I'M THE ONLY ONE WHO CAN HEAL YOU!
...THE ONLY ONE...

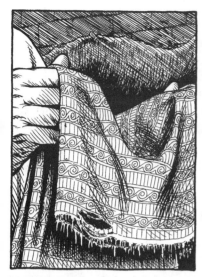

THE PACKING IS FINISHED.

HIS SWADDLING CLOTH.

I KNOW.

IT'S STILL SO *VIVID* -- THAT MORNING...

I KNOW.

WHERE HAVE THE YEARS GONE?

I KNOW. I KNOW. OUR CHILD IS A MAN NOW.

IT SEEMS THAT THE TIME HAS COME FOR HIM TO KNOW THE TRUTH.

THE *TRUTH* IS THAT HE IS OUR SON!

HIS BLOOD IS HIGHER THAN OURS.

NO! THEY DIDN'T WANT HIM!

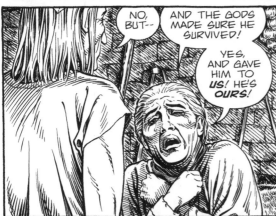

NO, BUT--

AND THE GODS MADE SURE HE SURVIVED!

YES, AND GAVE HIM TO *US!* HE'S *OURS!*

MAYBE... MAYBE YOU'RE RIGHT. ANYWAY, I DON'T KNOW WHERE I COULD FIND THE COURAGE TO TELL HIM.

TELL WHO WHAT?

PARIS!

TELL YOU THAT YOUR MOTHER WEEPS TO SEE YOU GO.

WE'LL BE BACK IN FIVE DAYS, MOTHER.

I--I KNOW... DON'T MIND ME. WHAT HARM CAN FIVE DAYS BRING?

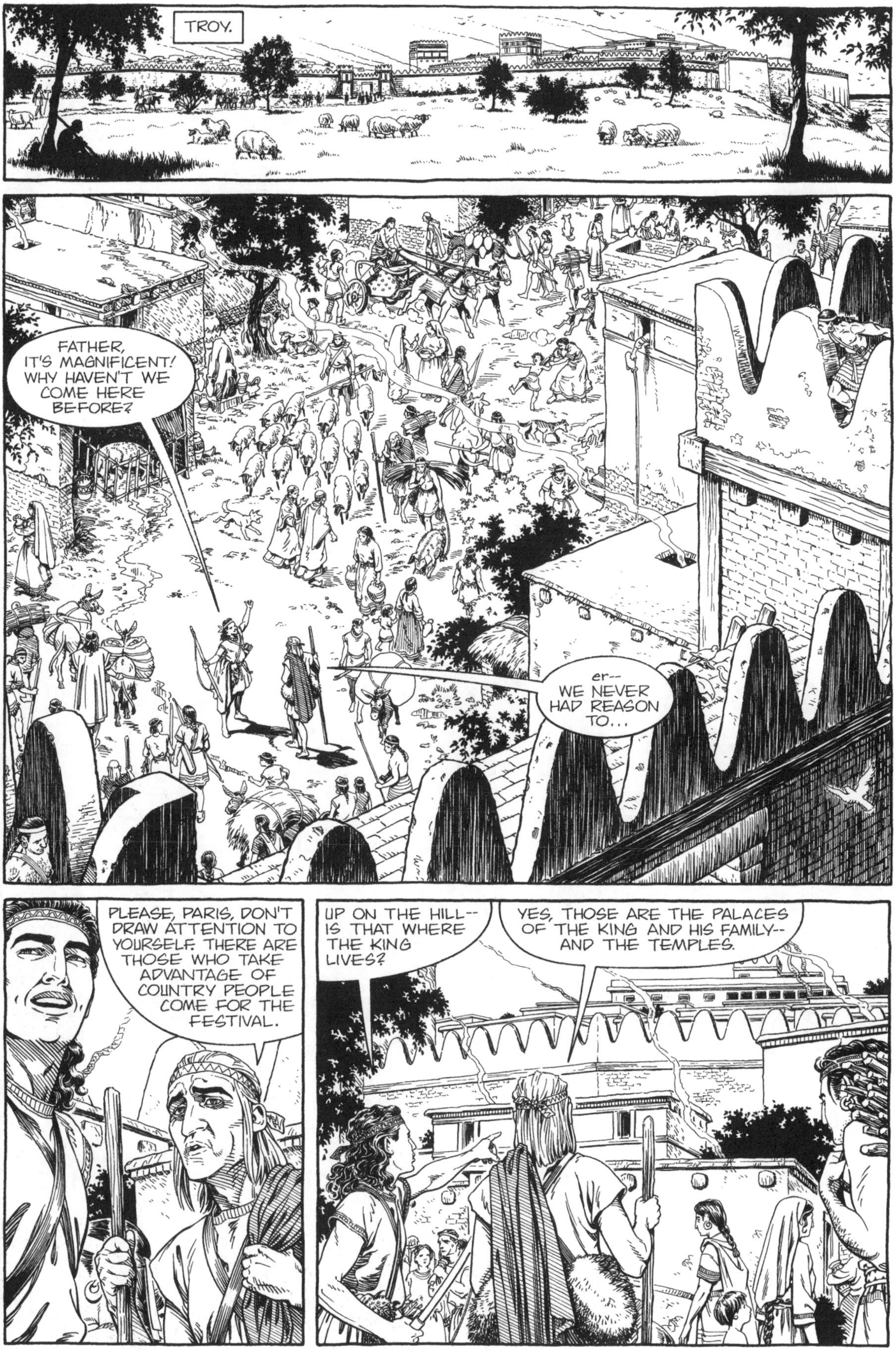
TROY.
FATHER, IT'S MAGNIFICENT! WHY HAVEN'T WE COME HERE BEFORE?
er-- WE NEVER HAD REASON TO...
PLEASE, PARIS, DON'T DRAW ATTENTION TO YOURSELF. THERE ARE THOSE WHO TAKE ADVANTAGE OF COUNTRY PEOPLE COME FOR THE FESTIVAL.
UP ON THE HILL-- IS THAT WHERE THE KING LIVES?
YES, THOSE ARE THE PALACES OF THE KING AND HIS FAMILY-- AND THE TEMPLES.

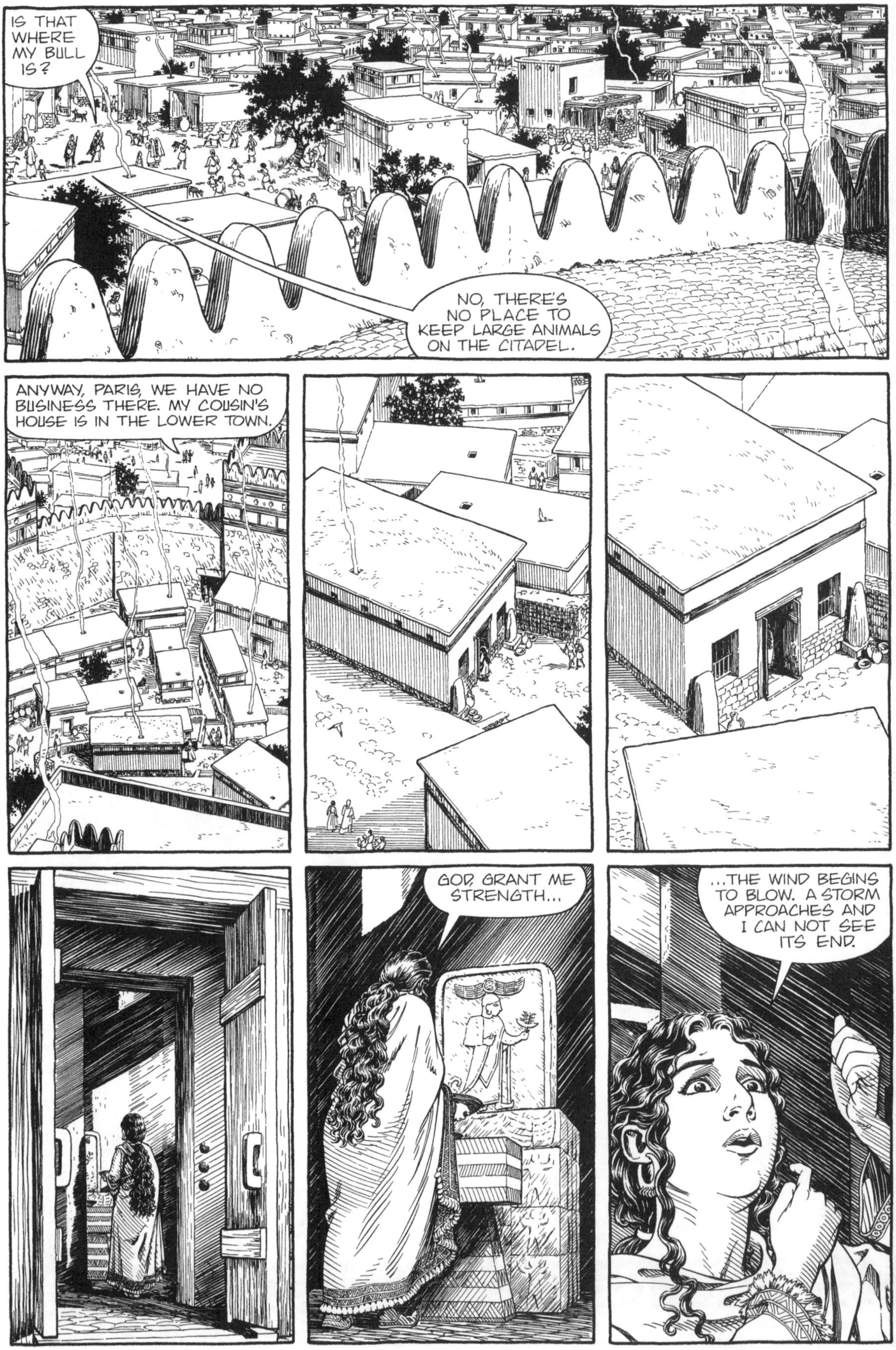
IS THAT WHERE MY BULL IS?
NO, THERE'S NO PLACE TO KEEP LARGE ANIMALS ON THE CITADEL.
ANYWAY, PARIS, WE HAVE NO BUSINESS THERE. MY COUSIN'S HOUSE IS IN THE LOWER TOWN.
GOD, GRANT ME STRENGTH...
...THE WIND BEGINS TO BLOW. A STORM APPROACHES AND I CAN NOT SEE ITS END.

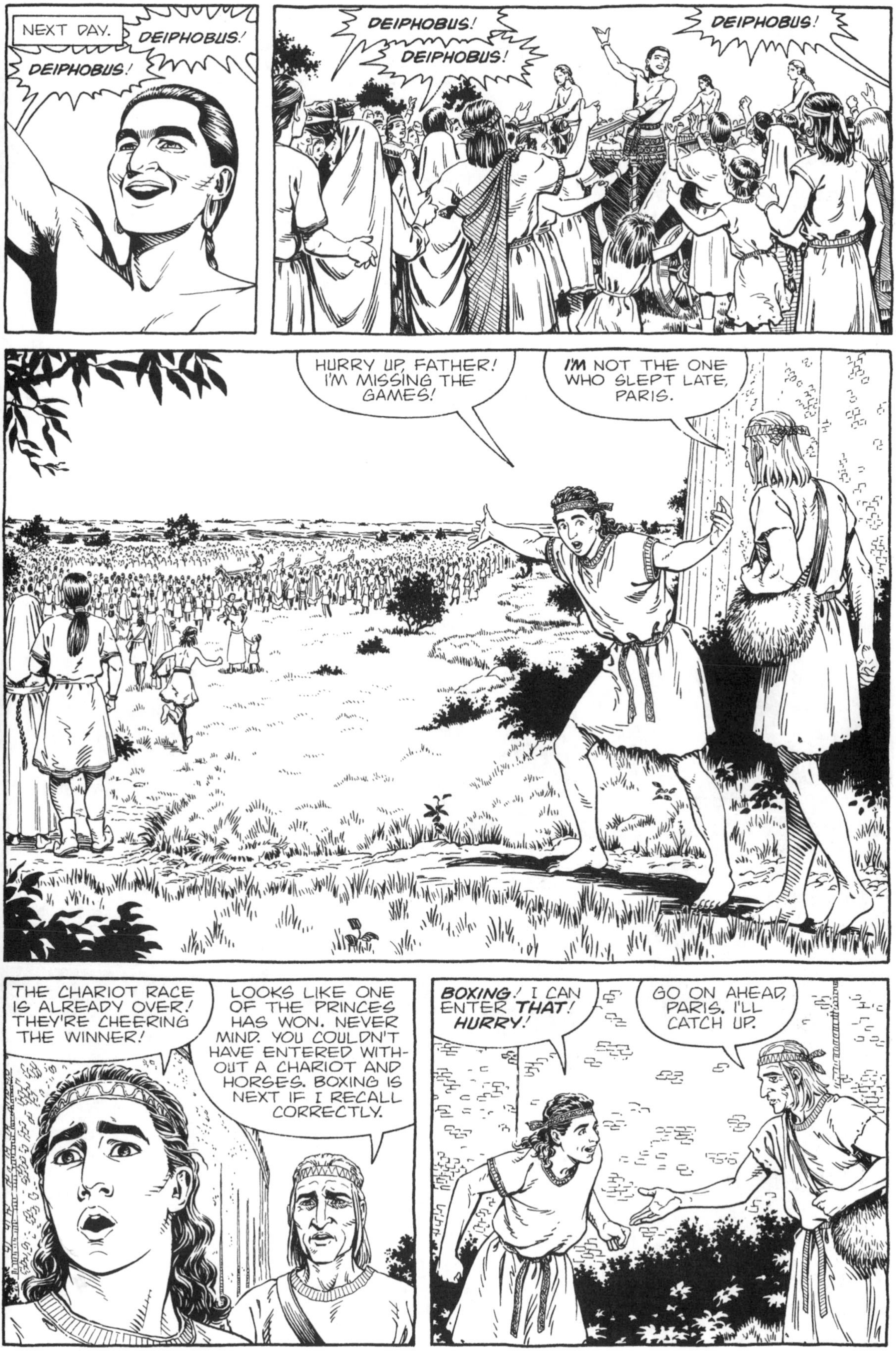
NEXT DAY.
DEIPHOBUS!
DEIPHOBUS!
DEIPHOBUS!
DEIPHOBUS!
DEIPHOBUS!
HURRY UP, FATHER! I'M MISSING THE GAMES!
I'M NOT THE ONE WHO SLEPT LATE, PARIS.
THE CHARIOT RACE IS ALREADY OVER! THEY'RE CHEERING THE WINNER!
LOOKS LIKE ONE OF THE PRINCES HAS WON. NEVER MIND. YOU COULDN'T HAVE ENTERED WITH-OUT A CHARIOT AND HORSES. BOXING IS NEXT IF I RECALL CORRECTLY.
BOXING! I CAN ENTER THAT! HURRY!
GO ON AHEAD, PARIS. I'LL CATCH UP.

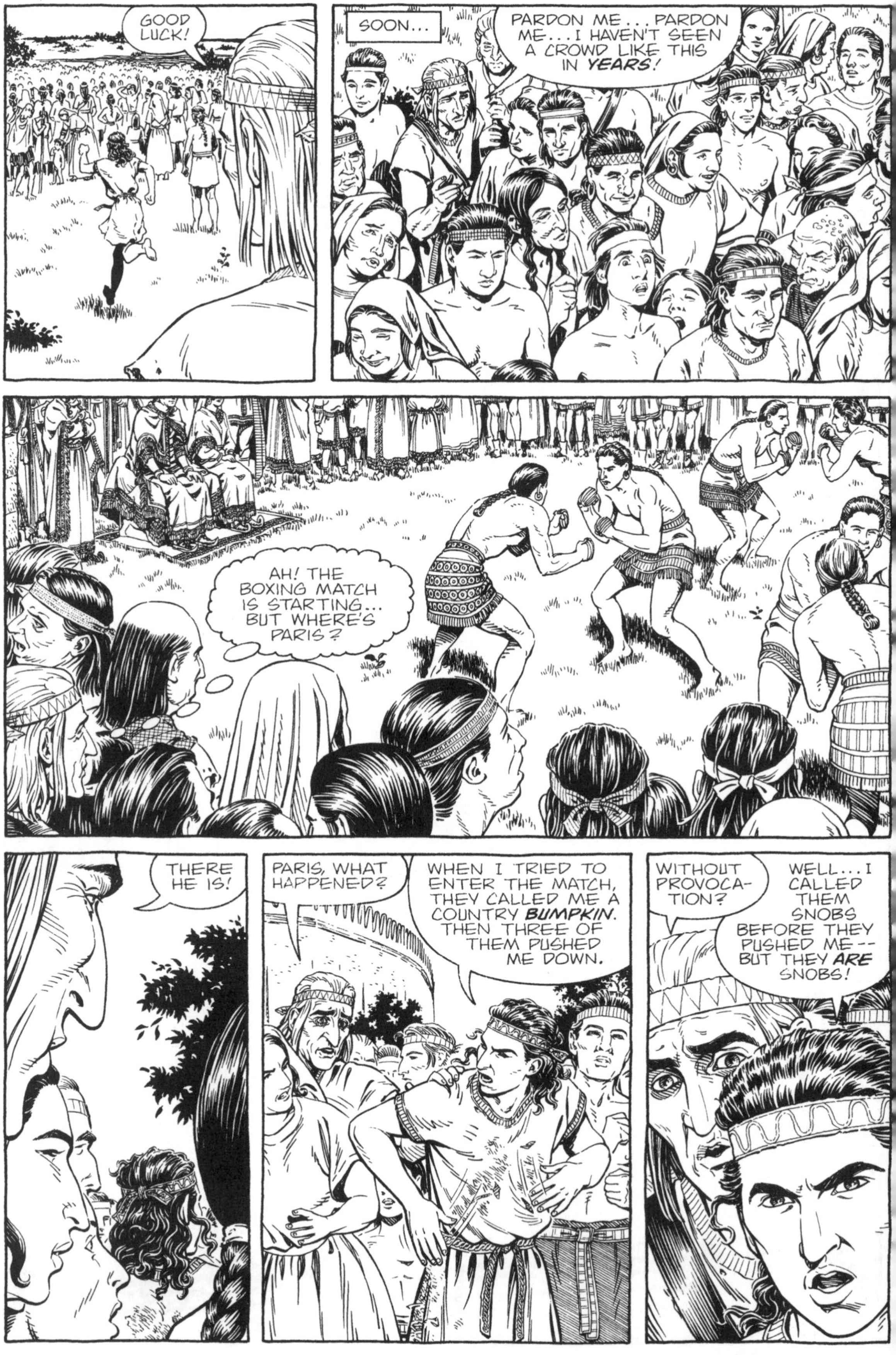
GOOD LUCK!
SOON...
PARDON ME... PARDON ME... I HAVEN'T SEEN A CROWD LIKE THIS IN *YEARS!*
AH! THE BOXING MATCH IS STARTING... BUT WHERE'S PARIS?
THERE HE IS!
PARIS, WHAT HAPPENED?
WHEN I TRIED TO ENTER THE MATCH, THEY CALLED ME A COUNTRY *BUMPKIN*. THEN THREE OF THEM PUSHED ME DOWN.
WITHOUT PROVOCATION?
WELL... I CALLED THEM SNOBS BEFORE THEY PUSHED ME -- BUT THEY *ARE* SNOBS!

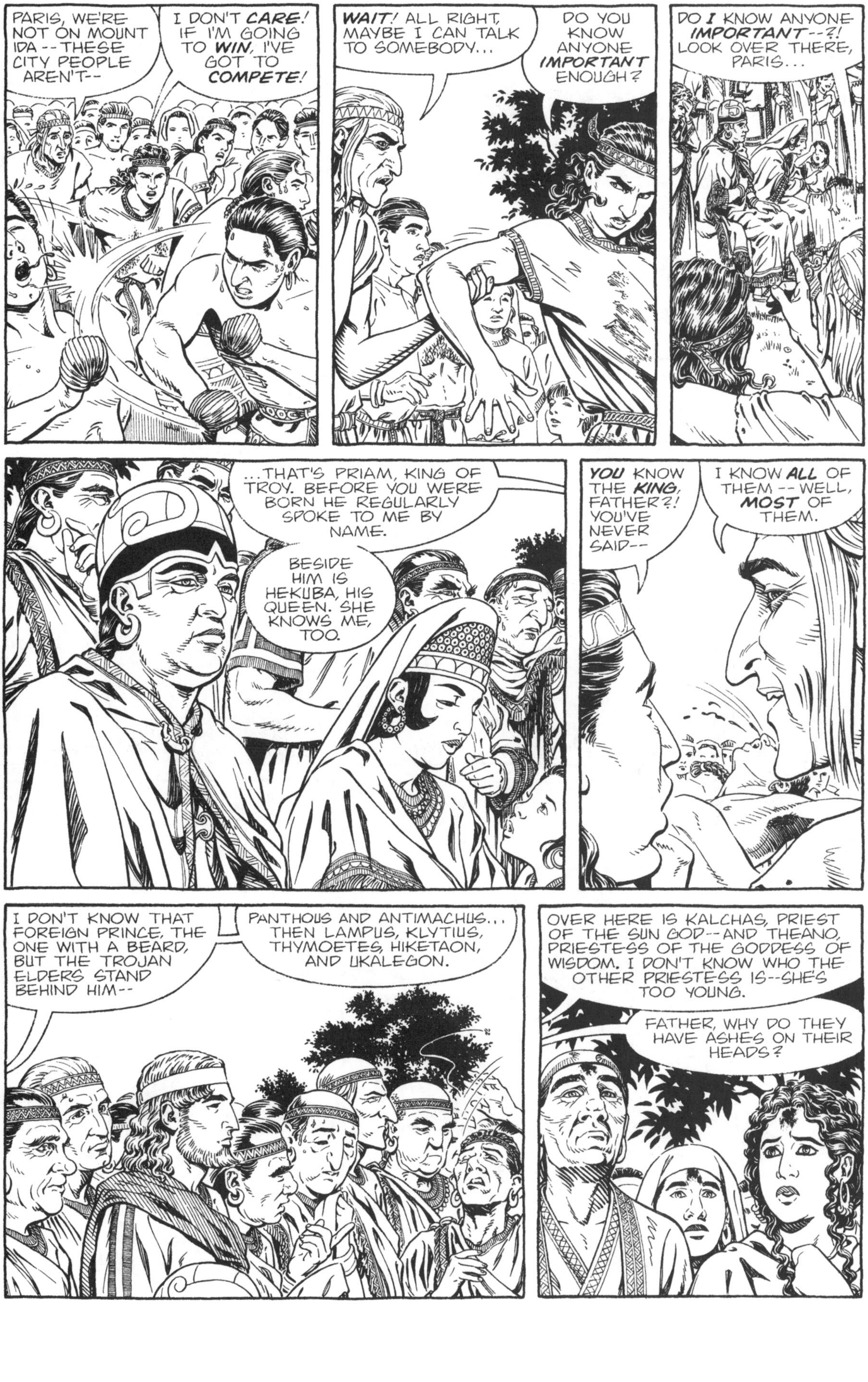
PARIS, WE'RE NOT ON MOUNT IDA -- THESE CITY PEOPLE AREN'T--
I DON'T CARE! IF I'M GOING TO WIN, I'VE GOT TO COMPETE!
WAIT! ALL RIGHT, MAYBE I CAN TALK TO SOMEBODY...
DO YOU KNOW ANYONE IMPORTANT ENOUGH?
DO I KNOW ANYONE IMPORTANT--?! LOOK OVER THERE, PARIS...
...THAT'S PRIAM, KING OF TROY. BEFORE YOU WERE BORN HE REGULARLY SPOKE TO ME BY NAME.
BESIDE HIM IS HEKUBA, HIS QUEEN. SHE KNOWS ME, TOO.
YOU KNOW THE KING, FATHER?! YOU'VE NEVER SAID--
I KNOW ALL OF THEM -- WELL, MOST OF THEM.
I DON'T KNOW THAT FOREIGN PRINCE, THE ONE WITH A BEARD, BUT THE TROJAN ELDERS STAND BEHIND HIM--
PANTHOUS AND ANTIMACHUS... THEN LAMPUS, KLYTIUS, THYMOETES, HIKETAON, AND UKALEGON.
OVER HERE IS KALCHAS, PRIEST OF THE SUN GOD--AND THEANO, PRIESTESS OF THE GODDESS OF WISDOM. I DON'T KNOW WHO THE OTHER PRIESTESS IS--SHE'S TOO YOUNG.
FATHER, WHY DO THEY HAVE ASHES ON THEIR HEADS?

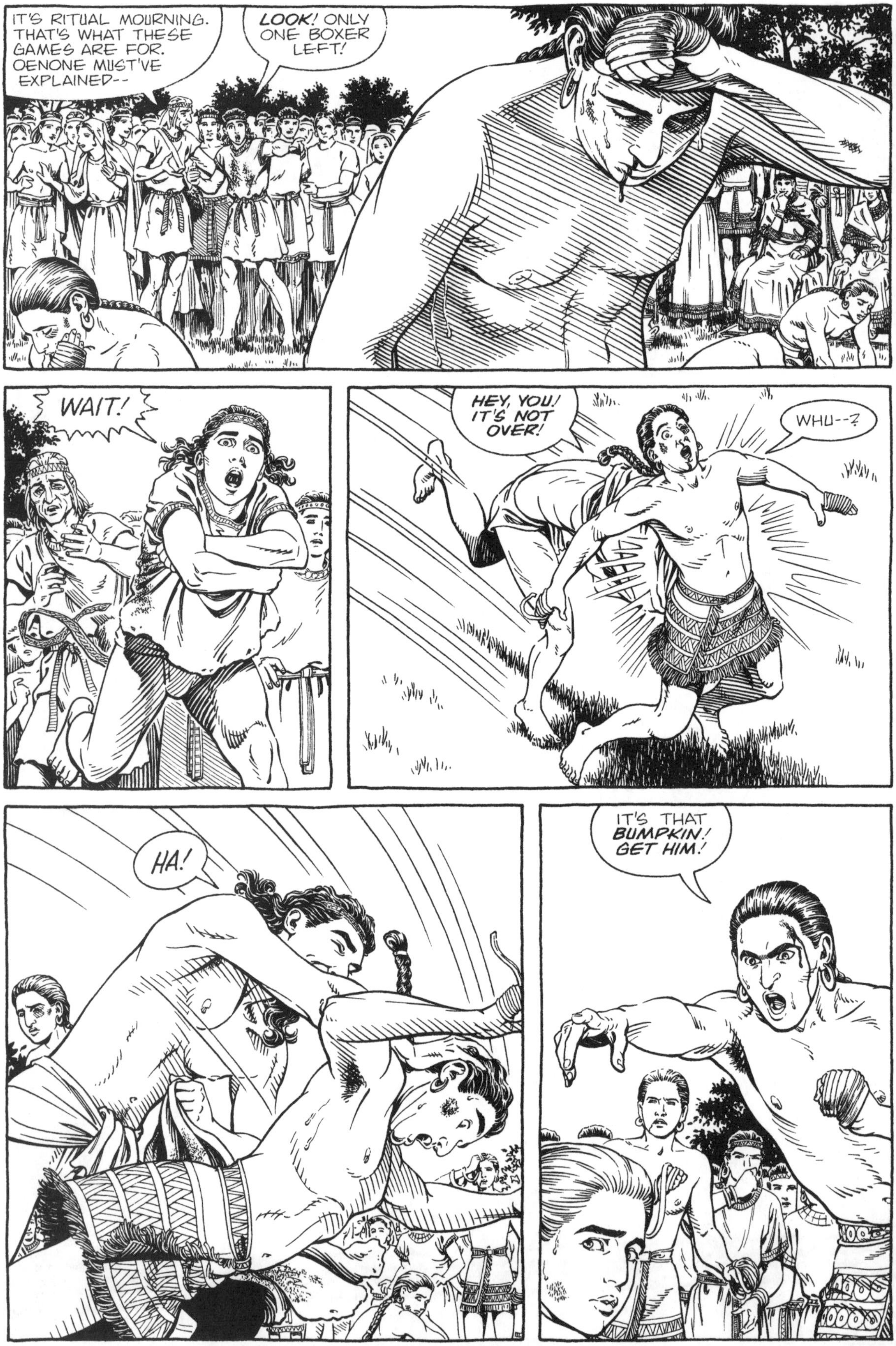
IT'S RITUAL MOURNING. THAT'S WHAT THESE GAMES ARE FOR. OENONE MUST'VE EXPLAINED--
LOOK! ONLY ONE BOXER LEFT!
WAIT!
HEY, YOU! IT'S NOT OVER!
WHU--?
HA!
IT'S THAT BUMPKIN! GET HIM!

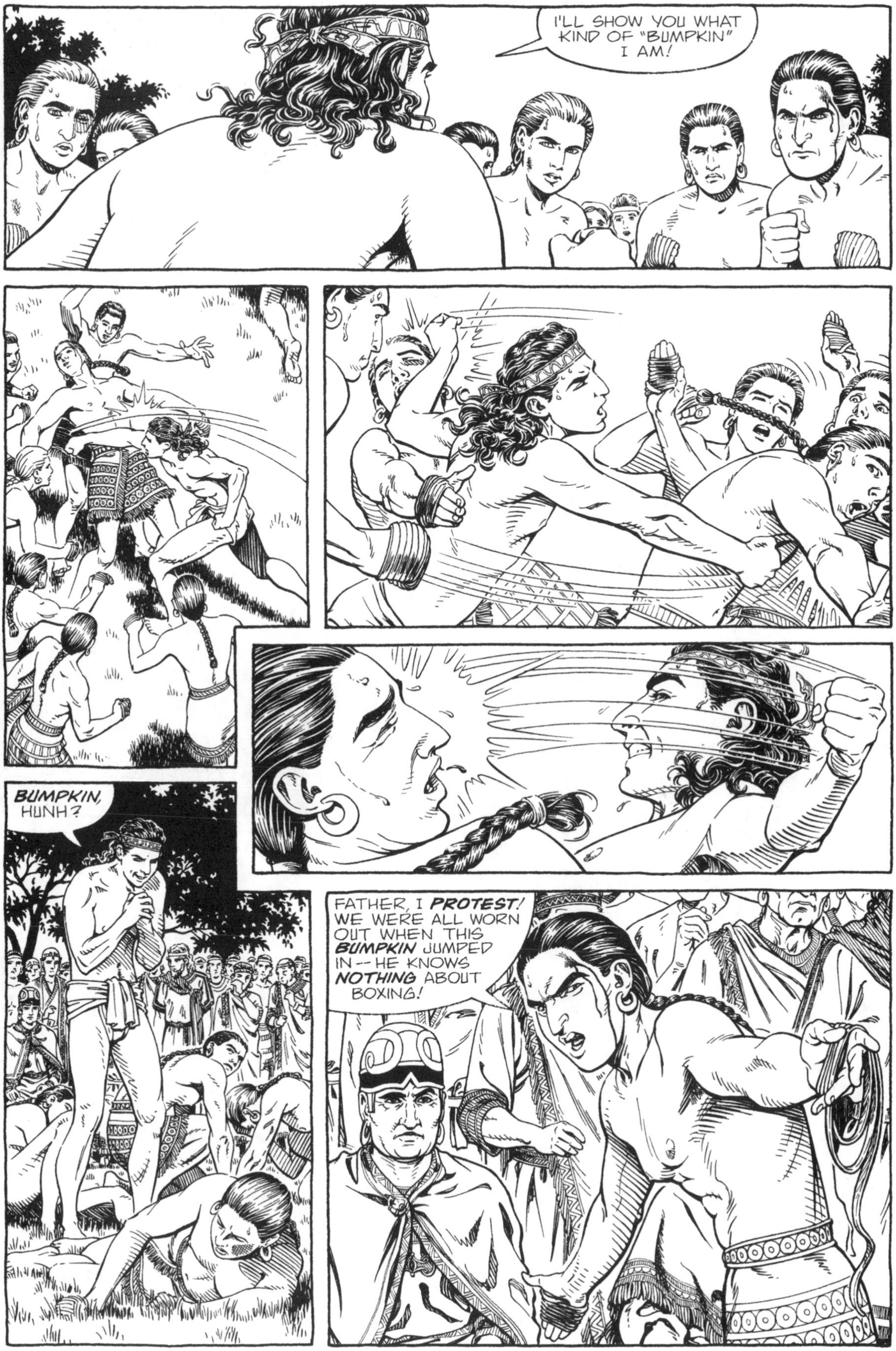
I'LL SHOW YOU WHAT KIND OF "BUMPKIN" I AM!
BUMPKIN, HUNH?
FATHER, I PROTEST! WE WERE ALL WORN OUT WHEN THIS BUMPKIN JUMPED IN -- HE KNOWS NOTHING ABOUT BOXING!

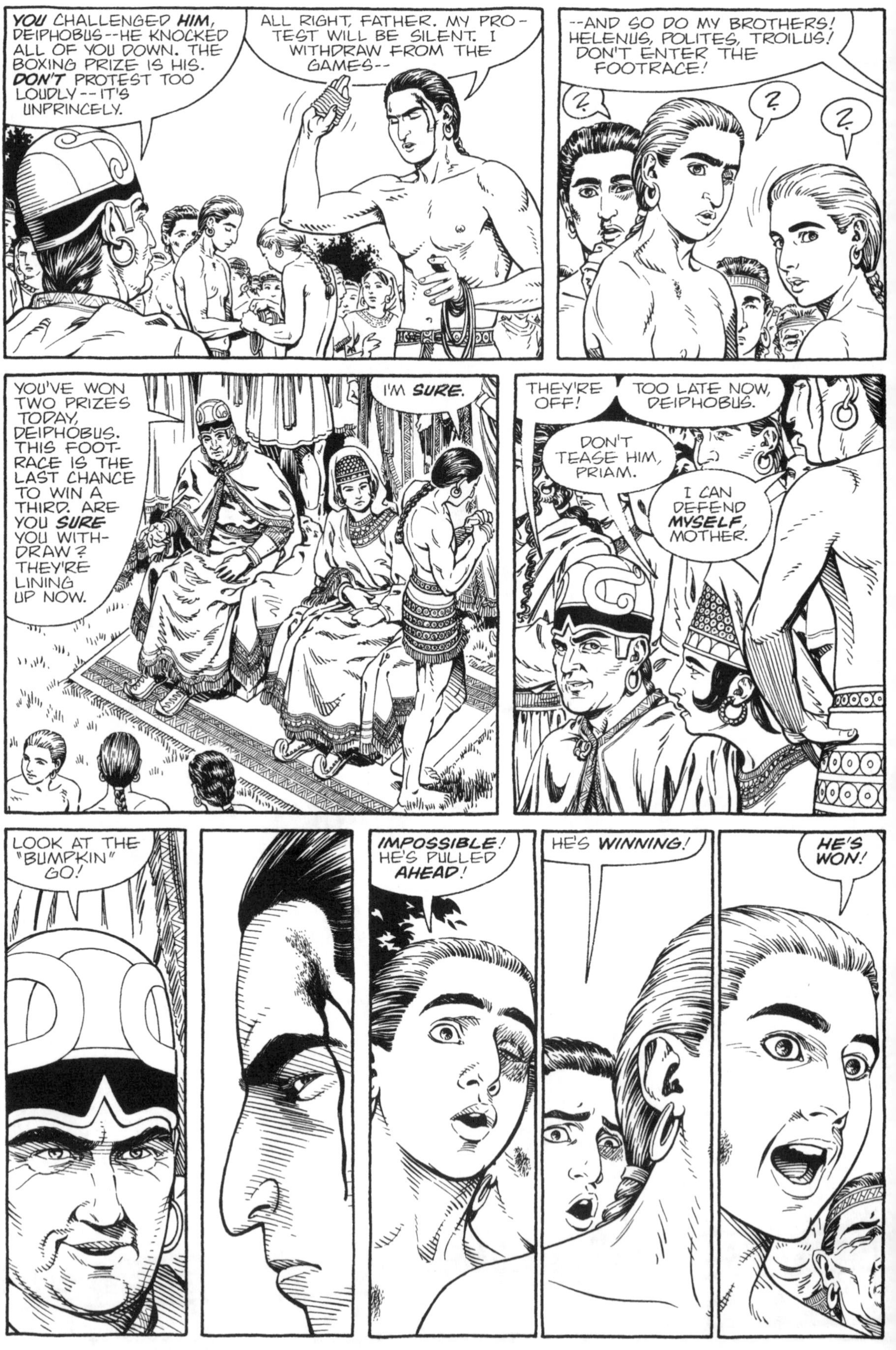
YOU CHALLENGED HIM, DEIPHOBUS--HE KNOCKED ALL OF YOU DOWN. THE BOXING PRIZE IS HIS. DON'T PROTEST TOO LOUDLY--IT'S UNPRINCELY.
ALL RIGHT, FATHER. MY PROTEST WILL BE SILENT. I WITHDRAW FROM THE GAMES--
--AND SO DO MY BROTHERS! HELENUS, POLITES, TROILUS! DON'T ENTER THE FOOTRACE!
?
?
?
YOU'VE WON TWO PRIZES TODAY, DEIPHOBUS. THIS FOOTRACE IS THE LAST CHANCE TO WIN A THIRD. ARE YOU SURE YOU WITHDRAW? THEY'RE LINING UP NOW.
I'M SURE.
THEY'RE OFF!
TOO LATE NOW, DEIPHOBUS.
DON'T TEASE HIM, PRIAM.
I CAN DEFEND MYSELF, MOTHER.
LOOK AT THE "BUMPKIN" GO!
IMPOSSIBLE! HE'S PULLED AHEAD!
HE'S WINNING!
HE'S WON!

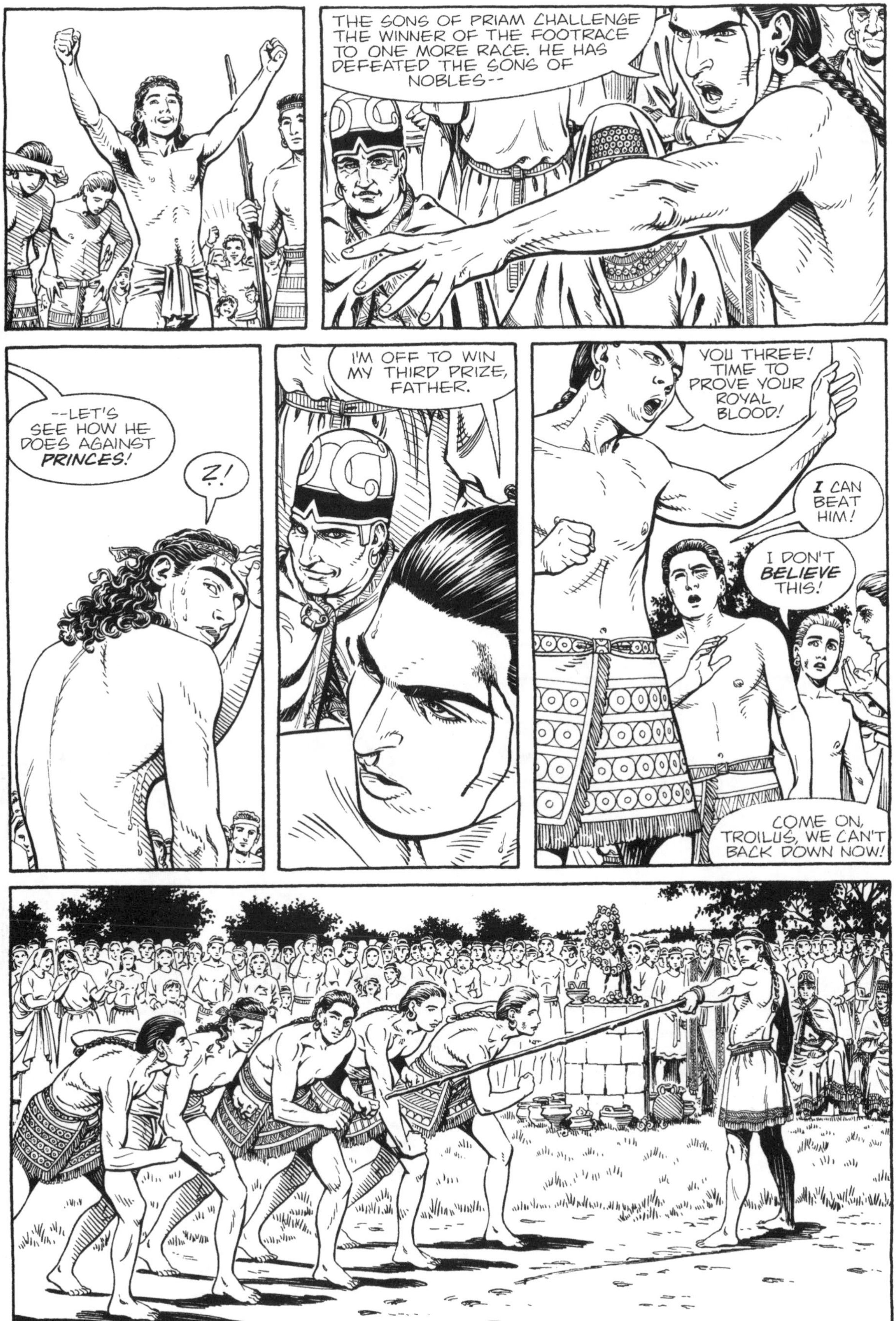
THE SONS OF PRIAM CHALLENGE THE WINNER OF THE FOOTRACE TO ONE MORE RACE. HE HAS DEFEATED THE SONS OF NOBLES--
--LET'S SEE HOW HE DOES AGAINST PRINCES!
Z!
I'M OFF TO WIN MY THIRD PRIZE, FATHER.
YOU THREE! TIME TO PROVE YOUR ROYAL BLOOD!
I CAN BEAT HIM!
I DON'T BELIEVE THIS!
COME ON, TROILUS, WE CAN'T BACK DOWN NOW!

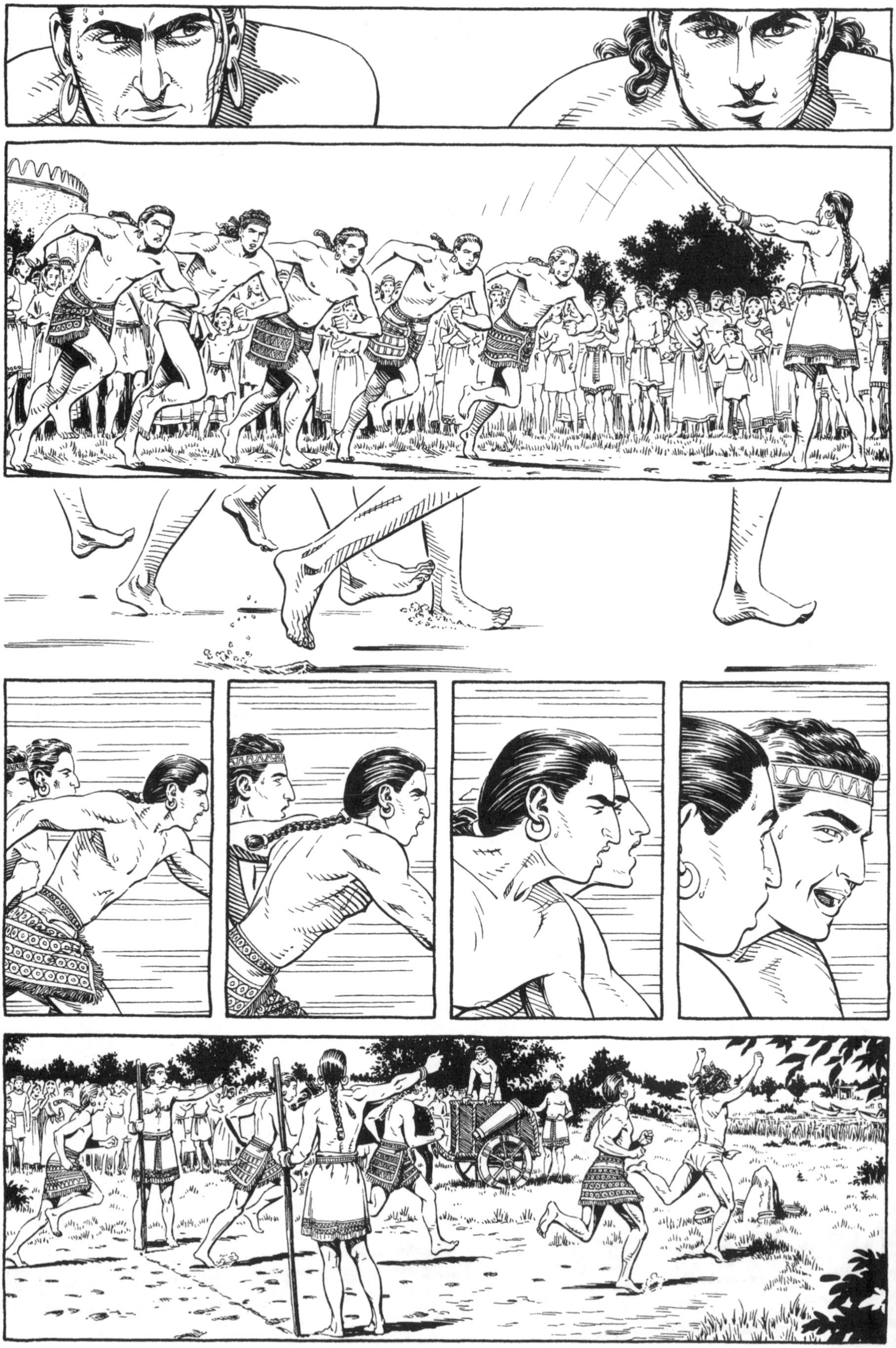

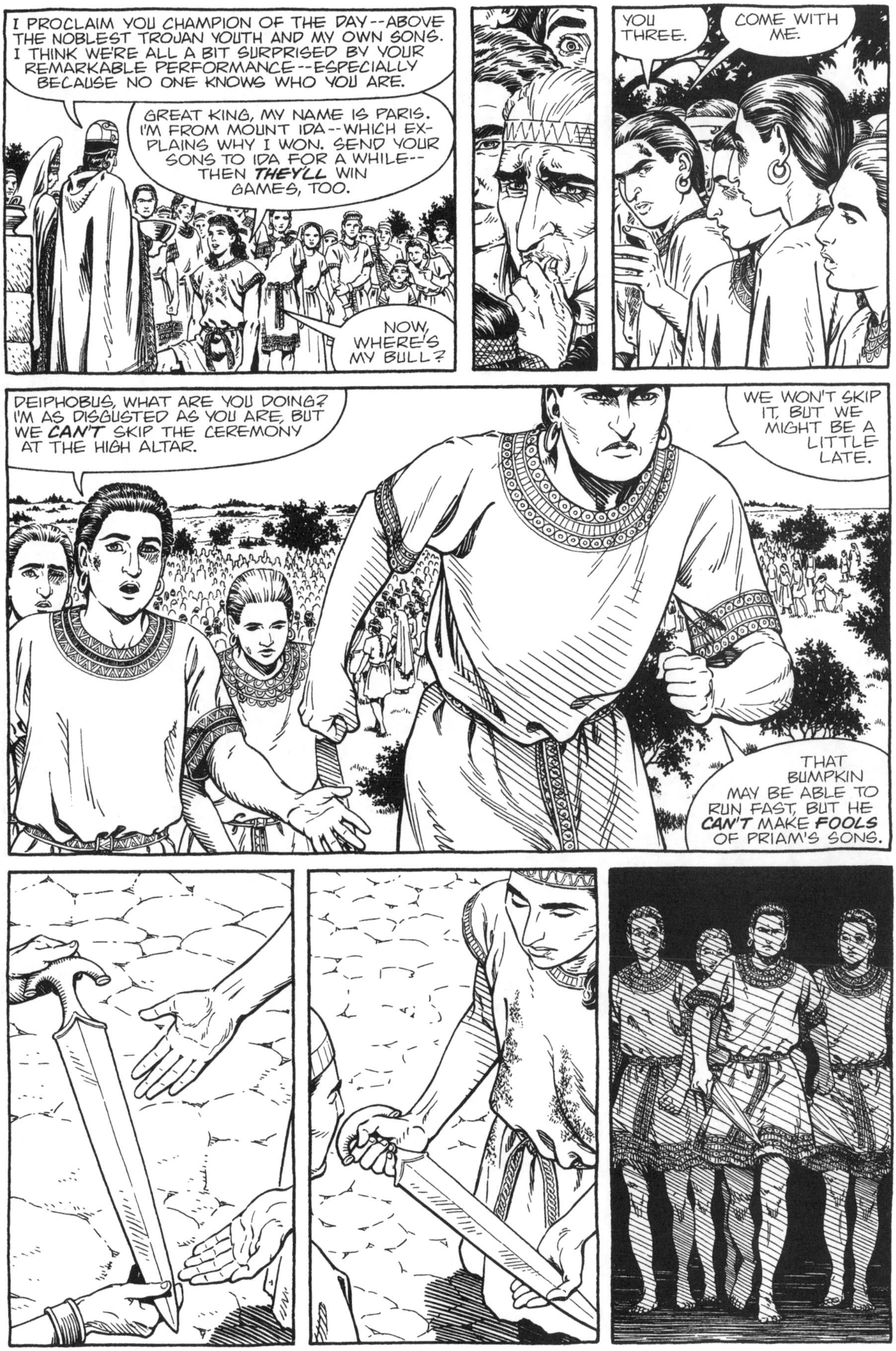
I PROCLAIM YOU CHAMPION OF THE DAY--ABOVE THE NOBLEST TROJAN YOUTH AND MY OWN SONS. I THINK WE'RE ALL A BIT SURPRISED BY YOUR REMARKABLE PERFORMANCE--ESPECIALLY BECAUSE NO ONE KNOWS WHO YOU ARE.
GREAT KING, MY NAME IS PARIS. I'M FROM MOUNT IDA--WHICH EXPLAINS WHY I WON. SEND YOUR SONS TO IDA FOR A WHILE--THEN THEY'LL WIN GAMES, TOO.
NOW, WHERE'S MY BULL?
YOU THREE.
COME WITH ME.
DEIPHOBUS, WHAT ARE YOU DOING? I'M AS DISGUSTED AS YOU ARE, BUT WE CAN'T SKIP THE CEREMONY AT THE HIGH ALTAR.
WE WON'T SKIP IT, BUT WE MIGHT BE A LITTLE LATE.
THAT BUMPKIN MAY BE ABLE TO RUN FAST, BUT HE CAN'T MAKE FOOLS OF PRIAM'S SONS.

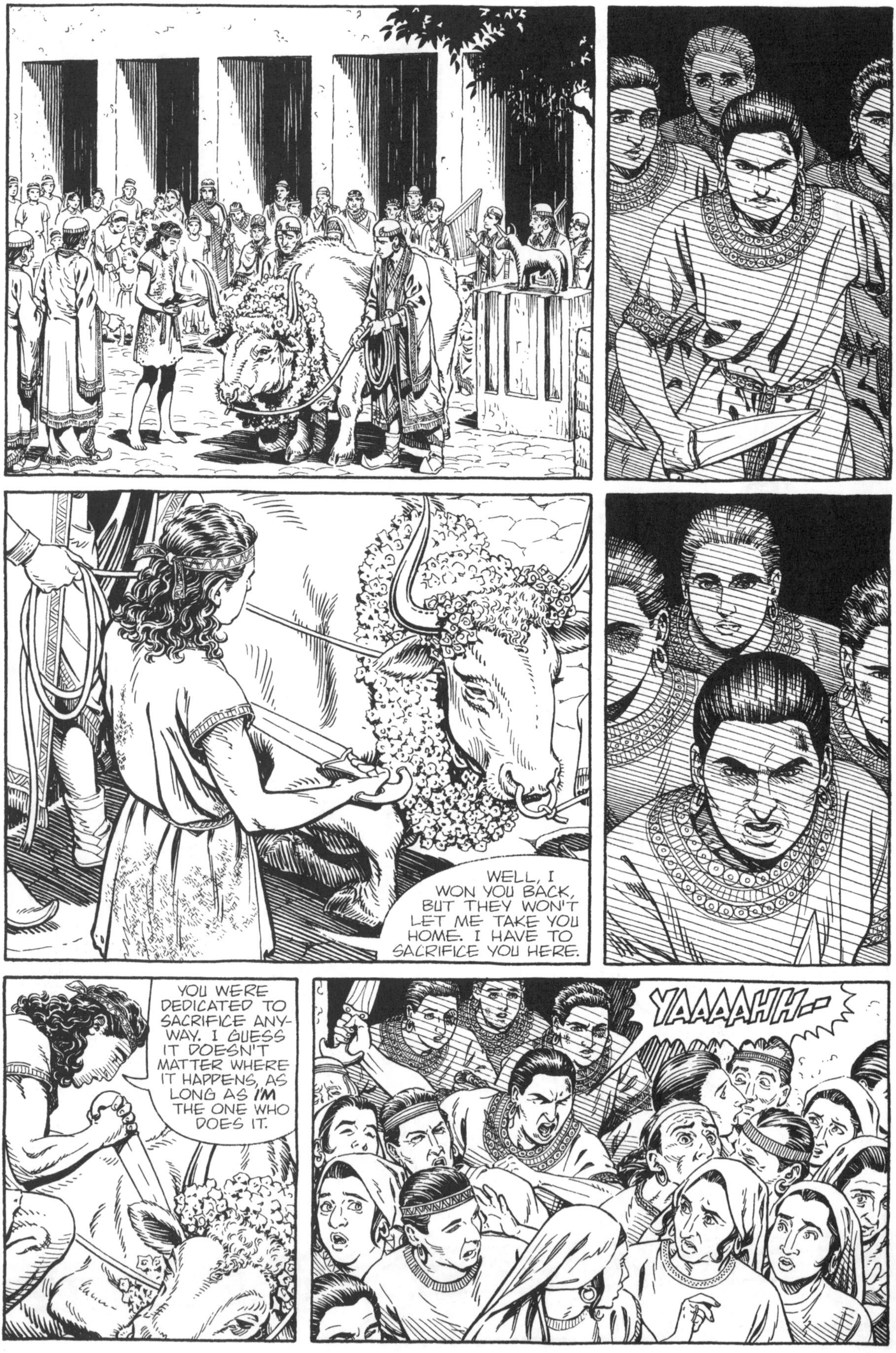
WELL, I WON YOU BACK, BUT THEY WON'T LET ME TAKE YOU HOME. I HAVE TO SACRIFICE YOU HERE.
YOU WERE DEDICATED TO SACRIFICE ANY-WAY. I GUESS IT DOESN'T MATTER WHERE IT HAPPENS, AS LONG AS *I'M* THE ONE WHO DOES IT.
YAAAAHH--

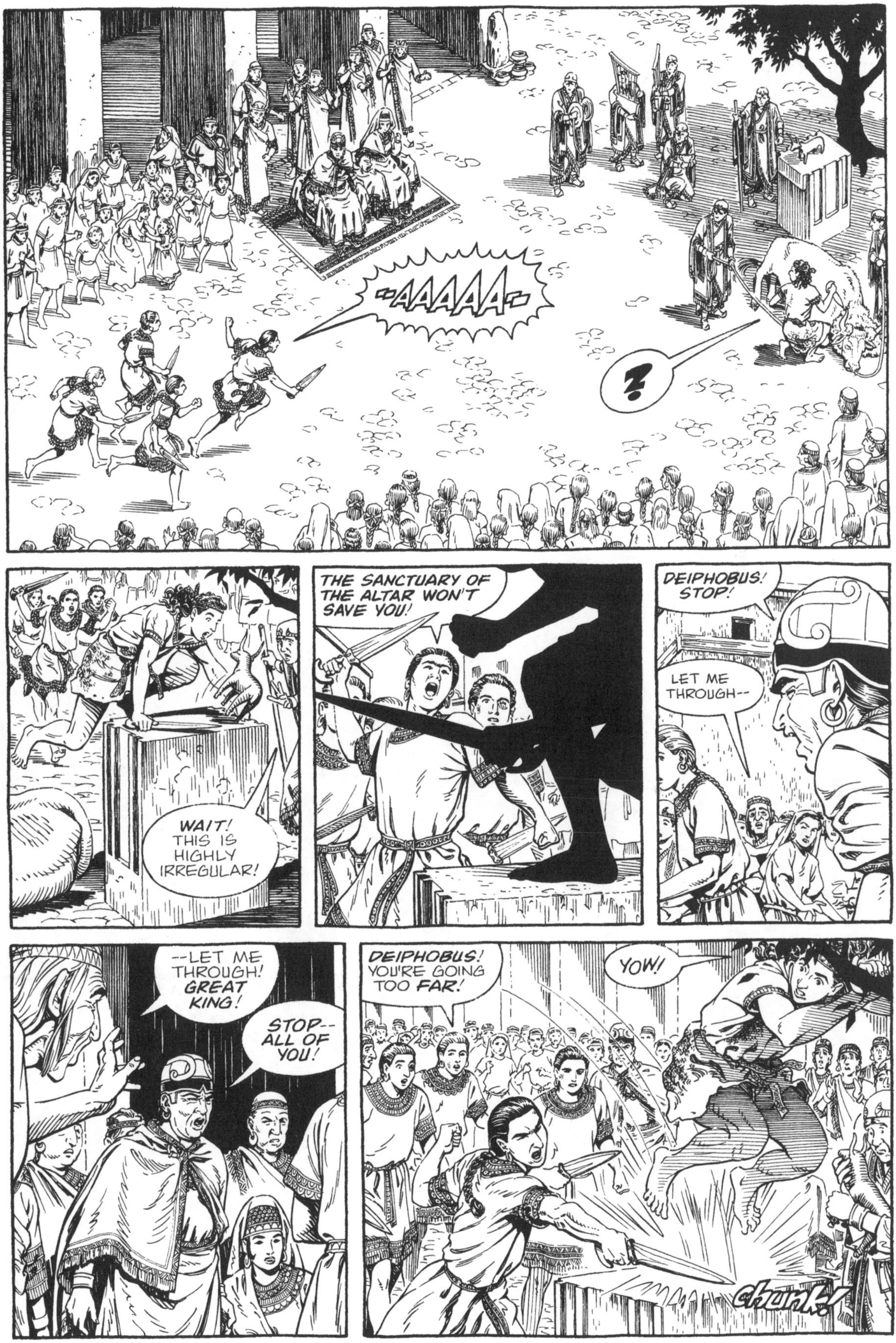
-AAAAA-
?
WAIT! THIS IS HIGHLY IRREGULAR!
THE SANCTUARY OF THE ALTAR WON'T SAVE YOU!
DEIPHOBUS! STOP!
LET ME THROUGH--
--LET ME THROUGH! GREAT KING!
STOP-- ALL OF YOU!
DEIPHOBUS! YOU'RE GOING TOO FAR!
YOW!
chunk!

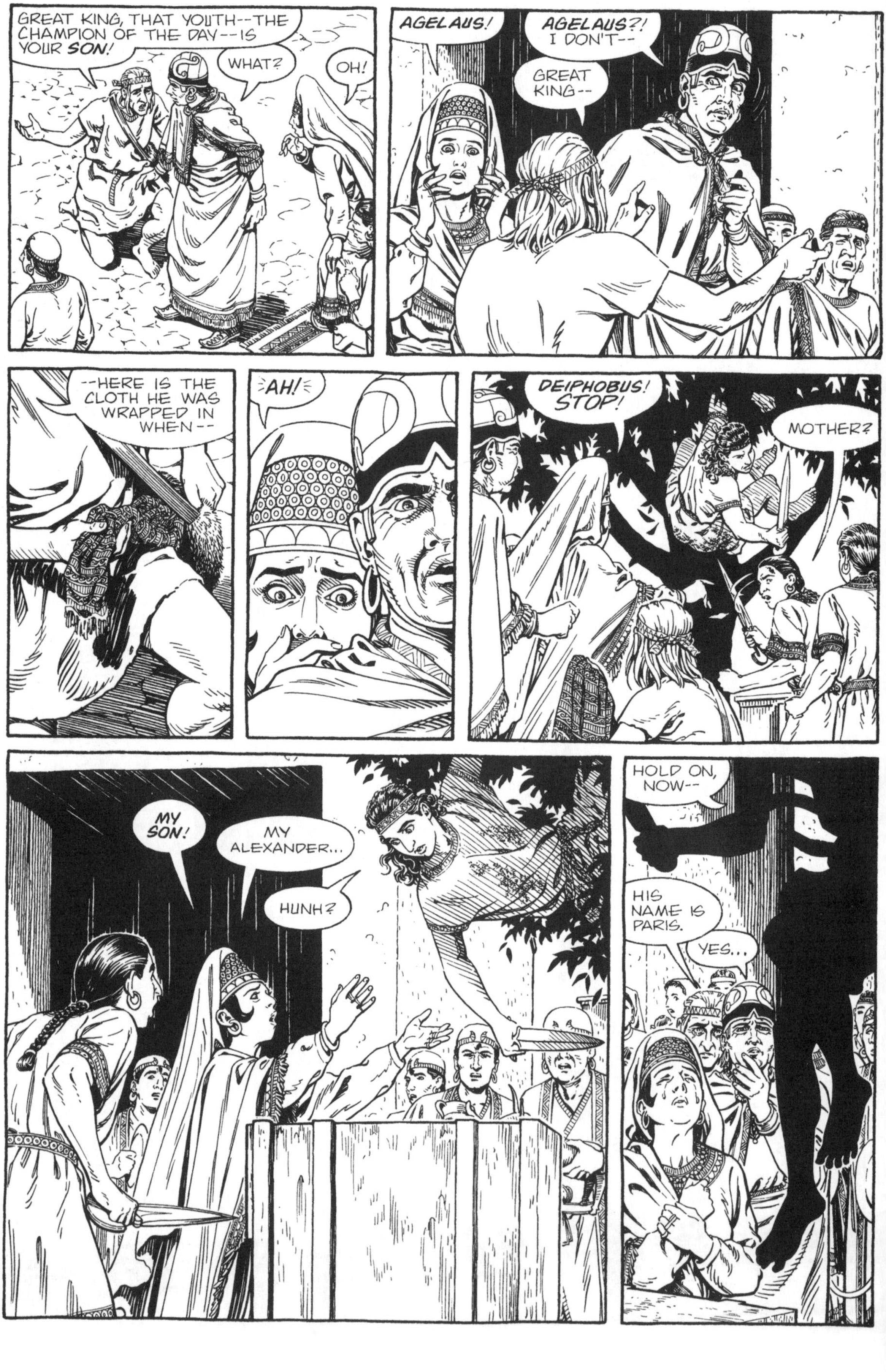
GREAT KING, THAT YOUTH--THE CHAMPION OF THE DAY--IS YOUR SON!
WHAT?
OH!
AGELAUS!
AGELAUS?! I DON'T--
GREAT KING--
--HERE IS THE CLOTH HE WAS WRAPPED IN WHEN--
AH!
DEIPHOBUS! STOP!
MOTHER?
MY SON!
MY ALEXANDER...
HUNH?
HOLD ON, NOW--
HIS NAME IS PARIS.
YES...

FATHER, WHAT'S GOING ON? I DON'T UNDERSTAND--

FORGIVE ME, PARIS. I'VE NEVER TOLD YOU. I'M SORRY...

YOU'RE A PRINCE OF TROY.

WHAT--?

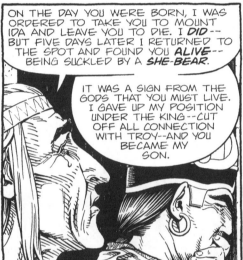
ON THE DAY YOU WERE BORN, I WAS ORDERED TO TAKE YOU TO MOUNT IDA AND LEAVE YOU TO DIE. I *DID*-- BUT FIVE DAYS LATER I RETURNED TO THE SPOT AND FOUND YOU *ALIVE*-- BEING SUCKLED BY A *SHE-BEAR*.

IT WAS A SIGN FROM THE GODS THAT YOU MUST LIVE. I GAVE UP MY POSITION UNDER THE KING--CUT OFF ALL CONNECTION WITH TROY--AND YOU BECAME MY SON.

HERE'S THE PROOF --THIS SWADDLING CLOTH--KEPT SAFE FOR SIXTEEN YEARS. THERE'S NO BLOOD ON IT--NO MARKS OF VIOLENCE OR WEATHER--

YES, HE *IS* MY SON...

NO... heh...

SILENCE.

LISTEN, EVERYONE! MY LONG LOST SON HAS BEEN *FOUND*! WELCOME PARIS, *PRINCE OF TROY*!

WELL, DEIPHOBUS, NOW THAT THE "BUMPKIN" IS A PRINCE--*AND OUR BROTHER*--IT'S NO DISGRACE THAT HE'S CHAMPION OF THE DAY, IS IT?

uh

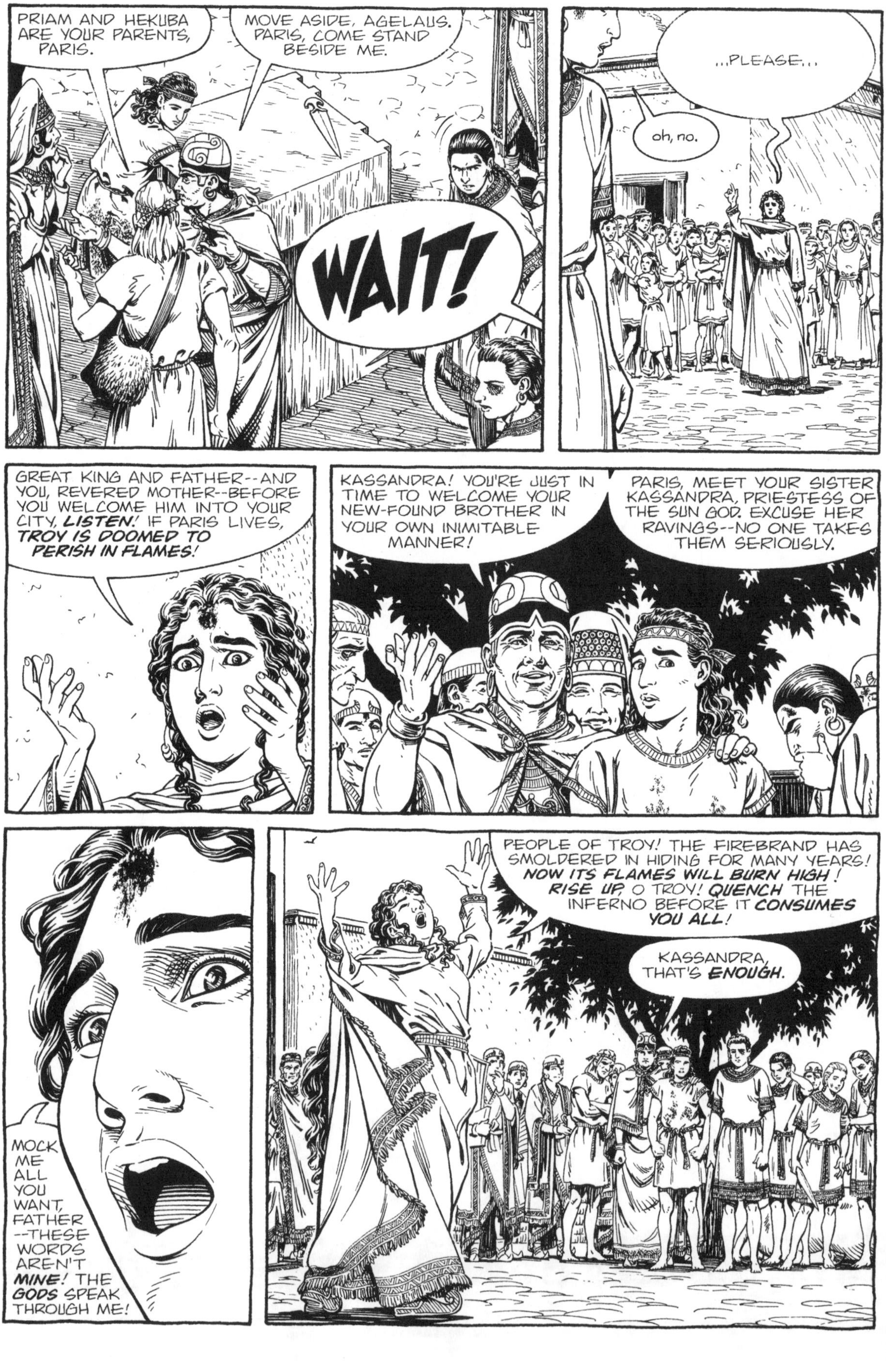
PRIAM AND HEKUBA ARE YOUR PARENTS, PARIS.
MOVE ASIDE, AGELAUS. PARIS, COME STAND BESIDE ME.
WAIT!
...PLEASE...
oh, no.
GREAT KING AND FATHER--AND YOU, REVERED MOTHER--BEFORE YOU WELCOME HIM INTO YOUR CITY, LISTEN! IF PARIS LIVES, TROY IS DOOMED TO PERISH IN FLAMES!
KASSANDRA! YOU'RE JUST IN TIME TO WELCOME YOUR NEW-FOUND BROTHER IN YOUR OWN INIMITABLE MANNER!
PARIS, MEET YOUR SISTER KASSANDRA, PRIESTESS OF THE SUN GOD. EXCUSE HER RAVINGS--NO ONE TAKES THEM SERIOUSLY.
MOCK ME ALL YOU WANT, FATHER --THESE WORDS AREN'T MINE! THE GODS SPEAK THROUGH ME!
PEOPLE OF TROY! THE FIREBRAND HAS SMOLDERED IN HIDING FOR MANY YEARS! NOW ITS FLAMES WILL BURN HIGH! RISE UP, O TROY! QUENCH THE INFERNO BEFORE IT CONSUMES YOU ALL!
KASSANDRA, THAT'S ENOUGH.

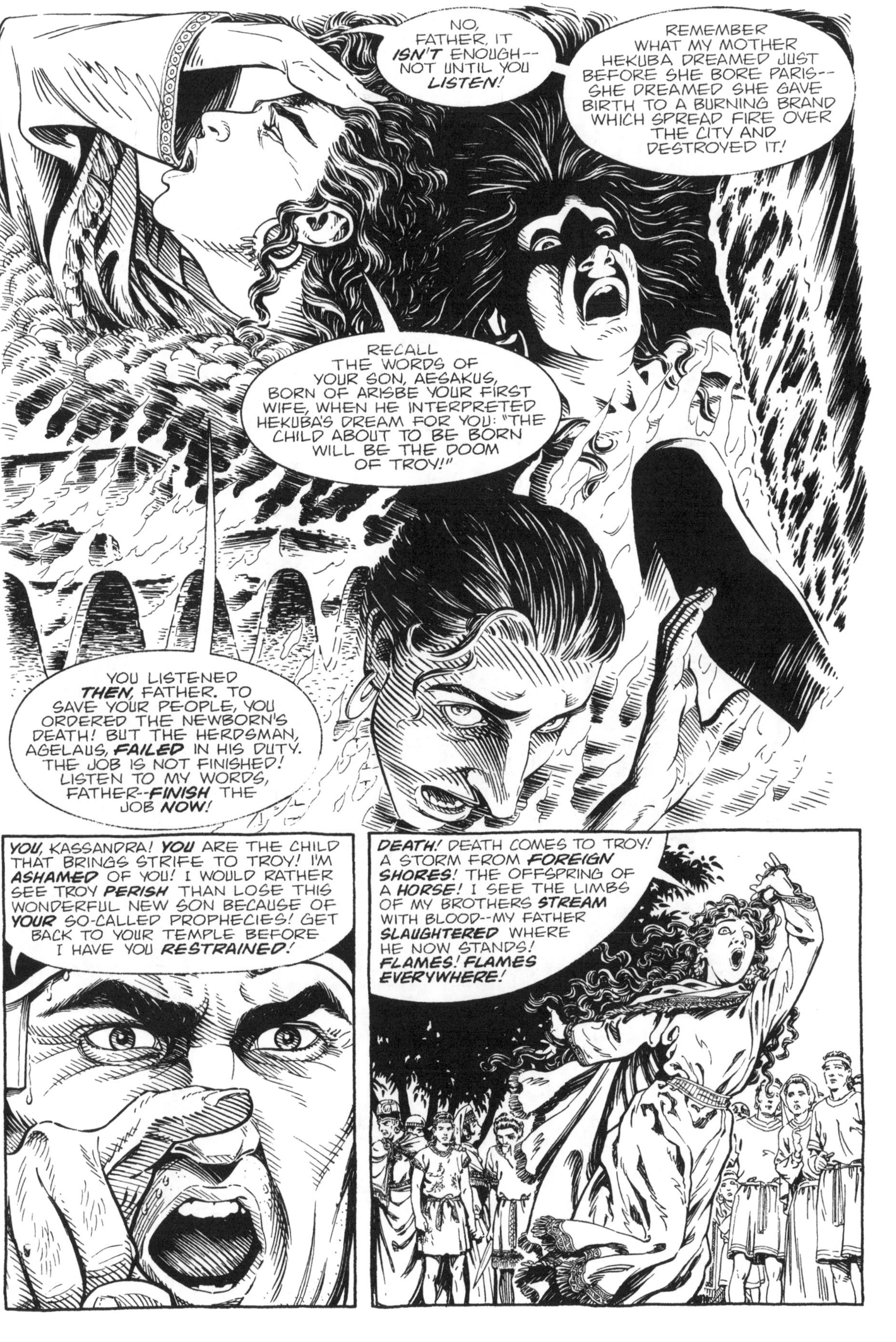
NO, FATHER, IT ISN'T ENOUGH-- NOT UNTIL YOU LISTEN!
REMEMBER WHAT MY MOTHER HEKUBA DREAMED JUST BEFORE SHE BORE PARIS-- SHE DREAMED SHE GAVE BIRTH TO A BURNING BRAND WHICH SPREAD FIRE OVER THE CITY AND DESTROYED IT!
RECALL THE WORDS OF YOUR SON, AESAKUS, BORN OF ARISBE YOUR FIRST WIFE, WHEN HE INTERPRETED HEKUBA'S DREAM FOR YOU: "THE CHILD ABOUT TO BE BORN WILL BE THE DOOM OF TROY!"
YOU LISTENED THEN, FATHER. TO SAVE YOUR PEOPLE, YOU ORDERED THE NEWBORN'S DEATH! BUT THE HERDSMAN, AGELAUS, FAILED IN HIS DUTY. THE JOB IS NOT FINISHED! LISTEN TO MY WORDS, FATHER--FINISH THE JOB NOW!
YOU, KASSANDRA! YOU ARE THE CHILD THAT BRINGS STRIFE TO TROY! I'M ASHAMED OF YOU! I WOULD RATHER SEE TROY PERISH THAN LOSE THIS WONDERFUL NEW SON BECAUSE OF YOUR SO-CALLED PROPHECIES! GET BACK TO YOUR TEMPLE BEFORE I HAVE YOU RESTRAINED!
DEATH! DEATH COMES TO TROY! A STORM FROM FOREIGN SHORES! THE OFFSPRING OF A HORSE! I SEE THE LIMBS OF MY BROTHERS STREAM WITH BLOOD--MY FATHER SLAUGHTERED WHERE HE NOW STANDS! FLAMES! FLAMES EVERYWHERE!

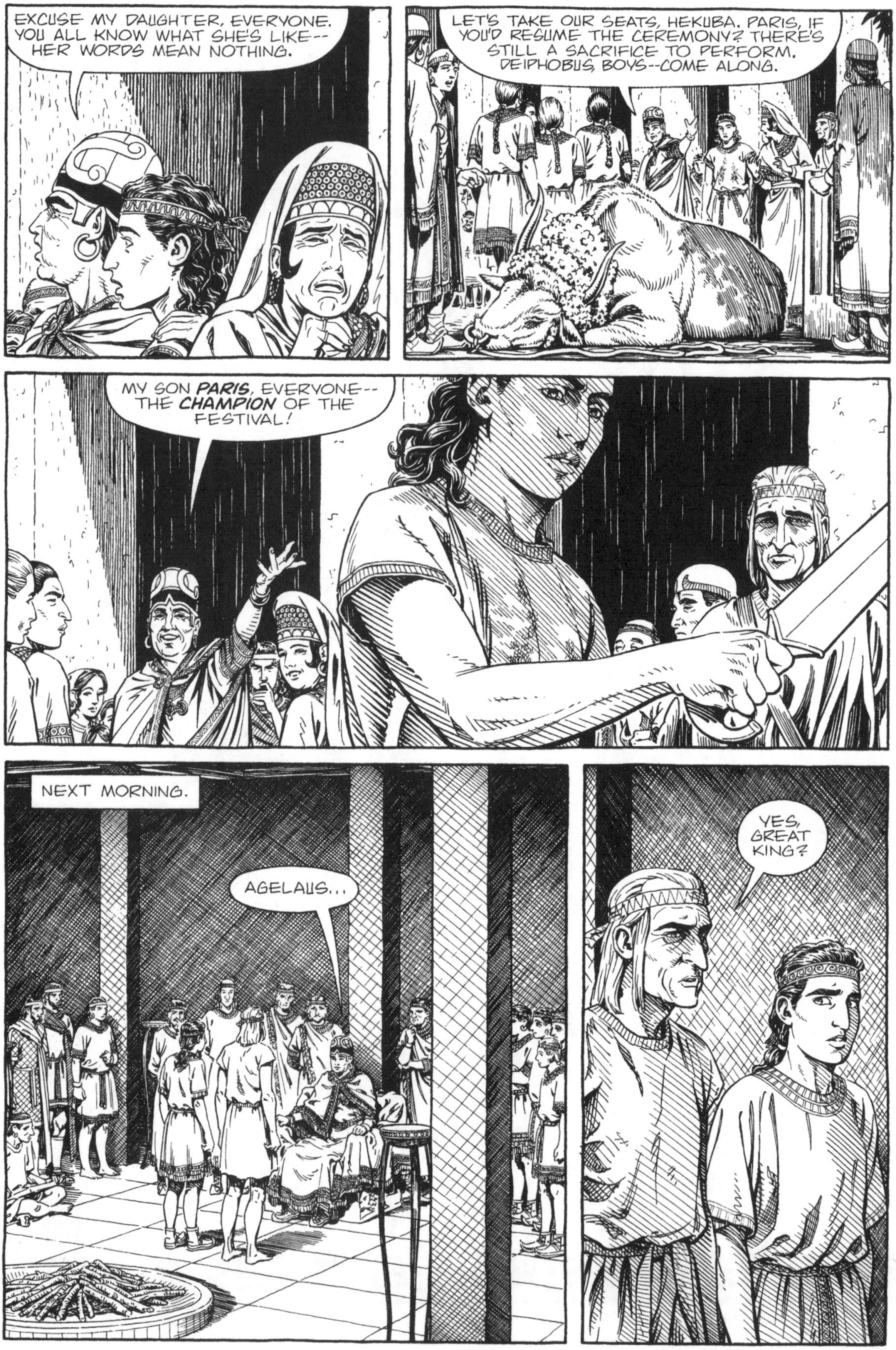
EXCUSE MY DAUGHTER, EVERYONE. YOU ALL KNOW WHAT SHE'S LIKE-- HER WORDS MEAN NOTHING.
LET'S TAKE OUR SEATS, HEKUBA. PARIS, IF YOU'D RESUME THE CEREMONY? THERE'S STILL A SACRIFICE TO PERFORM. DEIPHOBUS, BOYS--COME ALONG.
MY SON PARIS, EVERYONE-- THE CHAMPION OF THE FESTIVAL!
NEXT MORNING.
AGELAUS...
YES, GREAT KING?

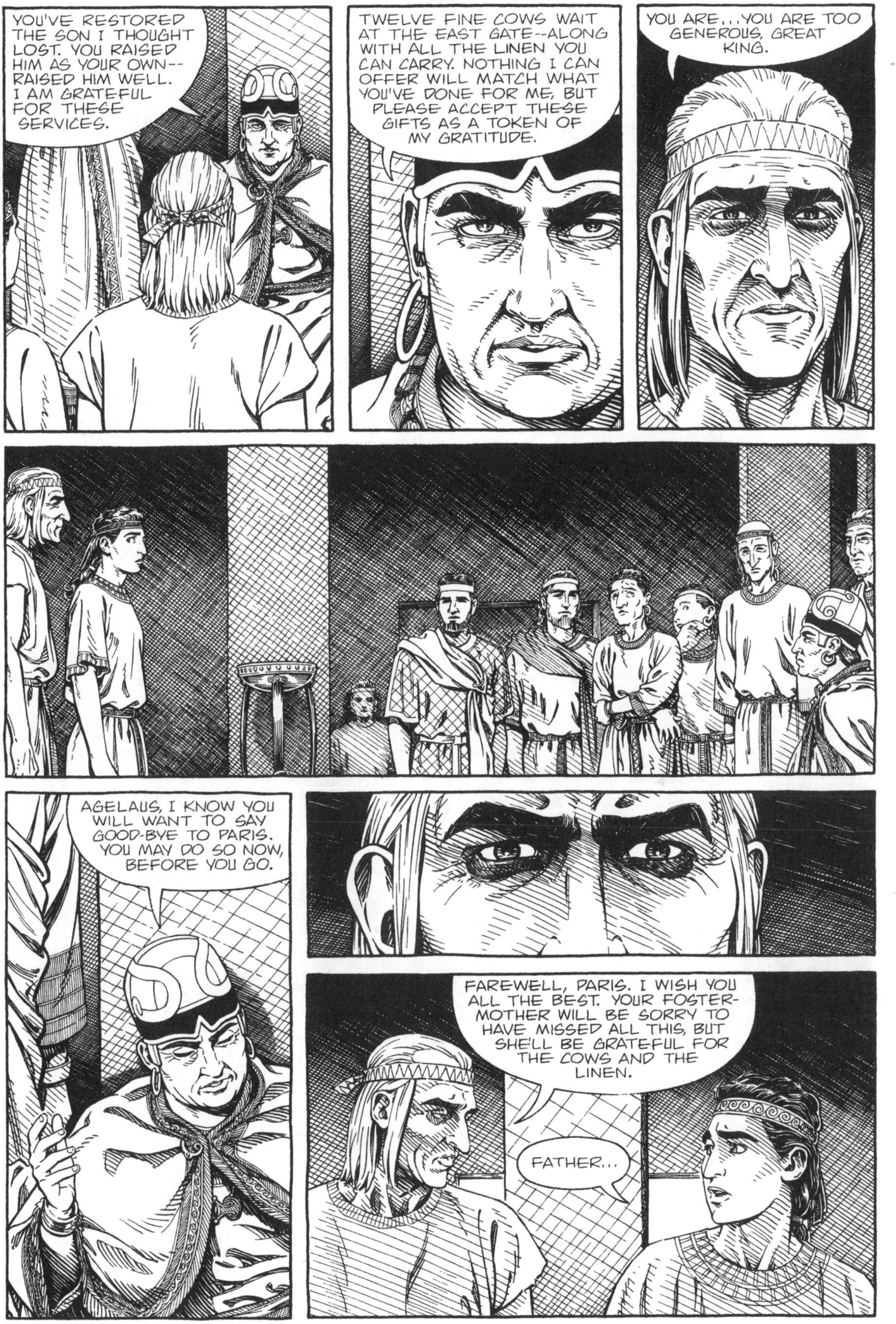
YOU'VE RESTORED THE SON I THOUGHT LOST. YOU RAISED HIM AS YOUR OWN-- RAISED HIM WELL. I AM GRATEFUL FOR THESE SERVICES.
TWELVE FINE COWS WAIT AT THE EAST GATE--ALONG WITH ALL THE LINEN YOU CAN CARRY. NOTHING I CAN OFFER WILL MATCH WHAT YOU'VE DONE FOR ME, BUT PLEASE ACCEPT THESE GIFTS AS A TOKEN OF MY GRATITUDE.
YOU ARE...YOU ARE TOO GENEROUS, GREAT KING.
AGELAUS, I KNOW YOU WILL WANT TO SAY GOOD-BYE TO PARIS. YOU MAY DO SO NOW, BEFORE YOU GO.
FAREWELL, PARIS. I WISH YOU ALL THE BEST. YOUR FOSTER-MOTHER WILL BE SORRY TO HAVE MISSED ALL THIS, BUT SHE'LL BE GRATEFUL FOR THE COWS AND THE LINEN.
FATHER...

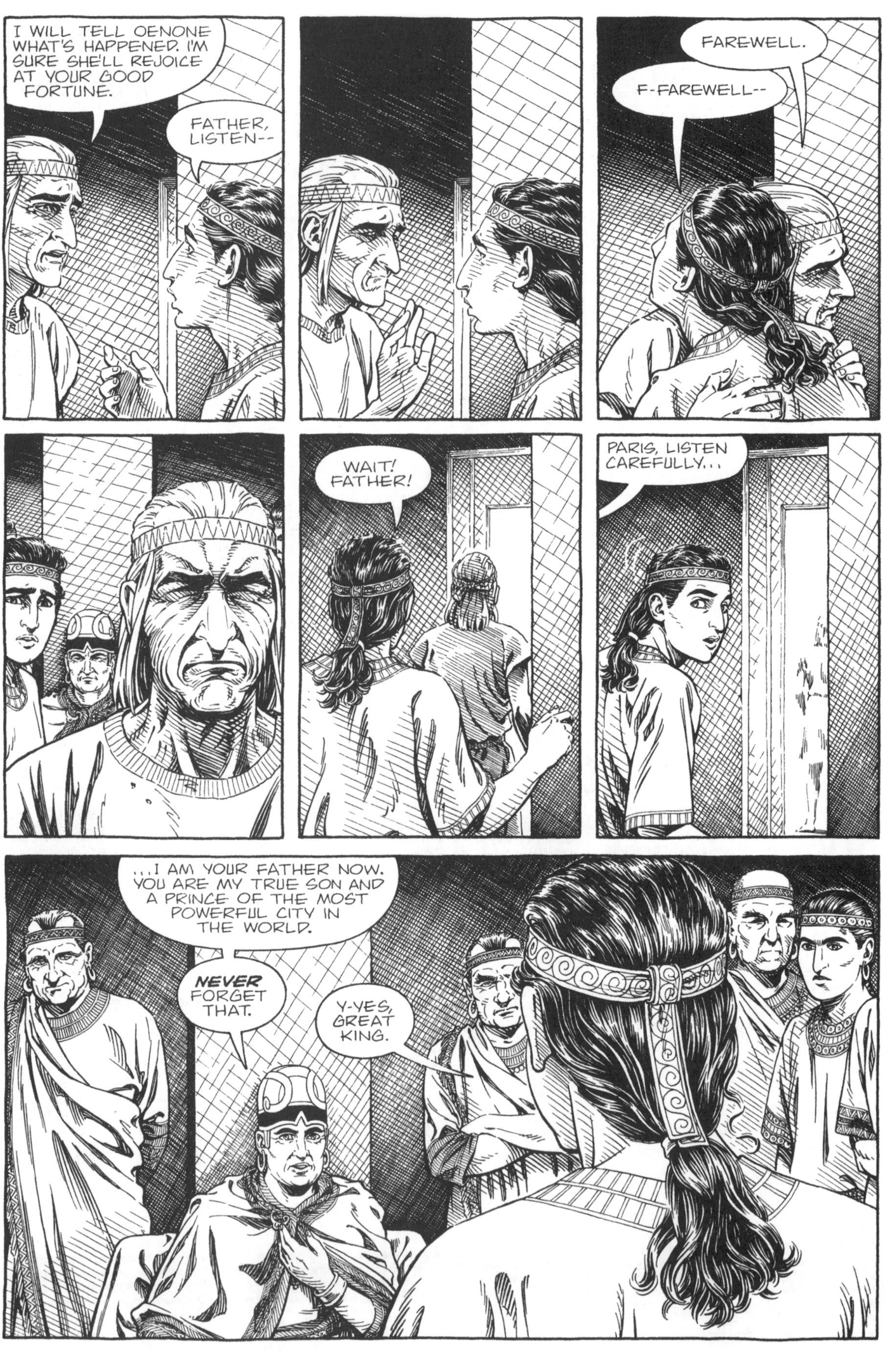
I WILL TELL OENONE WHAT'S HAPPENED. I'M SURE SHE'LL REJOICE AT YOUR GOOD FORTUNE.
FATHER, LISTEN--
FAREWELL.
F-FAREWELL--
WAIT! FATHER!
PARIS, LISTEN CAREFULLY...
...I AM YOUR FATHER NOW. YOU ARE MY TRUE SON AND A PRINCE OF THE MOST POWERFUL CITY IN THE WORLD.
NEVER FORGET THAT.
Y-YES, GREAT KING.

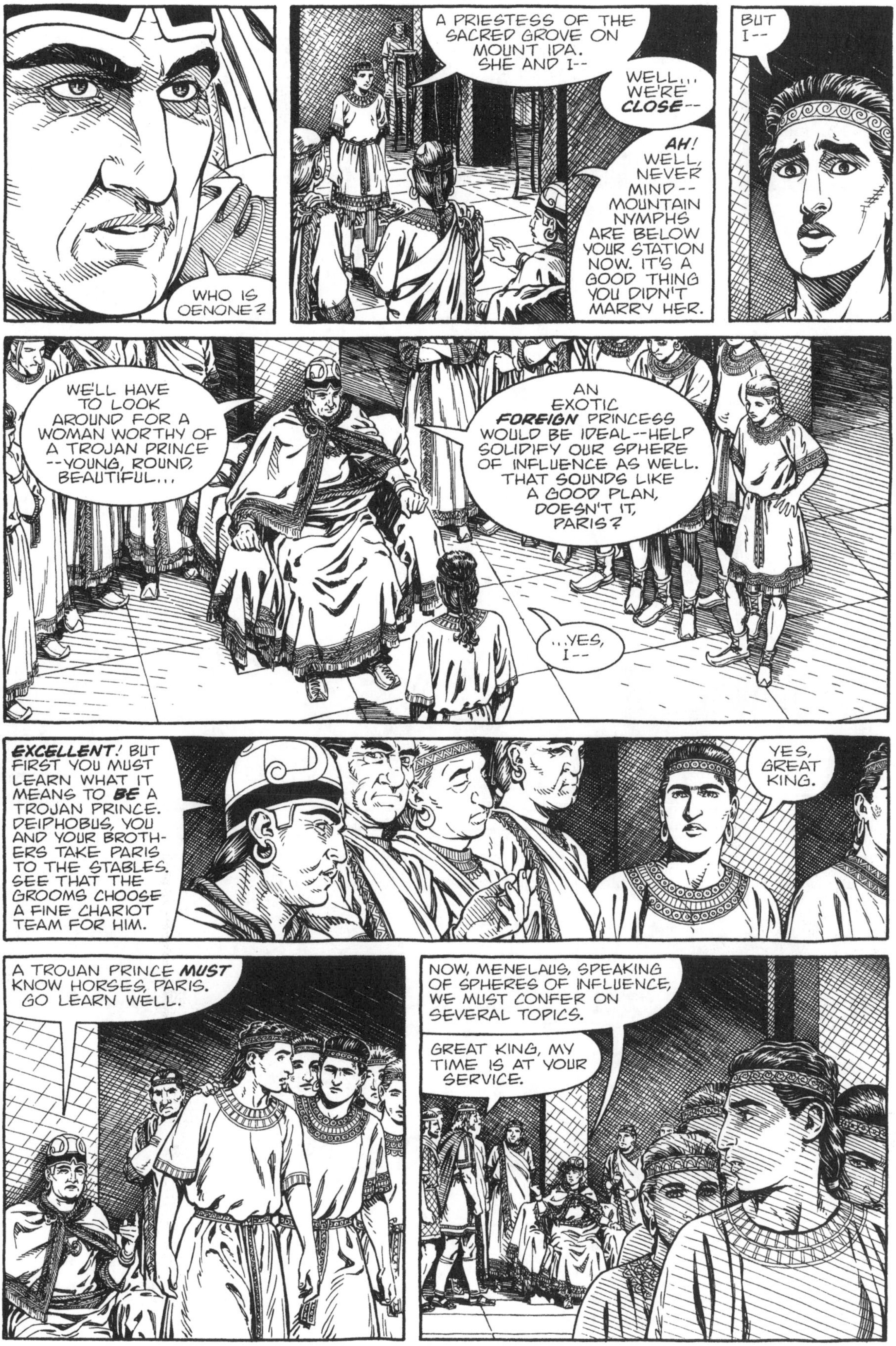
WHO IS OENONE?
A PRIESTESS OF THE SACRED GROVE ON MOUNT IDA. SHE AND I--
WELL... WE'RE **CLOSE**--
AH! WELL, NEVER MIND--MOUNTAIN NYMPHS ARE BELOW YOUR STATION NOW. IT'S A GOOD THING YOU DIDN'T MARRY HER.
BUT I--
WE'LL HAVE TO LOOK AROUND FOR A WOMAN WORTHY OF A TROJAN PRINCE --YOUNG, ROUND, BEAUTIFUL...
AN EXOTIC **FOREIGN** PRINCESS WOULD BE IDEAL--HELP SOLIDIFY OUR SPHERE OF INFLUENCE AS WELL. THAT SOUNDS LIKE A GOOD PLAN, DOESN'T IT, PARIS?
...YES, I--
EXCELLENT! BUT FIRST YOU MUST LEARN WHAT IT MEANS TO **BE** A TROJAN PRINCE. DEIPHOBUS, YOU AND YOUR BROTHERS TAKE PARIS TO THE STABLES. SEE THAT THE GROOMS CHOOSE A FINE CHARIOT TEAM FOR HIM.
YES, GREAT KING.
A TROJAN PRINCE **MUST** KNOW HORSES, PARIS. GO LEARN WELL.
NOW, MENELAUS, SPEAKING OF SPHERES OF INFLUENCE, WE MUST CONFER ON SEVERAL TOPICS.
GREAT KING, MY TIME IS AT YOUR SERVICE.

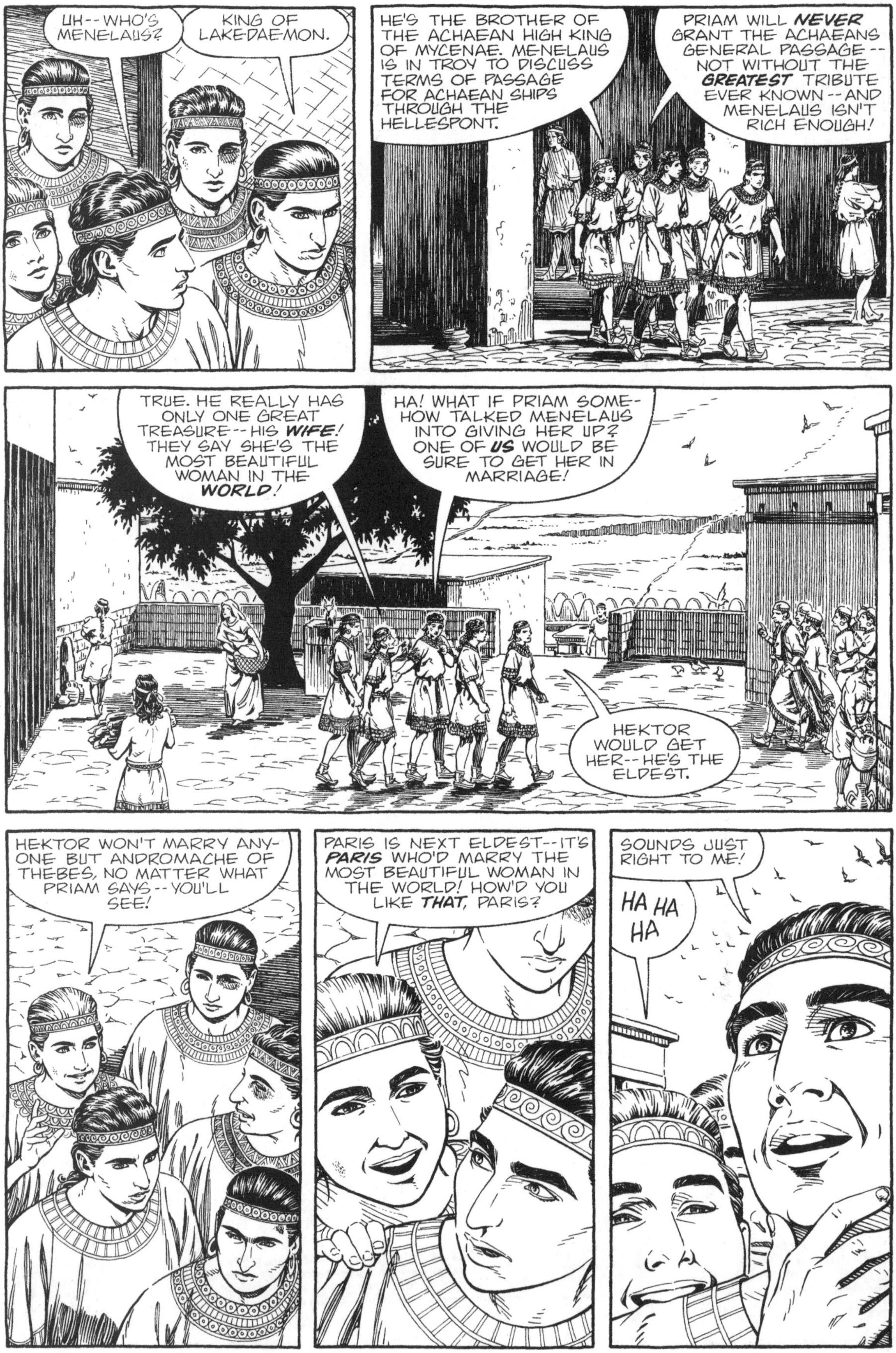
UH--WHO'S MENELAUS?
KING OF LAKEDAEMON.
HE'S THE BROTHER OF THE ACHAEAN HIGH KING OF MYCENAE. MENELAUS IS IN TROY TO DISCUSS TERMS OF PASSAGE FOR ACHAEAN SHIPS THROUGH THE HELLESPONT.
PRIAM WILL NEVER GRANT THE ACHAEANS GENERAL PASSAGE--NOT WITHOUT THE GREATEST TRIBUTE EVER KNOWN--AND MENELAUS ISN'T RICH ENOUGH!
TRUE. HE REALLY HAS ONLY ONE GREAT TREASURE--HIS WIFE! THEY SAY SHE'S THE MOST BEAUTIFUL WOMAN IN THE WORLD!
HA! WHAT IF PRIAM SOMEHOW TALKED MENELAUS INTO GIVING HER UP? ONE OF US WOULD BE SURE TO GET HER IN MARRIAGE!
HEKTOR WOULD GET HER--HE'S THE ELDEST.
HEKTOR WON'T MARRY ANYONE BUT ANDROMACHE OF THEBES, NO MATTER WHAT PRIAM SAYS--YOU'LL SEE!
PARIS IS NEXT ELDEST--IT'S PARIS WHO'D MARRY THE MOST BEAUTIFUL WOMAN IN THE WORLD! HOW'D YOU LIKE THAT, PARIS?
SOUNDS JUST RIGHT TO ME!
HA HA HA

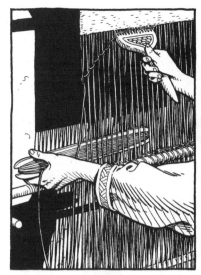

PHILOMELA! STOP PULLING YOUR BROTHER'S HAIR!

MAY I COME IN?

HAS THE COUNCIL MEETING BEGUN? △-◎-▽-◎-▽ ◎

IS THIS THE KIND OF GREETING I GET AFTER ALL THESE MONTHS?

WHAT?

△-◎-▽-◎-▽ △-◎

HEKTOR!

MOTHER! I'M SO GLAD TO SEE YOU AGAIN!

HEKTOR! I THOUGHT YOU WERE ONE OF THE SERVANTS!

IS THAT WHY YOU DIDN'T COME DOWN TO MEET MY SHIP?

HA HA! NO--

△-◎-▽ △-◎-▽

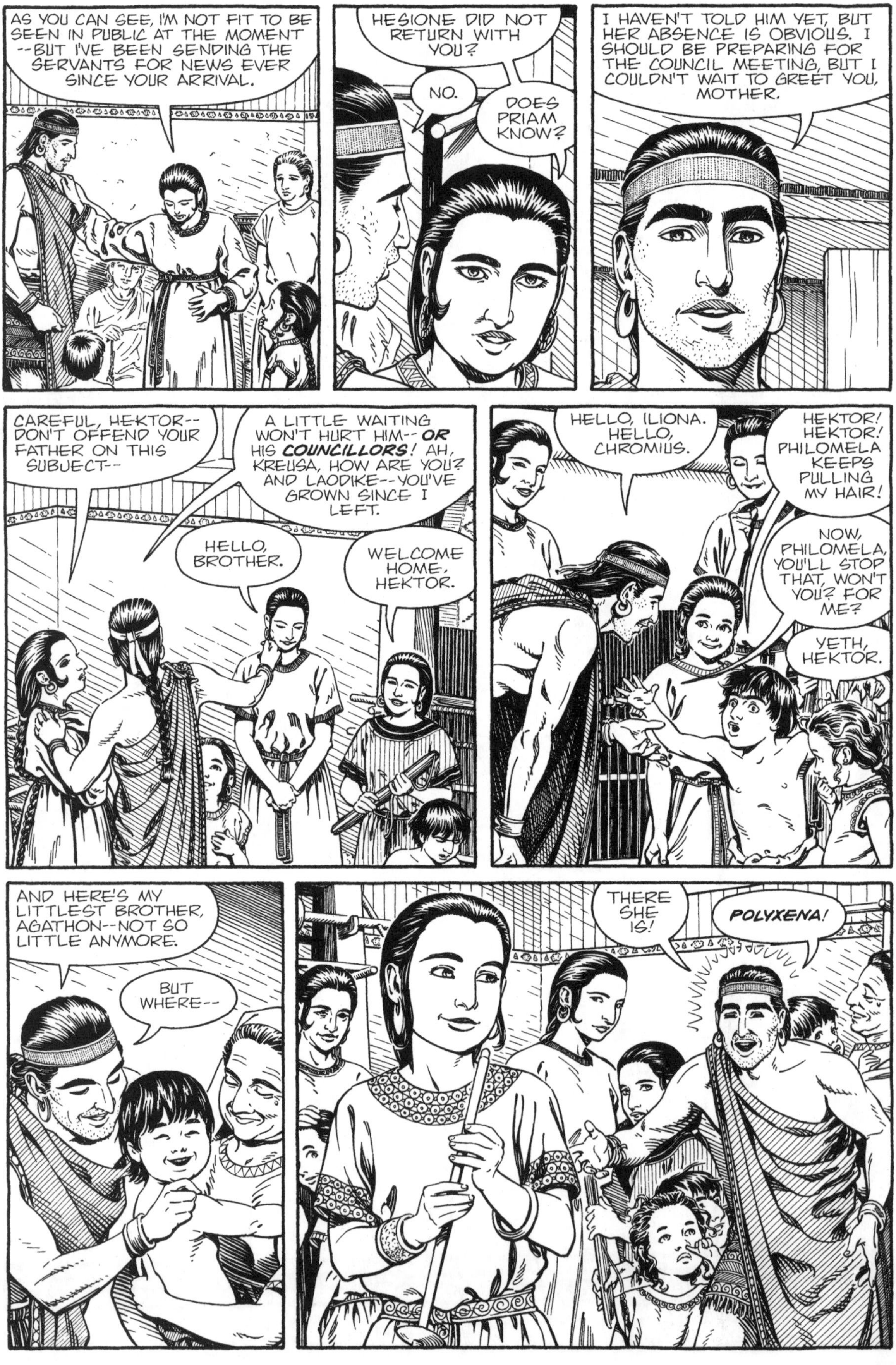
AS YOU CAN SEE, I'M NOT FIT TO BE SEEN IN PUBLIC AT THE MOMENT --BUT I'VE BEEN SENDING THE SERVANTS FOR NEWS EVER SINCE YOUR ARRIVAL.
HESIONE DID NOT RETURN WITH YOU?
NO.
DOES PRIAM KNOW?
I HAVEN'T TOLD HIM YET, BUT HER ABSENCE IS OBVIOUS. I SHOULD BE PREPARING FOR THE COUNCIL MEETING, BUT I COULDN'T WAIT TO GREET YOU, MOTHER.
CAREFUL, HEKTOR-- DON'T OFFEND YOUR FATHER ON THIS SUBUECT--
A LITTLE WAITING WON'T HURT HIM--OR HIS COUNCILLORS! AH, KREUSA, HOW ARE YOU? AND LAODIKE--YOU'VE GROWN SINCE I LEFT.
HELLO, BROTHER.
WELCOME HOME, HEKTOR.
HELLO, ILIONA. HELLO, CHROMIUS.
HEKTOR! HEKTOR! PHILOMELA KEEPS PULLING MY HAIR!
NOW, PHILOMELA, YOU'LL STOP THAT, WON'T YOU? FOR ME?
YETH, HEKTOR.
AND HERE'S MY LITTLEST BROTHER, AGATHON--NOT SO LITTLE ANYMORE.
BUT WHERE--
THERE SHE IS!
POLYXENA!

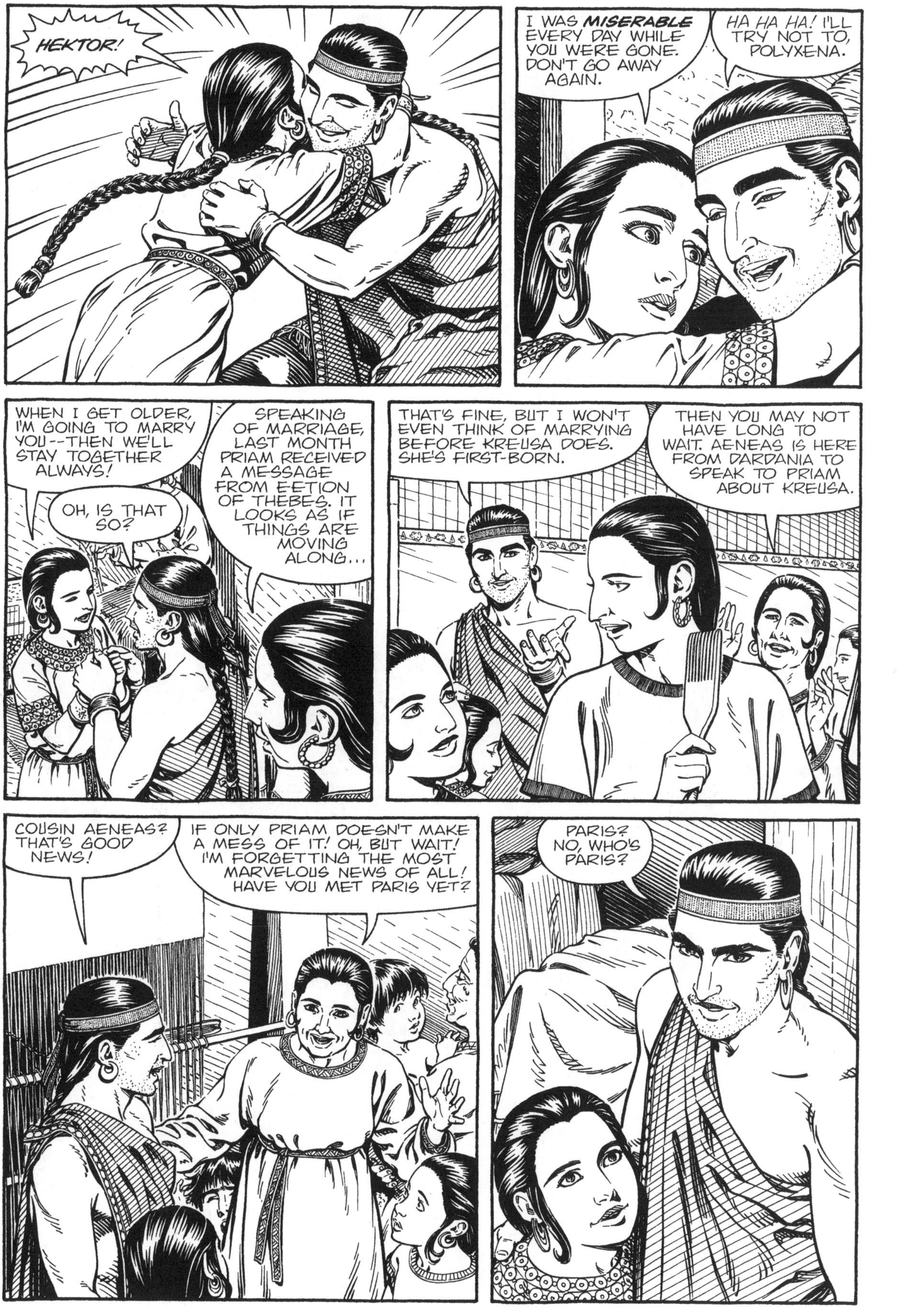
HEKTOR!
I WAS MISERABLE EVERY DAY WHILE YOU WERE GONE. DON'T GO AWAY AGAIN.
HA HA HA! I'LL TRY NOT TO, POLYXENA.
WHEN I GET OLDER, I'M GOING TO MARRY YOU--THEN WE'LL STAY TOGETHER ALWAYS!
OH, IS THAT SO?
SPEAKING OF MARRIAGE, LAST MONTH PRIAM RECEIVED A MESSAGE FROM EETION OF THEBES. IT LOOKS AS IF THINGS ARE MOVING ALONG...
THAT'S FINE, BUT I WON'T EVEN THINK OF MARRYING BEFORE KREUSA DOES. SHE'S FIRST-BORN.
THEN YOU MAY NOT HAVE LONG TO WAIT. AENEAS IS HERE FROM DARDANIA TO SPEAK TO PRIAM ABOUT KREUSA.
COUSIN AENEAS? THAT'S GOOD NEWS!
IF ONLY PRIAM DOESN'T MAKE A MESS OF IT! OH, BUT WAIT! I'M FORGETTING THE MOST MARVELOUS NEWS OF ALL! HAVE YOU MET PARIS YET?
PARIS? NO, WHO'S PARIS?

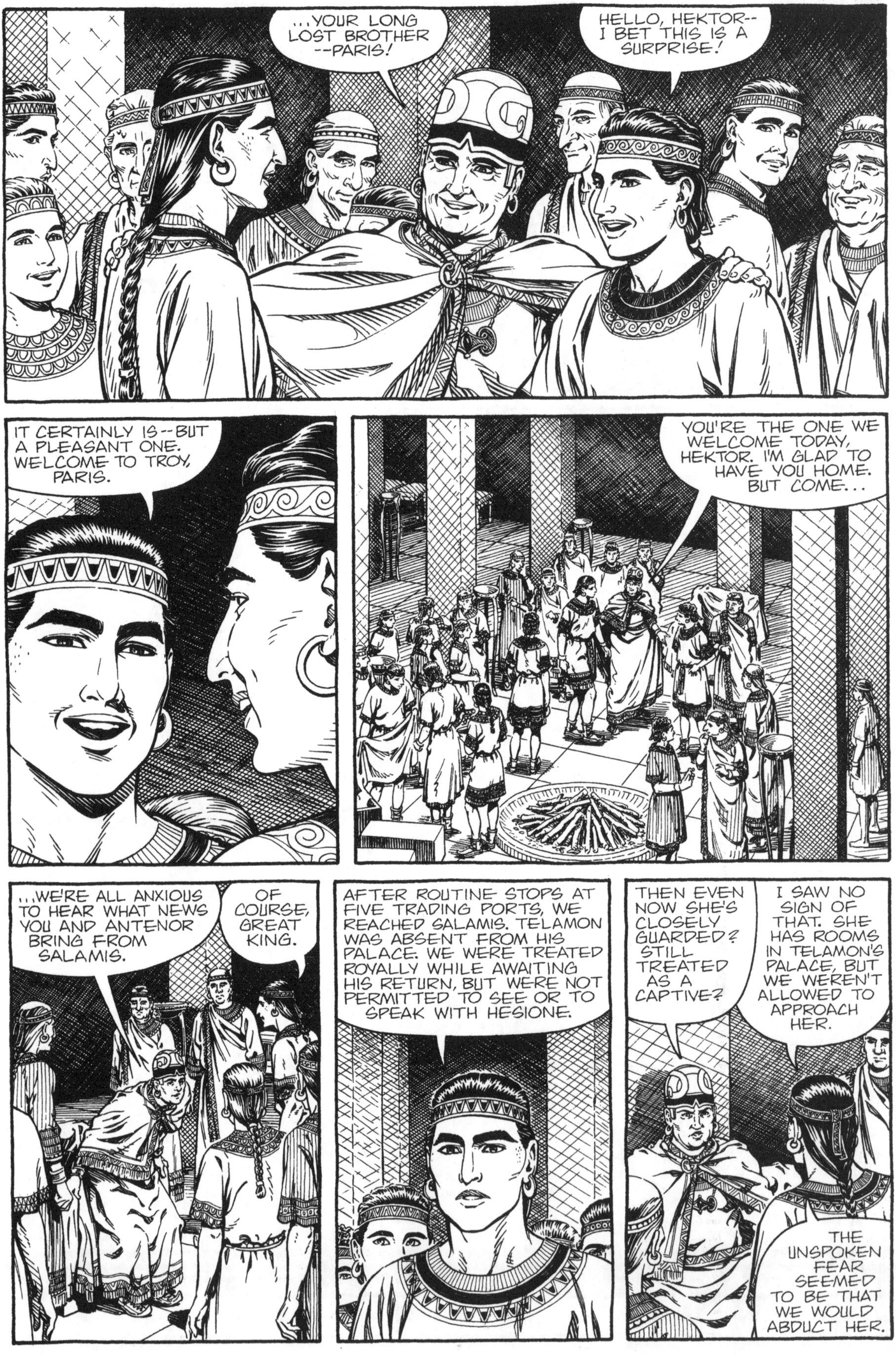
...YOUR LONG LOST BROTHER --PARIS!
HELLO, HEKTOR-- I BET THIS IS A SURPRISE!
IT CERTAINLY IS--BUT A PLEASANT ONE. WELCOME TO TROY, PARIS.
YOU'RE THE ONE WE WELCOME TODAY, HEKTOR. I'M GLAD TO HAVE YOU HOME. BUT COME...
...WE'RE ALL ANXIOUS TO HEAR WHAT NEWS YOU AND ANTENOR BRING FROM SALAMIS.
OF COURSE, GREAT KING.
AFTER ROUTINE STOPS AT FIVE TRADING PORTS, WE REACHED SALAMIS. TELAMON WAS ABSENT FROM HIS PALACE. WE WERE TREATED ROYALLY WHILE AWAITING HIS RETURN, BUT WERE NOT PERMITTED TO SEE OR TO SPEAK WITH HESIONE.
THEN EVEN NOW SHE'S CLOSELY GUARDED? STILL TREATED AS A CAPTIVE?
I SAW NO SIGN OF THAT. SHE HAS ROOMS IN TELAMON'S PALACE, BUT WE WEREN'T ALLOWED TO APPROACH HER.
THE UNSPOKEN FEAR SEEMED TO BE THAT WE WOULD ABDUCT HER.

 DID YOU GIVE THEM ANY BASIS FOR SUCH FEAR?

 NO! WE DECLARED OURSELVES A PEACEFUL EMBASSY AND CONDUCTED OURSELVES WITHIN THOSE BOUNDS!

GOOD. GO ON.

 AFTER SEVERAL WEEKS, TELAMON RETURNED AND GRANTED US AUDIENCE. HIS SONS--AJAX BY HIS WIFE PERIBOEA AND TEUKROS BY HESIONE--ATTENDED AS WELL. I PRESENTED OUR REQUEST THAT HE SURRENDER HESIONE SO WE COULD RETURN HER TO HER HOME.

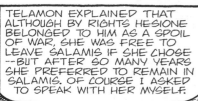 TELAMON EXPLAINED THAT ALTHOUGH BY RIGHTS HESIONE BELONGED TO HIM AS A SPOIL OF WAR, SHE WAS FREE TO LEAVE SALAMIS IF SHE CHOSE --BUT AFTER SO MANY YEARS SHE PREFERRED TO REMAIN IN SALAMIS. OF COURSE I ASKED TO SPEAK WITH HER MYSELF.

AND?

WHEN SHE APPEARED I TOLD HER THAT HEKTOR, PRINCE OF TROY, HELD A SHIP TO CARRY HER BACK ACROSS THE SEA TO WHERE HER LOVED ONES ANXIOUSLY AWAITED HER.

AND...SHE LAUGHED--

LAUGHED?

YES, SHE SEEMED *FLATTERED*, ACTUALLY--

--AS IF...

AS IF? WHAT?

SHE SEEMED SURPRISED THAT ANYONE IN TROY REMEMBERED HER. SHE WAS VERY GRACIOUS AS SHE DECLINED OUR OFFER. SHE EXPLAINED THAT SHE WAS ALREADY WITH HER LOVED ONES--IN SALAMIS--AND WAS TOO OLD FOR SUCH A LONG SEA JOURNEY.

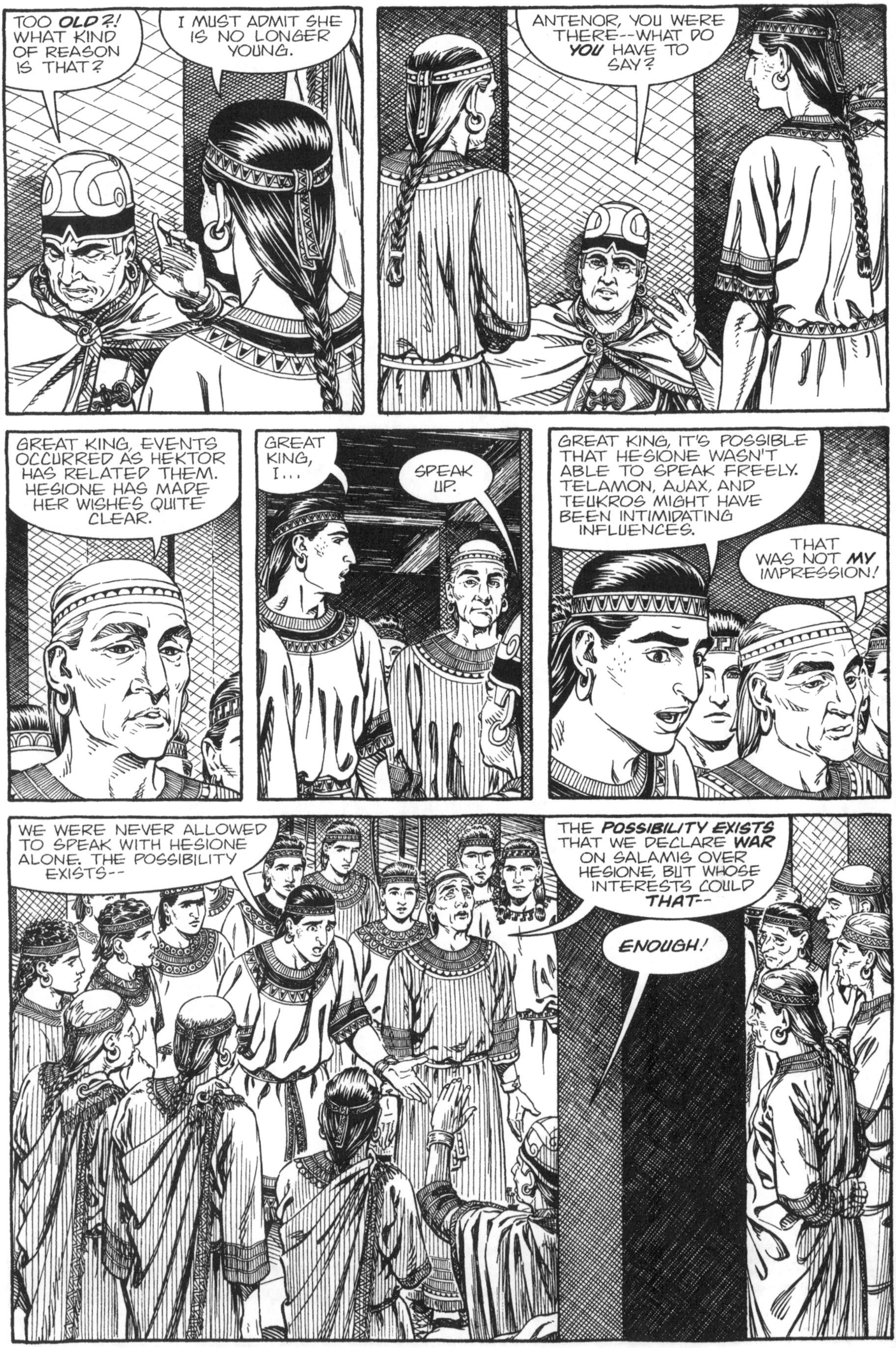
TOO OLD?! WHAT KIND OF REASON IS THAT?
I MUST ADMIT SHE IS NO LONGER YOUNG.
ANTENOR, YOU WERE THERE--WHAT DO YOU HAVE TO SAY?
GREAT KING, EVENTS OCCURRED AS HEKTOR HAS RELATED THEM. HESIONE HAS MADE HER WISHES QUITE CLEAR.
GREAT KING, I...
SPEAK UP.
GREAT KING, IT'S POSSIBLE THAT HESIONE WASN'T ABLE TO SPEAK FREELY. TELAMON, AJAX, AND TEUKROS MIGHT HAVE BEEN INTIMIDATING INFLUENCES.
THAT WAS NOT MY IMPRESSION!
WE WERE NEVER ALLOWED TO SPEAK WITH HESIONE ALONE. THE POSSIBILITY EXISTS--
THE POSSIBILITY EXISTS THAT WE DECLARE WAR ON SALAMIS OVER HESIONE, BUT WHOSE INTERESTS COULD THAT--
ENOUGH!

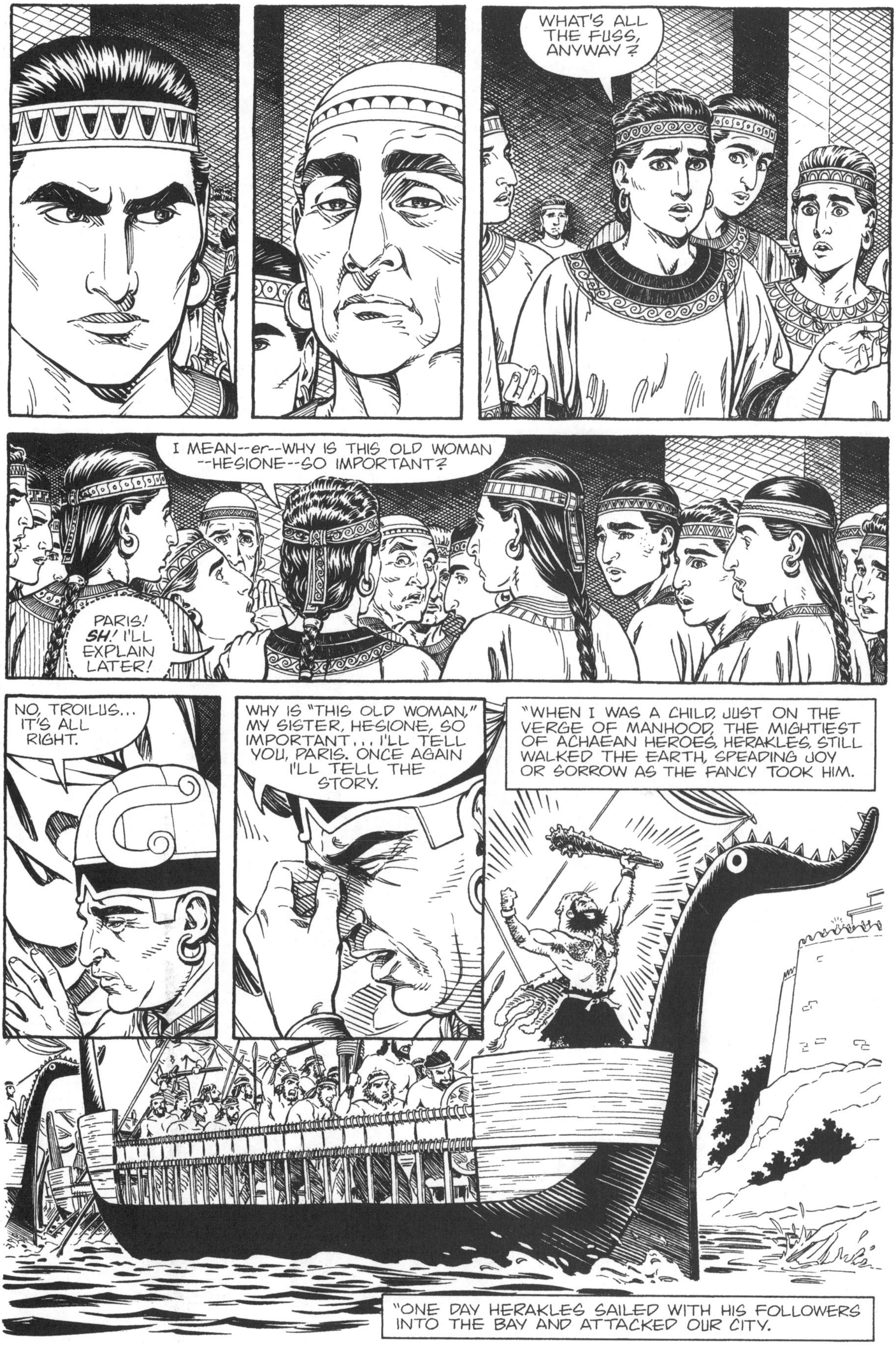
WHAT'S ALL THE FUSS, ANYWAY?
I MEAN--er--WHY IS THIS OLD WOMAN --HESIONE--SO IMPORTANT?
PARIS! SH! I'LL EXPLAIN LATER!
NO, TROILUS... IT'S ALL RIGHT.
WHY IS "THIS OLD WOMAN," MY SISTER, HESIONE, SO IMPORTANT... I'LL TELL YOU, PARIS. ONCE AGAIN I'LL TELL THE STORY.
"WHEN I WAS A CHILD, JUST ON THE VERGE OF MANHOOD, THE MIGHTIEST OF ACHAEAN HEROES, HERAKLES, STILL WALKED THE EARTH, SPEADING JOY OR SORROW AS THE FANCY TOOK HIM.
"ONE DAY HERAKLES SAILED WITH HIS FOLLOWERS INTO THE BAY AND ATTACKED OUR CITY.

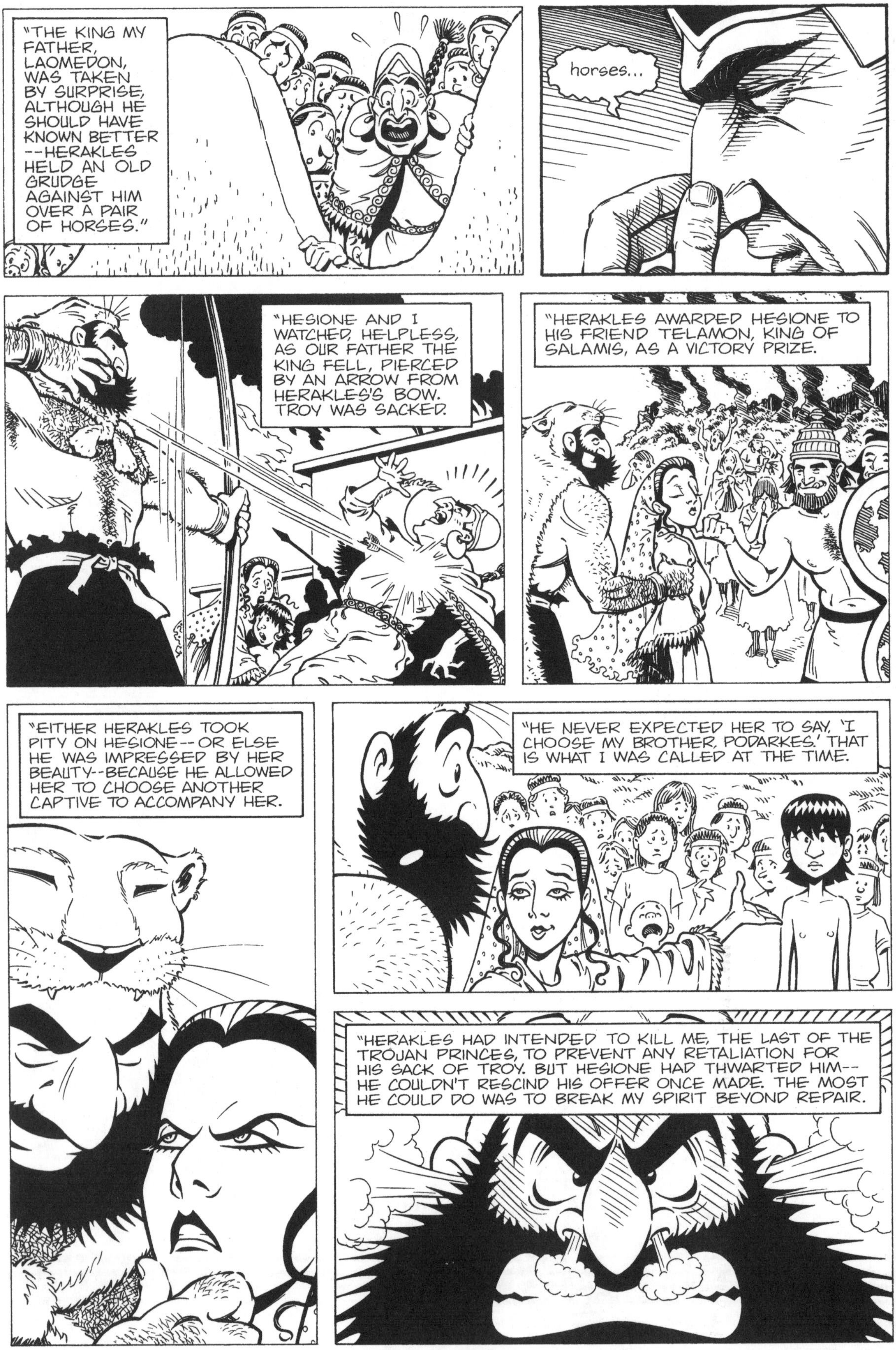
"THE KING MY FATHER, LAOMEDON, WAS TAKEN BY SURPRISE, ALTHOUGH HE SHOULD HAVE KNOWN BETTER --HERAKLES HELD AN OLD GRUDGE AGAINST HIM OVER A PAIR OF HORSES."
horses...
"HESIONE AND I WATCHED, HELPLESS, AS OUR FATHER THE KING FELL, PIERCED BY AN ARROW FROM HERAKLES'S BOW. TROY WAS SACKED.
"HERAKLES AWARDED HESIONE TO HIS FRIEND TELAMON, KING OF SALAMIS, AS A VICTORY PRIZE.
"EITHER HERAKLES TOOK PITY ON HESIONE--OR ELSE HE WAS IMPRESSED BY HER BEAUTY--BECAUSE HE ALLOWED HER TO CHOOSE ANOTHER CAPTIVE TO ACCOMPANY HER.
"HE NEVER EXPECTED HER TO SAY, 'I CHOOSE MY BROTHER, PODARKES.' THAT IS WHAT I WAS CALLED AT THE TIME.
"HERAKLES HAD INTENDED TO KILL ME, THE LAST OF THE TROJAN PRINCES, TO PREVENT ANY RETALIATION FOR HIS SACK OF TROY. BUT HESIONE HAD THWARTED HIM--HE COULDN'T RESCIND HIS OFFER ONCE MADE. THE MOST HE COULD DO WAS TO BREAK MY SPIRIT BEYOND REPAIR.

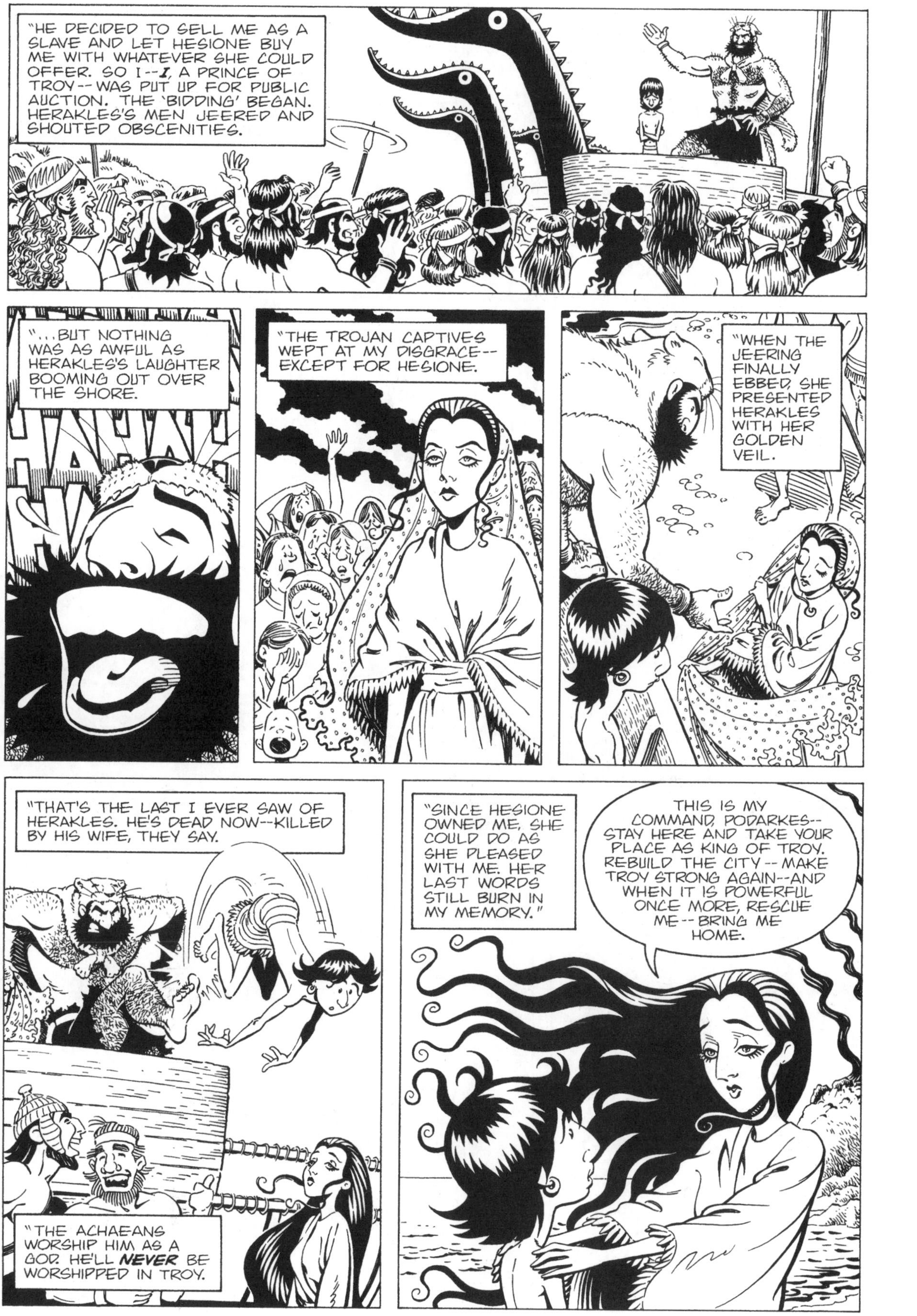
"HE DECIDED TO SELL ME AS A SLAVE AND LET HESIONE BUY ME WITH WHATEVER SHE COULD OFFER. SO I--*I*, A PRINCE OF TROY--WAS PUT UP FOR PUBLIC AUCTION. THE 'BIDDING' BEGAN. HERAKLES'S MEN JEERED AND SHOUTED OBSCENITIES.
"...BUT NOTHING WAS AS AWFUL AS HERAKLES'S LAUGHTER BOOMING OUT OVER THE SHORE.
"THE TROJAN CAPTIVES WEPT AT MY DISGRACE--EXCEPT FOR HESIONE.
"WHEN THE JEERING FINALLY EBBED, SHE PRESENTED HERAKLES WITH HER GOLDEN VEIL.
"THAT'S THE LAST I EVER SAW OF HERAKLES. HE'S DEAD NOW--KILLED BY HIS WIFE, THEY SAY.
"THE ACHAEANS WORSHIP HIM AS A GOD. HE'LL ***NEVER*** BE WORSHIPPED IN TROY.
"SINCE HESIONE OWNED ME, SHE COULD DO AS SHE PLEASED WITH ME. HER LAST WORDS STILL BURN IN MY MEMORY."
THIS IS MY COMMAND, PODARKES--STAY HERE AND TAKE YOUR PLACE AS KING OF TROY. REBUILD THE CITY--MAKE TROY STRONG AGAIN--AND WHEN IT IS POWERFUL ONCE MORE, RESCUE ME--BRING ME HOME.

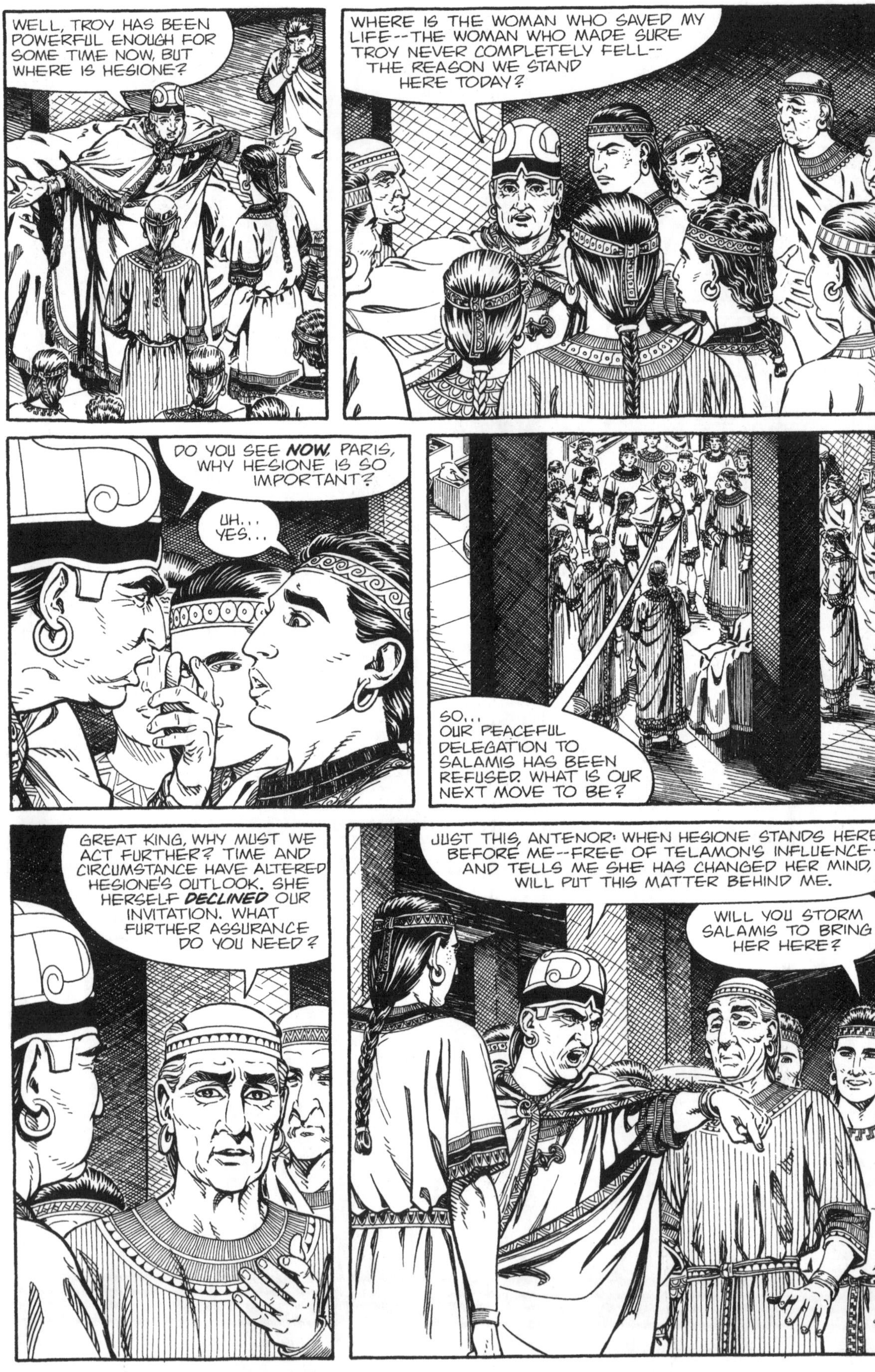
WELL, TROY HAS BEEN POWERFUL ENOUGH FOR SOME TIME NOW, BUT WHERE IS HESIONE?
WHERE IS THE WOMAN WHO SAVED MY LIFE--THE WOMAN WHO MADE SURE TROY NEVER COMPLETELY FELL--THE REASON WE STAND HERE TODAY?
DO YOU SEE **NOW**, PARIS, WHY HESIONE IS SO IMPORTANT?
UH... YES...
SO... OUR PEACEFUL DELEGATION TO SALAMIS HAS BEEN REFUSED. WHAT IS OUR NEXT MOVE TO BE?
GREAT KING, WHY MUST WE ACT FURTHER? TIME AND CIRCUMSTANCE HAVE ALTERED HESIONE'S OUTLOOK. SHE HERSELF **DECLINED** OUR INVITATION. WHAT FURTHER ASSURANCE DO YOU NEED?
JUST THIS, ANTENOR: WHEN HESIONE STANDS HERE BEFORE ME--FREE OF TELAMON'S INFLUENCE--AND TELLS ME SHE HAS CHANGED HER MIND, I WILL PUT THIS MATTER BEHIND ME.
WILL YOU STORM SALAMIS TO BRING HER HERE?

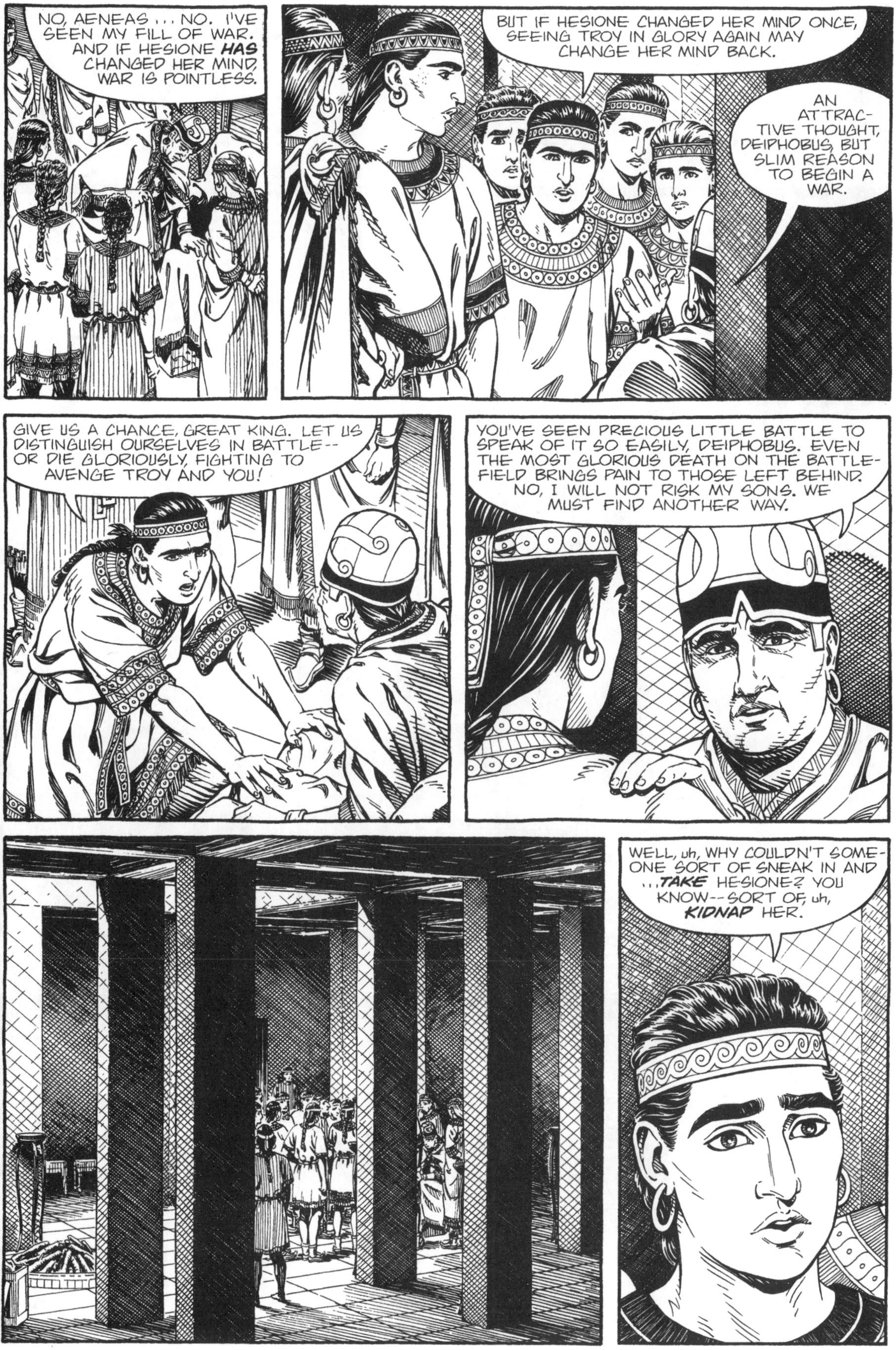
NO, AENEAS . . . NO. I'VE SEEN MY FILL OF WAR. AND IF HESIONE **HAS** CHANGED HER MIND, WAR IS POINTLESS.
BUT IF HESIONE CHANGED HER MIND ONCE, SEEING TROY IN GLORY AGAIN MAY CHANGE HER MIND BACK.
AN ATTRACTIVE THOUGHT, DEIPHOBUS, BUT SLIM REASON TO BEGIN A WAR.
GIVE US A CHANCE, GREAT KING. LET US DISTINGUISH OURSELVES IN BATTLE-- OR DIE GLORIOUSLY, FIGHTING TO AVENGE TROY AND YOU!
YOU'VE SEEN PRECIOUS LITTLE BATTLE TO SPEAK OF IT SO EASILY, DEIPHOBUS. EVEN THE MOST GLORIOUS DEATH ON THE BATTLEFIELD BRINGS PAIN TO THOSE LEFT BEHIND. NO, I WILL NOT RISK MY SONS. WE MUST FIND ANOTHER WAY.
WELL, uh, WHY COULDN'T SOMEONE SORT OF SNEAK IN AND . . ***TAKE*** HESIONE? YOU KNOW--SORT OF, uh, ***KIDNAP*** HER.

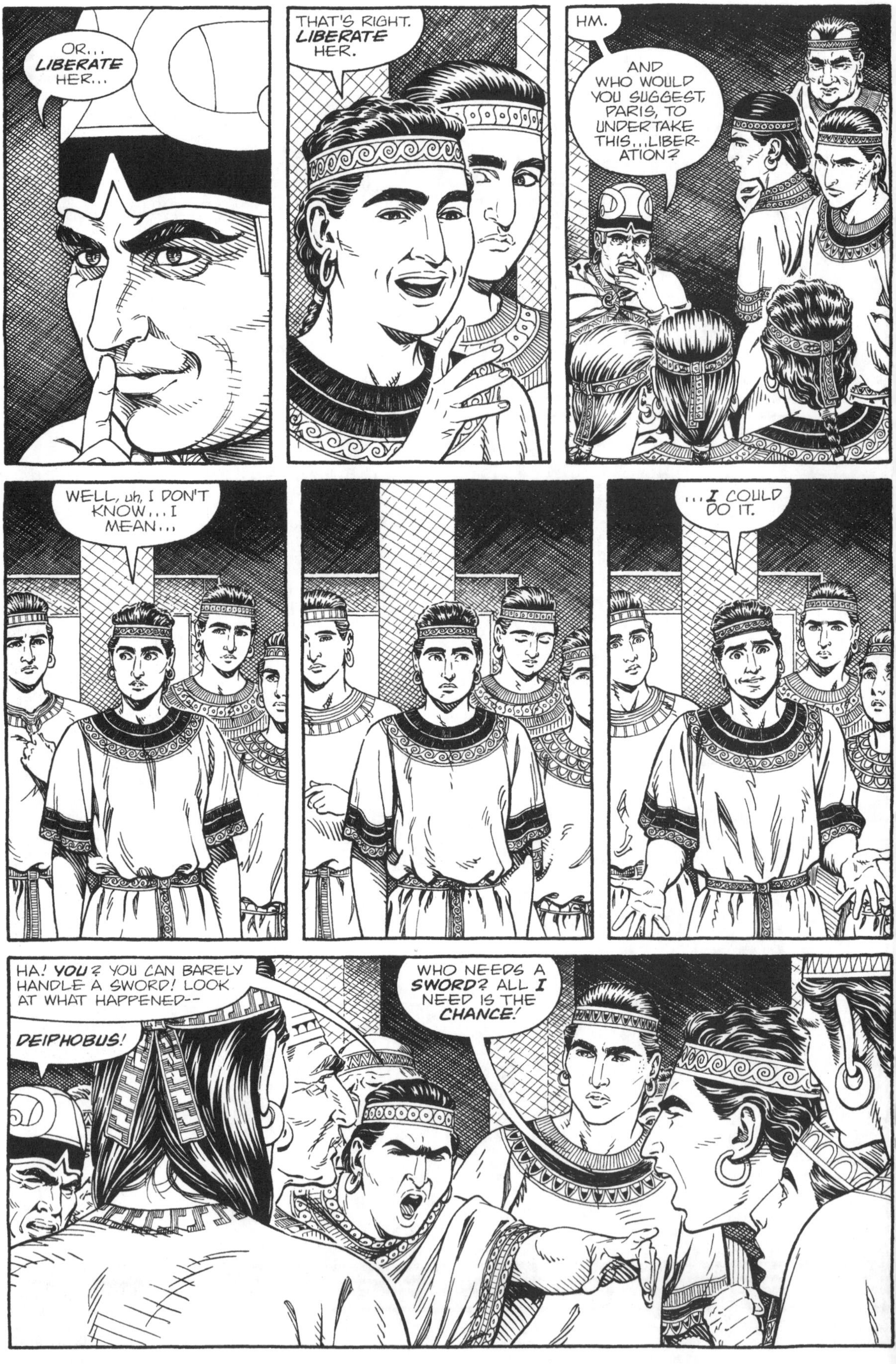
OR... LIBERATE HER...
THAT'S RIGHT. LIBERATE HER.
HM.
AND WHO WOULD YOU SUGGEST, PARIS, TO UNDERTAKE THIS...LIBER-ATION?
WELL, uh, I DON'T KNOW... I MEAN...
...I COULD DO IT.
HA! YOU? YOU CAN BARELY HANDLE A SWORD! LOOK AT WHAT HAPPENED--
DEIPHOBUS!
WHO NEEDS A SWORD? ALL I NEED IS THE CHANCE!

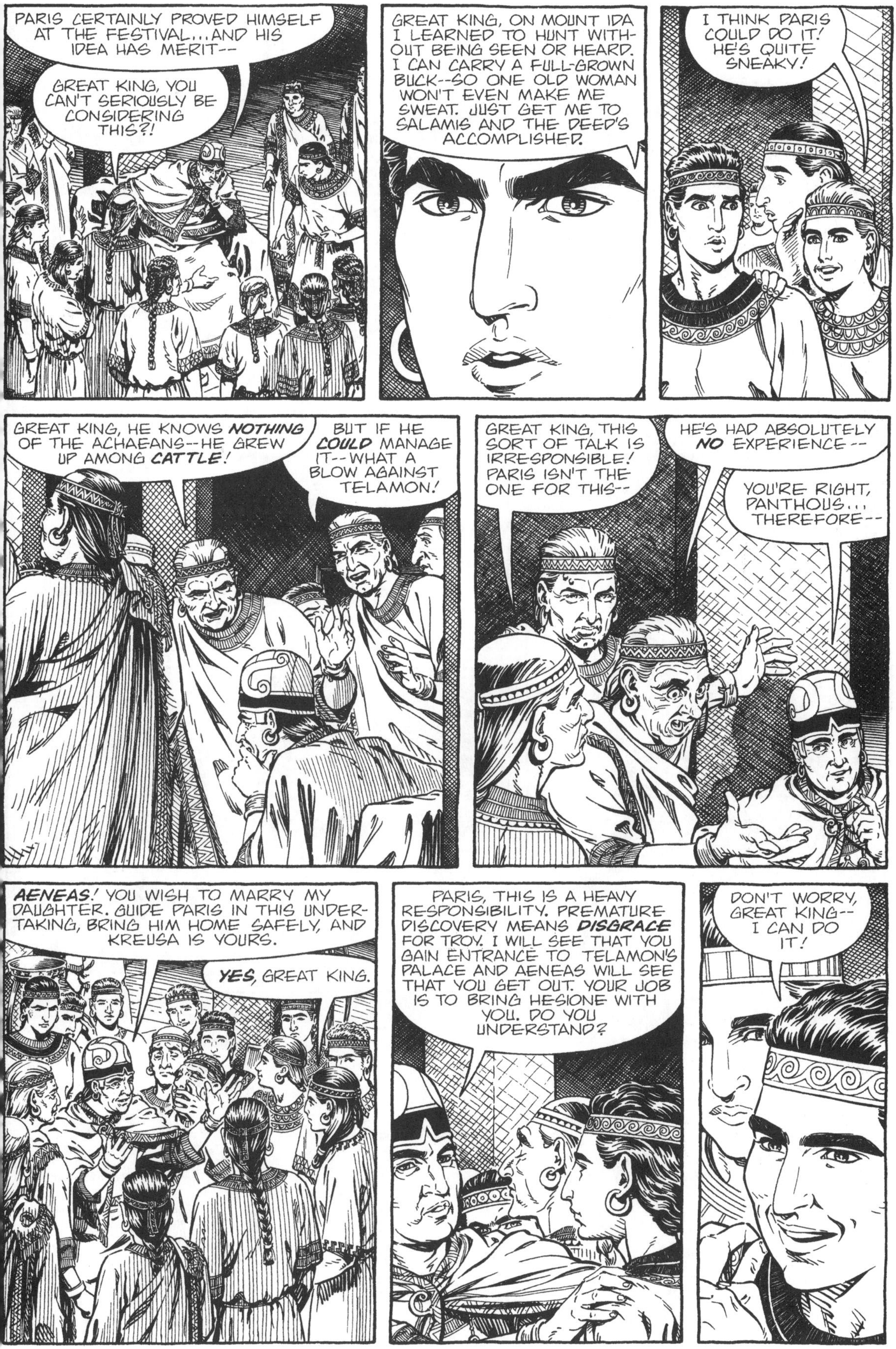
PARIS CERTAINLY PROVED HIMSELF AT THE FESTIVAL... AND HIS IDEA HAS MERIT--
GREAT KING, YOU CAN'T SERIOUSLY BE CONSIDERING THIS?!
GREAT KING, ON MOUNT IDA I LEARNED TO HUNT WITHOUT BEING SEEN OR HEARD. I CAN CARRY A FULL-GROWN BUCK--SO ONE OLD WOMAN WON'T EVEN MAKE ME SWEAT. JUST GET ME TO SALAMIS AND THE DEED'S ACCOMPLISHED.
I THINK PARIS COULD DO IT! HE'S QUITE SNEAKY!
GREAT KING, HE KNOWS NOTHING OF THE ACHAEANS--HE GREW UP AMONG CATTLE!
BUT IF HE COULD MANAGE IT--WHAT A BLOW AGAINST TELAMON!
GREAT KING, THIS SORT OF TALK IS IRRESPONSIBLE! PARIS ISN'T THE ONE FOR THIS--
HE'S HAD ABSOLUTELY NO EXPERIENCE--
YOU'RE RIGHT, PANTHOUS... THEREFORE--
AENEAS! YOU WISH TO MARRY MY DAUGHTER. GUIDE PARIS IN THIS UNDERTAKING, BRING HIM HOME SAFELY, AND KREUSA IS YOURS.
YES, GREAT KING.
PARIS, THIS IS A HEAVY RESPONSIBILITY. PREMATURE DISCOVERY MEANS DISGRACE FOR TROY. I WILL SEE THAT YOU GAIN ENTRANCE TO TELAMON'S PALACE AND AENEAS WILL SEE THAT YOU GET OUT. YOUR JOB IS TO BRING HESIONE WITH YOU. DO YOU UNDERSTAND?
DON'T WORRY, GREAT KING-- I CAN DO IT!

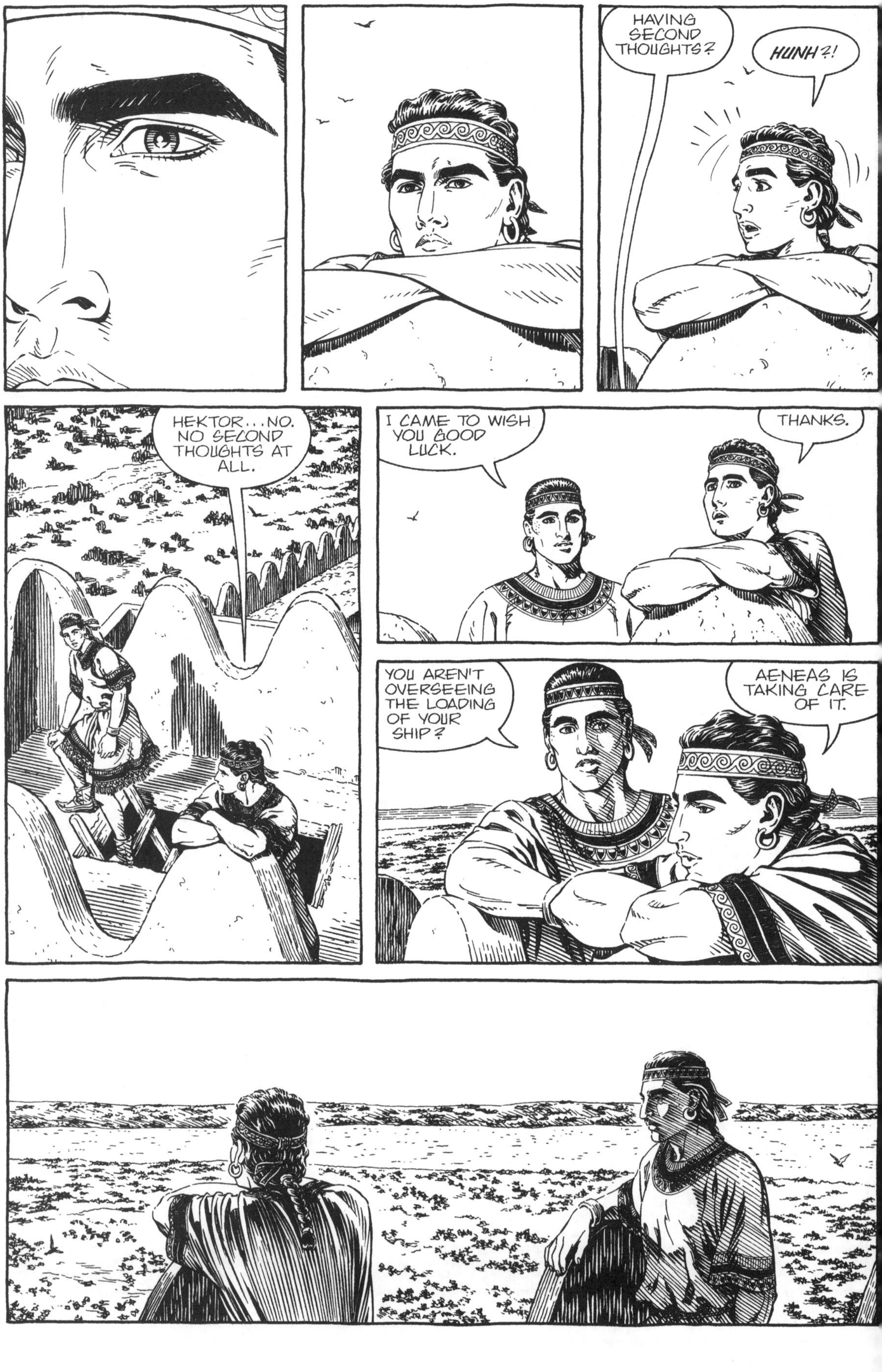
HAVING SECOND THOUGHTS?
HUNH?!
HEKTOR...NO. NO SECOND THOUGHTS AT ALL.
I CAME TO WISH YOU GOOD LUCK.
THANKS.
YOU AREN'T OVERSEEING THE LOADING OF YOUR SHIP?
AENEAS IS TAKING CARE OF IT.

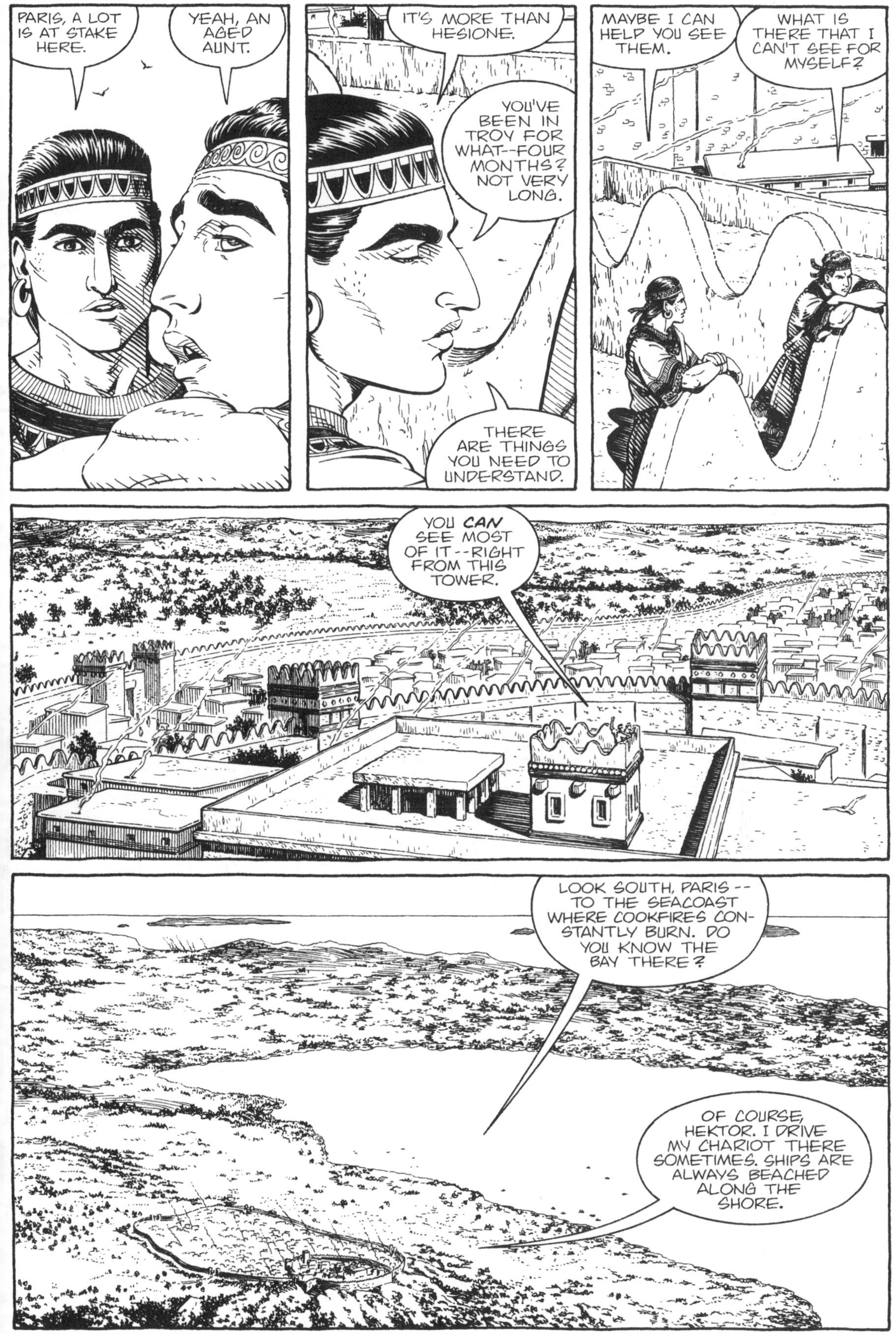
PARIS, A LOT IS AT STAKE HERE.
YEAH, AN AGED AUNT.
IT'S MORE THAN HESIONE.
YOU'VE BEEN IN TROY FOR WHAT--FOUR MONTHS? NOT VERY LONG.
THERE ARE THINGS YOU NEED TO UNDERSTAND.
MAYBE I CAN HELP YOU SEE THEM.
WHAT IS THERE THAT I CAN'T SEE FOR MYSELF?
YOU CAN SEE MOST OF IT--RIGHT FROM THIS TOWER.
LOOK SOUTH, PARIS--TO THE SEACOAST WHERE COOKFIRES CONSTANTLY BURN. DO YOU KNOW THE BAY THERE?
OF COURSE, HEKTOR. I DRIVE MY CHARIOT THERE SOMETIMES. SHIPS ARE ALWAYS BEACHED ALONG THE SHORE.

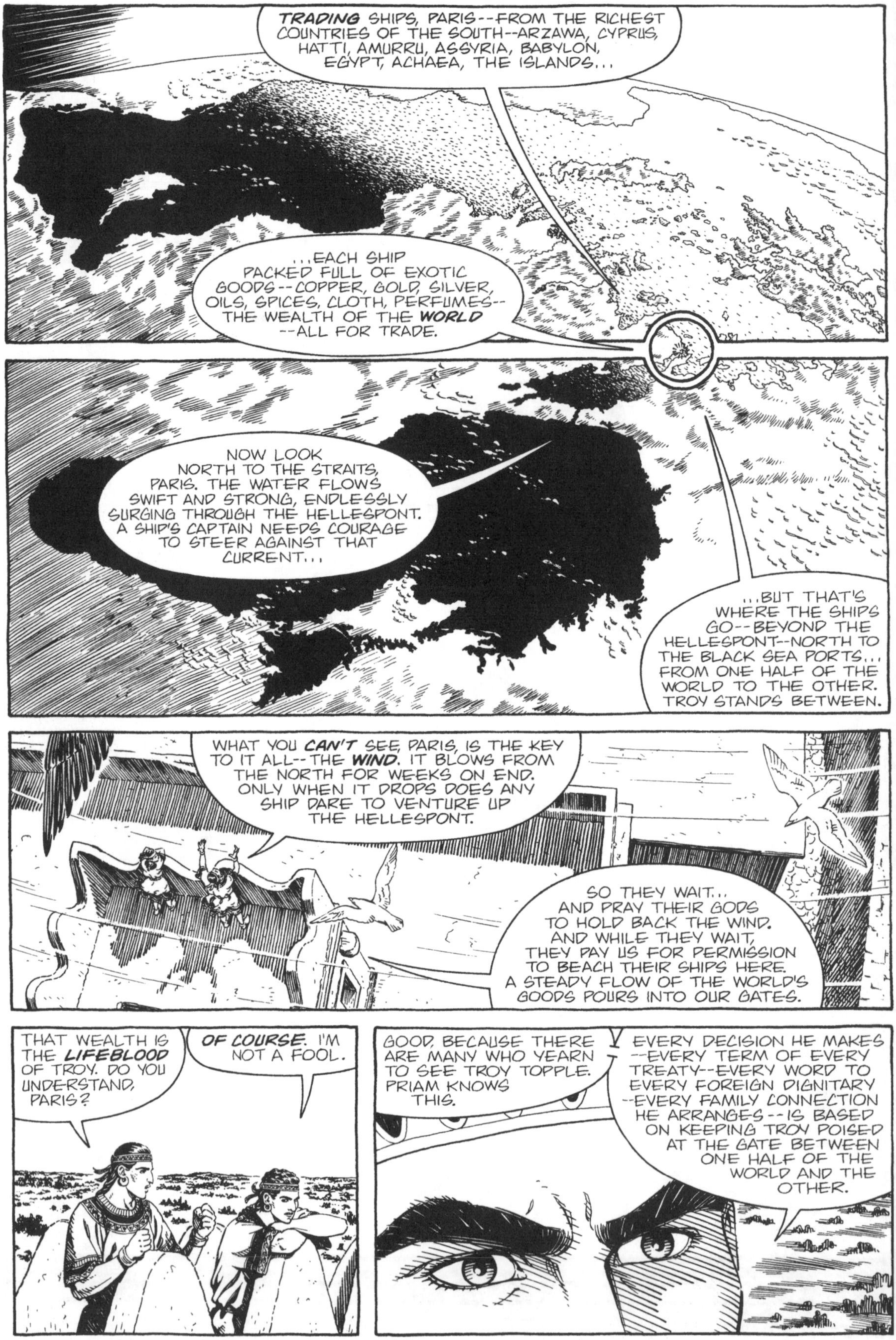
TRADING SHIPS, PARIS--FROM THE RICHEST COUNTRIES OF THE SOUTH--ARZAWA, CYPRUS, HATTI, AMURRU, ASSYRIA, BABYLON, EGYPT, ACHAEA, THE ISLANDS...
...EACH SHIP PACKED FULL OF EXOTIC GOODS--COPPER, GOLD, SILVER, OILS, SPICES, CLOTH, PERFUMES--THE WEALTH OF THE WORLD--ALL FOR TRADE.
NOW LOOK NORTH TO THE STRAITS, PARIS. THE WATER FLOWS SWIFT AND STRONG, ENDLESSLY SURGING THROUGH THE HELLESPONT. A SHIP'S CAPTAIN NEEDS COURAGE TO STEER AGAINST THAT CURRENT...
...BUT THAT'S WHERE THE SHIPS GO--BEYOND THE HELLESPONT--NORTH TO THE BLACK SEA PORTS... FROM ONE HALF OF THE WORLD TO THE OTHER. TROY STANDS BETWEEN.
WHAT YOU CAN'T SEE, PARIS, IS THE KEY TO IT ALL--THE WIND. IT BLOWS FROM THE NORTH FOR WEEKS ON END. ONLY WHEN IT DROPS DOES ANY SHIP DARE TO VENTURE UP THE HELLESPONT.
SO THEY WAIT... AND PRAY THEIR GODS TO HOLD BACK THE WIND. AND WHILE THEY WAIT, THEY PAY US FOR PERMISSION TO BEACH THEIR SHIPS HERE. A STEADY FLOW OF THE WORLD'S GOODS POURS INTO OUR GATES.
THAT WEALTH IS THE LIFEBLOOD OF TROY. DO YOU UNDERSTAND, PARIS?
OF COURSE. I'M NOT A FOOL.
GOOD, BECAUSE THERE ARE MANY WHO YEARN TO SEE TROY TOPPLE. PRIAM KNOWS THIS.
EVERY DECISION HE MAKES--EVERY TERM OF EVERY TREATY--EVERY WORD TO EVERY FOREIGN DIGNITARY--EVERY FAMILY CONNECTION HE ARRANGES--IS BASED ON KEEPING TROY POISED AT THE GATE BETWEEN ONE HALF OF THE WORLD AND THE OTHER.

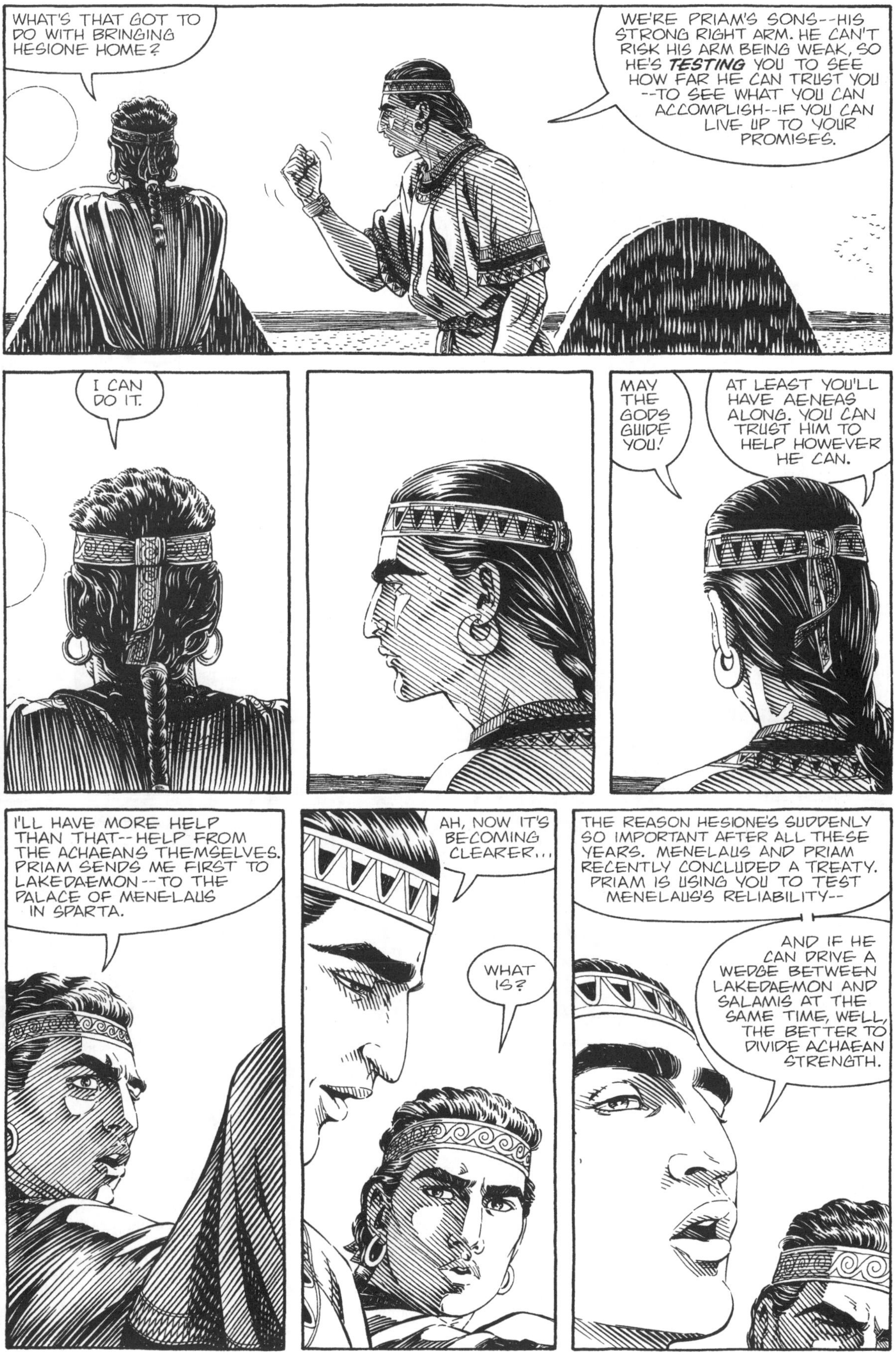

WHAT'S THAT GOT TO DO WITH BRINGING HESIONE HOME?
WE'RE PRIAM'S SONS--HIS STRONG RIGHT ARM. HE CAN'T RISK HIS ARM BEING WEAK, SO HE'S **TESTING** YOU TO SEE HOW FAR HE CAN TRUST YOU --TO SEE WHAT YOU CAN ACCOMPLISH--IF YOU CAN LIVE UP TO YOUR PROMISES.
I CAN DO IT.
MAY THE GODS GUIDE YOU!
AT LEAST YOU'LL HAVE AENEAS ALONG. YOU CAN TRUST HIM TO HELP HOWEVER HE CAN.
I'LL HAVE MORE HELP THAN THAT--HELP FROM THE ACHAEANS THEMSELVES. PRIAM SENDS ME FIRST TO LAKEDAEMON--TO THE PALACE OF MENELAUS IN SPARTA.
AH, NOW IT'S BECOMING CLEARER...
WHAT IS?
THE REASON HESIONE'S SUDDENLY SO IMPORTANT AFTER ALL THESE YEARS. MENELAUS AND PRIAM RECENTLY CONCLUDED A TREATY. PRIAM IS USING YOU TO TEST MENELAUS'S RELIABILITY--
AND IF HE CAN DRIVE A WEDGE BETWEEN LAKEDAEMON AND SALAMIS AT THE SAME TIME, WELL, THE BETTER TO DIVIDE ACHAEAN STRENGTH.

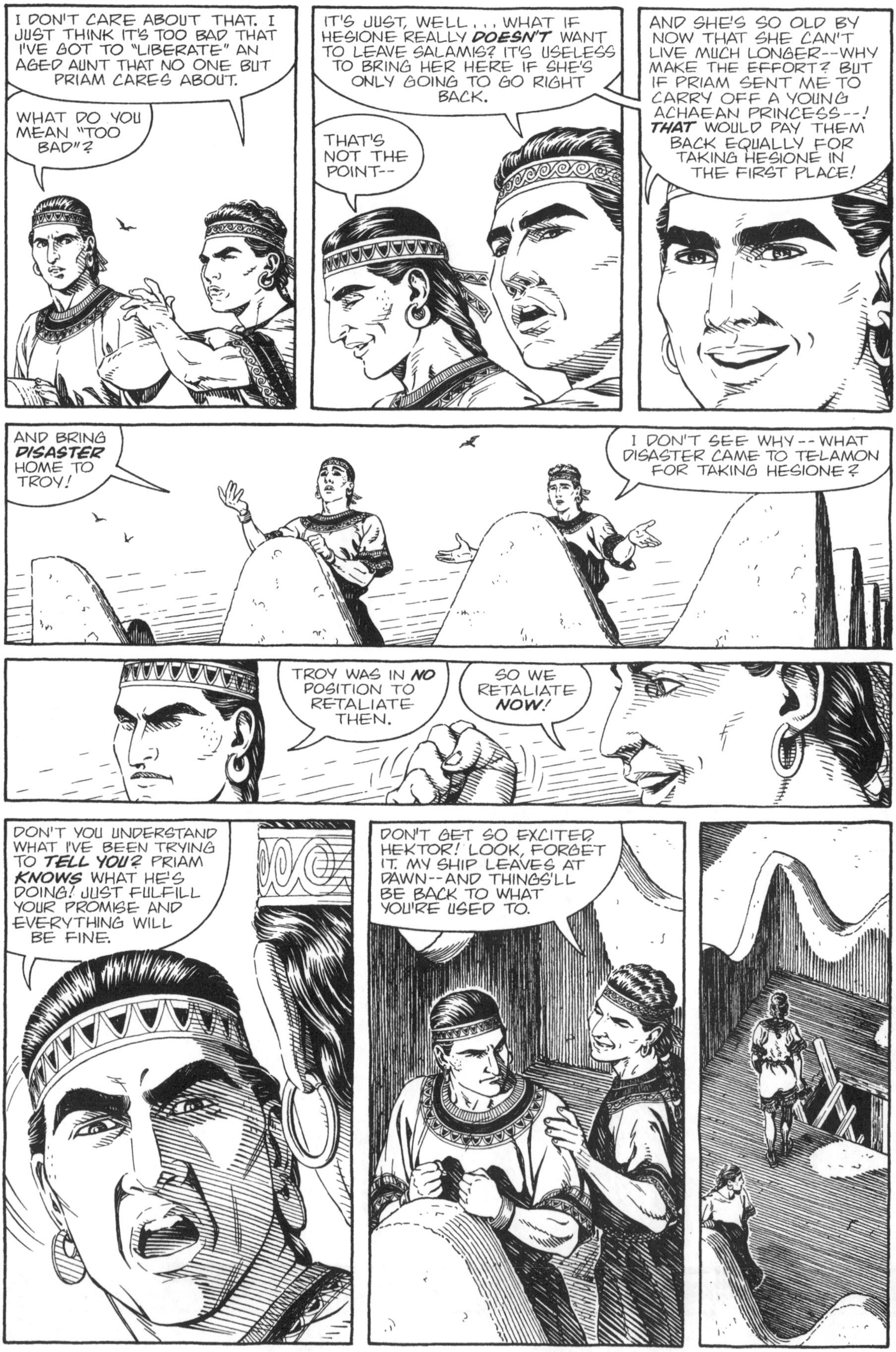
I DON'T CARE ABOUT THAT. I JUST THINK IT'S TOO BAD THAT I'VE GOT TO "LIBERATE" AN AGED AUNT THAT NO ONE BUT PRIAM CARES ABOUT.
WHAT DO YOU MEAN "TOO BAD"?
IT'S JUST, WELL . . . WHAT IF HESIONE REALLY DOESN'T WANT TO LEAVE SALAMIS? IT'S USELESS TO BRING HER HERE IF SHE'S ONLY GOING TO GO RIGHT BACK.
THAT'S NOT THE POINT--
AND SHE'S SO OLD BY NOW THAT SHE CAN'T LIVE MUCH LONGER--WHY MAKE THE EFFORT? BUT IF PRIAM SENT ME TO CARRY OFF A YOUNG ACHAEAN PRINCESS--! THAT WOULD PAY THEM BACK EQUALLY FOR TAKING HESIONE IN THE FIRST PLACE!
AND BRING DISASTER HOME TO TROY!
I DON'T SEE WHY--WHAT DISASTER CAME TO TELAMON FOR TAKING HESIONE?
TROY WAS IN NO POSITION TO RETALIATE THEN.
SO WE RETALIATE NOW!
DON'T YOU UNDERSTAND WHAT I'VE BEEN TRYING TO TELL YOU? PRIAM KNOWS WHAT HE'S DOING! JUST FULFILL YOUR PROMISE AND EVERYTHING WILL BE FINE.
DON'T GET SO EXCITED HEKTOR! LOOK, FORGET IT. MY SHIP LEAVES AT DAWN--AND THINGS'LL BE BACK TO WHAT YOU'RE USED TO.

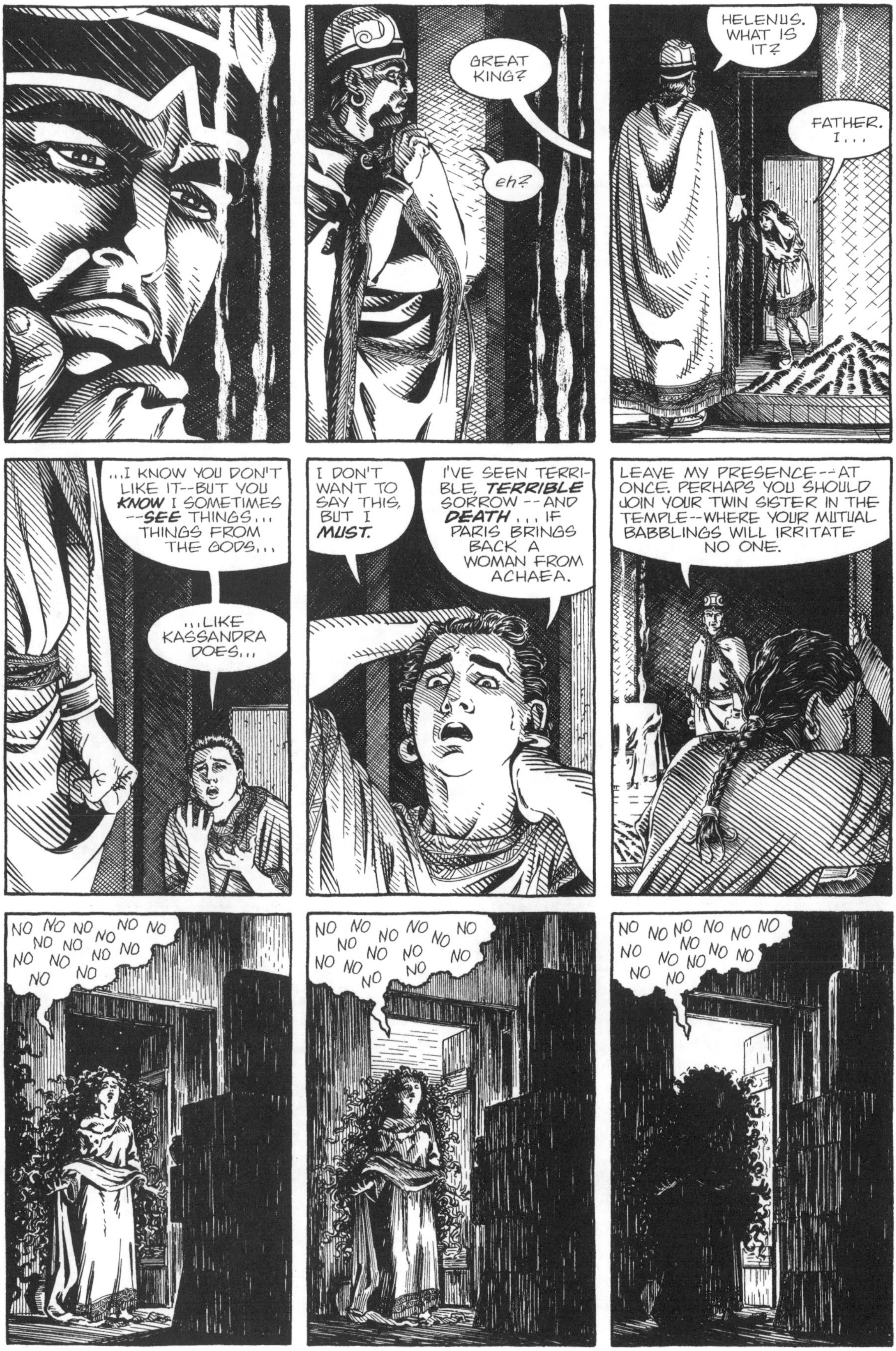
GREAT KING?
eh?
HELENUS. WHAT IS IT?
FATHER. I...
...I KNOW YOU DON'T LIKE IT--BUT YOU KNOW I SOMETIMES --SEE THINGS... THINGS FROM THE GODS...
...LIKE KASSANDRA DOES...
I DON'T WANT TO SAY THIS, BUT I MUST.
I'VE SEEN TERRIBLE, TERRIBLE SORROW--AND DEATH... IF PARIS BRINGS BACK A WOMAN FROM ACHAEA.
LEAVE MY PRESENCE--AT ONCE. PERHAPS YOU SHOULD JOIN YOUR TWIN SISTER IN THE TEMPLE--WHERE YOUR MUTUAL BABBLINGS WILL IRRITATE NO ONE.
NO NO NO NO NO NO NO NO NO NO NO NO NO NO NO NO NO NO
NO NO NO NO NO NO NO NO NO NO NO NO NO NO NO NO
NO NO NO NO NO NO NO NO NO NO NO NO NO NO NO NO

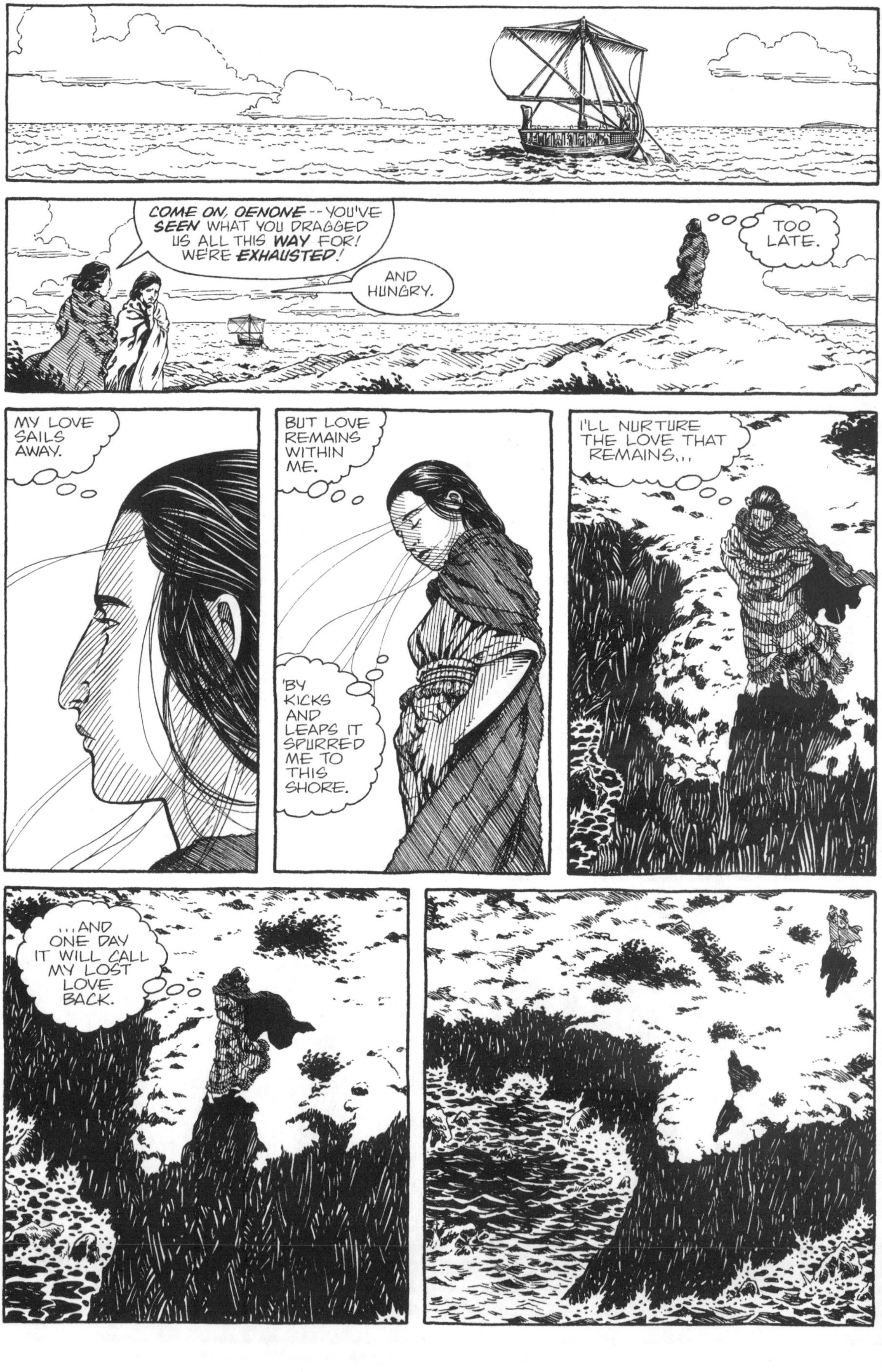
COME ON, OENONE--YOU'VE SEEN WHAT YOU DRAGGED US ALL THIS WAY FOR! WE'RE EXHAUSTED!
AND HUNGRY.
TOO LATE.
MY LOVE SAILS AWAY.
BUT LOVE REMAINS WITHIN ME.
'BY KICKS AND LEAPS IT SPURRED ME TO THIS SHORE.
I'LL NURTURE THE LOVE THAT REMAINS...
...AND ONE DAY IT WILL CALL MY LOST LOVE BACK.

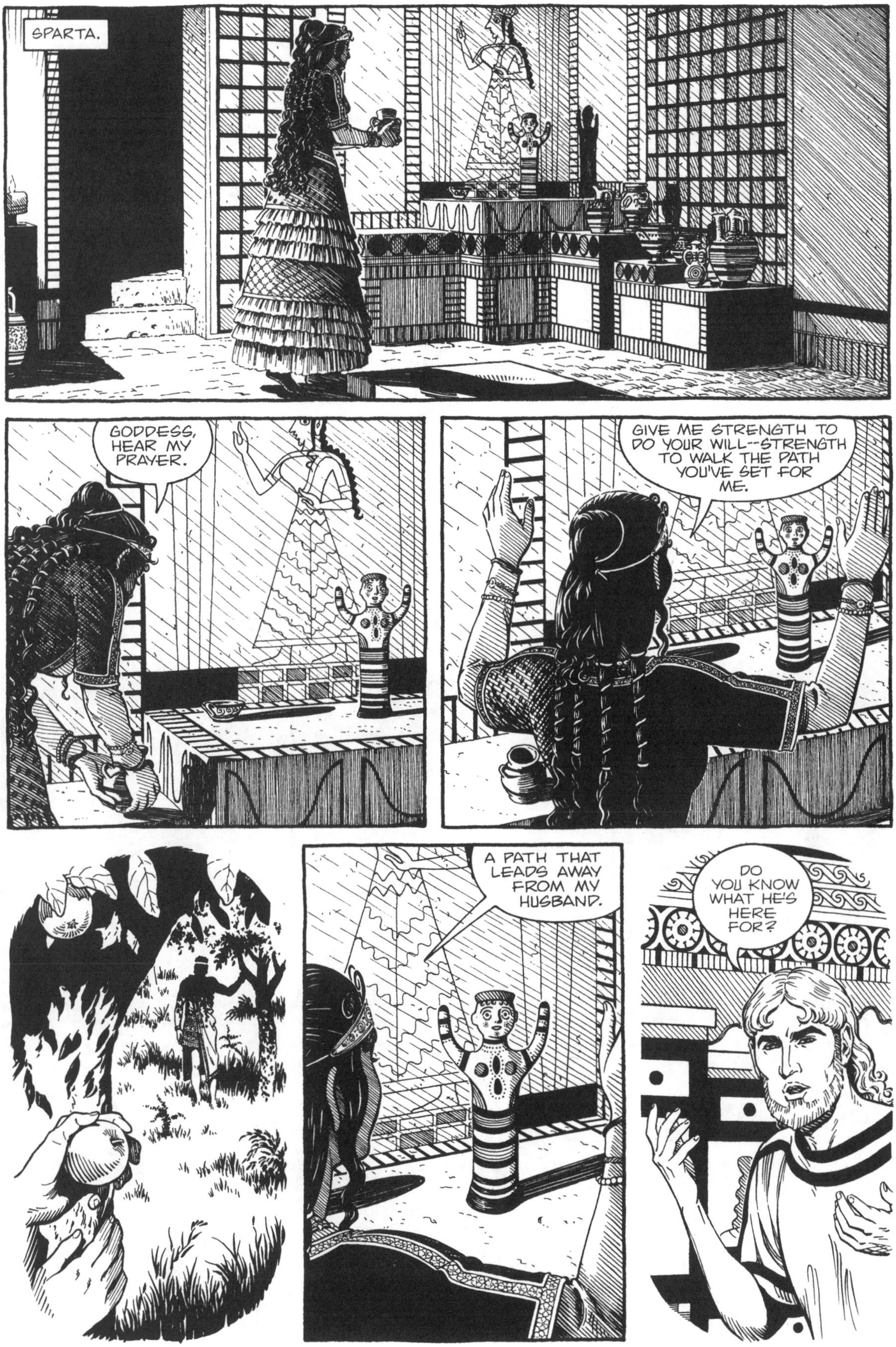
SPARTA.
GODDESS, HEAR MY PRAYER.
GIVE ME STRENGTH TO DO YOUR WILL--STRENGTH TO WALK THE PATH YOU'VE SET FOR ME.
A PATH THAT LEADS AWAY FROM MY HUSBAND.
DO YOU KNOW WHAT HE'S HERE FOR?

ALL MY LIFE, EVEN WHILE I WAS A CHILD MEN HAVE DESIRED ME.

ALL THE ACHAEAN KINGS SOUGHT TO MARRY ME. I YIELDED ONLY WHEN MY FATHER CHOSE MENELAUS AS MY HUSBAND.

DO YOU KNOW WHAT HE'S HERE FOR?

I YIELDED WILLING-LY.

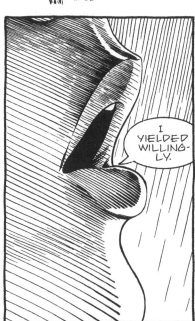

NOW MY WILL IS GONE...

...EATEN BY THE BLAZE YOU SET WITHIN ME, GODDESS.

I THOUGHT I KNEW FIRE, BUT I ONLY KNEW THE WARMTH OF LAMP AND HEARTH. THIS FIRE BURNS BEYOND CONTROL.

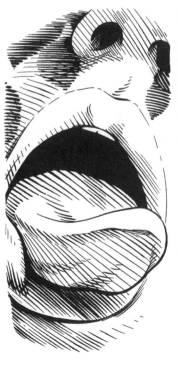

MY BODY FUELS THE FLAMES--FIRE CONSUMES ME.

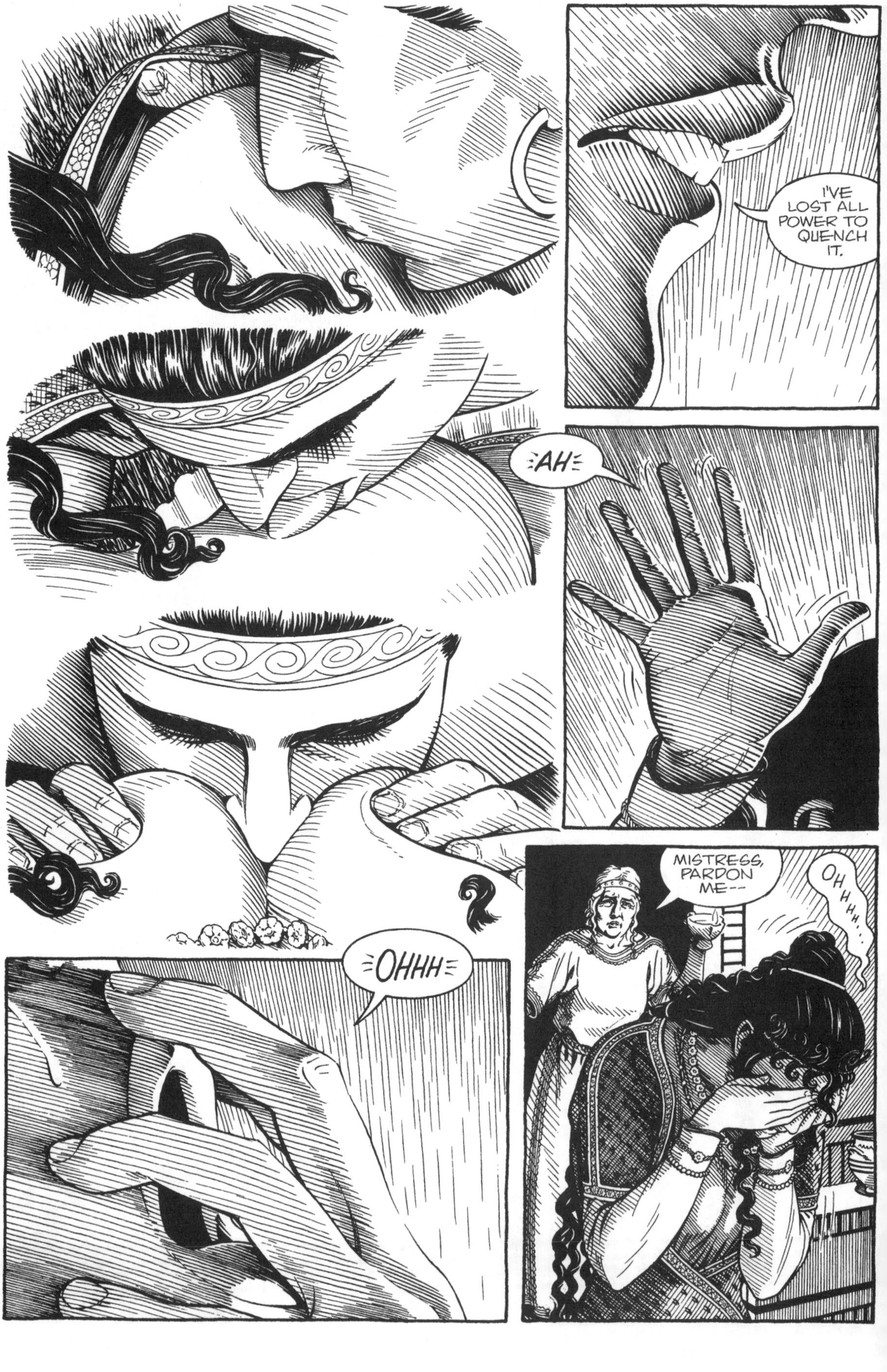
I'VE LOST ALL POWER TO QUENCH IT.
AH
OHHH
MISTRESS, PARDON ME--
OHHHH...

EVERYTHING'S BEEN DONE AS YOU INSTRUCTED-- THE WATCHMEN DISMISSED --THE BASKETS PACKED...

YES, THANK YOU, AITHRA. I'M FINISHED HERE...

OH, AITHRA, *HELP* ME!

MY DARLING CHILD, I WILL! BUT I DON'T UNDERSTAND-- TELL ME WHAT'S HAPPENING!

I--I'M LEAVING SPARTA--TONIGHT --*NOW*! I SAIL WITH PARIS AT DAWN.

WHAT? BUT *WHY*?

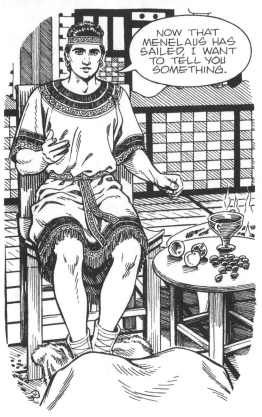

NOW THAT MENELAUS HAS SAILED I WANT TO TELL YOU SOMETHING.

BECAUSE I MUST.

MADNESS!

DO YOU KNOW WHAT HE'S HERE FOR?

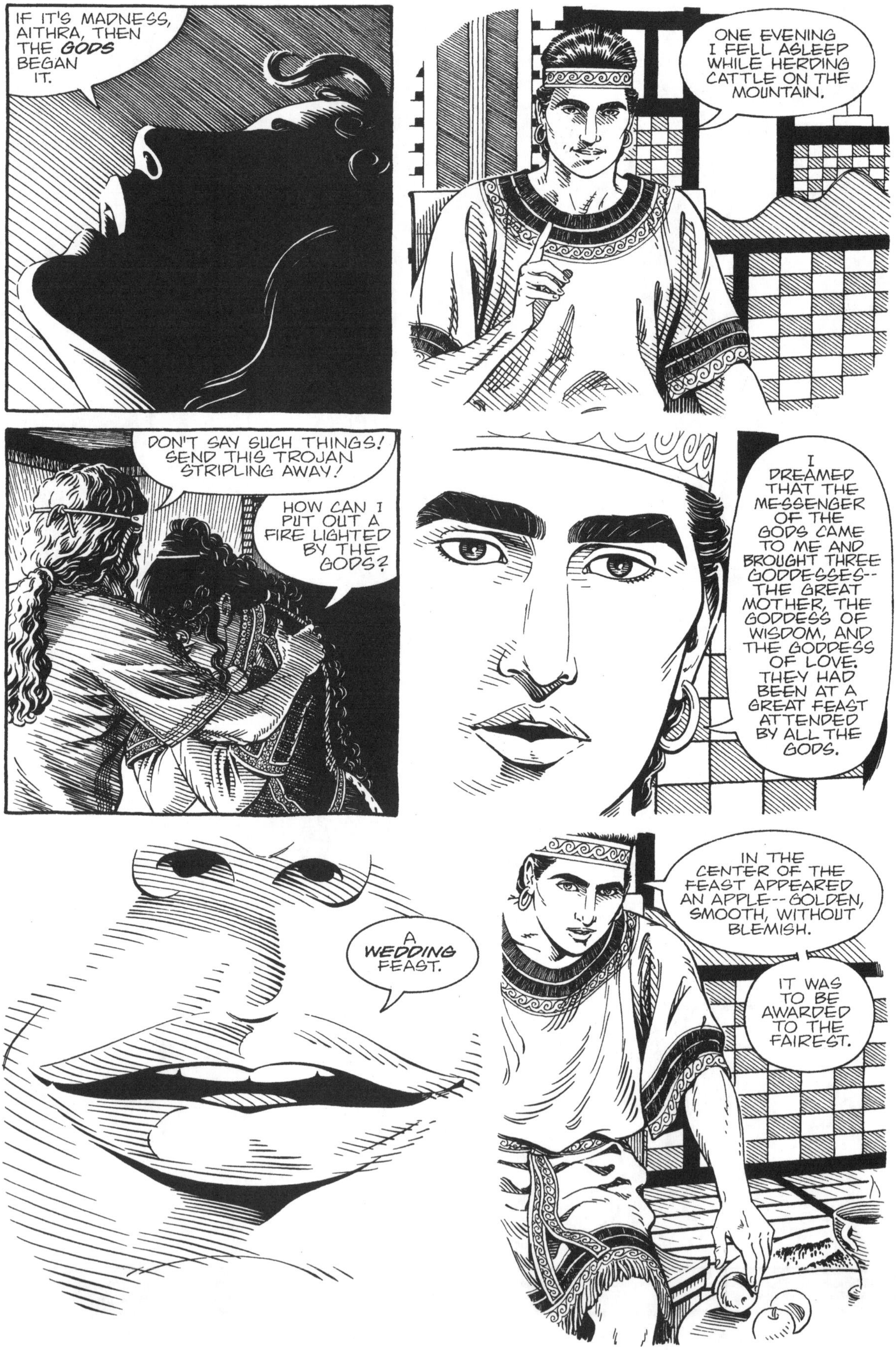

IF IT'S MADNESS, AITHRA, THEN THE GODS BEGAN IT.
ONE EVENING I FELL ASLEEP WHILE HERDING CATTLE ON THE MOUNTAIN.
DON'T SAY SUCH THINGS! SEND THIS TROJAN STRIPLING AWAY!
HOW CAN I PUT OUT A FIRE LIGHTED BY THE GODS?
I DREAMED THAT THE MESSENGER OF THE GODS CAME TO ME AND BROUGHT THREE GODDESSES-- THE GREAT MOTHER, THE GODDESS OF WISDOM, AND THE GODDESS OF LOVE. THEY HAD BEEN AT A GREAT FEAST ATTENDED BY ALL THE GODS.
A WEDDING FEAST.
IN THE CENTER OF THE FEAST APPEARED AN APPLE-- GOLDEN, SMOOTH, WITHOUT BLEMISH.
IT WAS TO BE AWARDED TO THE FAIREST.

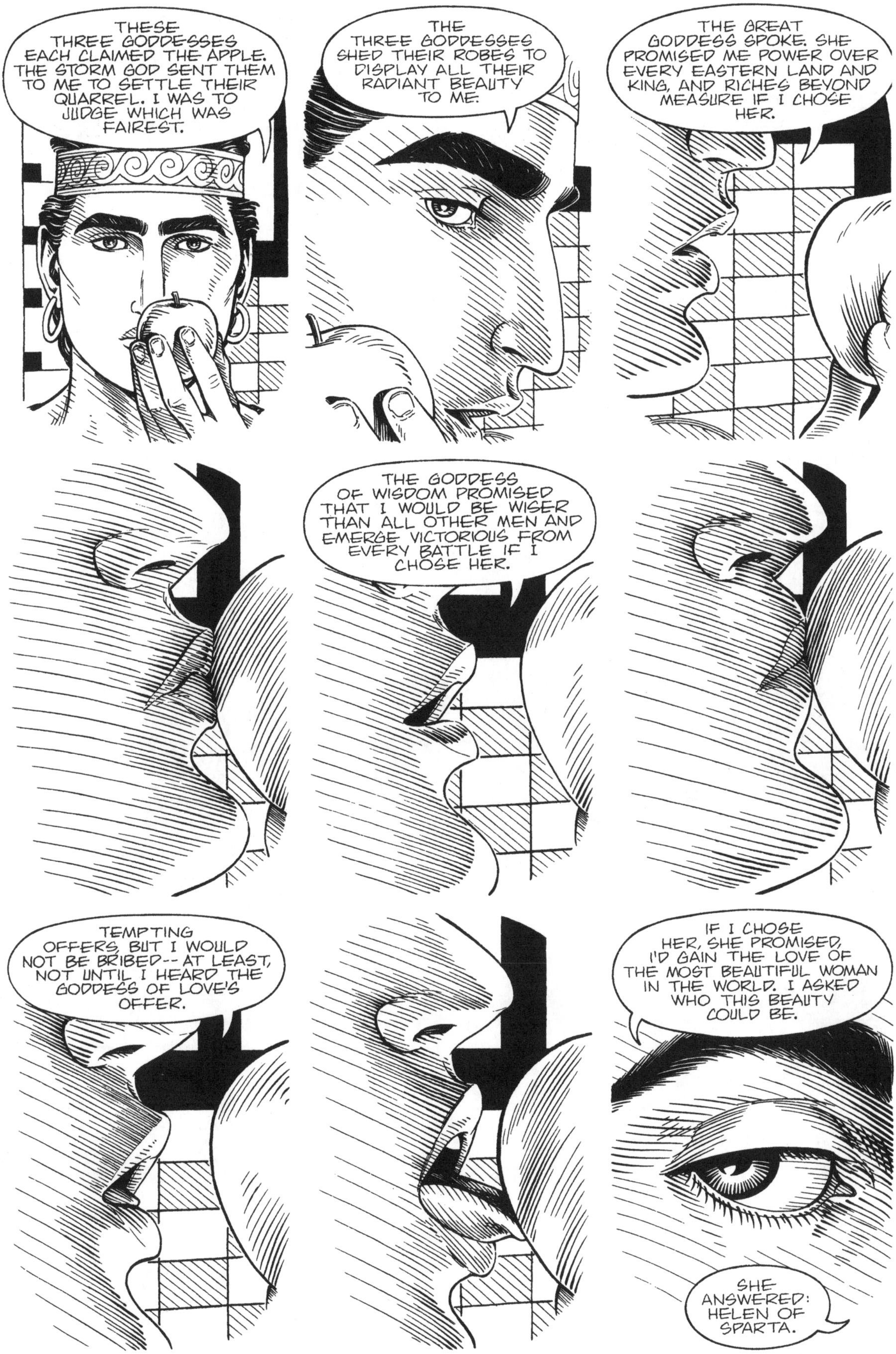
THESE THREE GODDESSES EACH CLAIMED THE APPLE. THE STORM GOD SENT THEM TO ME TO SETTLE THEIR QUARREL. I WAS TO JUDGE WHICH WAS FAIREST.
THE THREE GODDESSES SHED THEIR ROBES TO DISPLAY ALL THEIR RADIANT BEAUTY TO ME.
THE GREAT GODDESS SPOKE. SHE PROMISED ME POWER OVER EVERY EASTERN LAND AND KING, AND RICHES BEYOND MEASURE IF I CHOSE HER.
THE GODDESS OF WISDOM PROMISED THAT I WOULD BE WISER THAN ALL OTHER MEN AND EMERGE VICTORIOUS FROM EVERY BATTLE IF I CHOSE HER.
TEMPTING OFFERS, BUT I WOULD NOT BE BRIBED-- AT LEAST, NOT UNTIL I HEARD THE GODDESS OF LOVE'S OFFER.
IF I CHOSE HER, SHE PROMISED, I'D GAIN THE LOVE OF THE MOST BEAUTIFUL WOMAN IN THE WORLD. I ASKED WHO THIS BEAUTY COULD BE.
SHE ANSWERED: HELEN OF SPARTA.

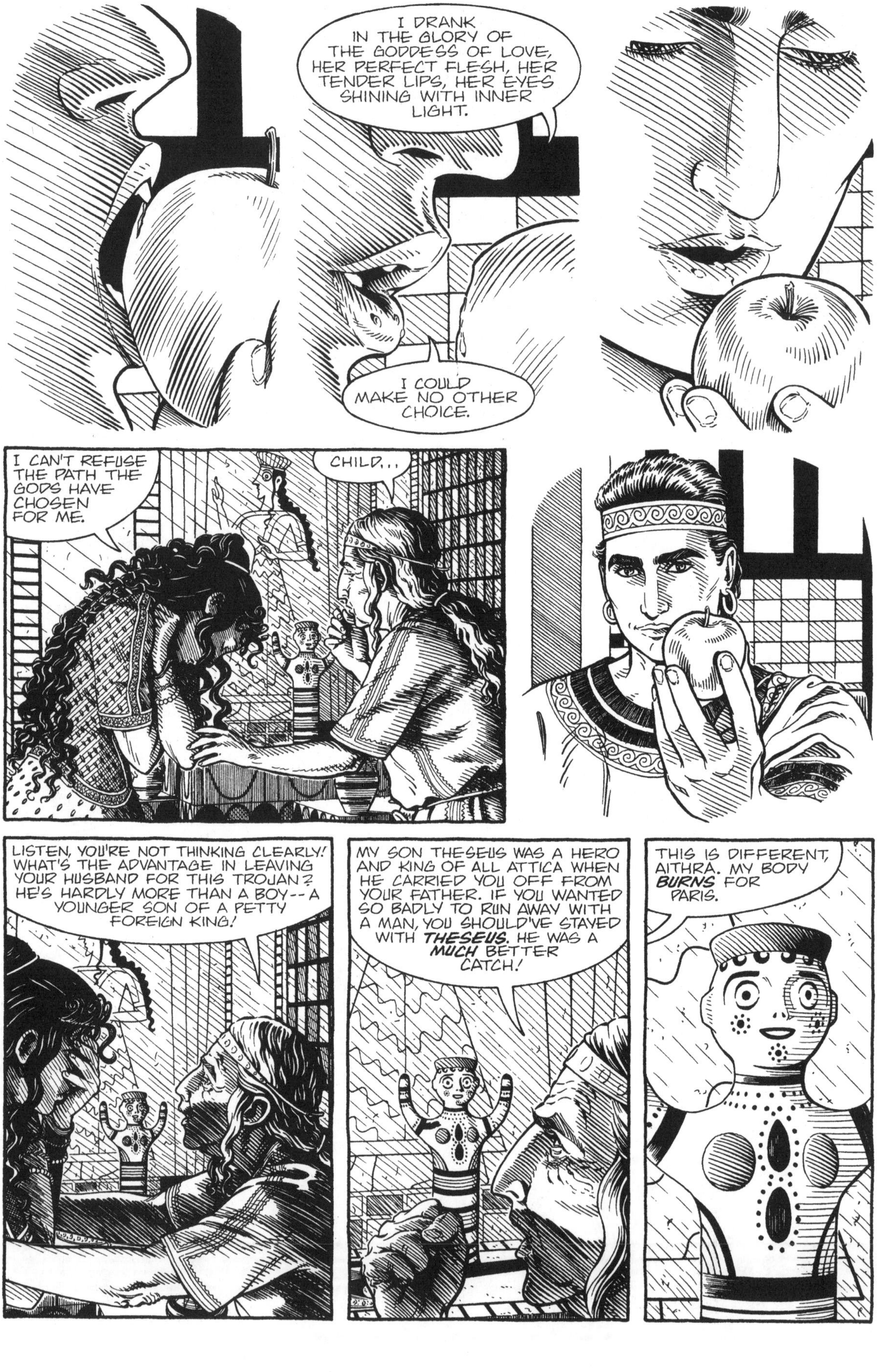
I DRANK IN THE GLORY OF THE GODDESS OF LOVE, HER PERFECT FLESH, HER TENDER LIPS, HER EYES SHINING WITH INNER LIGHT.
I COULD MAKE NO OTHER CHOICE.
I CAN'T REFUSE THE PATH THE GODS HAVE CHOSEN FOR ME.
CHILD...
LISTEN, YOU'RE NOT THINKING CLEARLY! WHAT'S THE ADVANTAGE IN LEAVING YOUR HUSBAND FOR THIS TROJAN? HE'S HARDLY MORE THAN A BOY-- A YOUNGER SON OF A PETTY FOREIGN KING!
MY SON THESEUS WAS A HERO AND KING OF ALL ATTICA WHEN HE CARRIED YOU OFF FROM YOUR FATHER. IF YOU WANTED SO BADLY TO RUN AWAY WITH A MAN, YOU SHOULD'VE STAYED WITH THESEUS. HE WAS A MUCH BETTER CATCH!
THIS IS DIFFERENT, AITHRA. MY BODY BURNS FOR PARIS.

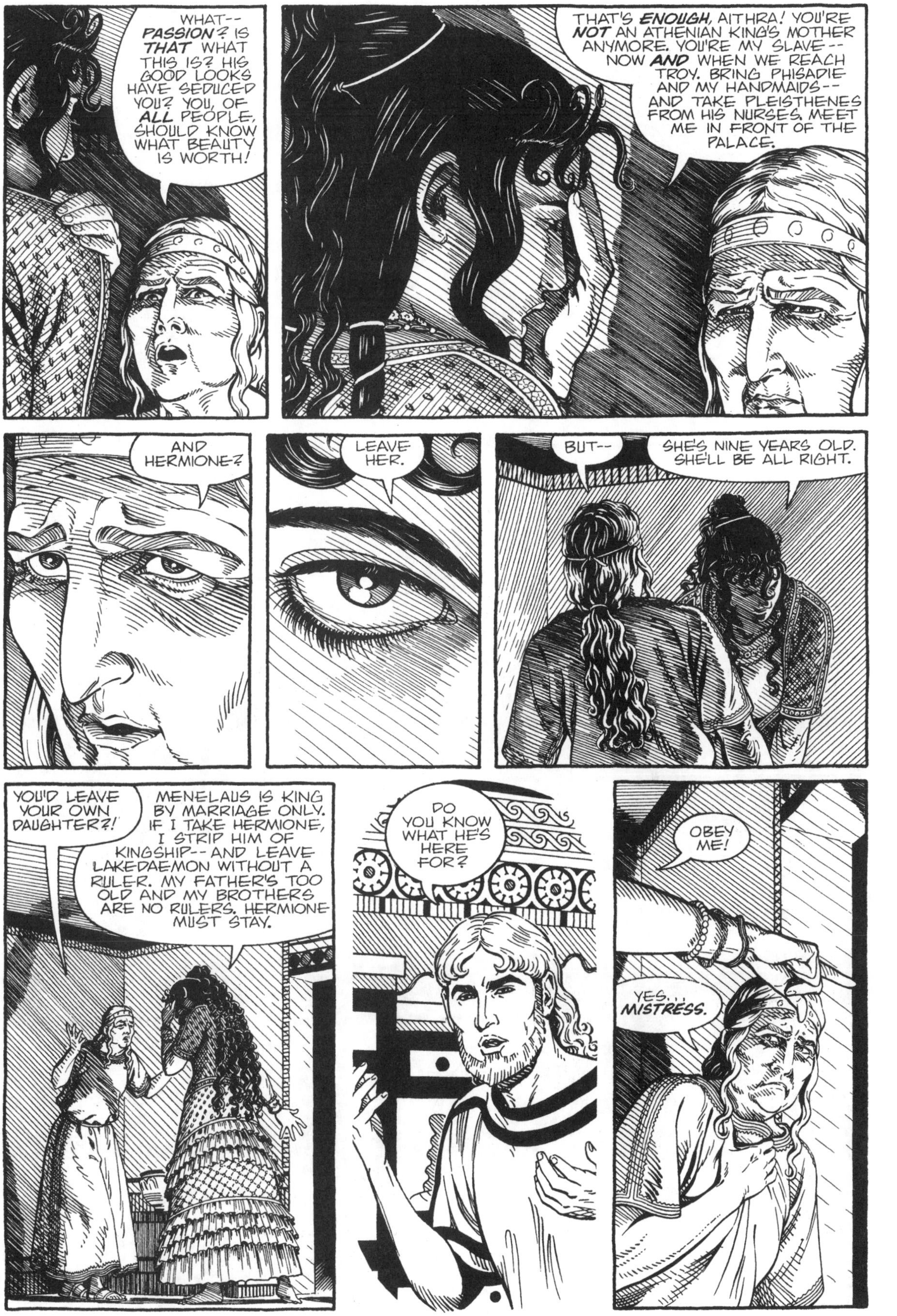
WHAT-- PASSION? IS THAT WHAT THIS IS? HIS GOOD LOOKS HAVE SEDUCED YOU? YOU, OF ALL PEOPLE, SHOULD KNOW WHAT BEAUTY IS WORTH!
THAT'S ENOUGH, AITHRA! YOU'RE NOT AN ATHENIAN KING'S MOTHER ANYMORE. YOU'RE MY SLAVE-- NOW AND WHEN WE REACH TROY. BRING PHISADIE AND MY HANDMAIDS-- AND TAKE PLEISTHENES FROM HIS NURSES. MEET ME IN FRONT OF THE PALACE.
AND HERMIONE?
LEAVE HER.
BUT--
SHE'S NINE YEARS OLD. SHE'LL BE ALL RIGHT.
YOU'D LEAVE YOUR OWN DAUGHTER?!
MENELAUS IS KING BY MARRIAGE ONLY. IF I TAKE HERMIONE, I STRIP HIM OF KINGSHIP-- AND LEAVE LAKEDAEMON WITHOUT A RULER. MY FATHER'S TOO OLD AND MY BROTHERS ARE NO RULERS. HERMIONE MUST STAY.
DO YOU KNOW WHAT HE'S HERE FOR?
OBEY ME!
YES... MISTRESS.

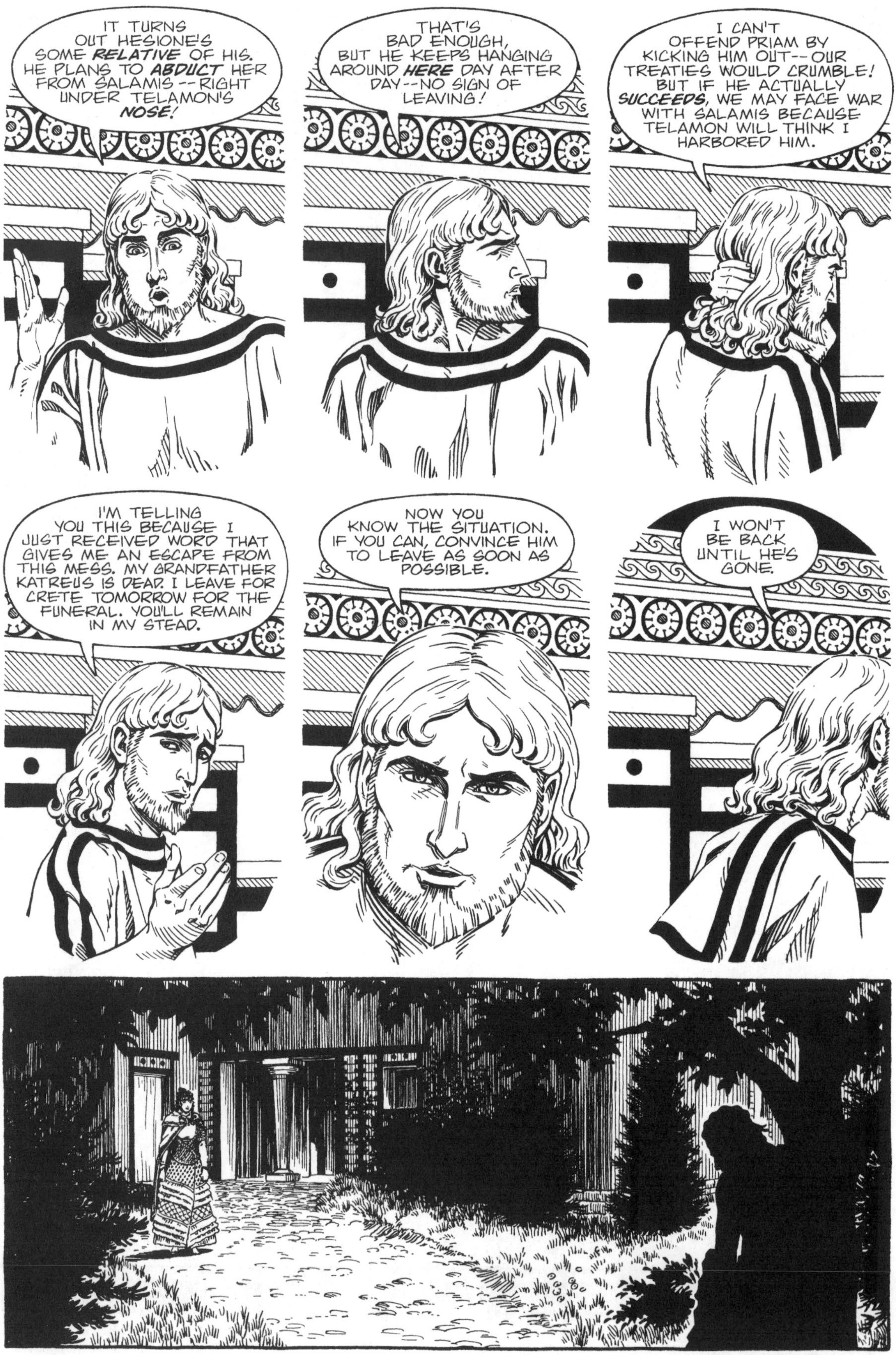
IT TURNS OUT HESIONE'S SOME RELATIVE OF HIS. HE PLANS TO ABDUCT HER FROM SALAMIS--RIGHT UNDER TELAMON'S NOSE!
THAT'S BAD ENOUGH, BUT HE KEEPS HANGING AROUND HERE DAY AFTER DAY--NO SIGN OF LEAVING!
I CAN'T OFFEND PRIAM BY KICKING HIM OUT--OUR TREATIES WOULD CRUMBLE! BUT IF HE ACTUALLY SUCCEEDS, WE MAY FACE WAR WITH SALAMIS BECAUSE TELAMON WILL THINK I HARBORED HIM.
I'M TELLING YOU THIS BECAUSE I JUST RECEIVED WORD THAT GIVES ME AN ESCAPE FROM THIS MESS. MY GRANDFATHER KATREUS IS DEAD. I LEAVE FOR CRETE TOMORROW FOR THE FUNERAL. YOU'LL REMAIN IN MY STEAD.
NOW YOU KNOW THE SITUATION. IF YOU CAN, CONVINCE HIM TO LEAVE AS SOON AS POSSIBLE.
I WON'T BE BACK UNTIL HE'S GONE.

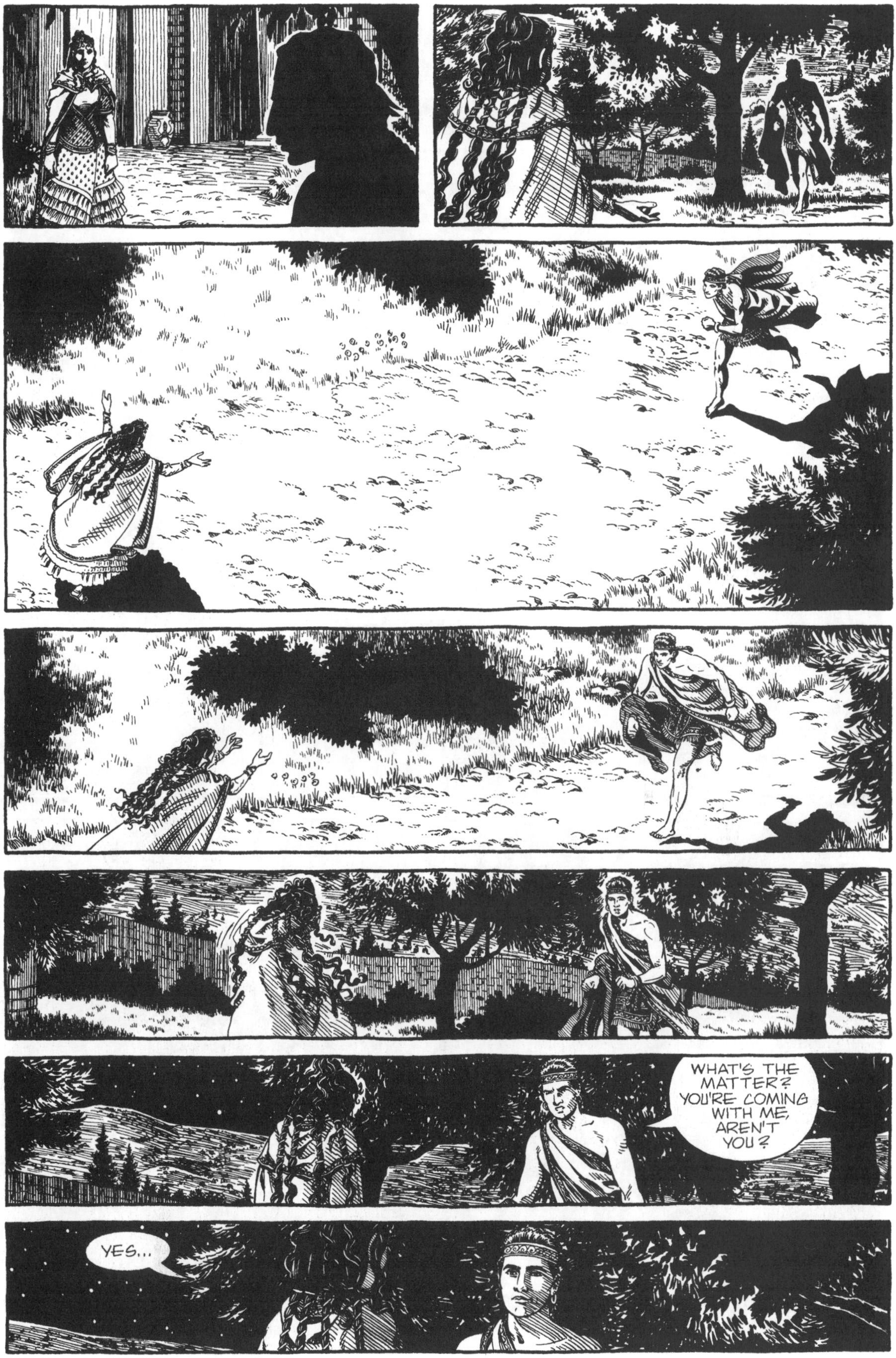
WHAT'S THE MATTER? YOU'RE COMING WITH ME, AREN'T YOU?
YES...

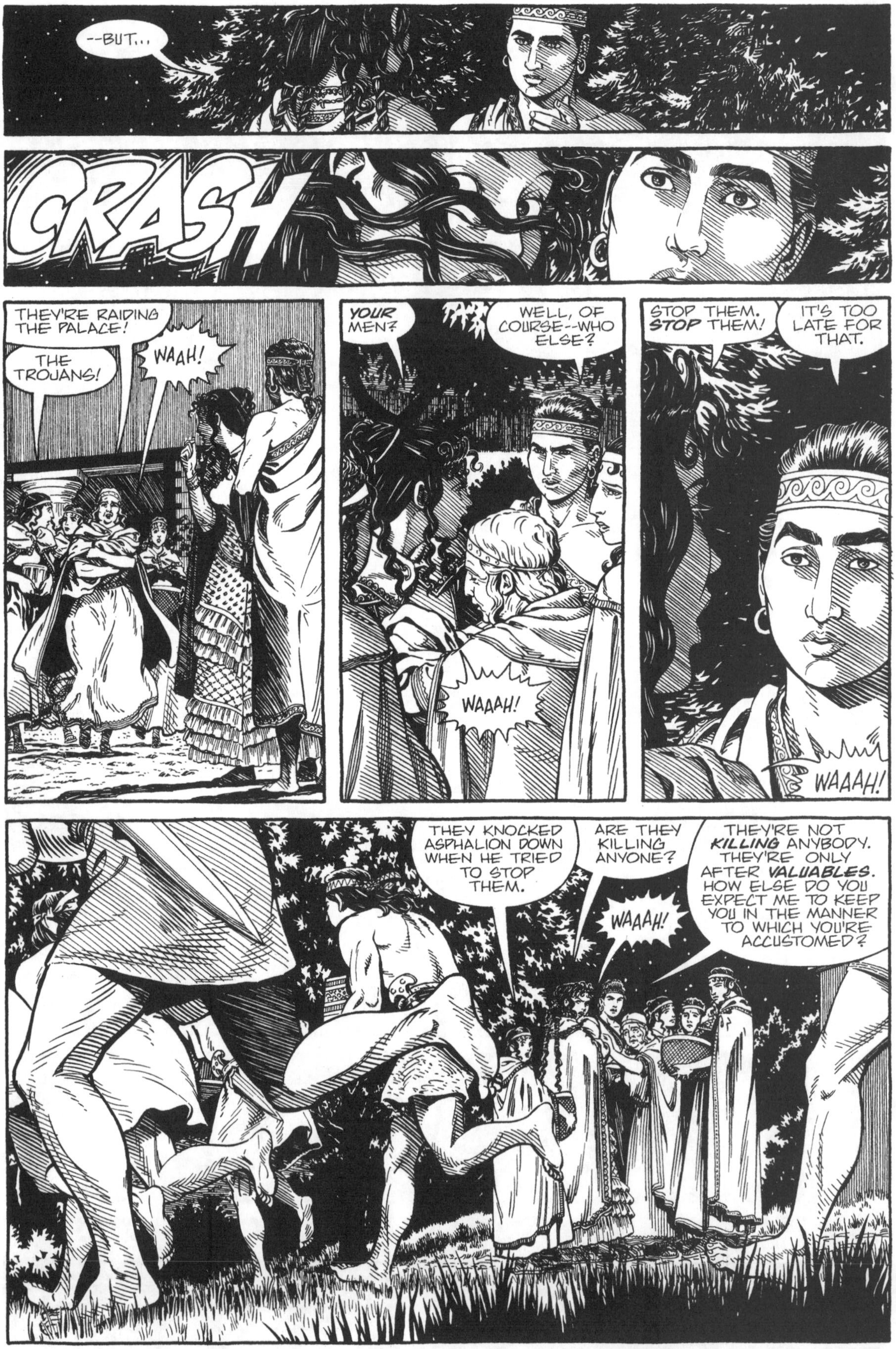
--BUT...
CRASH
THEY'RE RAIDING THE PALACE!
THE TROJANS!
WAAH!
YOUR MEN?
WELL, OF COURSE--WHO ELSE?
WAAAH!
STOP THEM. STOP THEM!
IT'S TOO LATE FOR THAT.
WAAAH!
THEY KNOCKED ASPHALION DOWN WHEN HE TRIED TO STOP THEM.
ARE THEY KILLING ANYONE?
WAAAH!
THEY'RE NOT KILLING ANYBODY. THEY'RE ONLY AFTER VALUABLES. HOW ELSE DO YOU EXPECT ME TO KEEP YOU IN THE MANNER TO WHICH YOU'RE ACCUSTOMED?

IT'S NOT ENOUGH TO DESPOIL MENELAUS OF HIS WIFE--YOU RAID HIS PALACE, *TOO?*

IT WAS SUPPOSED TO BE A DIVERSION SO NO ONE WOULD NOTICE YOU LEAVING. GREAT CHANCE FOR THAT NOW. SAY FAREWELL TO YOUR CROWD OF WOMEN AND THAT BAWLING CHILD, THEN COVER YOURSELF WITH THIS.

WAAAH!

THEY COME WITH ME. MY SON, TOO.

WAAAH!

NO-NO-NO-NO... IMPOSSIBLE.

THEN GO WITHOUT ME. EITHER THEY GO OR I STAY.

WAAAH!

YOU THINK YOU CAN BARGAIN WITH ME?

DECIDE.

WAAAH!

ALL RIGHT--BUT THEY'LL HAVE TO KEEP UP WITH THE CHARIOT. WE NEED TO REACH THE SHIP BEFORE DAWN.

WAAAH!

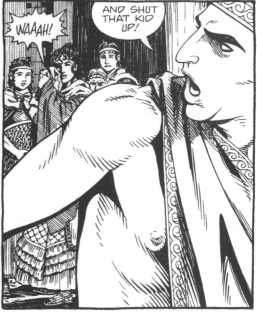

WAAAH!

AND SHUT THAT KID UP!

AITHRA... HELP ME--

GIVE PLEISTHENES TO ME.

WAAH!

MISTRESS, I DON'T UNDER-STAND--WHAT'S HAPPENING?

THAT TROJAN'S NOTHING BUT A RUDE BOY. I SAW THAT THE DAY HE LANDED.

WAAH!

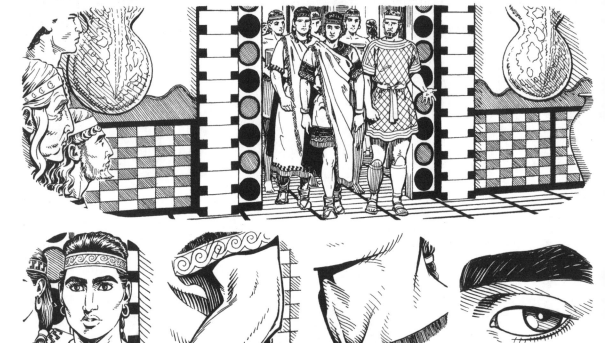

WE'RE LEAVING LAKEDAEMON, PHISADIE. WE SAIL FOR TROY.

WHAT MAKES YOU THINK YOUR BROTHERS WON'T COME AFTER HIM AS THEY DID THESEUS? THEY'RE DUE BACK AT ANY MOMENT.

WAAAH!

THAT'S WHY WE MUST SAIL BY DAWN.

COME!

WAAAH!

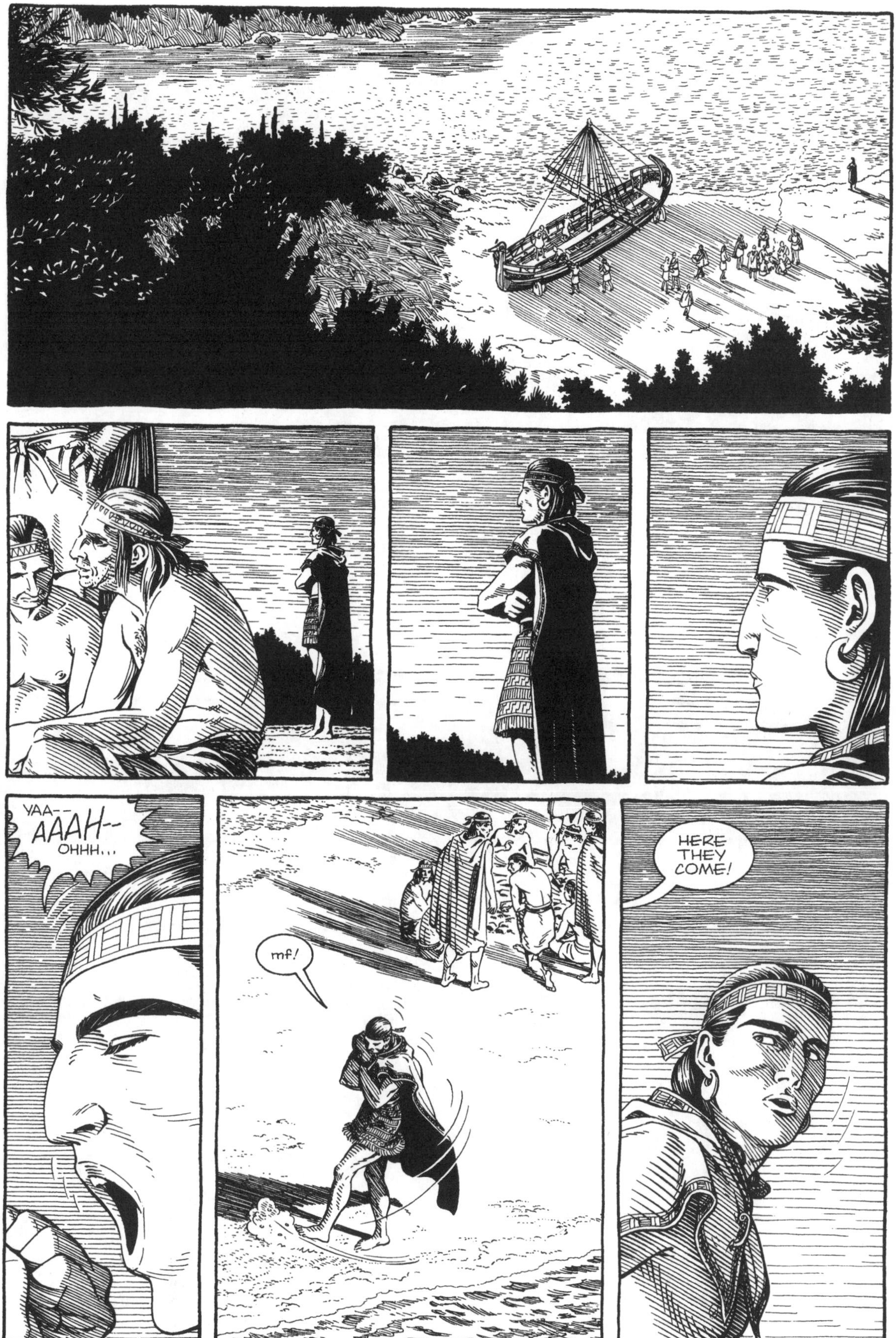
YAA--
AAAH--
OHHH...
mf!
HERE THEY COME!

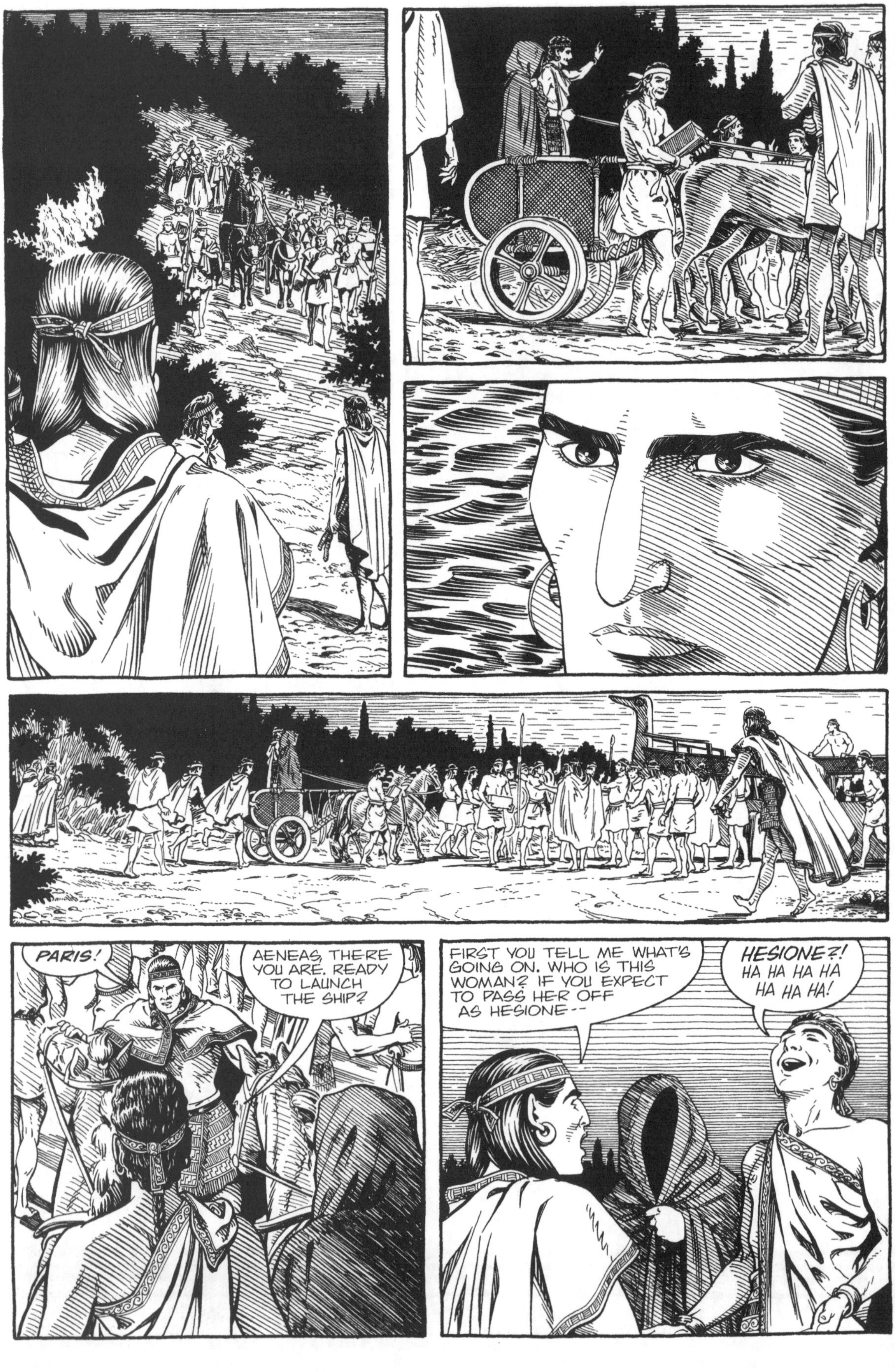
PARIS!
AENEAS, THERE YOU ARE. READY TO LAUNCH THE SHIP?
FIRST YOU TELL ME WHAT'S GOING ON. WHO IS THIS WOMAN? IF YOU EXPECT TO PASS HER OFF AS HESIONE--
HESIONE?! HA HA HA HA HA HA HA!

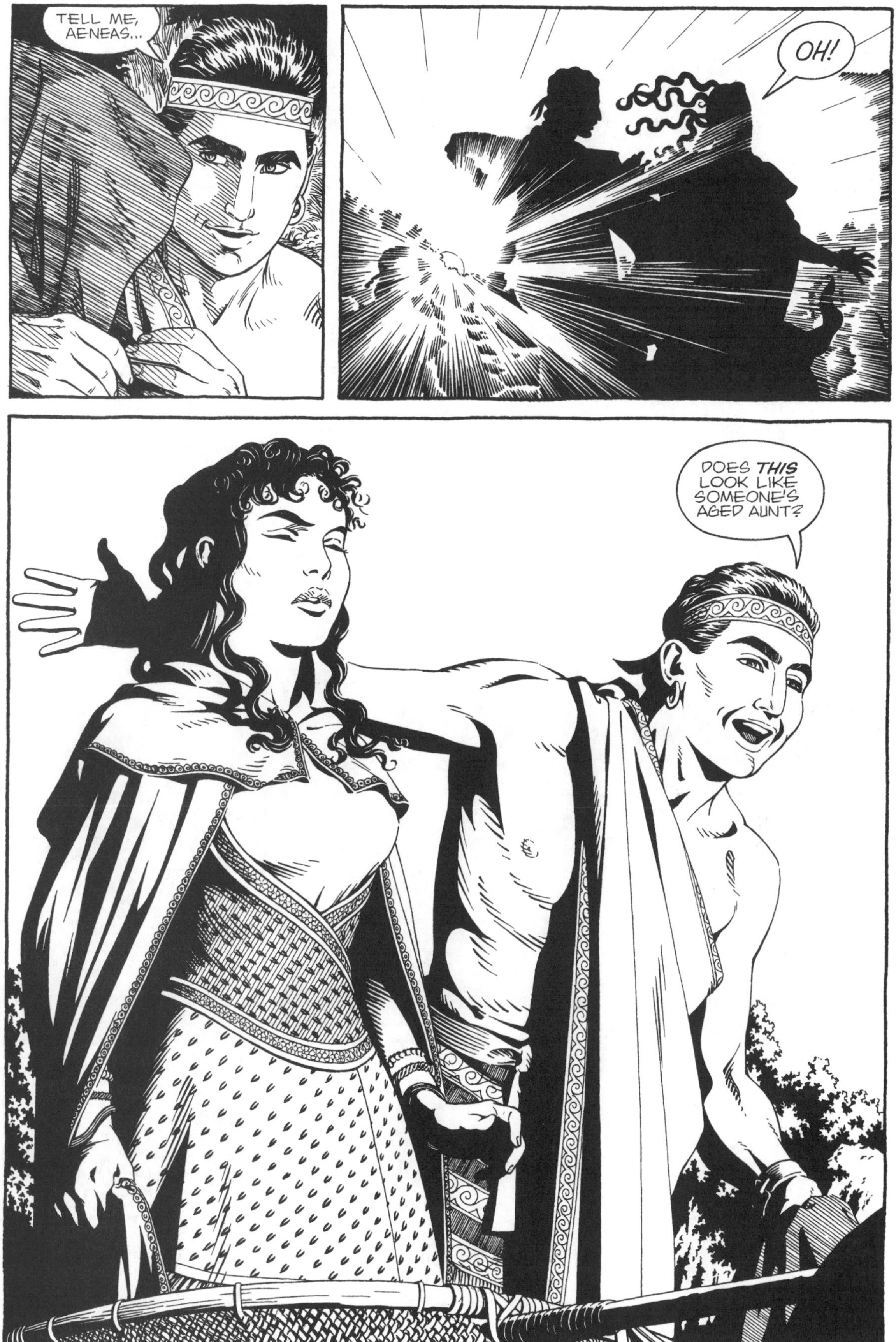
TELL ME, AENEAS...
OH!
DOES THIS LOOK LIKE SOMEONE'S AGED AUNT?

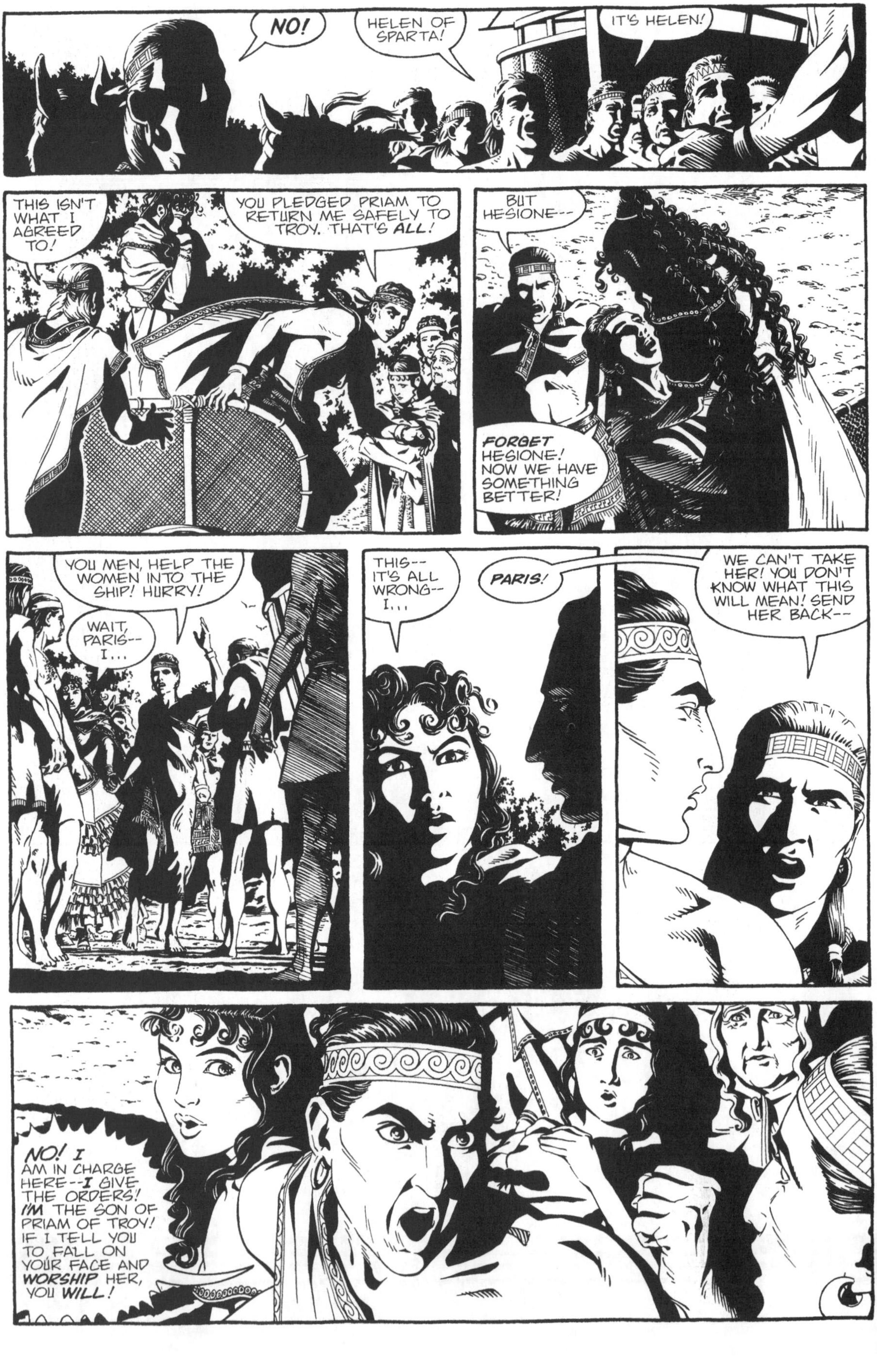
NO!
HELEN OF SPARTA!
IT'S HELEN!
THIS ISN'T WHAT I AGREED TO!
YOU PLEDGED PRIAM TO RETURN ME SAFELY TO TROY. THAT'S ALL!
BUT HESIONE--
FORGET HESIONE! NOW WE HAVE SOMETHING BETTER!
YOU MEN, HELP THE WOMEN INTO THE SHIP! HURRY!
WAIT, PARIS-- I...
THIS-- IT'S ALL WRONG-- I...
PARIS!
WE CAN'T TAKE HER! YOU DON'T KNOW WHAT THIS WILL MEAN! SEND HER BACK--
NO! I AM IN CHARGE HERE--I GIVE THE ORDERS! I'M THE SON OF PRIAM OF TROY! IF I TELL YOU TO FALL ON YOUR FACE AND WORSHIP HER, YOU WILL!

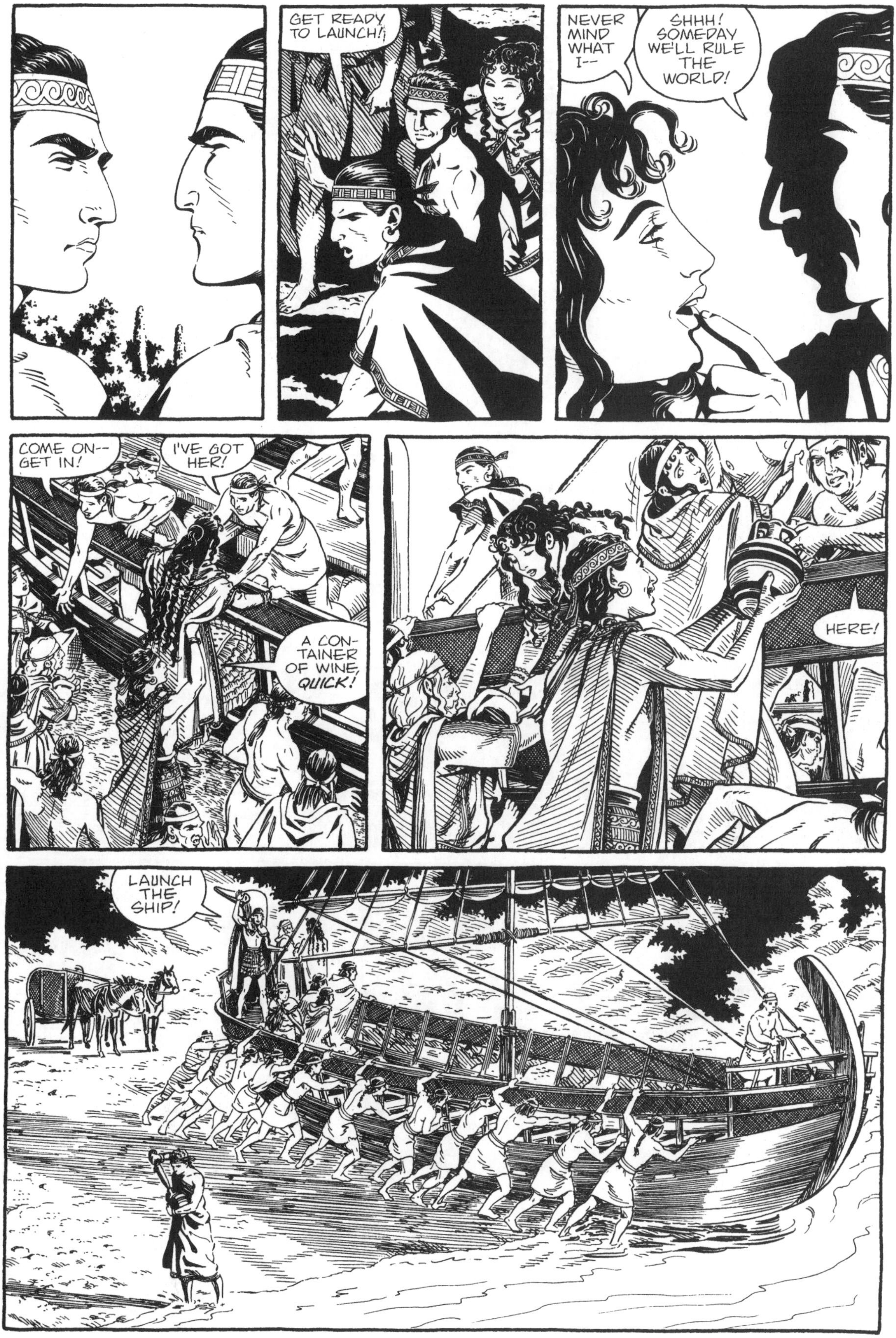
GET READY TO LAUNCH!
NEVER MIND WHAT I--
SHHH! SOMEDAY WE'LL RULE THE WORLD!
COME ON-- GET IN!
I'VE GOT HER!
A CONTAINER OF WINE, QUICK!
HERE!
LAUNCH THE SHIP!

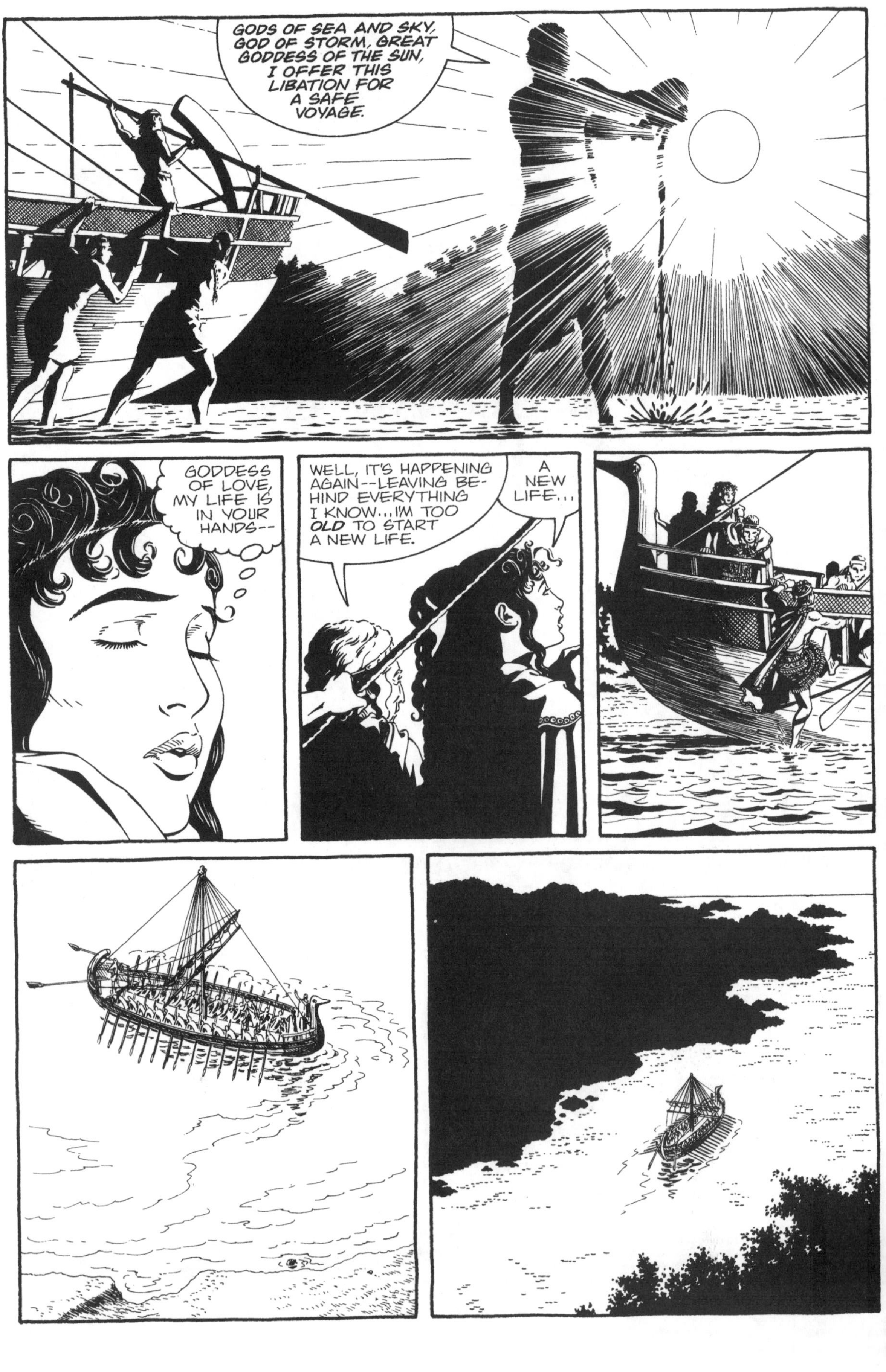
GODS OF SEA AND SKY, GOD OF STORM, GREAT GODDESS OF THE SUN, I OFFER THIS LIBATION FOR A SAFE VOYAGE.
GODDESS OF LOVE, MY LIFE IS IN YOUR HANDS--
WELL, IT'S HAPPENING AGAIN--LEAVING BEHIND EVERYTHING I KNOW...I'M TOO OLD TO START A NEW LIFE.
A NEW LIFE...

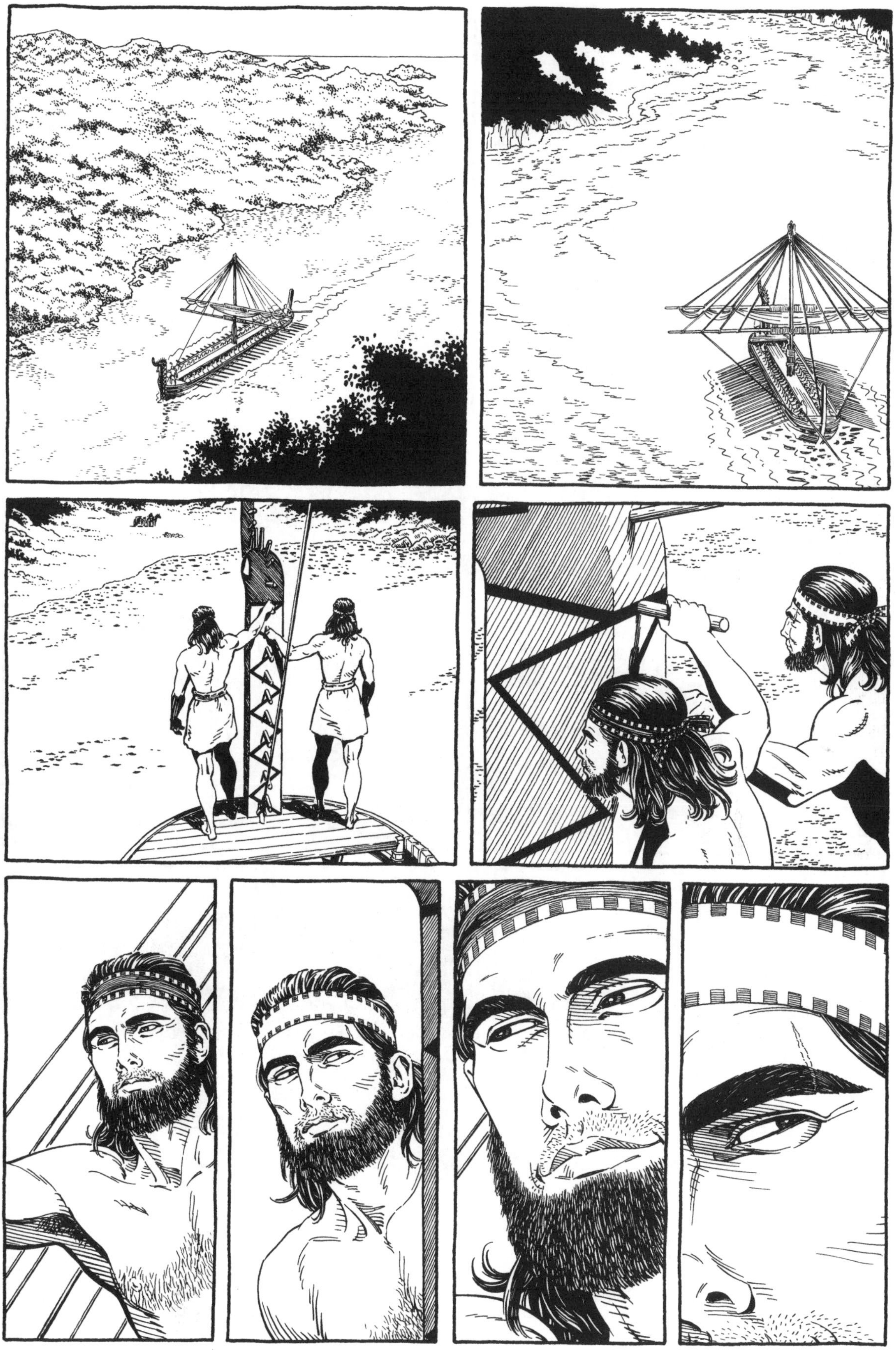

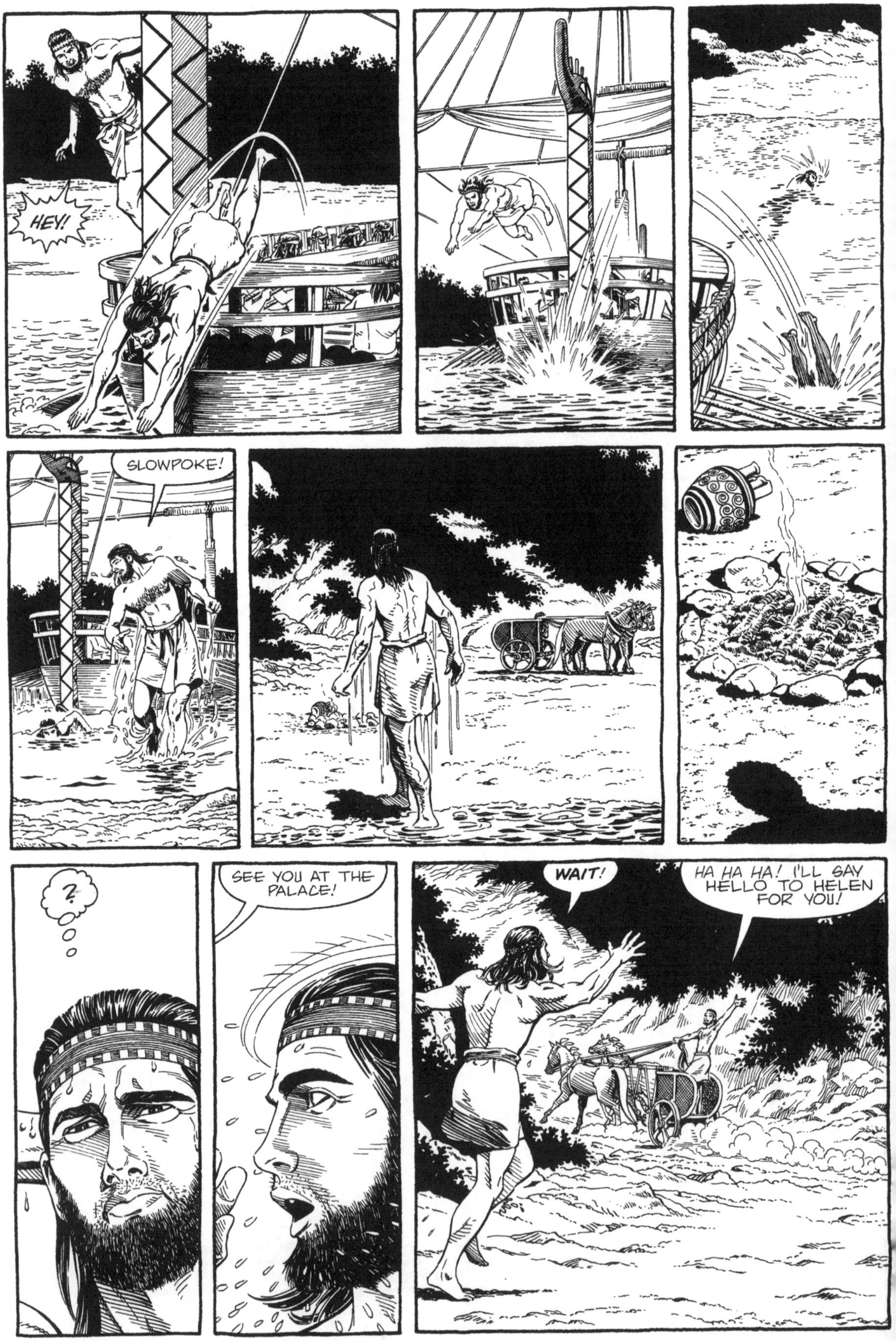
HEY!
SLOWPOKE!
?
SEE YOU AT THE PALACE!
WAIT!
HA HA HA! I'LL SAY HELLO TO HELEN FOR YOU!

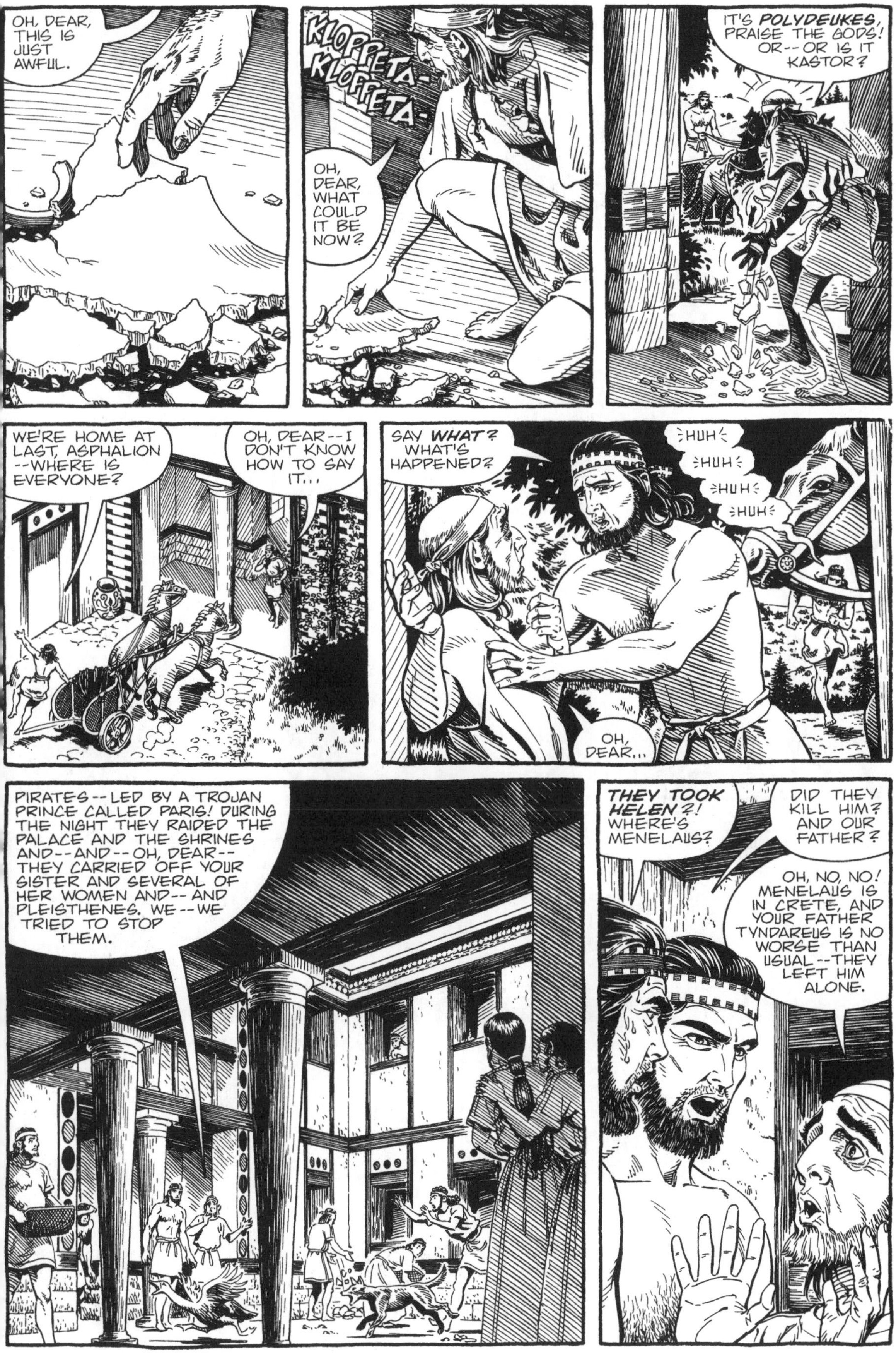

OH, DEAR, THIS IS JUST AWFUL.
KLOPPETA-KLOPPETA-
OH, DEAR, WHAT COULD IT BE NOW?
IT'S POLYDEUKES, PRAISE THE GODS! OR--OR IS IT KASTOR?
WE'RE HOME AT LAST, ASPHALION --WHERE IS EVERYONE?
OH, DEAR--I DON'T KNOW HOW TO SAY IT...
SAY WHAT? WHAT'S HAPPENED?
HUH
HUH
HUH
HUH
OH, DEAR...
PIRATES--LED BY A TROJAN PRINCE CALLED PARIS! DURING THE NIGHT THEY RAIDED THE PALACE AND THE SHRINES AND--AND--OH, DEAR--THEY CARRIED OFF YOUR SISTER AND SEVERAL OF HER WOMEN AND--AND PLEISTHENES. WE--WE TRIED TO STOP THEM.
THEY TOOK HELEN?! WHERE'S MENELAUS?
DID THEY KILL HIM? AND OUR FATHER?
OH, NO, NO! MENELAUS IS IN CRETE, AND YOUR FATHER TYNDAREUS IS NO WORSE THAN USUAL--THEY LEFT HIM ALONE.

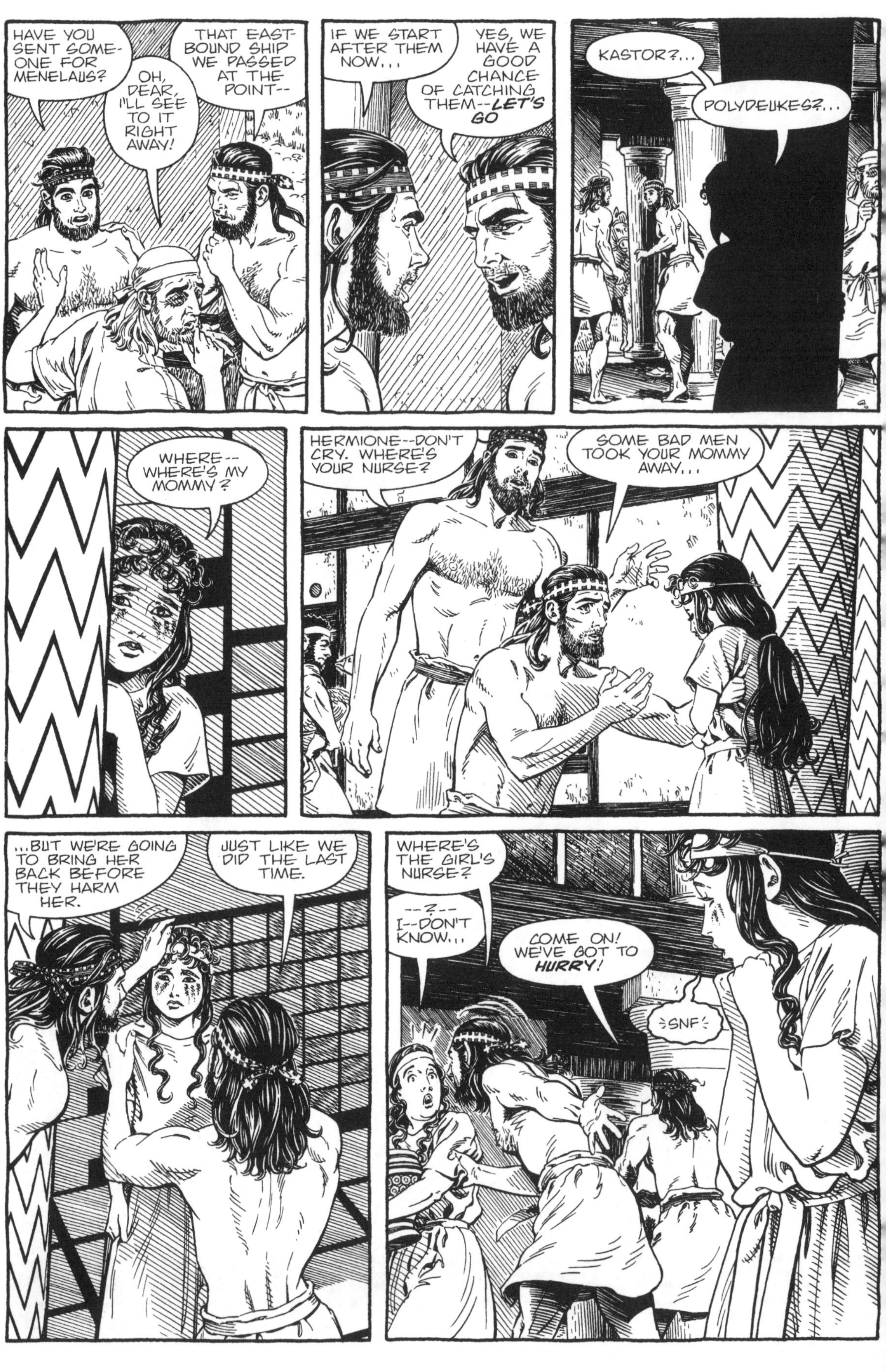
HAVE YOU SENT SOME-ONE FOR MENELAUS?
OH, DEAR, I'LL SEE TO IT RIGHT AWAY!
THAT EAST-BOUND SHIP WE PASSED AT THE POINT--
IF WE START AFTER THEM NOW...
YES, WE HAVE A GOOD CHANCE OF CATCHING THEM--LET'S GO
KASTOR?...
POLYDEUKES?...
WHERE-- WHERE'S MY MOMMY?
HERMIONE--DON'T CRY. WHERE'S YOUR NURSE?
SOME BAD MEN TOOK YOUR MOMMY AWAY...
...BUT WE'RE GOING TO BRING HER BACK BEFORE THEY HARM HER.
JUST LIKE WE DID THE LAST TIME.
WHERE'S THE GIRL'S NURSE?
--?-- I--DON'T KNOW...
COME ON! WE'VE GOT TO HURRY!
SNF

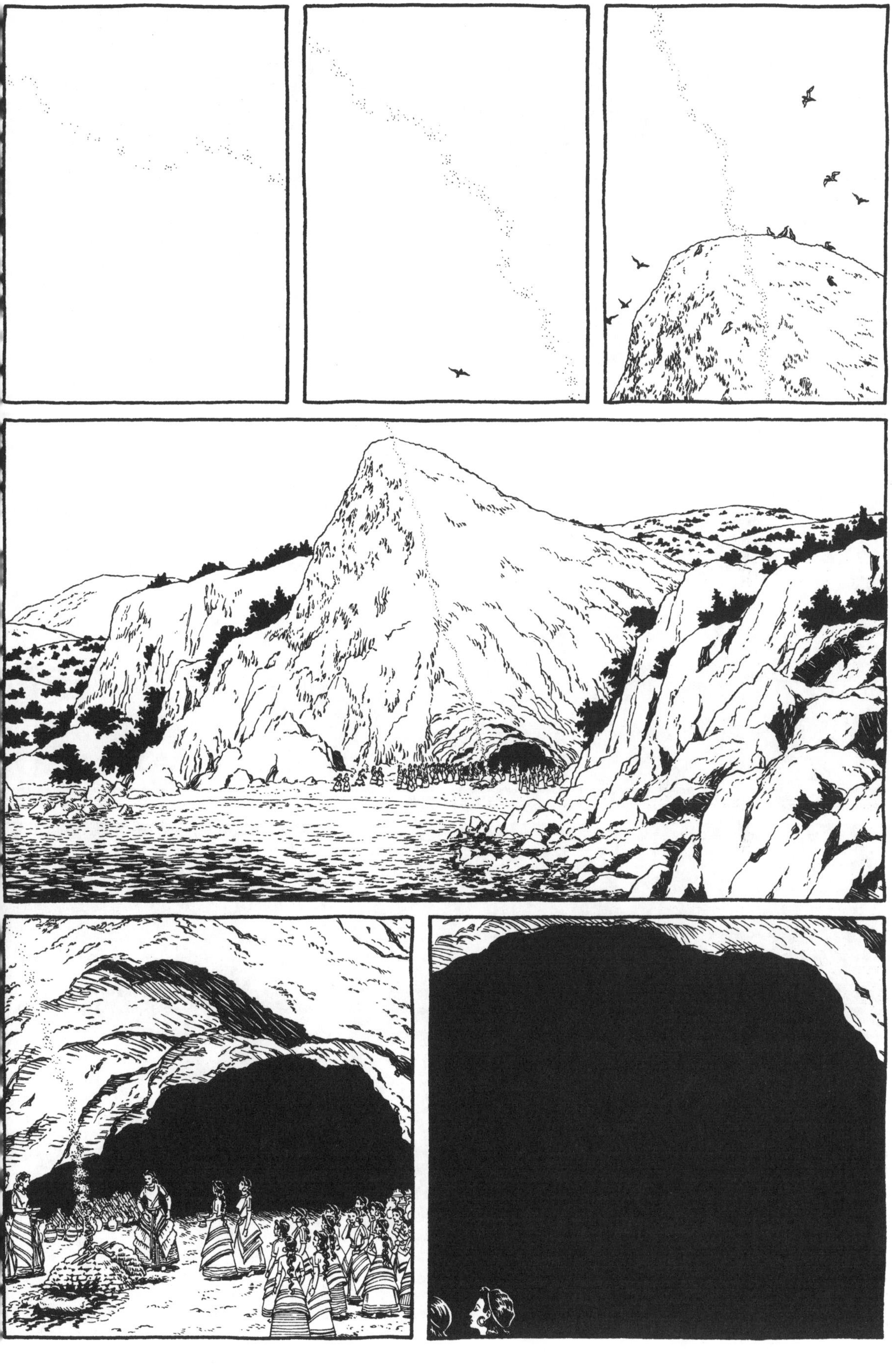

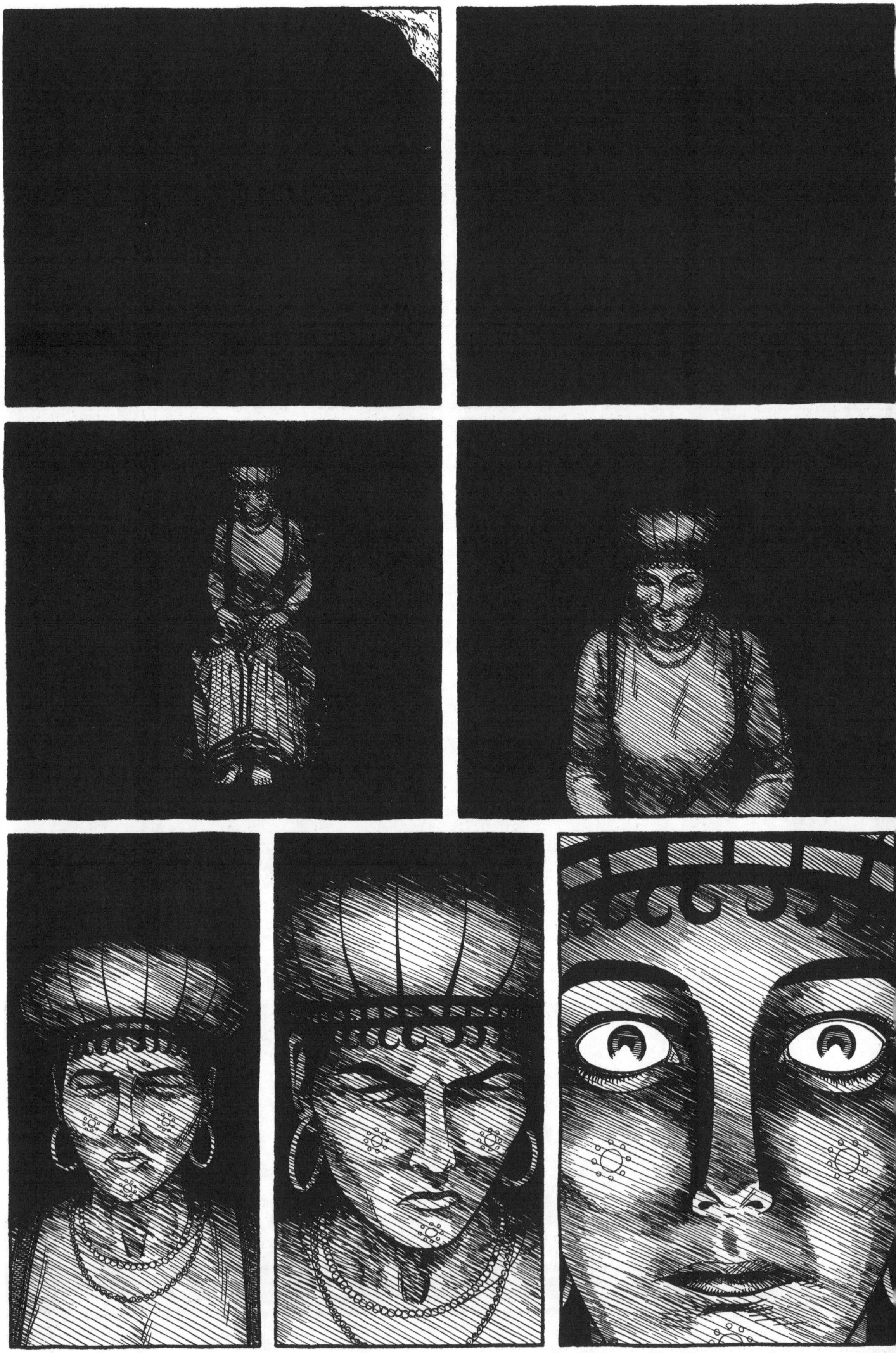

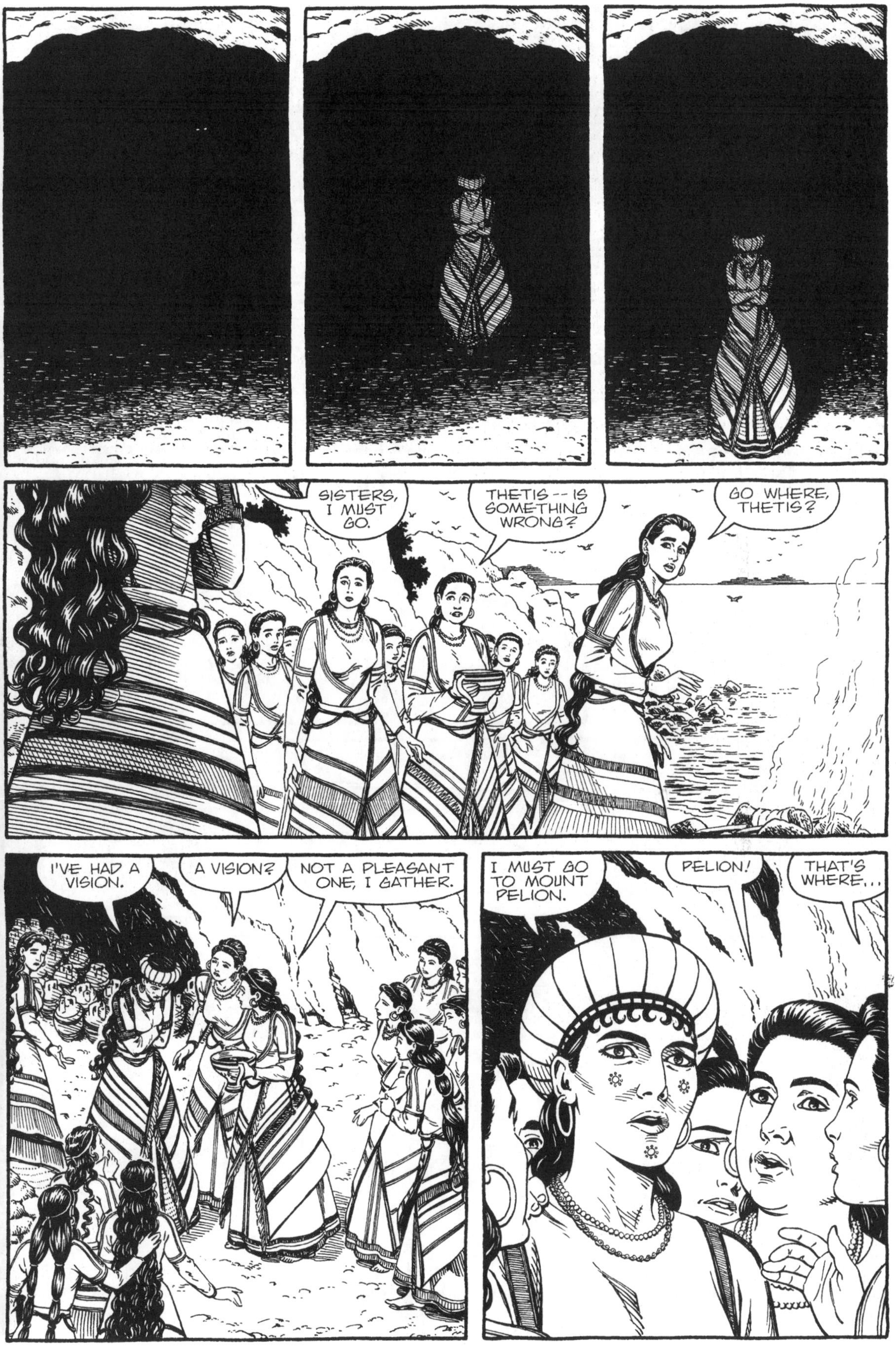
SISTERS, I MUST GO.
THETIS-- IS SOMETHING WRONG?
GO WHERE, THETIS?
I'VE HAD A VISION.
A VISION?
NOT A PLEASANT ONE, I GATHER.
I MUST GO TO MOUNT PELION.
PELION!
THAT'S WHERE...

THE MISTAKE OF MY LIFE WAS MARRYING PELEUS.

HOW DID I EVER IMAGINE A DAUGHTER OF OCEAN COULD LONG REMAIN WIFE TO A MORTAL--EVEN A MORTAL KING?

BUT THE ONE GOOD THING THAT CAME OF IT--MY *SON* --MY BEAUTIFUL BOY--THE FOOLISH MAN GRABBED HIS TINY HEEL AND TORE HIM FROM MY ARMS BEFORE THE GODS' BLESSING WAS COMPLETE...

PELEUS, YOU *DON'T* REALIZE WHAT YOU'VE *DONE*--YOU SENTENCED MY CHILD TO *DEATH!*

I TRIED TO LEAVE ALL THAT BEHIND IN PHTHIA--TRIED TO FORGET--BUT IT'S APPROACHING, THE DEATH THAT WILL TAKE MY SON--AND MANY OTHERS-- DEATH UPON DEATH UPON DEATH--

THETIS-- *STOP!*

WHAT AN *AWFUL* VISION!

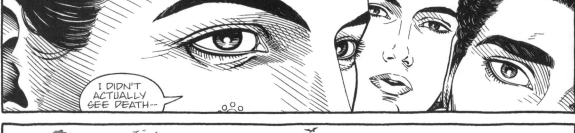

I DIDN'T ACTUALLY SEE DEATH--

I SAW A SHIP SAILING FAR OUT ON THE WATER--TOO FAR TO TURN BACK. IT CARRIES A MAN -- A BOY, REALLY--WHO BURNS WITH A FLAME THAT WILL CONSUME ALL HE TOUCHES. A WOMAN RIDES WITH HIM. SHE IS PROUD AND BEAUTIFUL...

...BUT WHERE SHE TREADS, DEATH FOLLOWS.

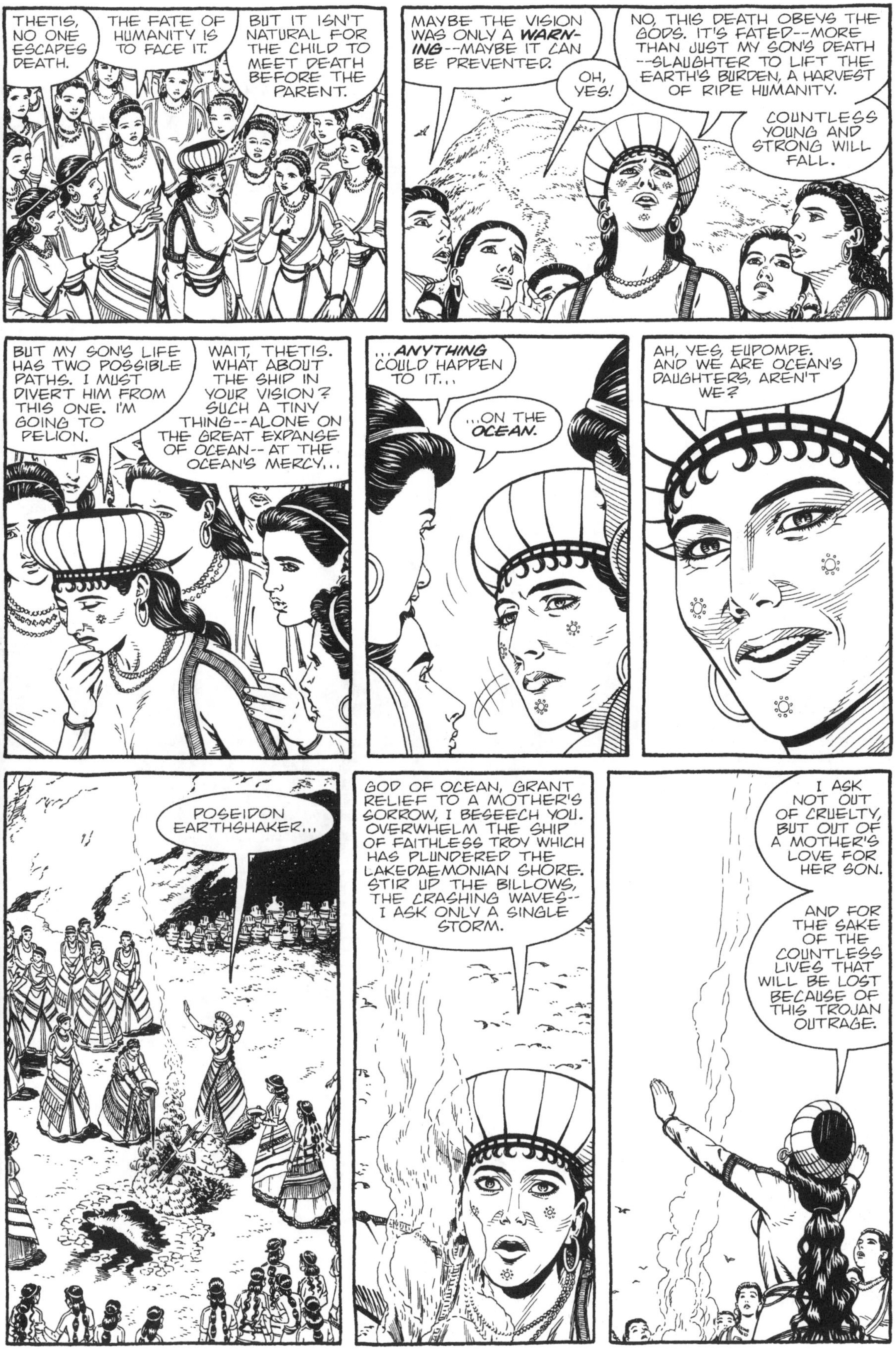
THETIS, NO ONE ESCAPES DEATH.
THE FATE OF HUMANITY IS TO FACE IT.
BUT IT ISN'T NATURAL FOR THE CHILD TO MEET DEATH BEFORE THE PARENT.
MAYBE THE VISION WAS ONLY A WARNING--MAYBE IT CAN BE PREVENTED.
OH, YES!
NO, THIS DEATH OBEYS THE GODS. IT'S FATED--MORE THAN JUST MY SON'S DEATH --SLAUGHTER TO LIFT THE EARTH'S BURDEN, A HARVEST OF RIPE HUMANITY.
COUNTLESS YOUNG AND STRONG WILL FALL.
BUT MY SON'S LIFE HAS TWO POSSIBLE PATHS. I MUST DIVERT HIM FROM THIS ONE. I'M GOING TO PELION.
WAIT, THETIS. WHAT ABOUT THE SHIP IN YOUR VISION? SUCH A TINY THING--ALONE ON THE GREAT EXPANSE OF OCEAN--AT THE OCEAN'S MERCY...
...ANYTHING COULD HAPPEN TO IT...
...ON THE OCEAN.
AH, YES, EUPOMPE. AND WE ARE OCEAN'S DAUGHTERS, AREN'T WE?
POSEIDON EARTHSHAKER...
GOD OF OCEAN, GRANT RELIEF TO A MOTHER'S SORROW, I BESEECH YOU. OVERWHELM THE SHIP OF FAITHLESS TROY WHICH HAS PLUNDERED THE LAKEDAEMONIAN SHORE. STIR UP THE BILLOWS, THE CRASHING WAVES-- I ASK ONLY A SINGLE STORM.
I ASK NOT OUT OF CRUELTY, BUT OUT OF A MOTHER'S LOVE FOR HER SON.
AND FOR THE SAKE OF THE COUNTLESS LIVES THAT WILL BE LOST BECAUSE OF THIS TROJAN OUTRAGE.

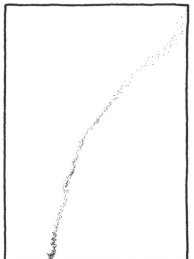
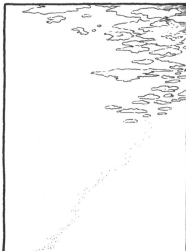

CAN WE OUTRUN IT, AENEAS?

AS LONG AS THIS WIND HOLDS, BUT NO TELLING WHERE IT'LL TAKE US.

NO ONE COULD PURSUE US THROUGH *THAT!* IT'S A BLESSING FROM THE GODS!

FOR US, YES --BUT A CURSE FOR ANYONE CAUGHT IN IT.

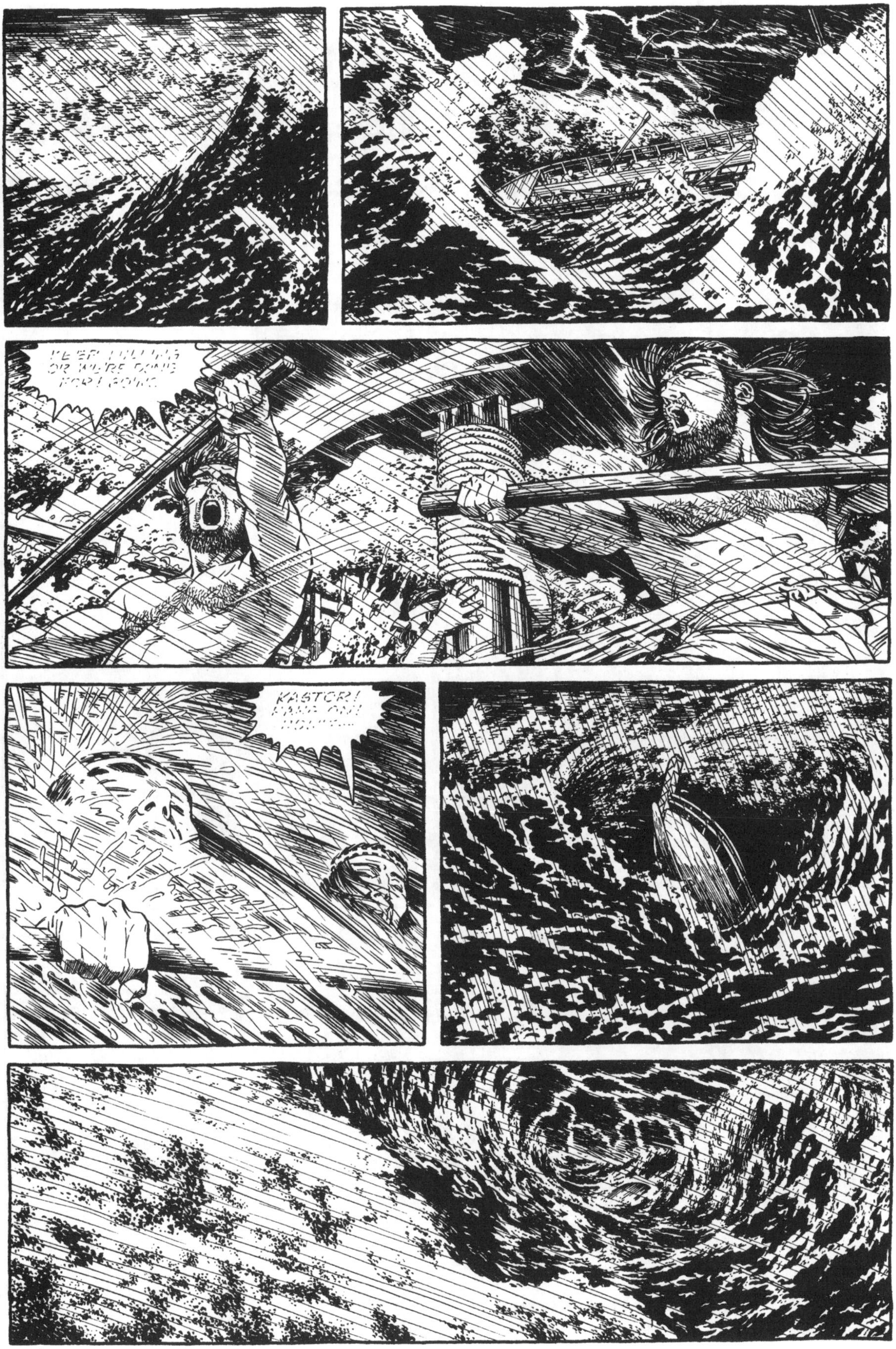
KEEP PULLING OR WE'RE DONE FOR!
KASTOR! HANG ON!

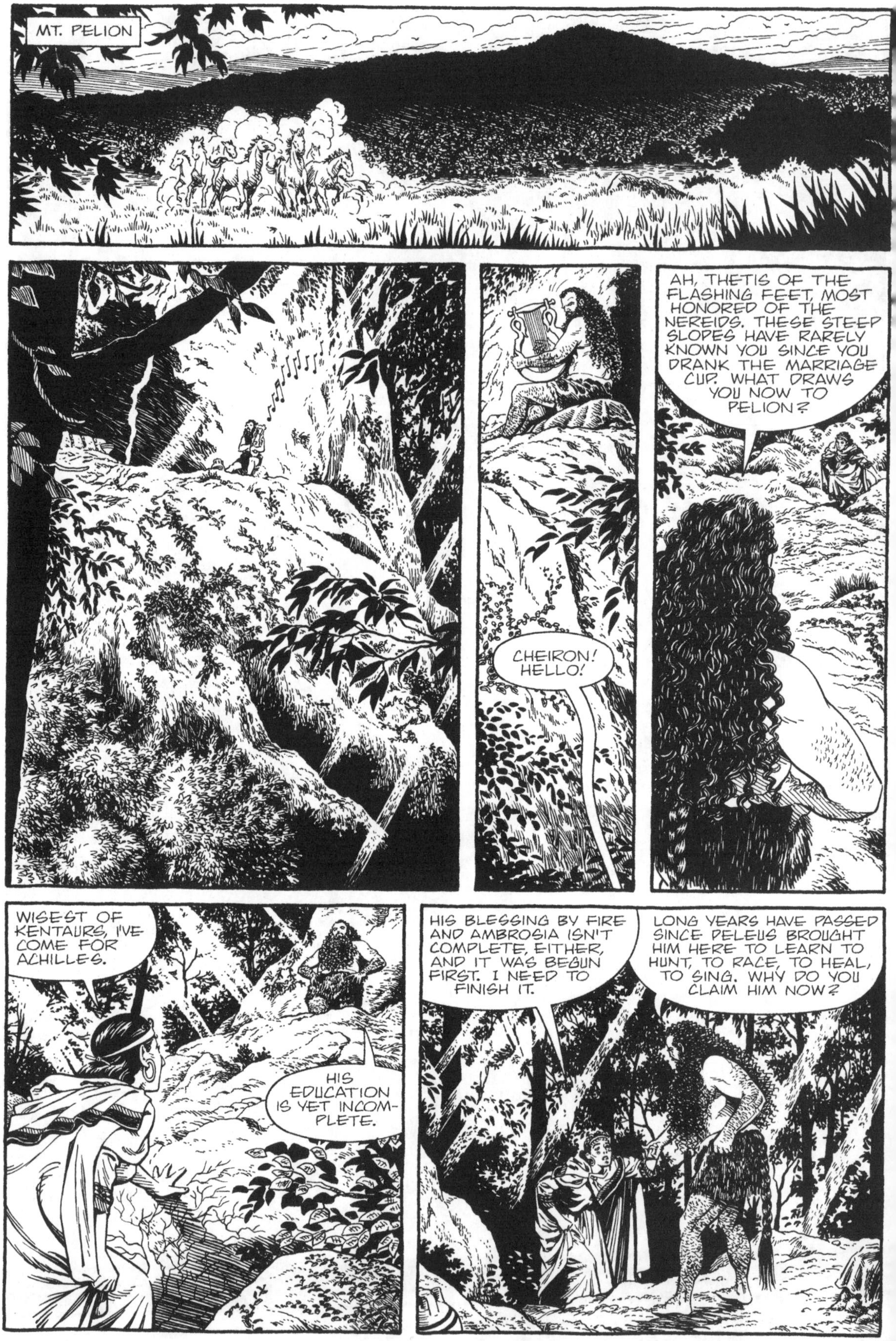
MT. PELION
CHEIRON! HELLO!
AH, THETIS OF THE FLASHING FEET, MOST HONORED OF THE NEREIDS. THESE STEEP SLOPES HAVE RARELY KNOWN YOU SINCE YOU DRANK THE MARRIAGE CUP. WHAT DRAWS YOU NOW TO PELION?
WISEST OF KENTAURS, I'VE COME FOR ACHILLES.
HIS EDUCATION IS YET INCOMPLETE.
HIS BLESSING BY FIRE AND AMBROSIA ISN'T COMPLETE, EITHER, AND IT WAS BEGUN FIRST. I NEED TO FINISH IT.
LONG YEARS HAVE PASSED SINCE PELEUS BROUGHT HIM HERE TO LEARN TO HUNT, TO RACE, TO HEAL, TO SING. WHY DO YOU CLAIM HIM NOW?

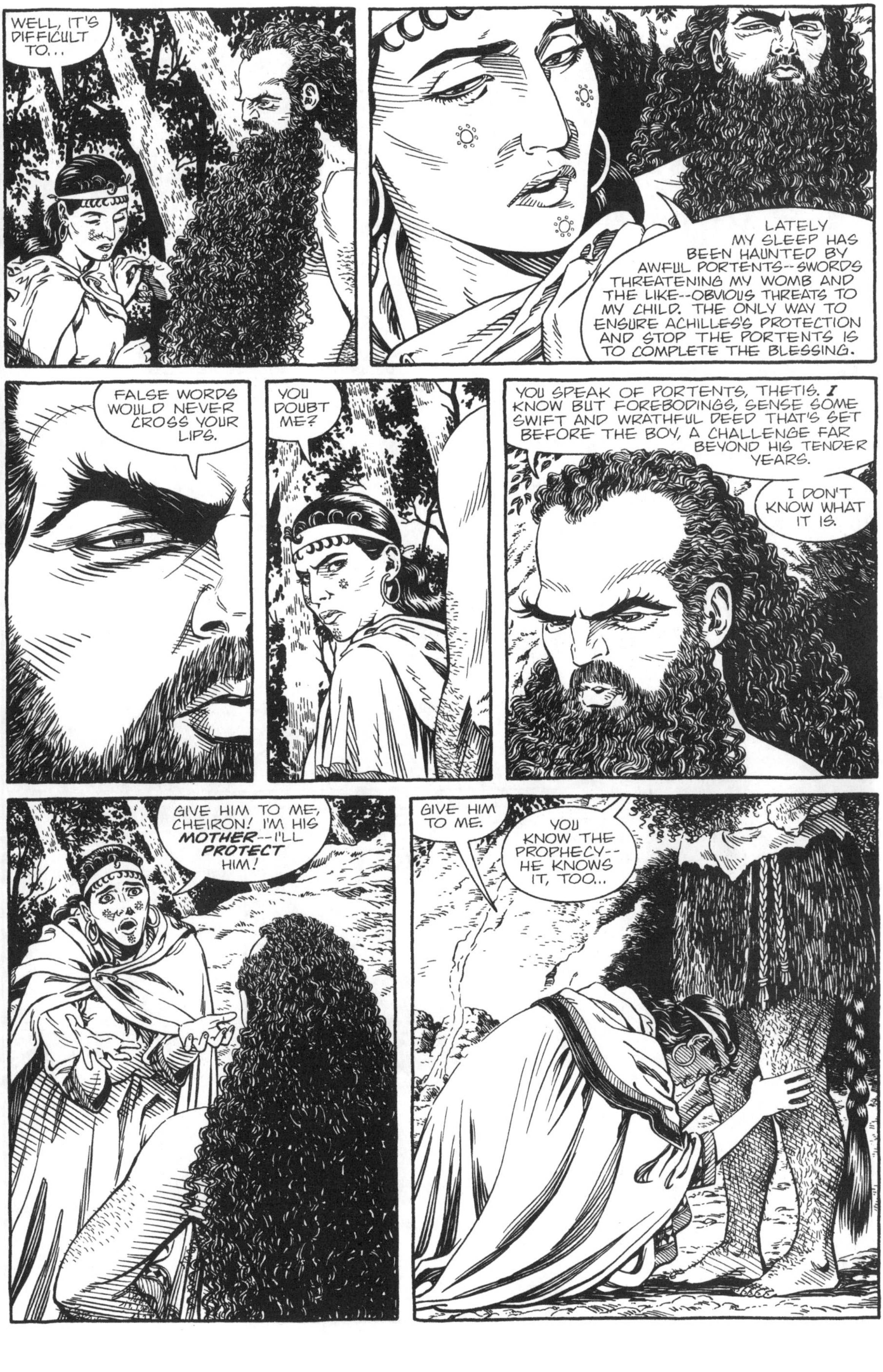
WELL, IT'S DIFFICULT TO...
LATELY MY SLEEP HAS BEEN HAUNTED BY AWFUL PORTENTS--SWORDS THREATENING MY WOMB AND THE LIKE--OBVIOUS THREATS TO MY CHILD. THE ONLY WAY TO ENSURE ACHILLES'S PROTECTION AND STOP THE PORTENTS IS TO COMPLETE THE BLESSING.
FALSE WORDS WOULD NEVER CROSS YOUR LIPS.
YOU DOUBT ME?
YOU SPEAK OF PORTENTS, THETIS. *I* KNOW BUT FOREBODINGS, SENSE SOME SWIFT AND WRATHFUL DEED THAT'S SET BEFORE THE BOY, A CHALLENGE FAR BEYOND HIS TENDER YEARS.
I DON'T KNOW WHAT IT IS.
GIVE HIM TO ME, CHEIRON! I'M HIS ***MOTHER***--I'LL ***PROTECT*** HIM!
GIVE HIM TO ME.
YOU KNOW THE PROPHECY--HE KNOWS IT, TOO...

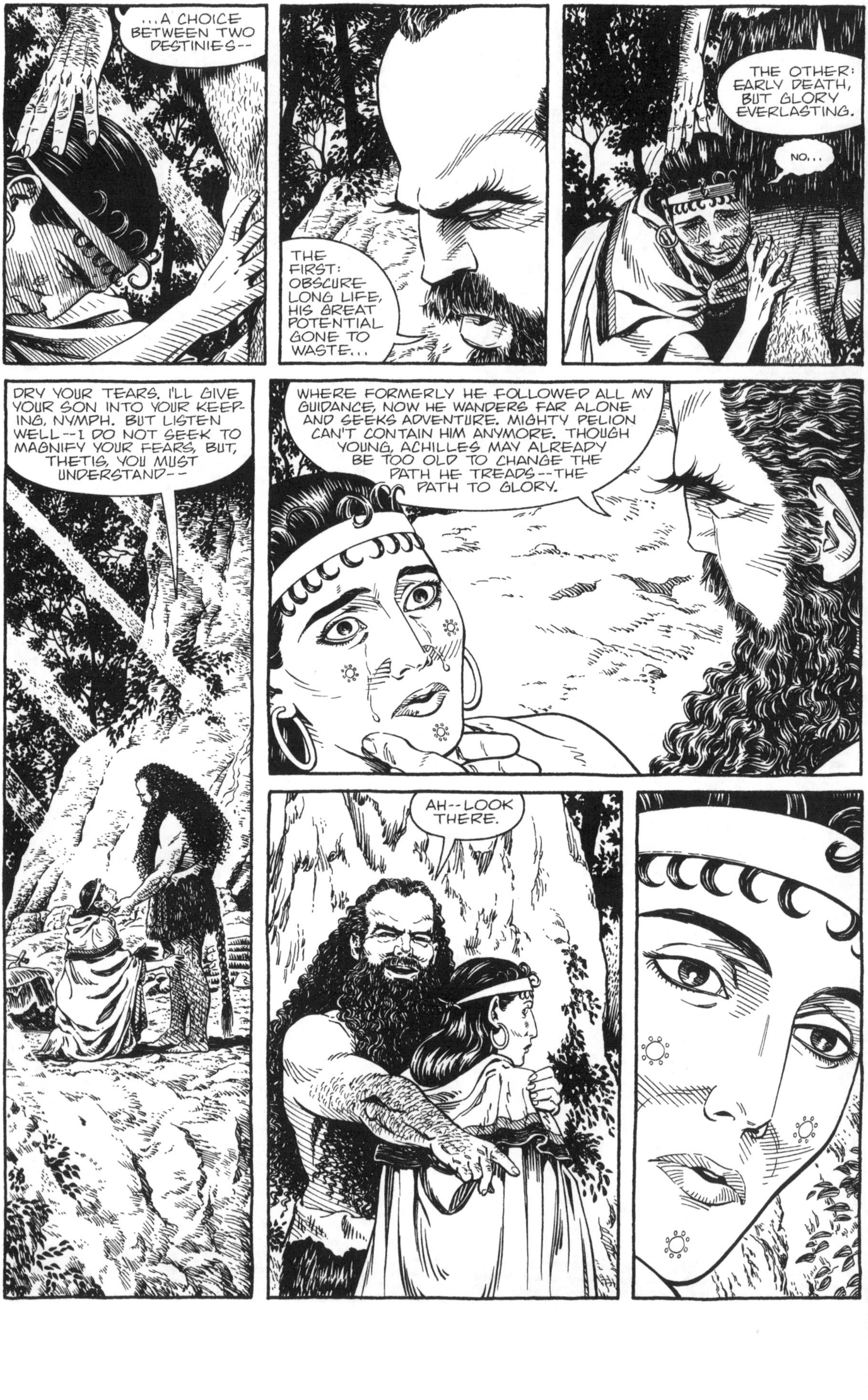
...A CHOICE BETWEEN TWO DESTINIES--
THE FIRST: OBSCURE LONG LIFE, HIS GREAT POTENTIAL GONE TO WASTE...
THE OTHER: EARLY DEATH, BUT GLORY EVERLASTING.
NO...
DRY YOUR TEARS. I'LL GIVE YOUR SON INTO YOUR KEEPING, NYMPH. BUT LISTEN WELL--I DO NOT SEEK TO MAGNIFY YOUR FEARS, BUT, THETIS, YOU MUST UNDERSTAND--
WHERE FORMERLY HE FOLLOWED ALL MY GUIDANCE, NOW HE WANDERS FAR ALONE AND SEEKS ADVENTURE. MIGHTY PELION CAN'T CONTAIN HIM ANYMORE. THOUGH YOUNG, ACHILLES MAY ALREADY BE TOO OLD TO CHANGE THE PATH HE TREADS--THE PATH TO GLORY.
AH--LOOK THERE.

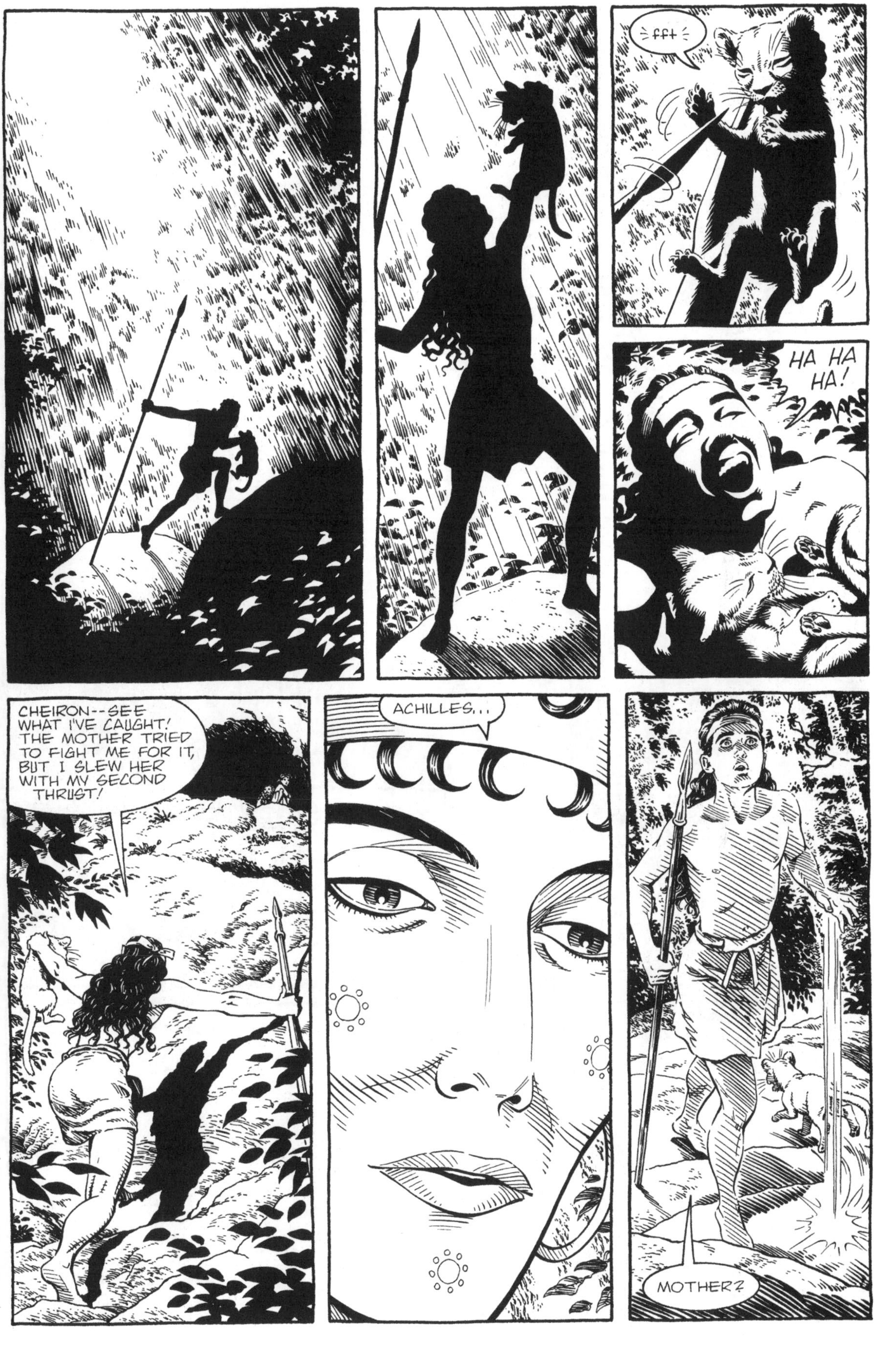
fft
HA HA HA!
CHEIRON--SEE WHAT I'VE CAUGHT! THE MOTHER TRIED TO FIGHT ME FOR IT, BUT I SLEW HER WITH MY SECOND THRUST!
ACHILLES...
MOTHER?

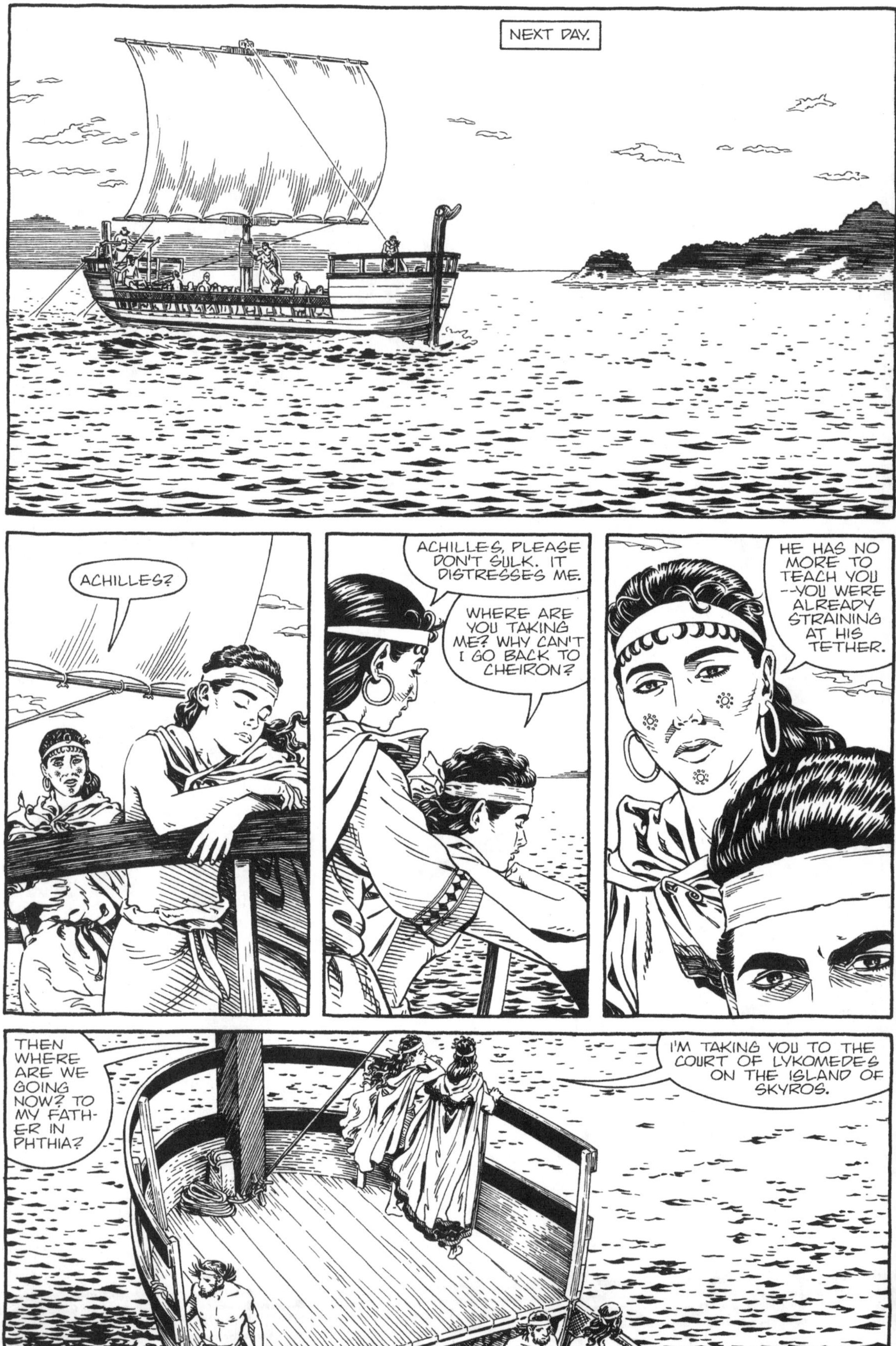
NEXT DAY.
ACHILLES?
ACHILLES, PLEASE DON'T SULK. IT DISTRESSES ME.
WHERE ARE YOU TAKING ME? WHY CAN'T I GO BACK TO CHEIRON?
HE HAS NO MORE TO TEACH YOU --YOU WERE ALREADY STRAINING AT HIS TETHER.
THEN WHERE ARE WE GOING NOW? TO MY FATHER IN PHTHIA?
I'M TAKING YOU TO THE COURT OF LYKOMEDES ON THE ISLAND OF SKYROS.

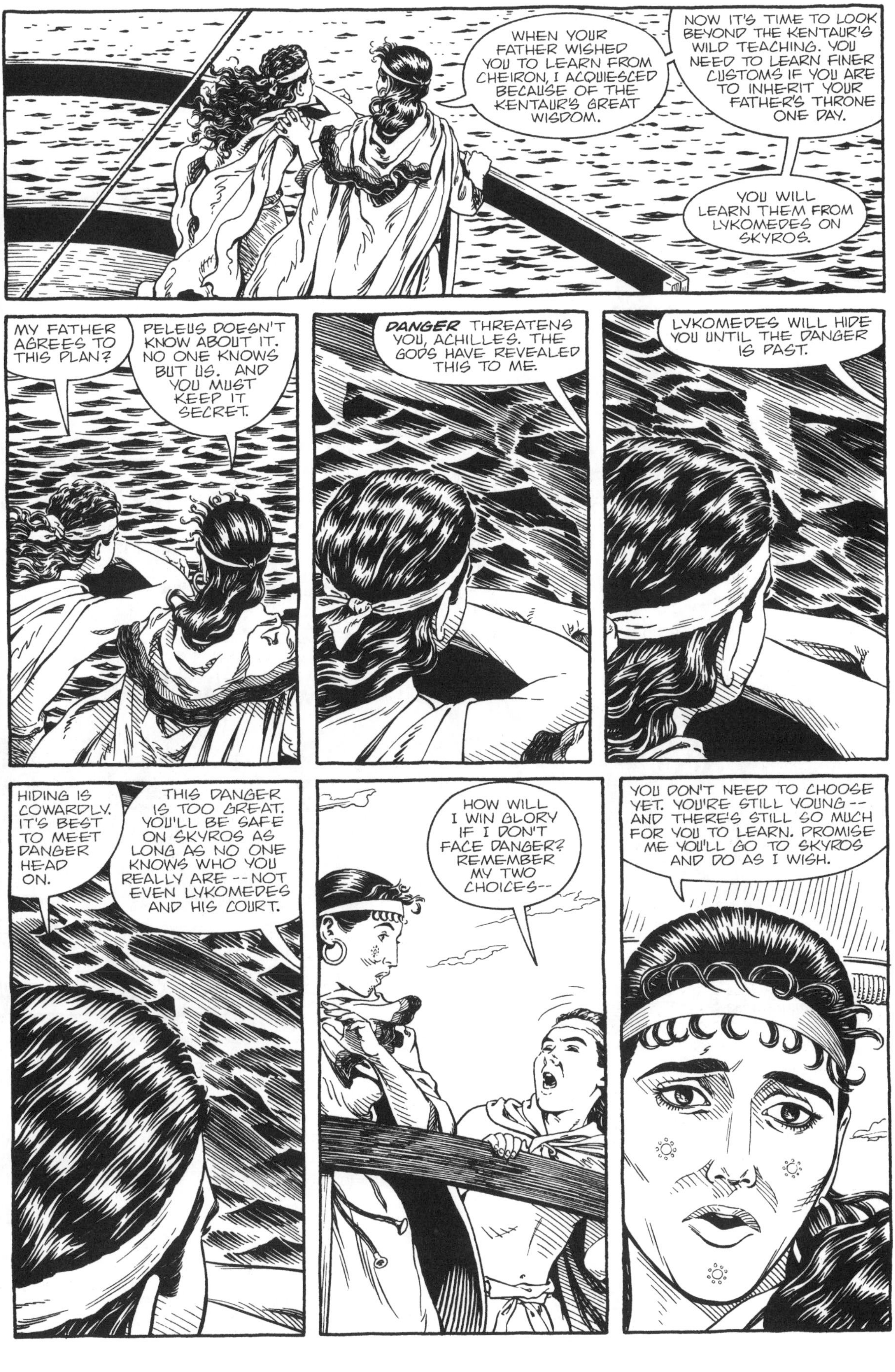
WHEN YOUR FATHER WISHED YOU TO LEARN FROM CHEIRON, I ACQUIESCED BECAUSE OF THE KENTAUR'S GREAT WISDOM.
NOW IT'S TIME TO LOOK BEYOND THE KENTAUR'S WILD TEACHING. YOU NEED TO LEARN FINER CUSTOMS IF YOU ARE TO INHERIT YOUR FATHER'S THRONE ONE DAY.
YOU WILL LEARN THEM FROM LYKOMEDES ON SKYROS.
MY FATHER AGREES TO THIS PLAN?
PELEUS DOESN'T KNOW ABOUT IT. NO ONE KNOWS BUT US. AND YOU MUST KEEP IT SECRET.
DANGER THREATENS YOU, ACHILLES. THE GODS HAVE REVEALED THIS TO ME.
LYKOMEDES WILL HIDE YOU UNTIL THE DANGER IS PAST.
HIDING IS COWARDLY. IT'S BEST TO MEET DANGER HEAD ON.
THIS DANGER IS TOO GREAT. YOU'LL BE SAFE ON SKYROS AS LONG AS NO ONE KNOWS WHO YOU REALLY ARE--NOT EVEN LYKOMEDES AND HIS COURT.
HOW WILL I WIN GLORY IF I DON'T FACE DANGER? REMEMBER MY TWO CHOICES--
YOU DON'T NEED TO CHOOSE YET. YOU'RE STILL YOUNG-- AND THERE'S STILL SO MUCH FOR YOU TO LEARN. PROMISE ME YOU'LL GO TO SKYROS AND DO AS I WISH.

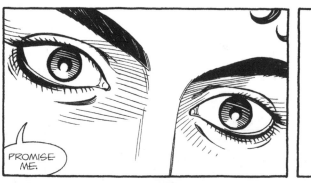

PROMISE ME.

OH, ALL RIGHT. I PROMISE.

YOUR PROMISE LACKS GRACE. REMEMBER WHO YOU ARE, ACHILLES--SON OF THE PRIESTESS WHO COMMANDS THE RESPECT OF ALL ACHAEA.

I PROMISE, MOTHER.

VERY GOOD--

LOOK! DOLPHINS!

YES, SENT BY MY FATHER OCEAN TO POINT OUT OUR DESTINATION. THERE'S SKYROS AHEAD.

WE'LL LAND TONIGHT AND IN THE MORNING I'LL PRESENT YOU TO LYKOMEDES.

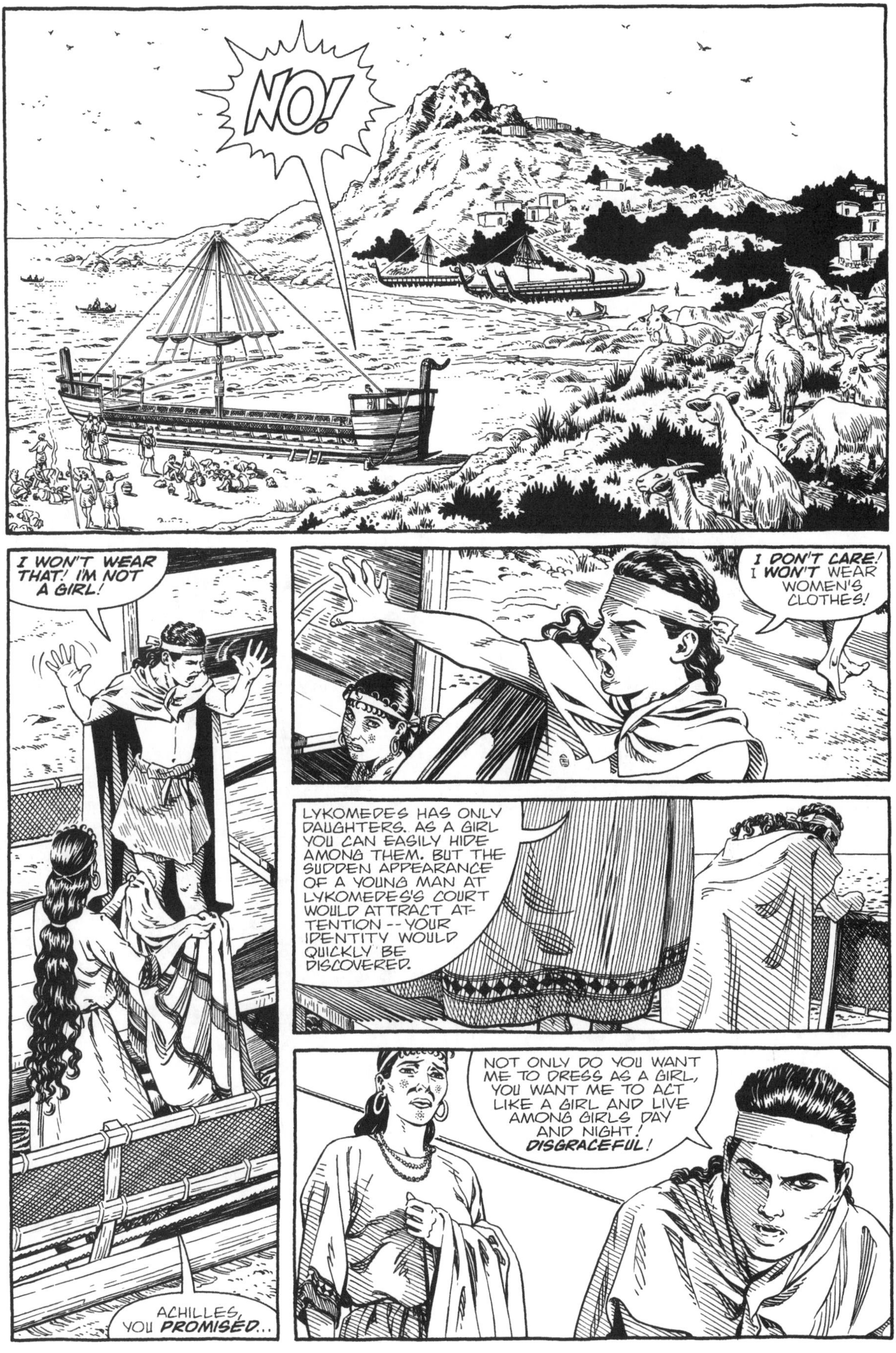
NO!
I WON'T WEAR THAT! I'M NOT A GIRL!
I DON'T CARE! I WON'T WEAR WOMEN'S CLOTHES!
LYKOMEDES HAS ONLY DAUGHTERS. AS A GIRL YOU CAN EASILY HIDE AMONG THEM. BUT THE SUDDEN APPEARANCE OF A YOUNG MAN AT LYKOMEDES'S COURT WOULD ATTRACT ATTENTION -- YOUR IDENTITY WOULD QUICKLY BE DISCOVERED.
NOT ONLY DO YOU WANT ME TO DRESS AS A GIRL, YOU WANT ME TO ACT LIKE A GIRL AND LIVE AMONG GIRLS DAY AND NIGHT! DISGRACEFUL!
ACHILLES, YOU PROMISED...

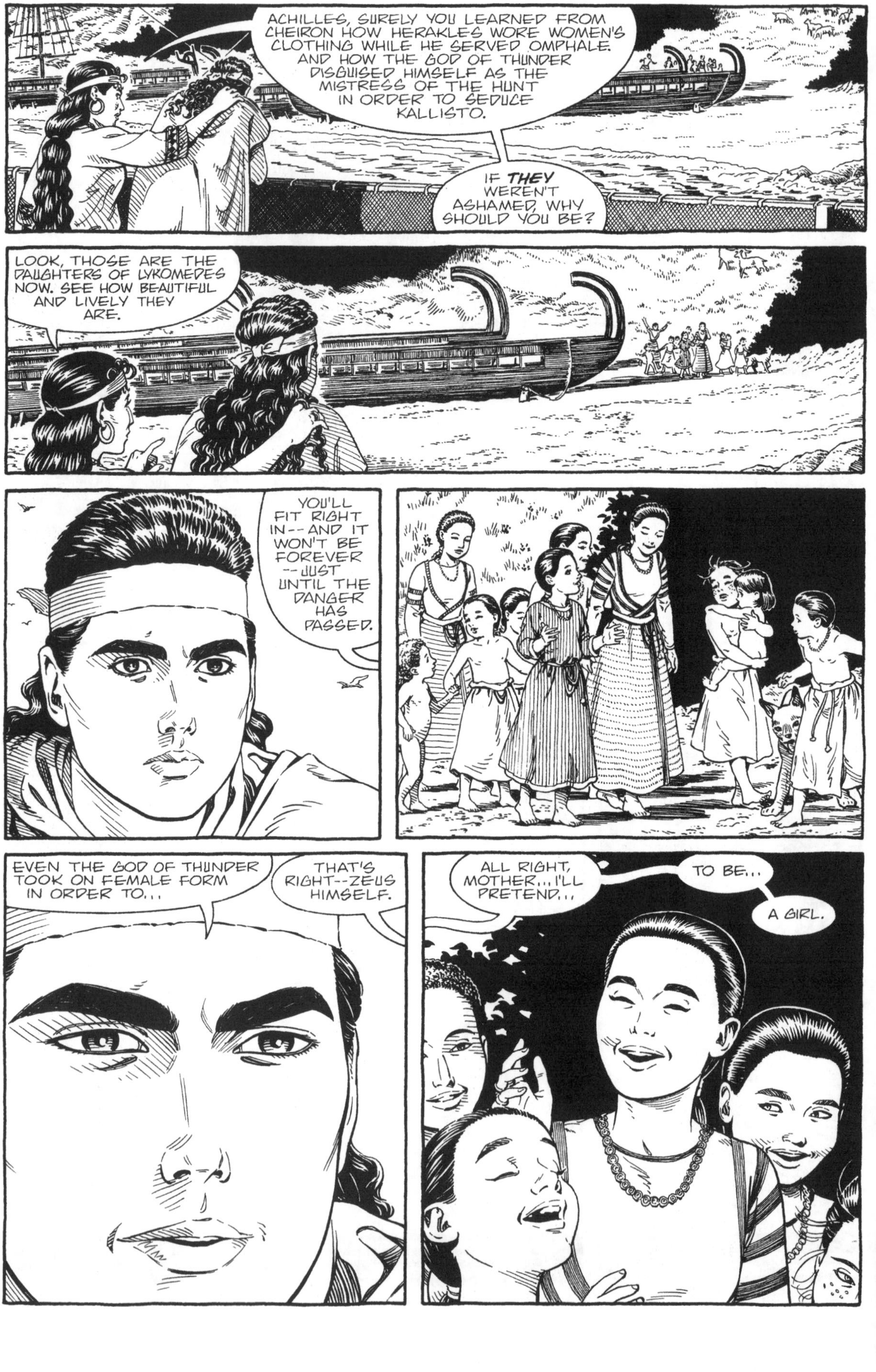
ACHILLES, SURELY YOU LEARNED FROM CHEIRON HOW HERAKLES WORE WOMEN'S CLOTHING WHILE HE SERVED OMPHALE. AND HOW THE GOD OF THUNDER DISGUISED HIMSELF AS THE MISTRESS OF THE HUNT IN ORDER TO SEDUCE KALLISTO.
IF THEY WEREN'T ASHAMED, WHY SHOULD YOU BE?
LOOK, THOSE ARE THE DAUGHTERS OF LYKOMEDES NOW. SEE HOW BEAUTIFUL AND LIVELY THEY ARE.
YOU'LL FIT RIGHT IN--AND IT WON'T BE FOREVER--JUST UNTIL THE DANGER HAS PASSED.
EVEN THE GOD OF THUNDER TOOK ON FEMALE FORM IN ORDER TO...
THAT'S RIGHT--ZEUS HIMSELF.
ALL RIGHT, MOTHER... I'LL PRETEND...
TO BE...
A GIRL.

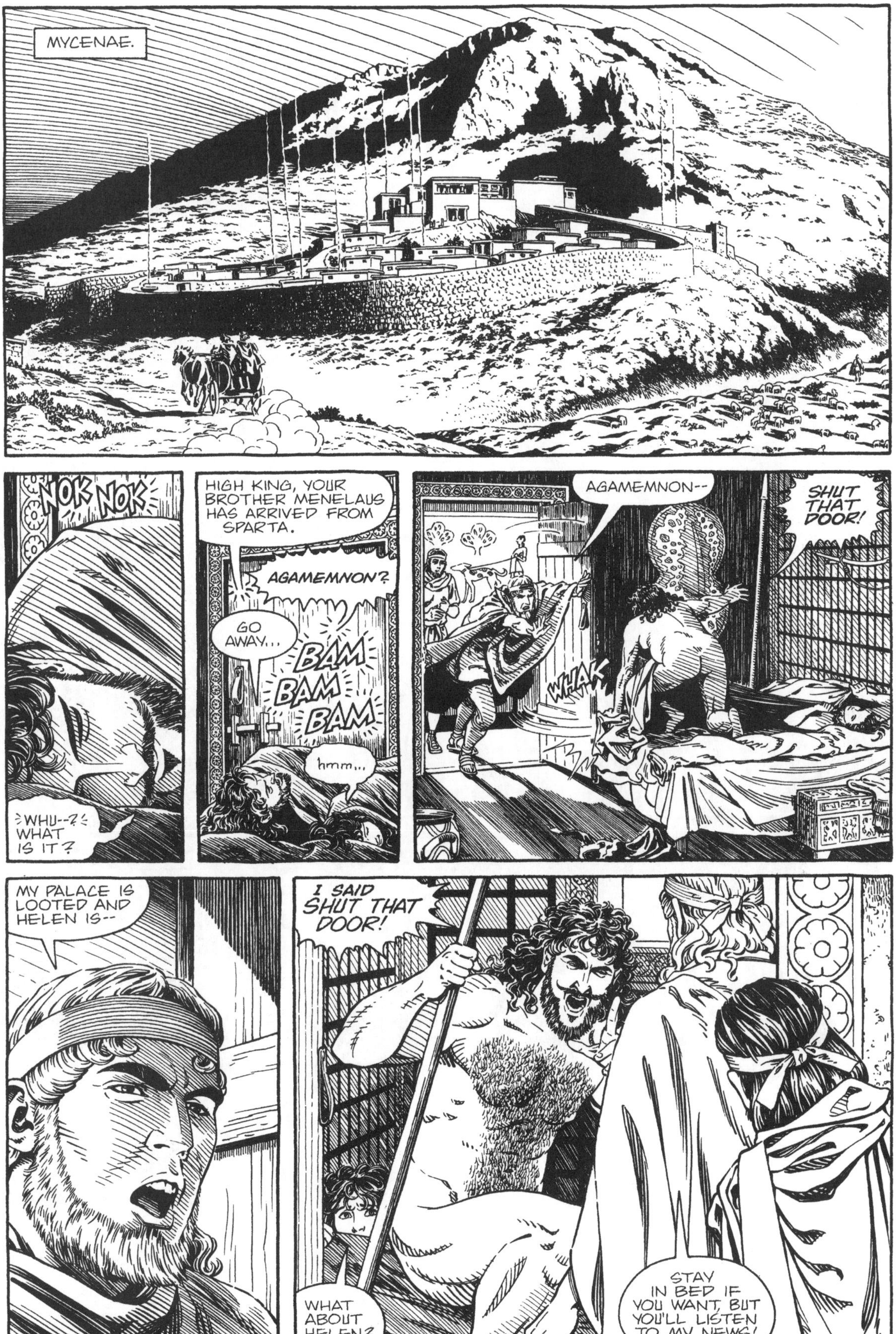
MYCENAE.
NOK NOK
WHU--? WHAT IS IT?
HIGH KING, YOUR BROTHER MENELAUS HAS ARRIVED FROM SPARTA.
AGAMEMNON?
GO AWAY...
BAM BAM BAM
hmm...
AGAMEMNON--
SHUT THAT DOOR!
WHAK
MY PALACE IS LOOTED AND HELEN IS--
I SAID SHUT THAT DOOR!
WHAT ABOUT HELEN?
STAY IN BED IF YOU WANT, BUT YOU'LL LISTEN TO MY NEWS!

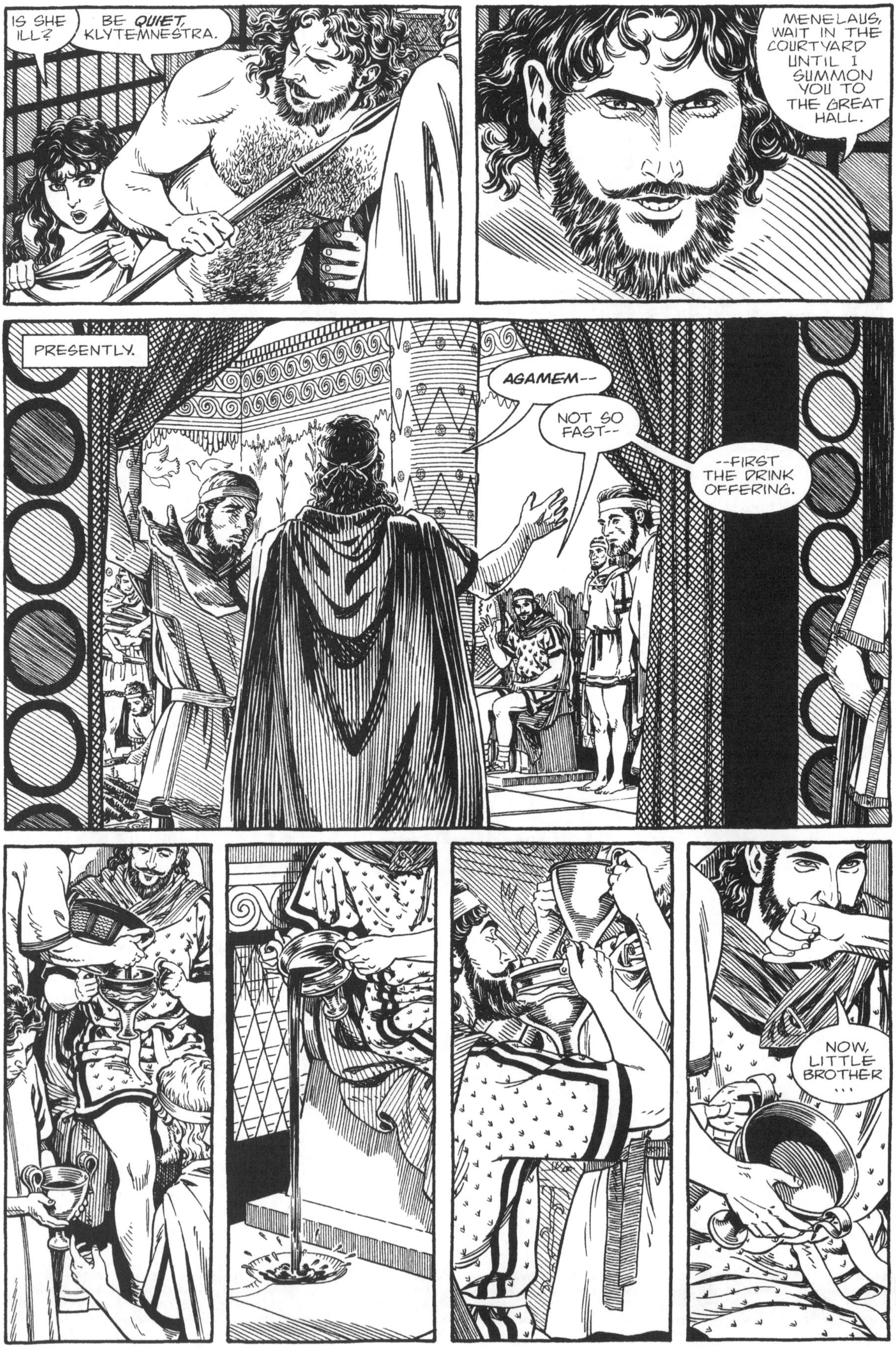
IS SHE ILL?
BE *QUIET*, KLYTEMNESTRA.
MENELAUS, WAIT IN THE COURTYARD UNTIL I SUMMON YOU TO THE GREAT HALL.
PRESENTLY.
AGAMEM--
NOT SO FAST--
--FIRST THE DRINK OFFERING.
NOW, LITTLE BROTHER ...

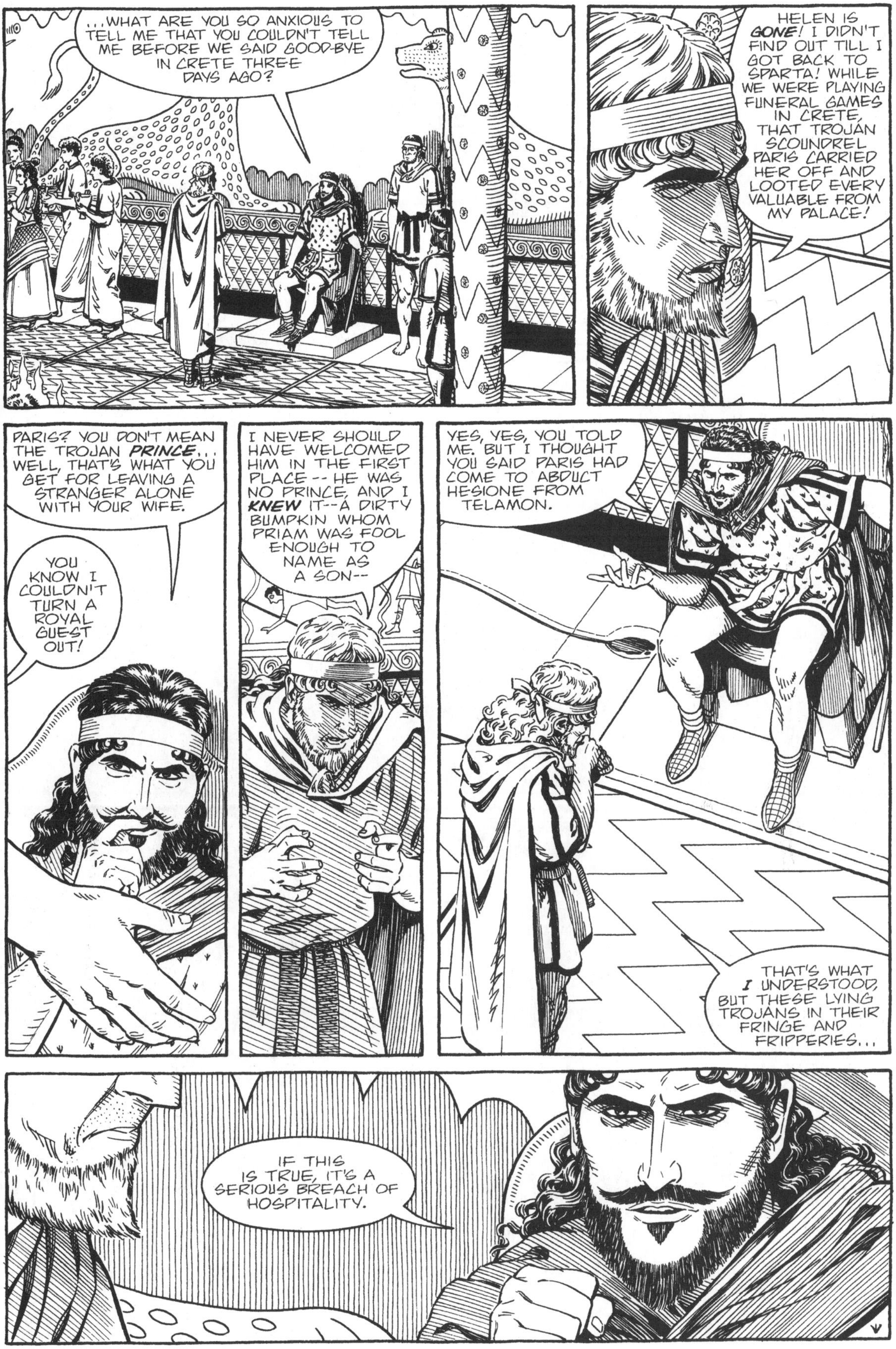
...WHAT ARE YOU SO ANXIOUS TO TELL ME THAT YOU COULDN'T TELL ME BEFORE WE SAID GOOD-BYE IN CRETE THREE DAYS AGO?
HELEN IS GONE! I DIDN'T FIND OUT TILL I GOT BACK TO SPARTA! WHILE WE WERE PLAYING FUNERAL GAMES IN CRETE, THAT TROJAN SCOUNDREL PARIS CARRIED HER OFF AND LOOTED EVERY VALUABLE FROM MY PALACE!
PARIS? YOU DON'T MEAN THE TROJAN PRINCE... WELL, THAT'S WHAT YOU GET FOR LEAVING A STRANGER ALONE WITH YOUR WIFE.
YOU KNOW I COULDN'T TURN A ROYAL GUEST OUT!
I NEVER SHOULD HAVE WELCOMED HIM IN THE FIRST PLACE -- HE WAS NO PRINCE, AND I KNEW IT--A DIRTY BUMPKIN WHOM PRIAM WAS FOOL ENOUGH TO NAME AS A SON--
YES, YES, YOU TOLD ME. BUT I THOUGHT YOU SAID PARIS HAD COME TO ABDUCT HESIONE FROM TELAMON.
THAT'S WHAT I UNDERSTOOD, BUT THESE LYING TROJANS IN THEIR FRINGE AND FRIPPERIES...
IF THIS IS TRUE, IT'S A SERIOUS BREACH OF HOSPITALITY.

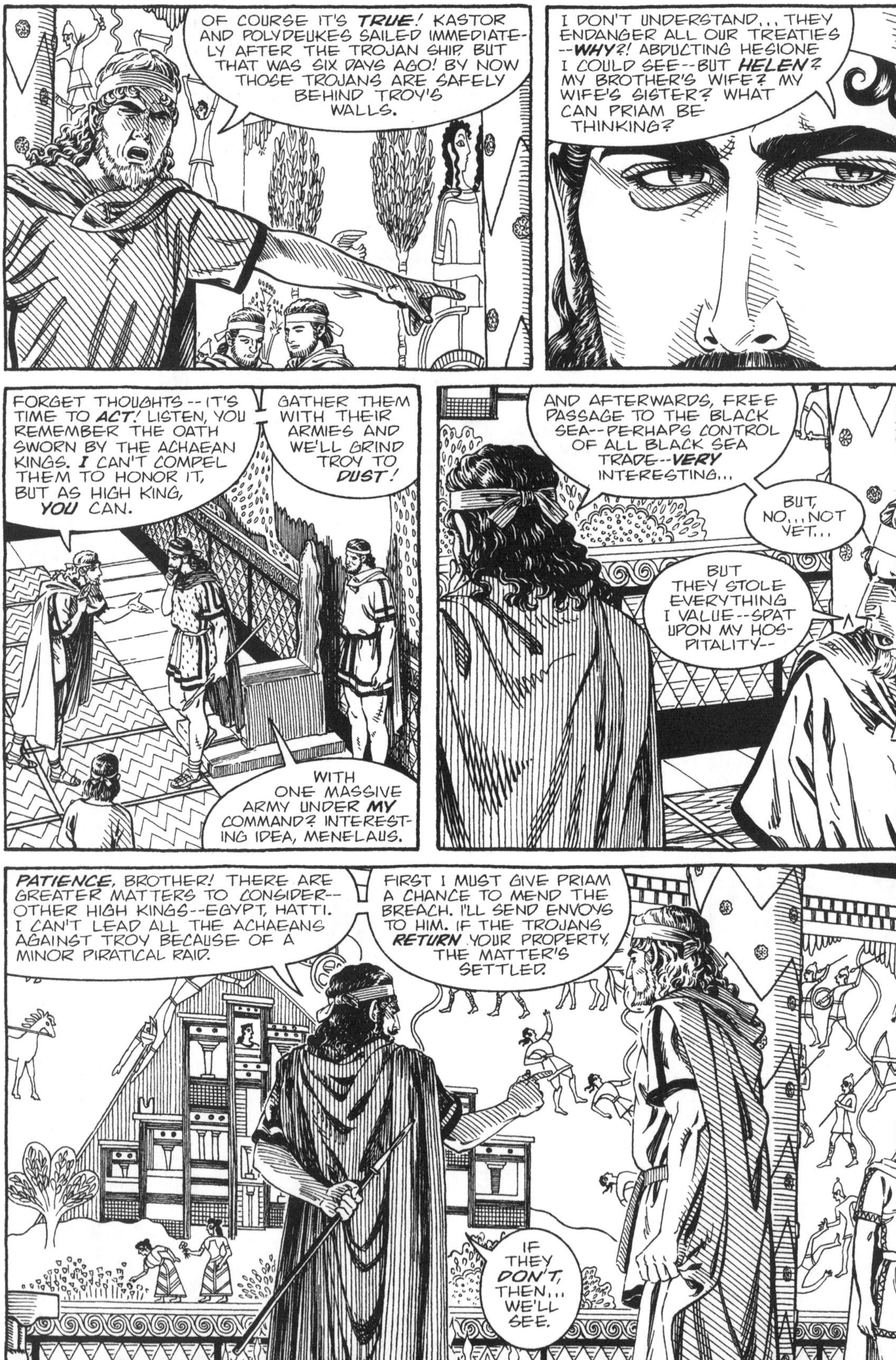
OF COURSE IT'S TRUE! KASTOR AND POLYDEUKES SAILED IMMEDIATELY AFTER THE TROJAN SHIP, BUT THAT WAS SIX DAYS AGO! BY NOW THOSE TROJANS ARE SAFELY BEHIND TROY'S WALLS.
I DON'T UNDERSTAND... THEY ENDANGER ALL OUR TREATIES --WHY?! ABDUCTING HESIONE I COULD SEE--BUT HELEN? MY BROTHER'S WIFE? MY WIFE'S SISTER? WHAT CAN PRIAM BE THINKING?
FORGET THOUGHTS -- IT'S TIME TO ACT! LISTEN, YOU REMEMBER THE OATH SWORN BY THE ACHAEAN KINGS. I CAN'T COMPEL THEM TO HONOR IT, BUT AS HIGH KING, YOU CAN.
GATHER THEM WITH THEIR ARMIES AND WE'LL GRIND TROY TO DUST!
WITH ONE MASSIVE ARMY UNDER MY COMMAND? INTERESTING IDEA, MENELAUS.
AND AFTERWARDS, FREE PASSAGE TO THE BLACK SEA--PERHAPS CONTROL OF ALL BLACK SEA TRADE--VERY INTERESTING...
BUT, NO... NOT YET...
BUT THEY STOLE EVERYTHING I VALUE--SPAT UPON MY HOSPITALITY--
PATIENCE, BROTHER! THERE ARE GREATER MATTERS TO CONSIDER-- OTHER HIGH KINGS--EGYPT, HATTI. I CAN'T LEAD ALL THE ACHAEANS AGAINST TROY BECAUSE OF A MINOR PIRATICAL RAID.
FIRST I MUST GIVE PRIAM A CHANCE TO MEND THE BREACH. I'LL SEND ENVOYS TO HIM. IF THE TROJANS RETURN YOUR PROPERTY, THE MATTER'S SETTLED.
IF THEY DON'T, THEN... WE'LL SEE.

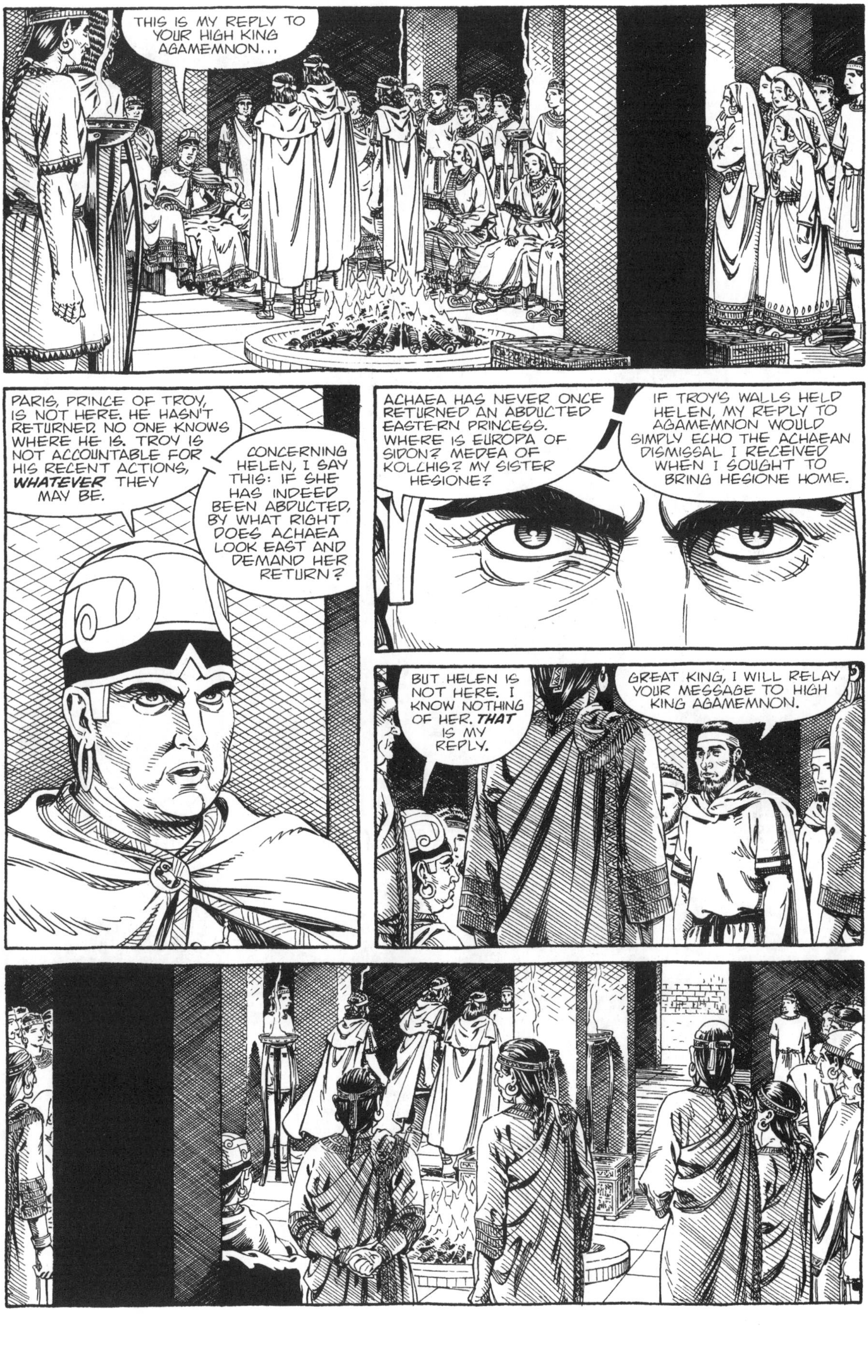
THIS IS MY REPLY TO YOUR HIGH KING AGAMEMNON...
PARIS, PRINCE OF TROY, IS NOT HERE. HE HASN'T RETURNED. NO ONE KNOWS WHERE HE IS. TROY IS NOT ACCOUNTABLE FOR HIS RECENT ACTIONS, **WHATEVER** THEY MAY BE.
CONCERNING HELEN, I SAY THIS: IF SHE HAS INDEED BEEN ABDUCTED, BY WHAT RIGHT DOES ACHAEA LOOK EAST AND DEMAND HER RETURN?
ACHAEA HAS NEVER ONCE RETURNED AN ABDUCTED EASTERN PRINCESS. WHERE IS EUROPA OF SIDON? MEDEA OF KOLCHIS? MY SISTER HESIONE?
IF TROY'S WALLS HELD HELEN, MY REPLY TO AGAMEMNON WOULD SIMPLY ECHO THE ACHAEAN DISMISSAL I RECEIVED WHEN I SOUGHT TO BRING HESIONE HOME.
BUT HELEN IS NOT HERE. I KNOW NOTHING OF HER. **THAT** IS MY REPLY.
GREAT KING, I WILL RELAY YOUR MESSAGE TO HIGH KING AGAMEMNON.

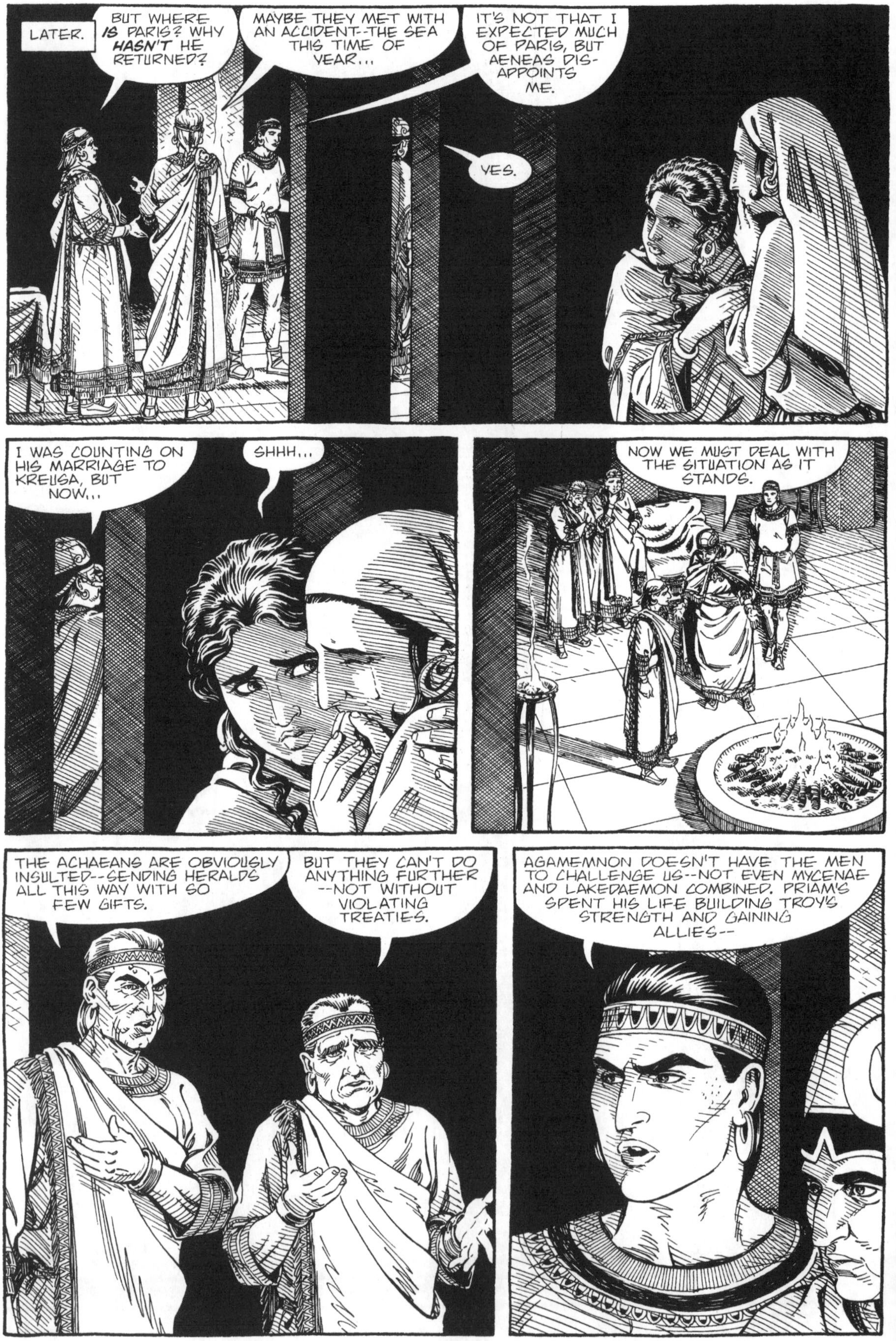
LATER.
BUT WHERE *IS* PARIS? WHY *HASN'T* HE RETURNED?
MAYBE THEY MET WITH AN ACCIDENT--THE SEA THIS TIME OF YEAR...
IT'S NOT THAT I EXPECTED MUCH OF PARIS, BUT AENEAS DIS-APPOINTS ME.
YES.
I WAS COUNTING ON HIS MARRIAGE TO KREUSA, BUT NOW...
SHHH...
NOW WE MUST DEAL WITH THE SITUATION AS IT STANDS.
THE ACHAEANS ARE OBVIOUSLY INSULTED--SENDING HERALDS ALL THIS WAY WITH SO FEW GIFTS.
BUT THEY CAN'T DO ANYTHING FURTHER --NOT WITHOUT VIOLATING TREATIES.
AGAMEMNON DOESN'T HAVE THE MEN TO CHALLENGE US--NOT EVEN MYCENAE AND LAKEDAEMON COMBINED. PRIAM'S SPENT HIS LIFE BUILDING TROY'S STRENGTH AND GAINING ALLIES--

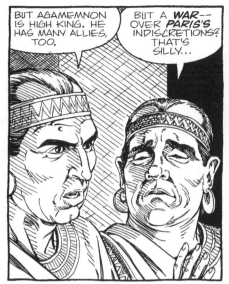

BUT AGAMEMNON IS HIGH KING. HE HAS MANY ALLIES, TOO.

BUT A *WAR*-- OVER *PARIS'S* INDISCRETIONS? THAT'S SILLY...

I HOPE YOU'RE RIGHT, PANTHOUS. BUT ANY PRETEXT MIGHT BE SUFFICIENT TO THOSE ENVIOUS OF TROY'S POWER AND WEALTH.

WE *MUST* LEARN WHAT THE ACHAEANS INTEND. SOMEONE MUST GO--

I'LL GO TO ACHAEA, GREAT KING.

NO, HEKTOR. I THINK THEY'VE HAD THEIR FILL OF TROJAN PRINCES.

GREAT KING--

AND NONE OF THE TROJAN ELDERS, EITHER. WHERE IS A TROJAN WHOM THE ACHAEANS HAVE NO REASON TO DISTRUST? SOMEONE WHO CAN WATCH AND LISTEN WITHOUT DRAWING ATTENTION...

A PRIEST.

HEH.

YOU'RE RIGHT, ANTENOR.

BRING KALCHAS TO ME.

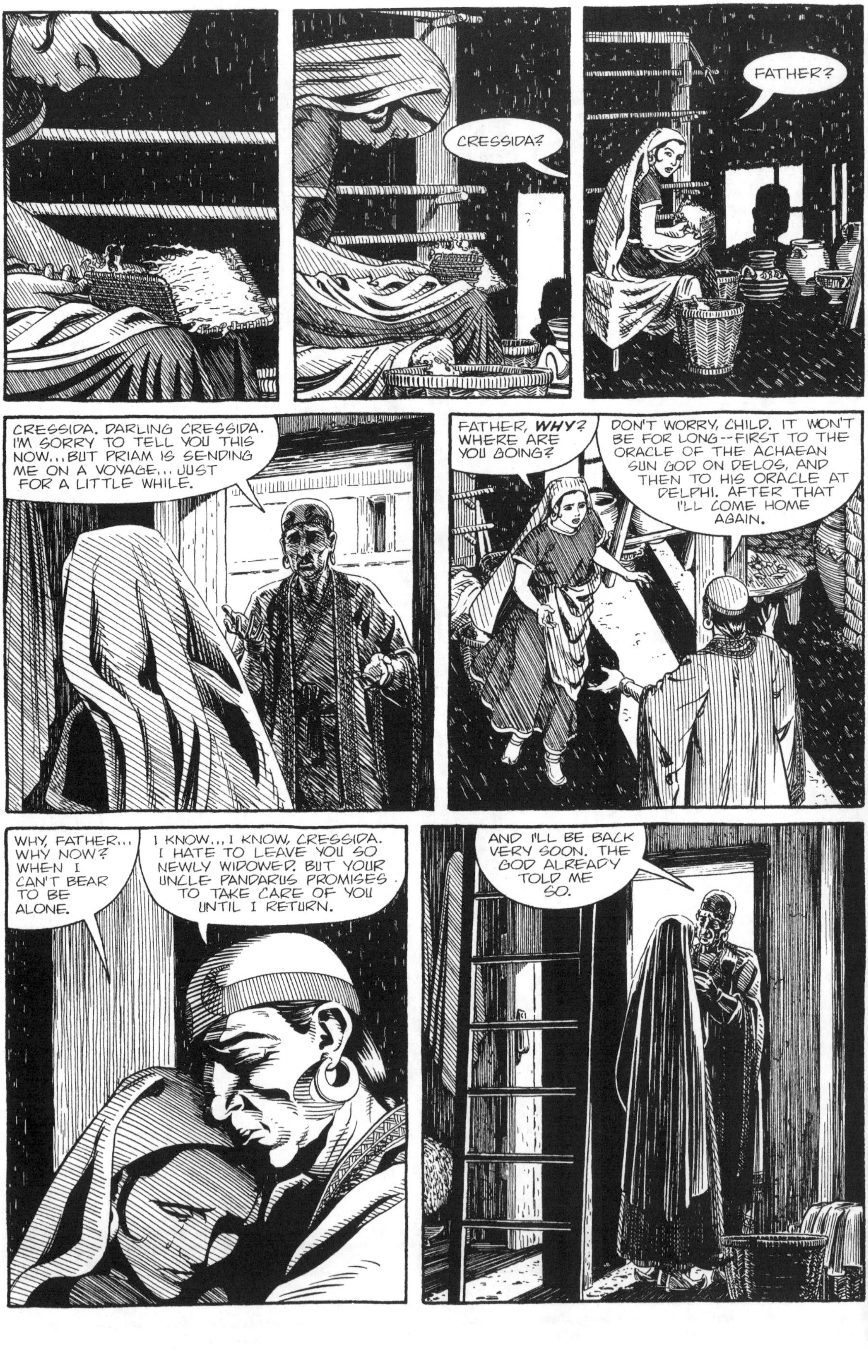
CRESSIDA?
FATHER?
CRESSIDA. DARLING CRESSIDA. I'M SORRY TO TELL YOU THIS NOW... BUT PRIAM IS SENDING ME ON A VOYAGE... JUST FOR A LITTLE WHILE.
FATHER, WHY? WHERE ARE YOU GOING?
DON'T WORRY, CHILD. IT WON'T BE FOR LONG--FIRST TO THE ORACLE OF THE ACHAEAN SUN GOD ON DELOS, AND THEN TO HIS ORACLE AT DELPHI. AFTER THAT I'LL COME HOME AGAIN.
WHY, FATHER... WHY NOW? WHEN I CAN'T BEAR TO BE ALONE.
I KNOW... I KNOW, CRESSIDA. I HATE TO LEAVE YOU SO NEWLY WIDOWED. BUT YOUR UNCLE PANDARUS PROMISES TO TAKE CARE OF YOU UNTIL I RETURN.
AND I'LL BE BACK VERY SOON. THE GOD ALREADY TOLD ME SO.

...AND THAT WAS HIS ANSWER, HIGH KING.

WELL SPOKEN, TALTHYBIUS. HAVE SOMETHING TO EAT.

MAY THE GODS BEAR WITNESS NOW TO THE JUSTICE OF MY WORDS,...

JUST AS A MAN VICTORIOUS IN BATTLE REFLECTS GLORY UPON HIS KINSMEN, SO HIS KINSMEN SHARE BLAME FOR HIS CRIMES. BUT THE KING OF TROY DISAVOWS THE INJURIES INFLICTED BY HIS SON. HE EXCUSES THEM BY NAMING WOMEN FAIRLY TAKEN--HESIONE BY LAOMEDON'S PROMISE, MEDEA BY HER OWN CHOICE, AND EUROPA BY GOD.

BUT TROY HAD NO CLAIM ON HELEN.

WE'RE NO STRANGERS TO BATTLE, MENELAUS--OR TO THE REWARDS OF VICTORY. THROUGH BATTLE I REGAINED OUR FATHER'S THRONE AND SCEPTER FROM HIS MURDERERS.

I WON MY WIFE BY FORCE OF ARMS, AND SHE HAS BORNE ME BEAUTIFUL DAUGHTERS WHOM I DELIGHT IN.

BUT THIS WILL BE NO SMALL BATTLE. TROY IS STRONGER NOW THAN IN HERAKLES'S DAY. IT WILL TAKE WARRIORS BY THE HUNDREDS -- BY THE *THOUSANDS*-- TO TOPPLE TROY. THE WORLD WILL SHAKE TO OUR CHARIOTS' THUNDER.

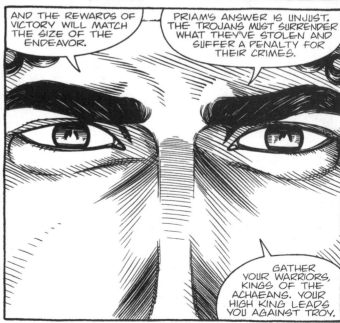

AND THE REWARDS OF VICTORY WILL MATCH THE SIZE OF THE ENDEAVOR.

PRIAM'S ANSWER IS UNJUST. THE TROJANS MUST SURRENDER WHAT THEY'VE STOLEN AND SUFFER A PENALTY FOR THEIR CRIMES.

GATHER YOUR WARRIORS, KINGS OF THE ACHAEANS. YOUR HIGH KING LEADS YOU AGAINST TROY.

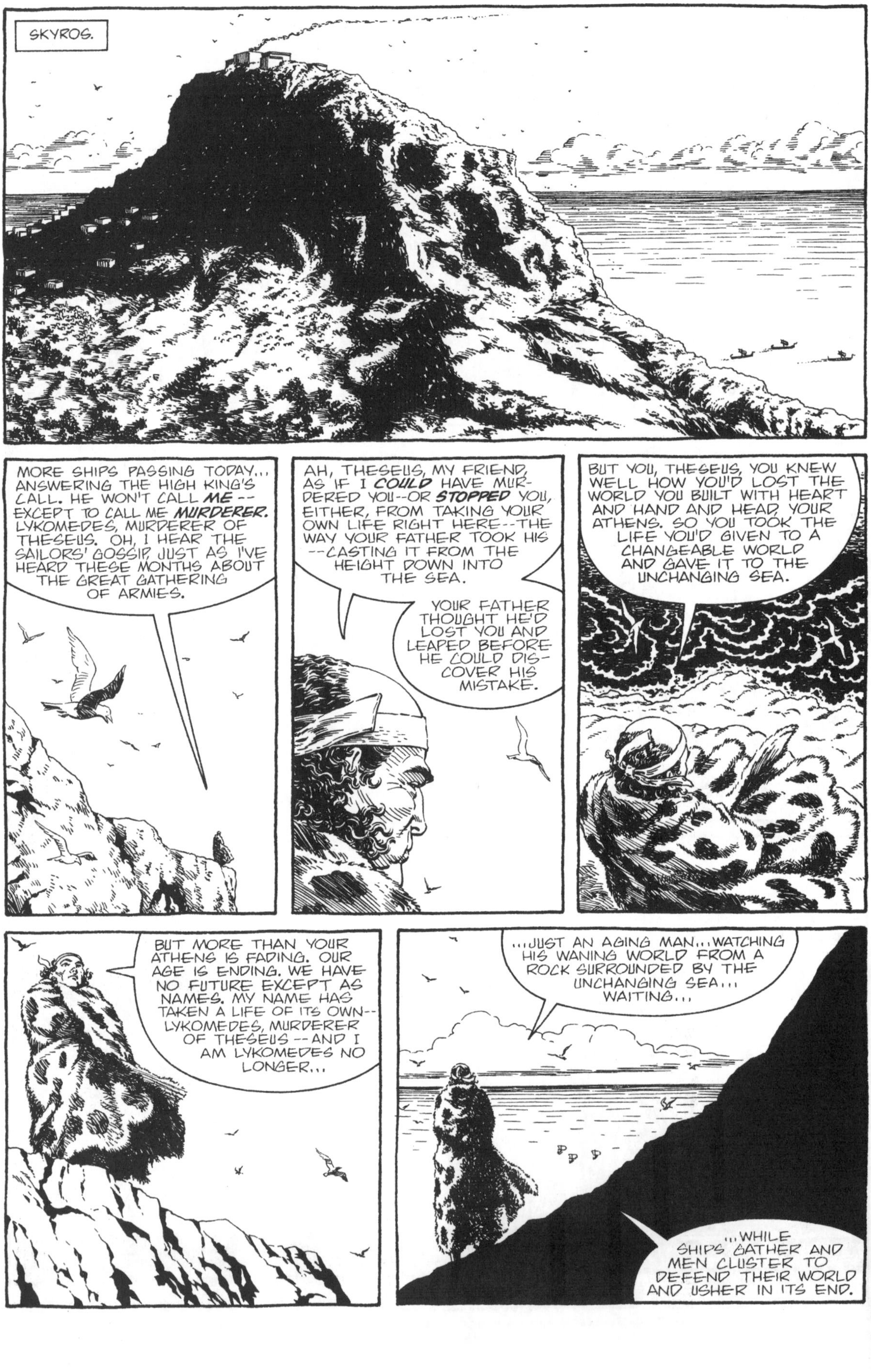
SKYROS.
MORE SHIPS PASSING TODAY... ANSWERING THE HIGH KING'S CALL. HE WON'T CALL ME -- EXCEPT TO CALL ME MURDERER. LYKOMEDES, MURDERER OF THESEUS. OH, I HEAR THE SAILORS' GOSSIP, JUST AS I'VE HEARD THESE MONTHS ABOUT THE GREAT GATHERING OF ARMIES.
AH, THESEUS, MY FRIEND, AS IF I COULD HAVE MURDERED YOU--OR STOPPED YOU, EITHER, FROM TAKING YOUR OWN LIFE RIGHT HERE--THE WAY YOUR FATHER TOOK HIS --CASTING IT FROM THE HEIGHT DOWN INTO THE SEA.
YOUR FATHER THOUGHT HE'D LOST YOU AND LEAPED BEFORE HE COULD DISCOVER HIS MISTAKE.
BUT YOU, THESEUS, YOU KNEW WELL HOW YOU'D LOST THE WORLD YOU BUILT WITH HEART AND HAND AND HEAD, YOUR ATHENS. SO YOU TOOK THE LIFE YOU'D GIVEN TO A CHANGEABLE WORLD AND GAVE IT TO THE UNCHANGING SEA.
BUT MORE THAN YOUR ATHENS IS FADING. OUR AGE IS ENDING. WE HAVE NO FUTURE EXCEPT AS NAMES. MY NAME HAS TAKEN A LIFE OF ITS OWN-- LYKOMEDES, MURDERER OF THESEUS --AND I AM LYKOMEDES NO LONGER...
...JUST AN AGING MAN... WATCHING HIS WANING WORLD FROM A ROCK SURROUNDED BY THE UNCHANGING SEA... WAITING...
...WHILE SHIPS GATHER AND MEN CLUSTER TO DEFEND THEIR WORLD AND USHER IN ITS END.

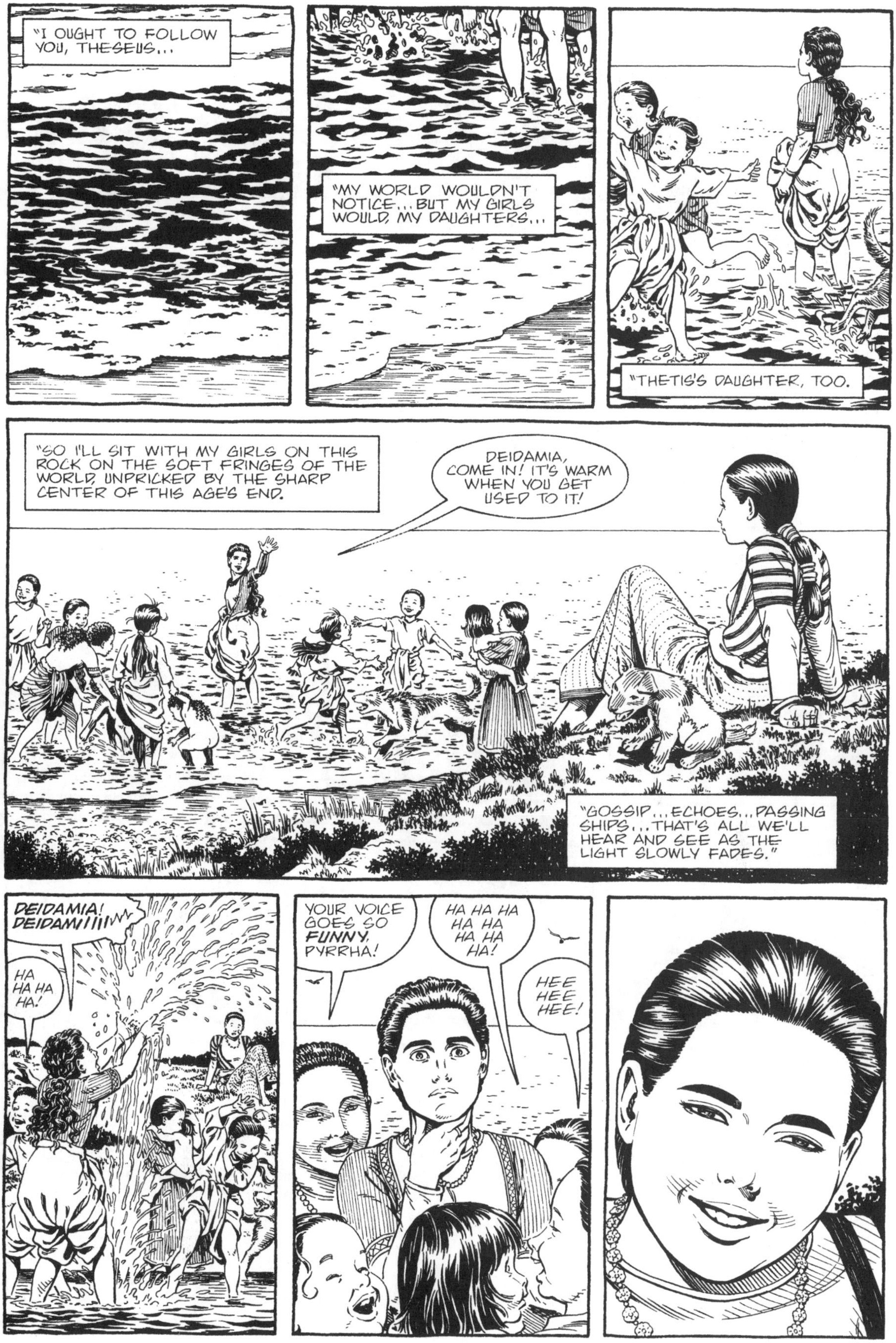
"I OUGHT TO FOLLOW YOU, THESEUS...
"MY WORLD WOULDN'T NOTICE... BUT MY GIRLS WOULD, MY DAUGHTERS...
"THETIS'S DAUGHTER, TOO.
"SO I'LL SIT WITH MY GIRLS ON THIS ROCK ON THE SOFT FRINGES OF THE WORLD, UNPRICKED BY THE SHARP CENTER OF THIS AGE'S END.
DEIDAMIA, COME IN! IT'S WARM WHEN YOU GET USED TO IT!
"GOSSIP... ECHOES... PASSING SHIPS... THAT'S ALL WE'LL HEAR AND SEE AS THE LIGHT SLOWLY FADES."
DEIDAMIA! DEIDAMIIIIII
HA HA HA HA!
YOUR VOICE GOES SO FUNNY, PYRRHA!
HA HA HA HA HA HA HA HA!
HEE HEE HEE!

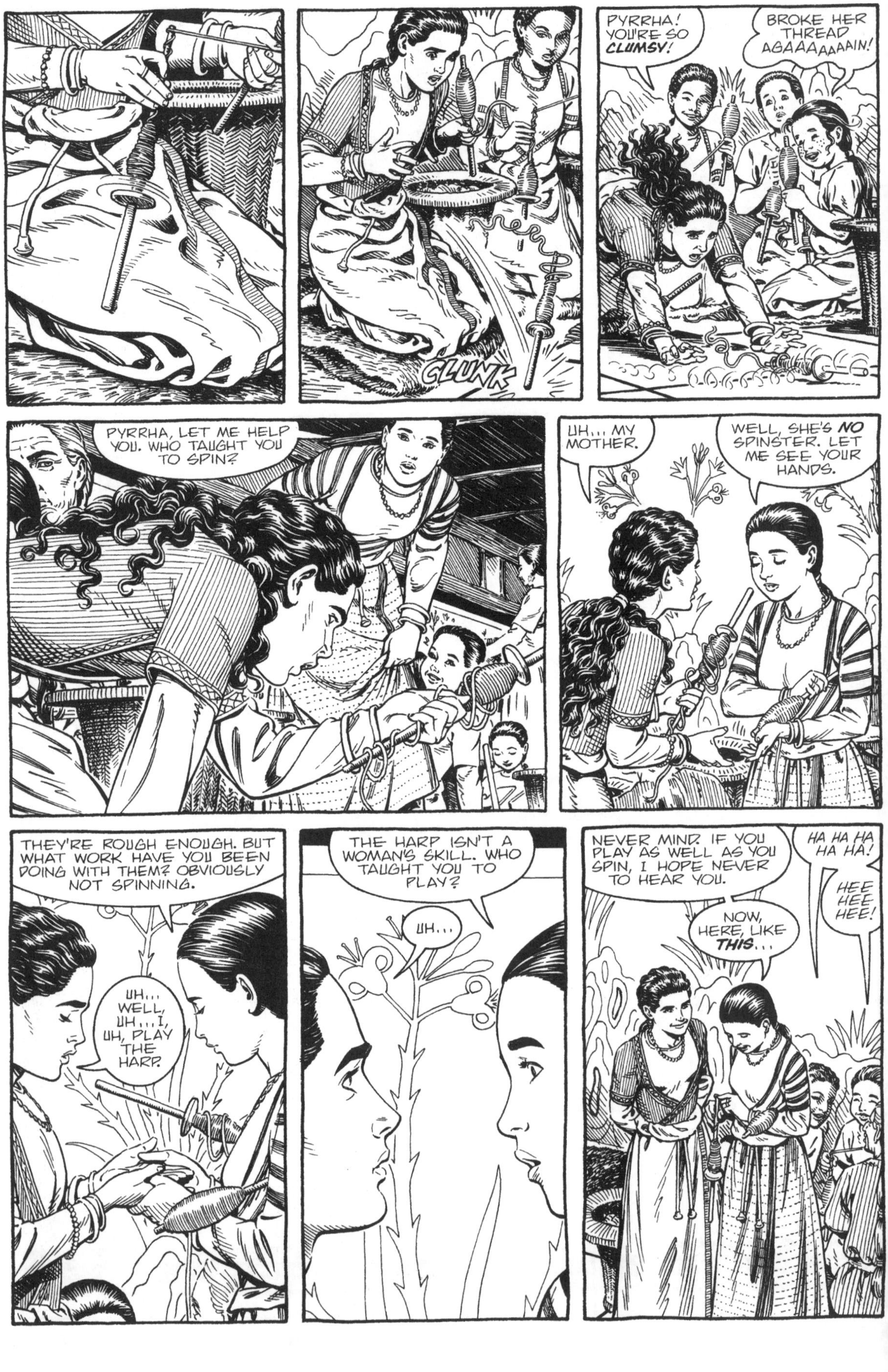
PYRRHA! YOU'RE SO CLUMSY!
BROKE HER THREAD AGAAAAAAAIN!
CLUNK
PYRRHA, LET ME HELP YOU. WHO TAUGHT YOU TO SPIN?
UH... MY MOTHER.
WELL, SHE'S NO SPINSTER. LET ME SEE YOUR HANDS.
THEY'RE ROUGH ENOUGH. BUT WHAT WORK HAVE YOU BEEN DOING WITH THEM? OBVIOUSLY NOT SPINNING.
UH... WELL, UH..., I, UH, PLAY THE HARP.
THE HARP ISN'T A WOMAN'S SKILL. WHO TAUGHT YOU TO PLAY?
UH...
NEVER MIND. IF YOU PLAY AS WELL AS YOU SPIN, I HOPE NEVER TO HEAR YOU.
NOW, HERE, LIKE THIS...
HA HA HA HA HA!
HEE HEE HEE!

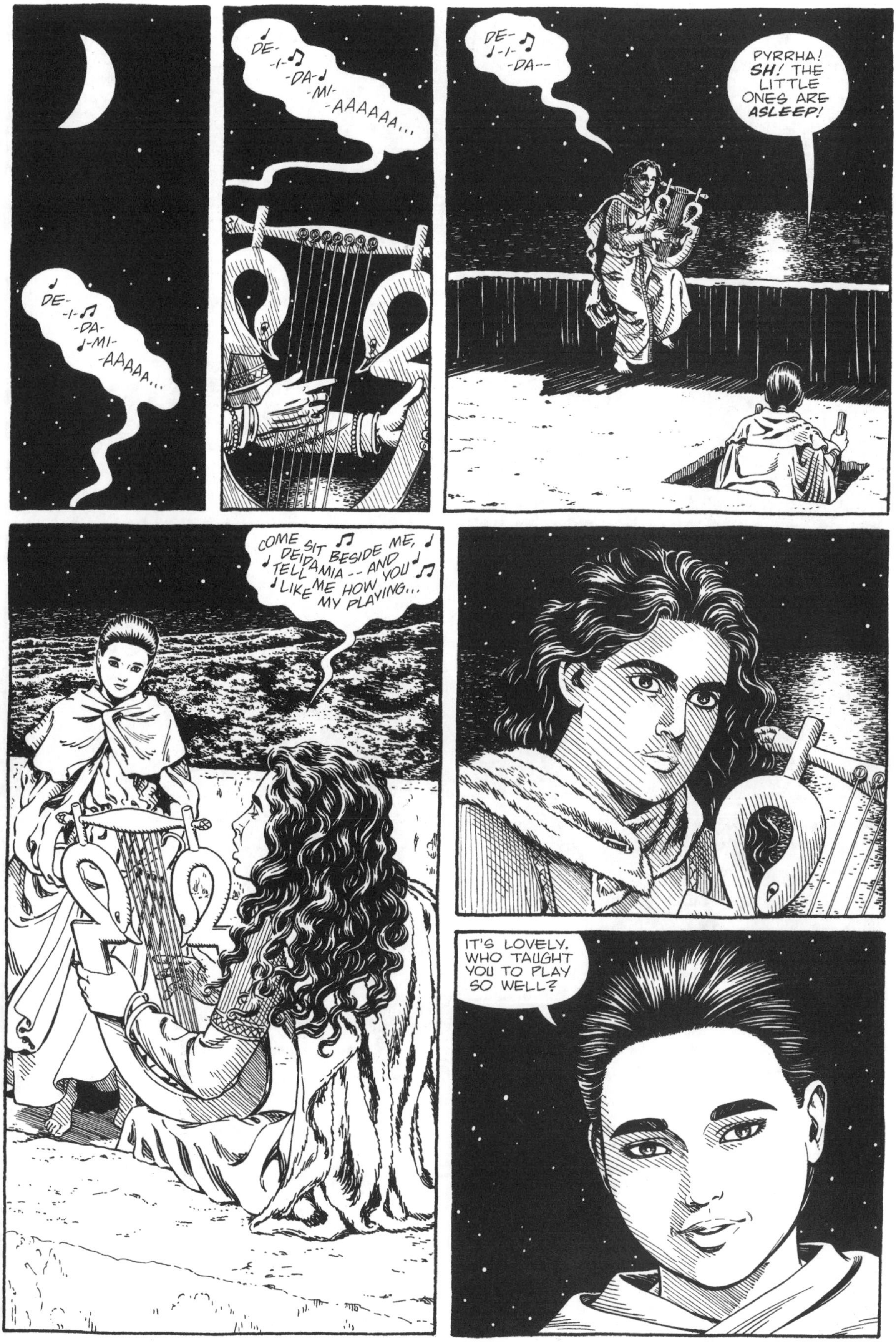

♩ DE- -I- ♫ -DA- ♩-MI- -AAAAA...
♩ DE- -I- ♫ -DA-♩ -MI- -AAAAAA...
DE- ♫ ♩-I- -DA--
PYRRHA! SH! THE LITTLE ONES ARE ASLEEP!
COME SIT ♫ BESIDE ME, ♩ ♩ DEIDAMIA -- AND TELL ME HOW YOU ♩ ♫ ♩ LIKE MY PLAYING...
IT'S LOVELY. WHO TAUGHT YOU TO PLAY SO WELL?

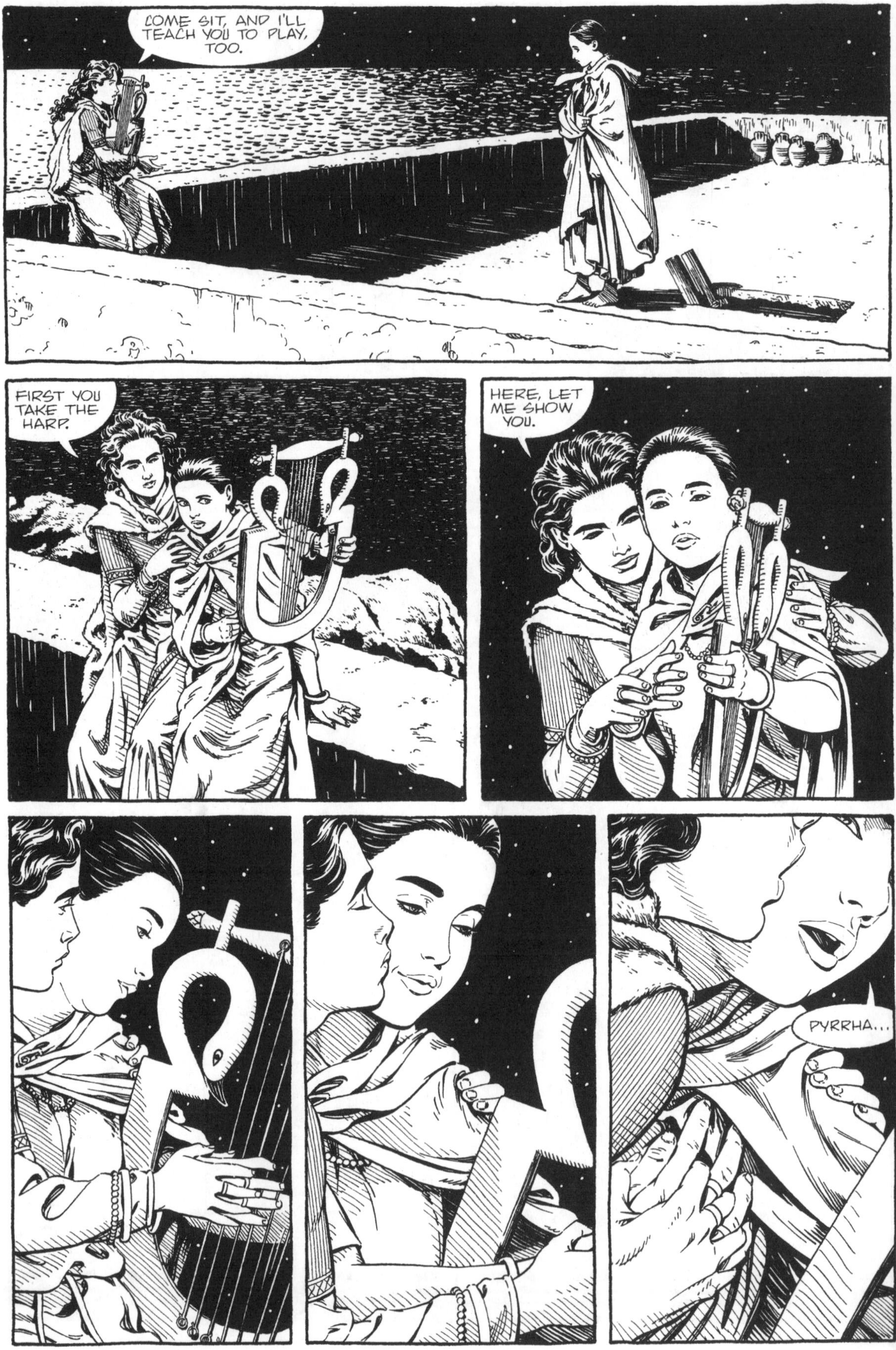
COME SIT, AND I'LL TEACH YOU TO PLAY, TOO.
FIRST YOU TAKE THE HARP.
HERE, LET ME SHOW YOU.
PYRRHA...

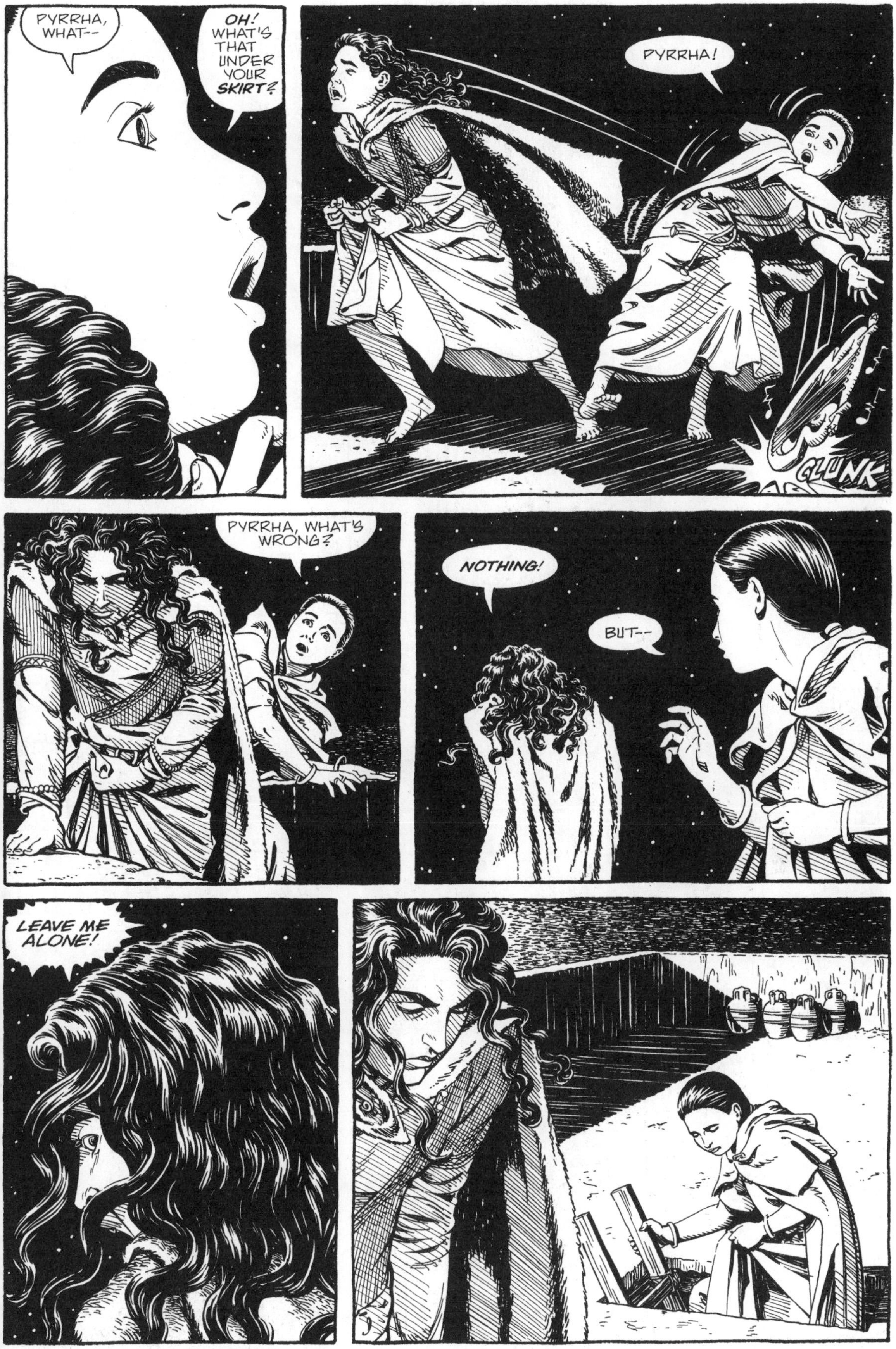

PYRRHA, WHAT--
OH! WHAT'S THAT UNDER YOUR SKIRT?
PYRRHA!
CLUNK
PYRRHA, WHAT'S WRONG?
NOTHING!
BUT--
LEAVE ME ALONE!

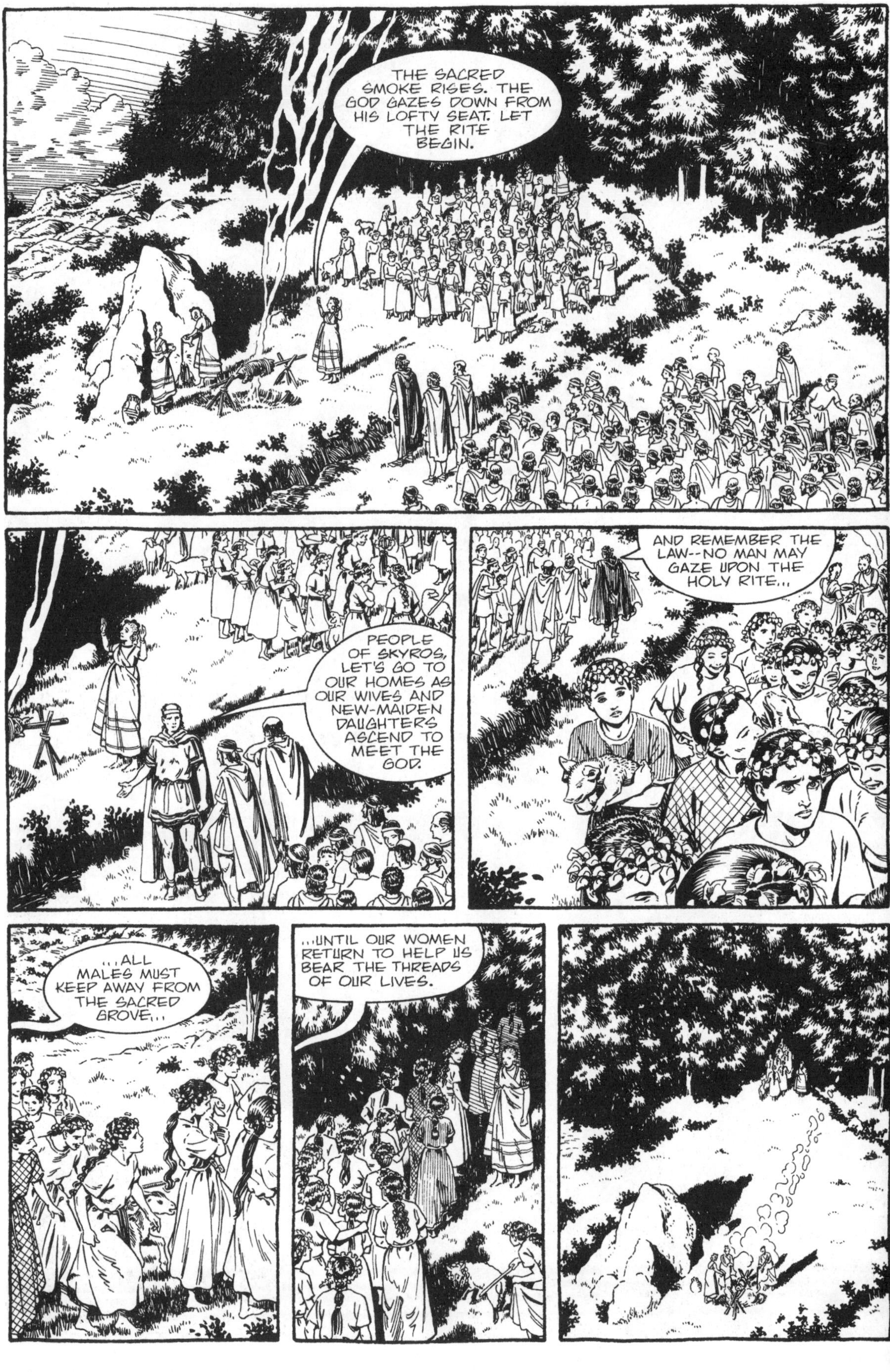
THE SACRED SMOKE RISES. THE GOD GAZES DOWN FROM HIS LOFTY SEAT. LET THE RITE BEGIN.
PEOPLE OF SKYROS, LET'S GO TO OUR HOMES AS OUR WIVES AND NEW-MAIDEN DAUGHTERS ASCEND TO MEET THE GOD.
AND REMEMBER THE LAW--NO MAN MAY GAZE UPON THE HOLY RITE...
...ALL MALES MUST KEEP AWAY FROM THE SACRED GROVE...
...UNTIL OUR WOMEN RETURN TO HELP US BEAR THE THREADS OF OUR LIVES.

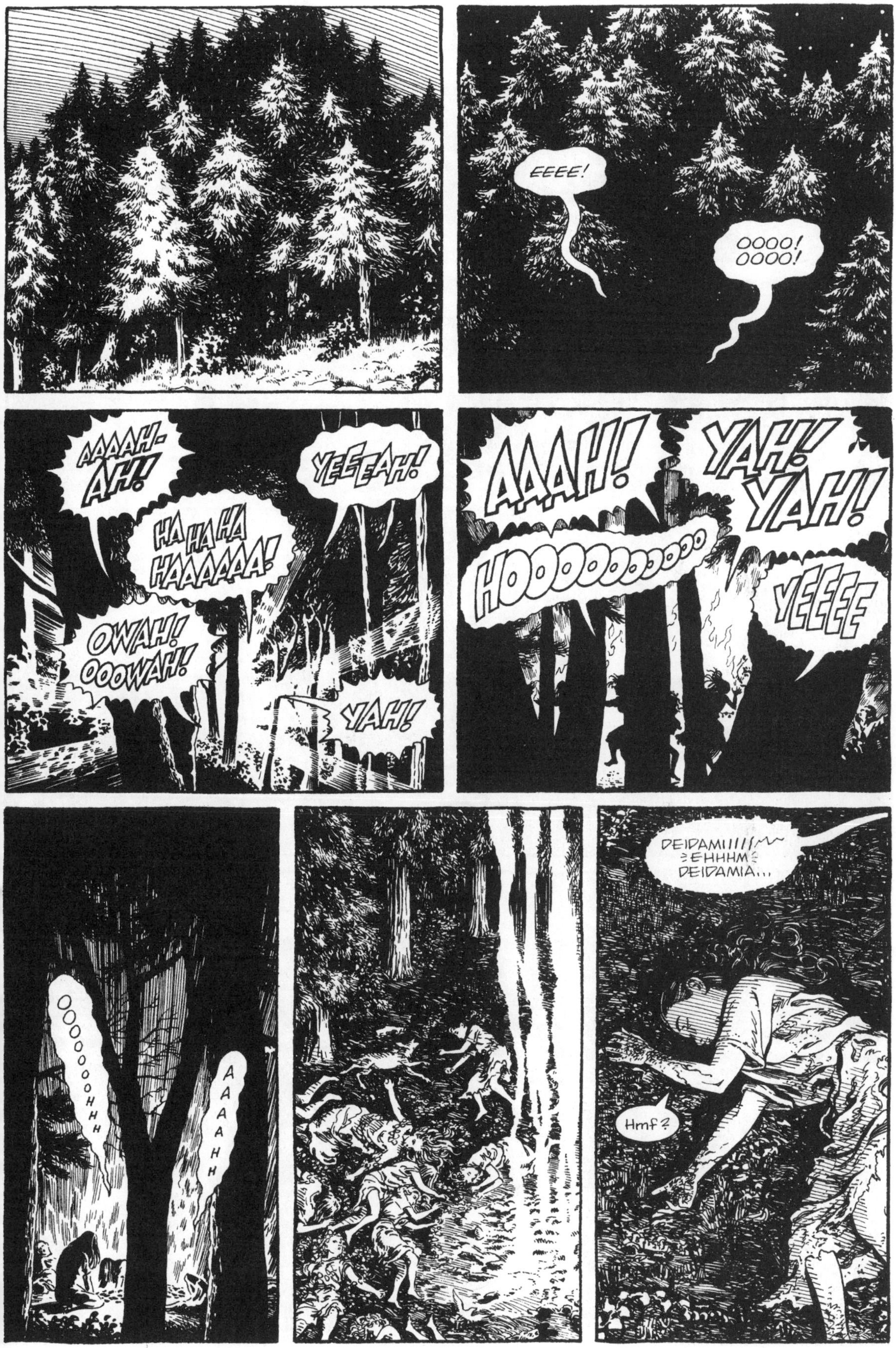
EEEE!
OOOO! OOOO!
AAAAH-AH!
HA HA HA HAAAAAA!
OWAH! OOOWAH!
YEEEAH!
YAH!
AAAH!
HOOOOOOOOOOO
YAH! YAH!
YEEEE
OOOOOOOOHHH
AAAAAHH
DEIDAMIIIII
EHHHM
DEIDAMIA...
Hmf?

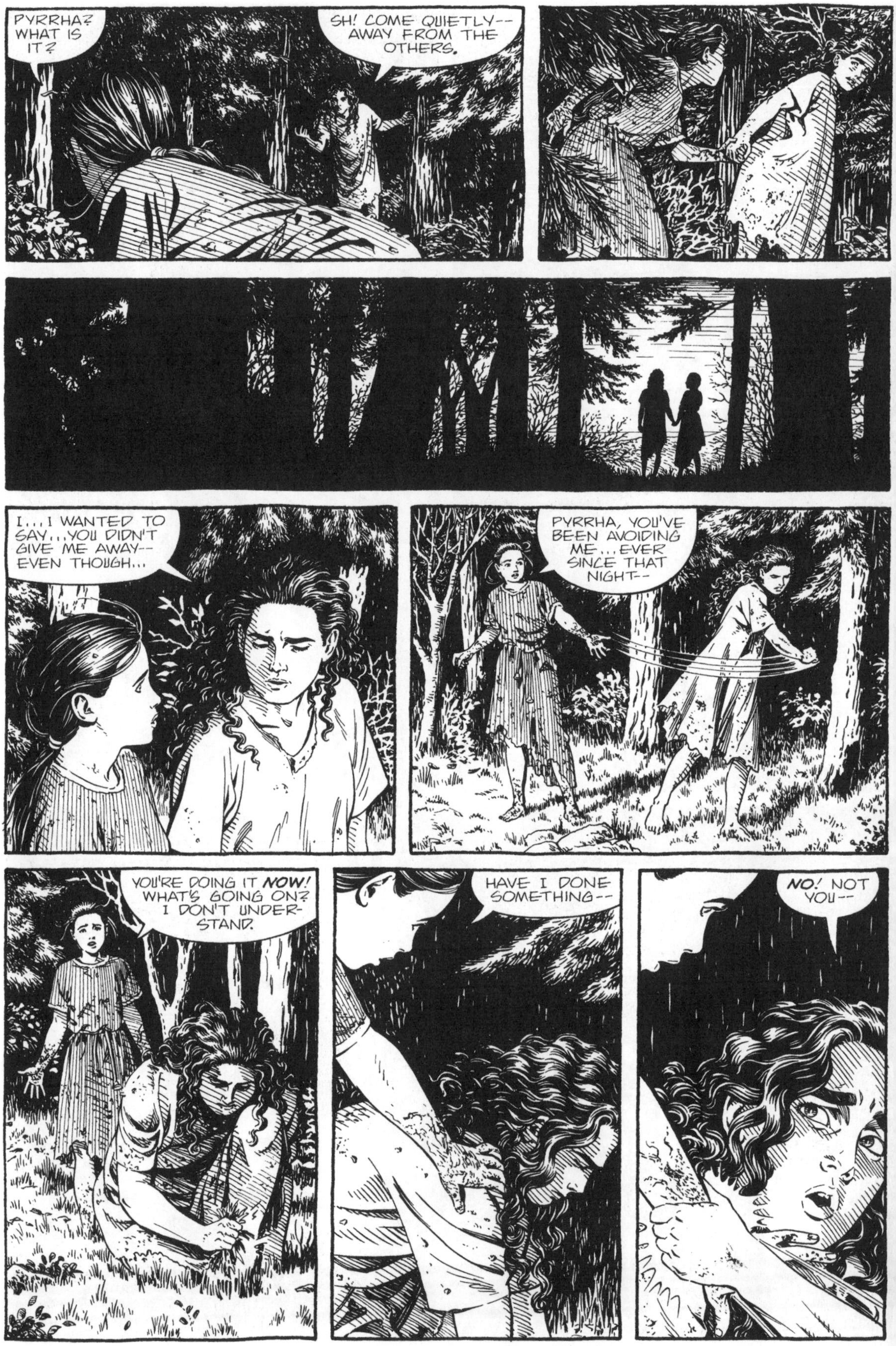
PYRRHA? WHAT IS IT?
SH! COME QUIETLY-- AWAY FROM THE OTHERS.
I...I WANTED TO SAY...YOU DIDN'T GIVE ME AWAY-- EVEN THOUGH...
PYRRHA, YOU'VE BEEN AVOIDING ME...EVER SINCE THAT NIGHT--
YOU'RE DOING IT NOW! WHAT'S GOING ON? I DON'T UNDER-STAND.
HAVE I DONE SOMETHING--
NO! NOT YOU--

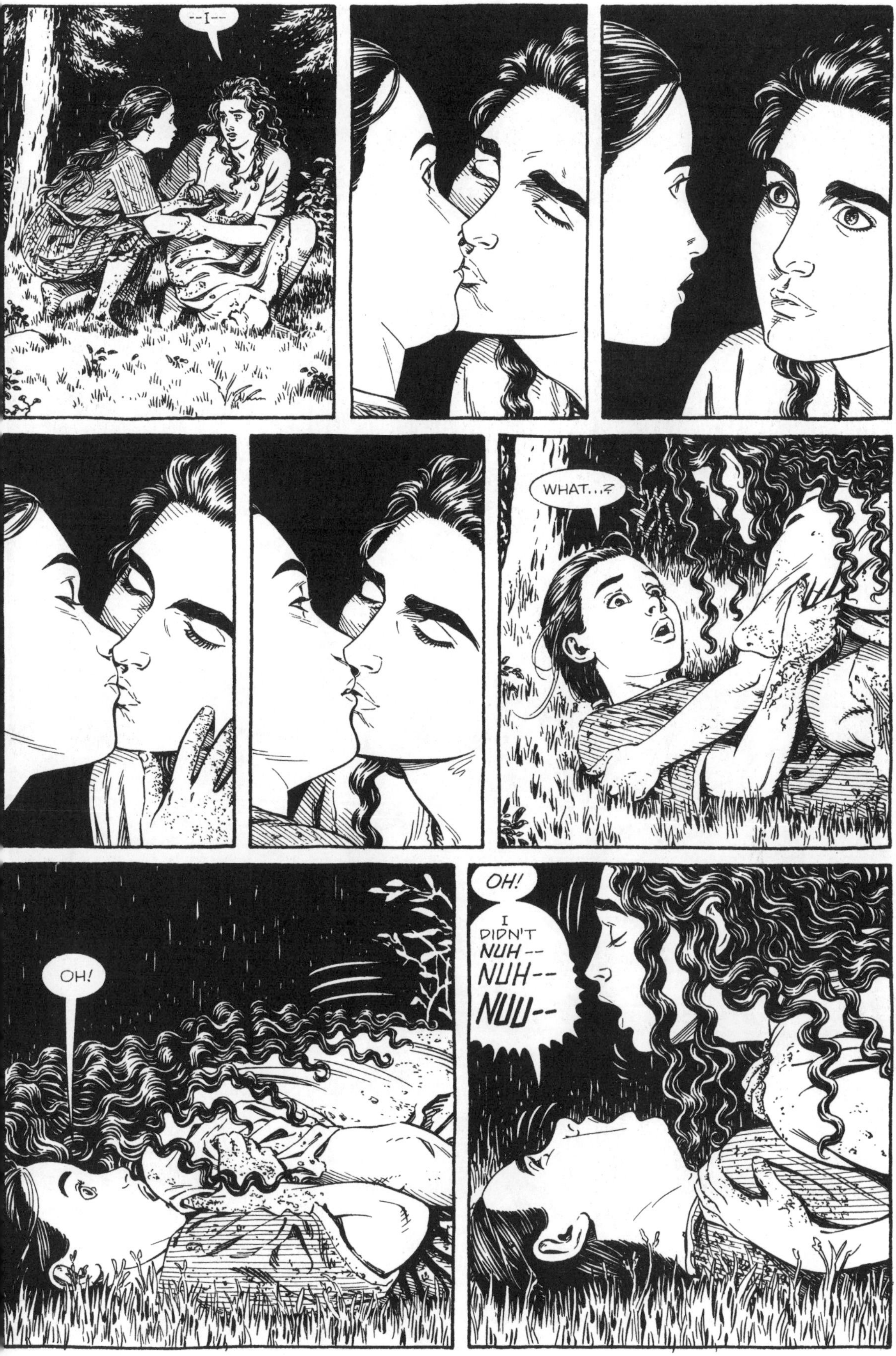
--I--
WHAT...?
OH!
OH!
I DIDN'T NUH-- NUH-- NUU--

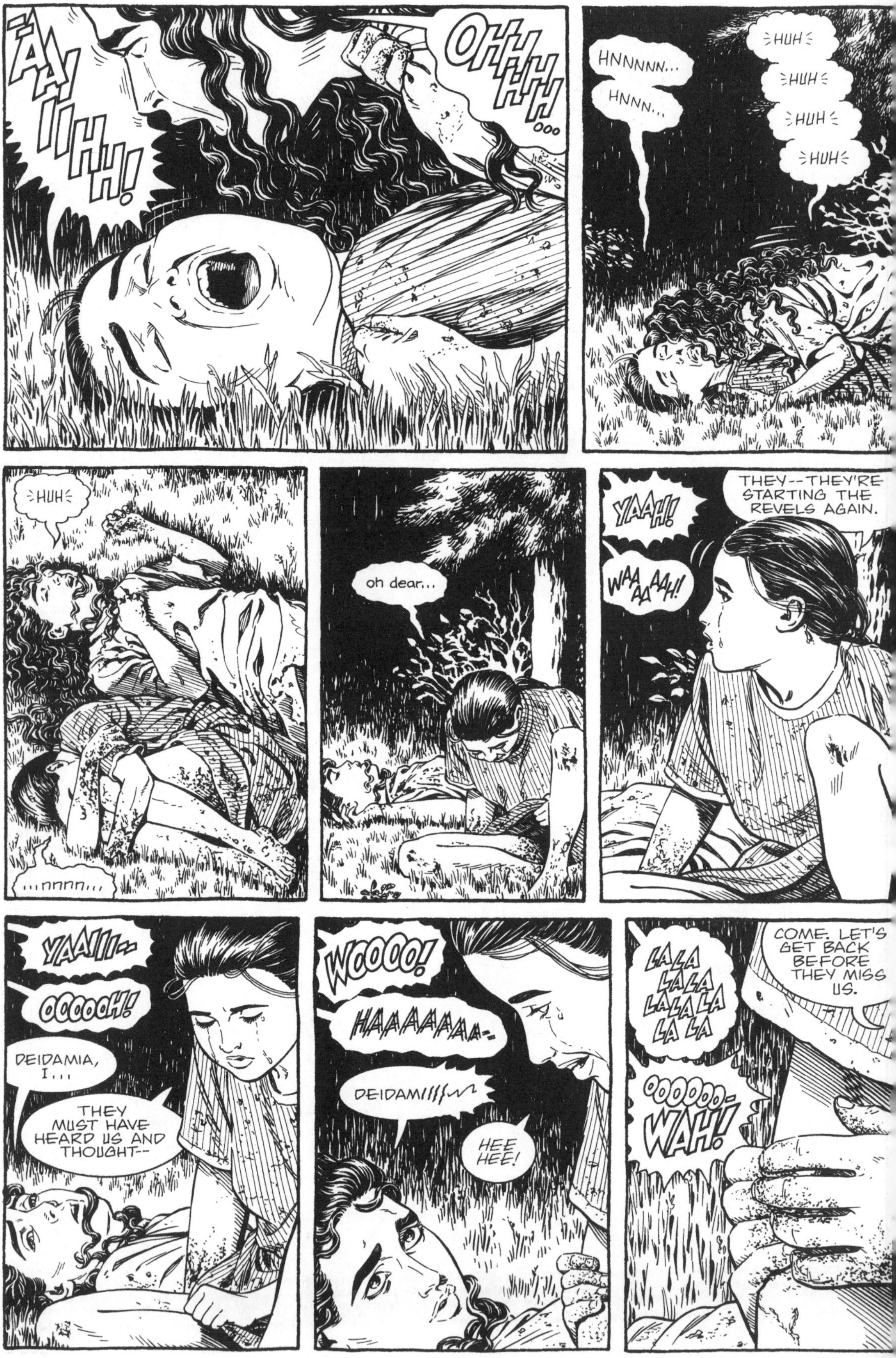
AAIIHH!
OHHHHH ooo
HNNNNN...
HNNN...
HUH
HUH
HUH
HUH
HUH
...nnnn...
oh dear...
YAAH!
WAAAAAH!
THEY--THEY'RE STARTING THE REVELS AGAIN.
YAAIII--
OOOOOH!
DEIDAMIA, I...
THEY MUST HAVE HEARD US AND THOUGHT--
WOOOO!
HAAAAAAAA--
DEIDAM
HEE HEE!
LA LA LA LA LA LA LA LA LA LA LA
OOOOOO-WAH!
COME. LET'S GET BACK BEFORE THEY MISS US.

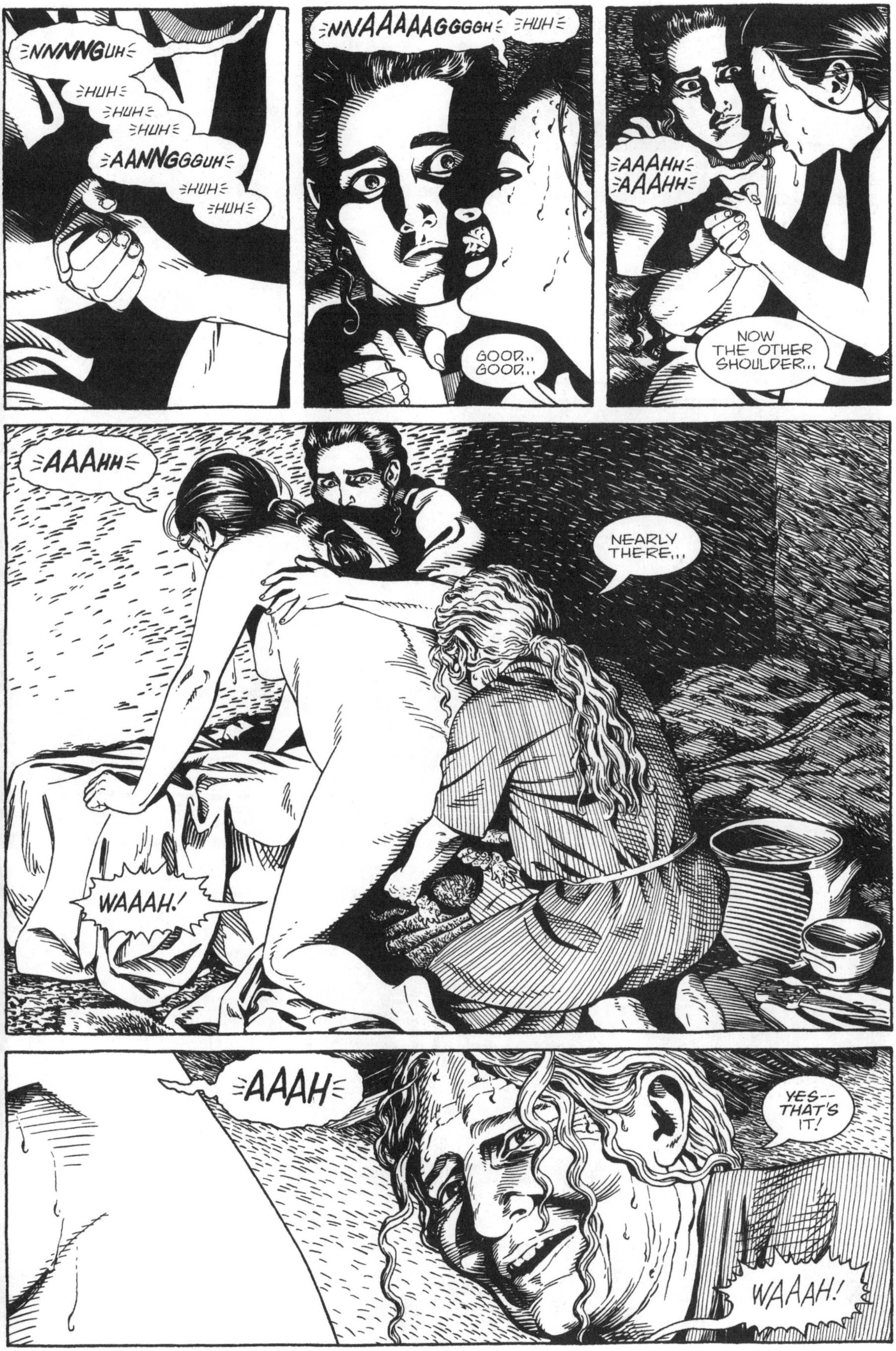
NNNNGUH
HUH
HUH
HUH
AANNGGGUH
HUH
HUH
NNAAAAAGGGGH
HUH
GOOD... GOOD...
AAAHH AAAHH
NOW THE OTHER SHOULDER...
AAAHH
NEARLY THERE...
WAAAH!
AAAH
YES-- THAT'S IT!
WAAAH!

A BOY!

≥HUH≥ LET ME HOLD HIM. ≥HUH≥ ≥HUH≥

WAAAH

≥HUH≥ A BOY! LOOK, PYRRHA! A BOY!

WAAAH!

OH, YES...

WAAAH!

SOON AS WE'RE FINISHED, I'LL BRING THE WET NURSE TO TAKE HIM--WE'D NEVER HIDE THAT VOICE AS WE DID YOUR PREGNANCY.

ALMOST OVER. PYRRHA, MAKE SURE THEY KEEP WARM.

SHH, BABY BOY...

WAAAH

WHAT'S TAKING HER SO LONG TO BRING THE WET NURSE?

OH, PYRRHA, ISN'T HE WONDERFUL?

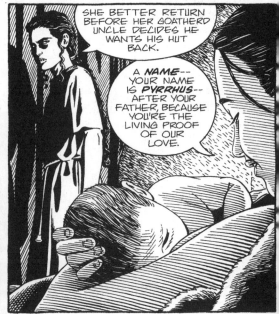

SHE BETTER RETURN BEFORE HER GOATHERD UNCLE DECIDES HE WANTS HIS HUT BACK.

A NAME-- YOUR NAME IS PYRRHUS-- AFTER YOUR FATHER, BECAUSE YOU'RE THE LIVING PROOF OF OUR LOVE.

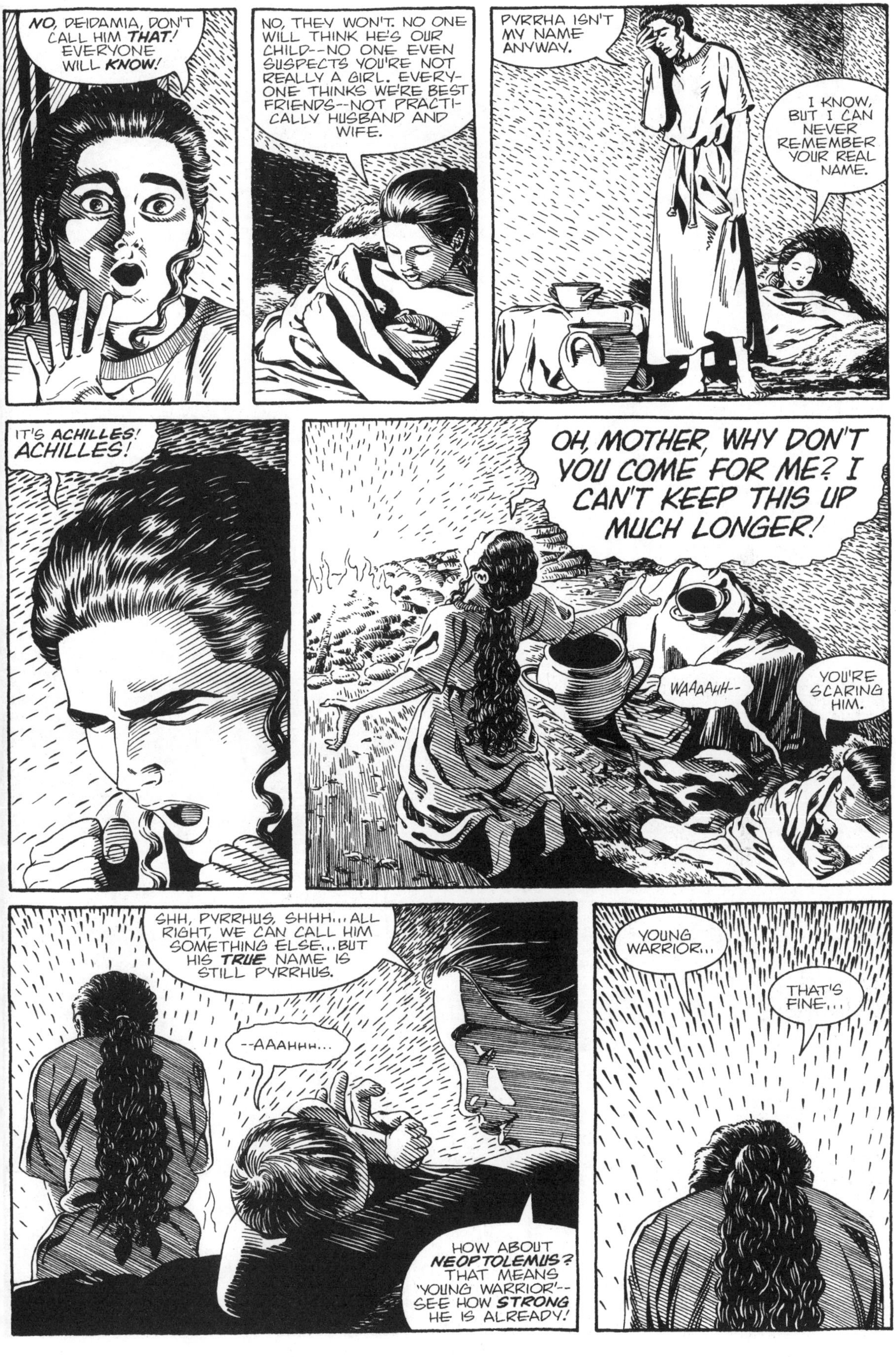
NO, DEIDAMIA, DON'T CALL HIM THAT! EVERYONE WILL KNOW!
NO, THEY WON'T. NO ONE WILL THINK HE'S OUR CHILD--NO ONE EVEN SUSPECTS YOU'RE NOT REALLY A GIRL. EVERYONE THINKS WE'RE BEST FRIENDS--NOT PRACTICALLY HUSBAND AND WIFE.
PYRRHA ISN'T MY NAME ANYWAY.
I KNOW, BUT I CAN NEVER REMEMBER YOUR REAL NAME.
IT'S ACHILLES! ACHILLES!
OH, MOTHER, WHY DON'T YOU COME FOR ME? I CAN'T KEEP THIS UP MUCH LONGER!
WAAAAHH--
YOU'RE SCARING HIM.
SHH, PYRRHUS, SHHH... ALL RIGHT, WE CAN CALL HIM SOMETHING ELSE... BUT HIS TRUE NAME IS STILL PYRRHUS.
--AAAHHH...
HOW ABOUT NEOPTOLEMUS? THAT MEANS 'YOUNG WARRIOR'--SEE HOW STRONG HE IS ALREADY!
YOUNG WARRIOR...
THAT'S FINE...

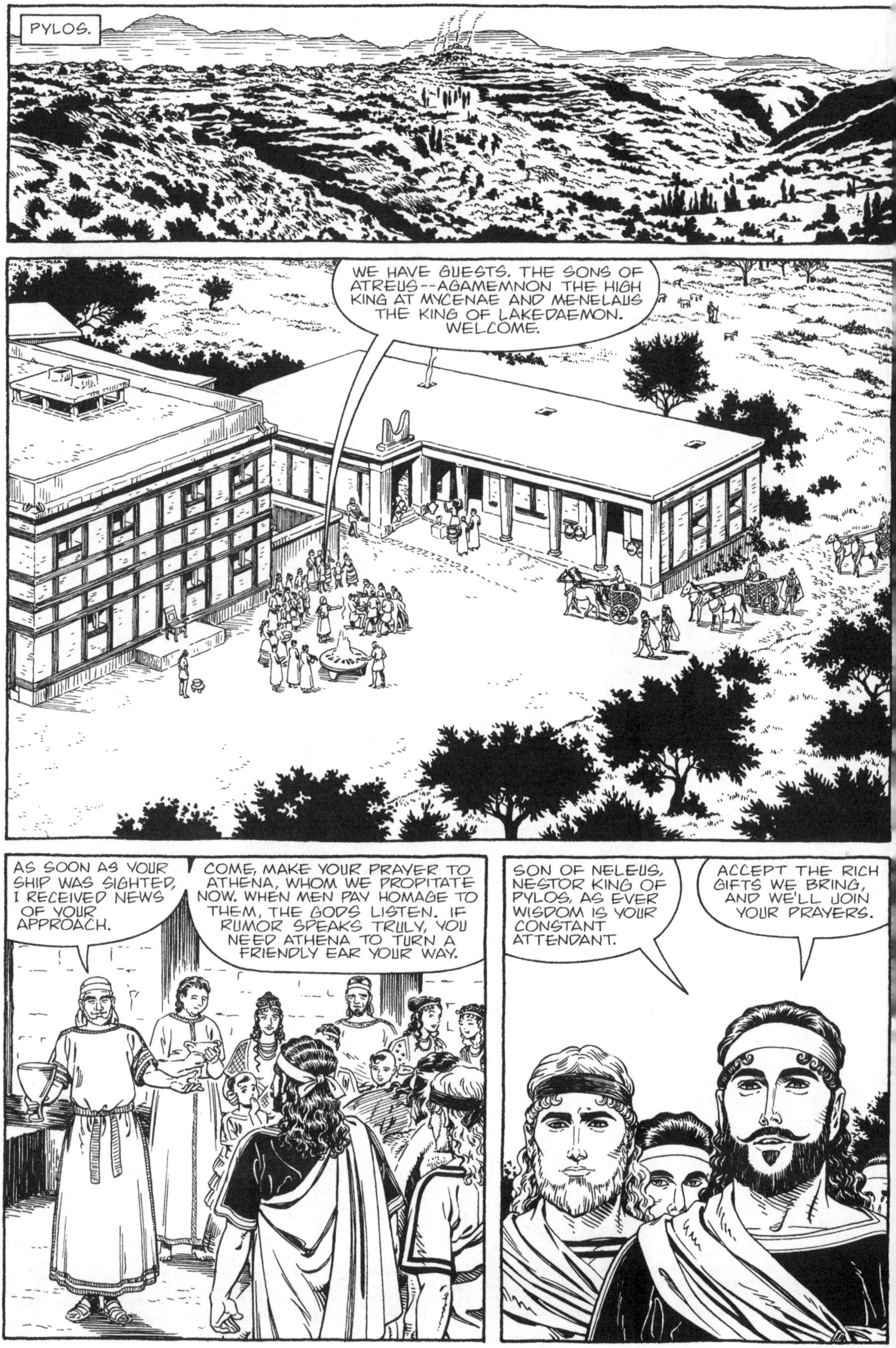
PYLOS.
WE HAVE GUESTS. THE SONS OF ATREUS--AGAMEMNON THE HIGH KING AT MYCENAE AND MENELAUS THE KING OF LAKEDAEMON. WELCOME.
AS SOON AS YOUR SHIP WAS SIGHTED, I RECEIVED NEWS OF YOUR APPROACH.
COME, MAKE YOUR PRAYER TO ATHENA, WHOM WE PROPITIATE NOW. WHEN MEN PAY HOMAGE TO THEM, THE GODS LISTEN. IF RUMOR SPEAKS TRULY, YOU NEED ATHENA TO TURN A FRIENDLY EAR YOUR WAY.
SON OF NELEUS, NESTOR KING OF PYLOS, AS EVER WISDOM IS YOUR CONSTANT ATTENDANT.
ACCEPT THE RICH GIFTS WE BRING, AND WE'LL JOIN YOUR PRAYERS.

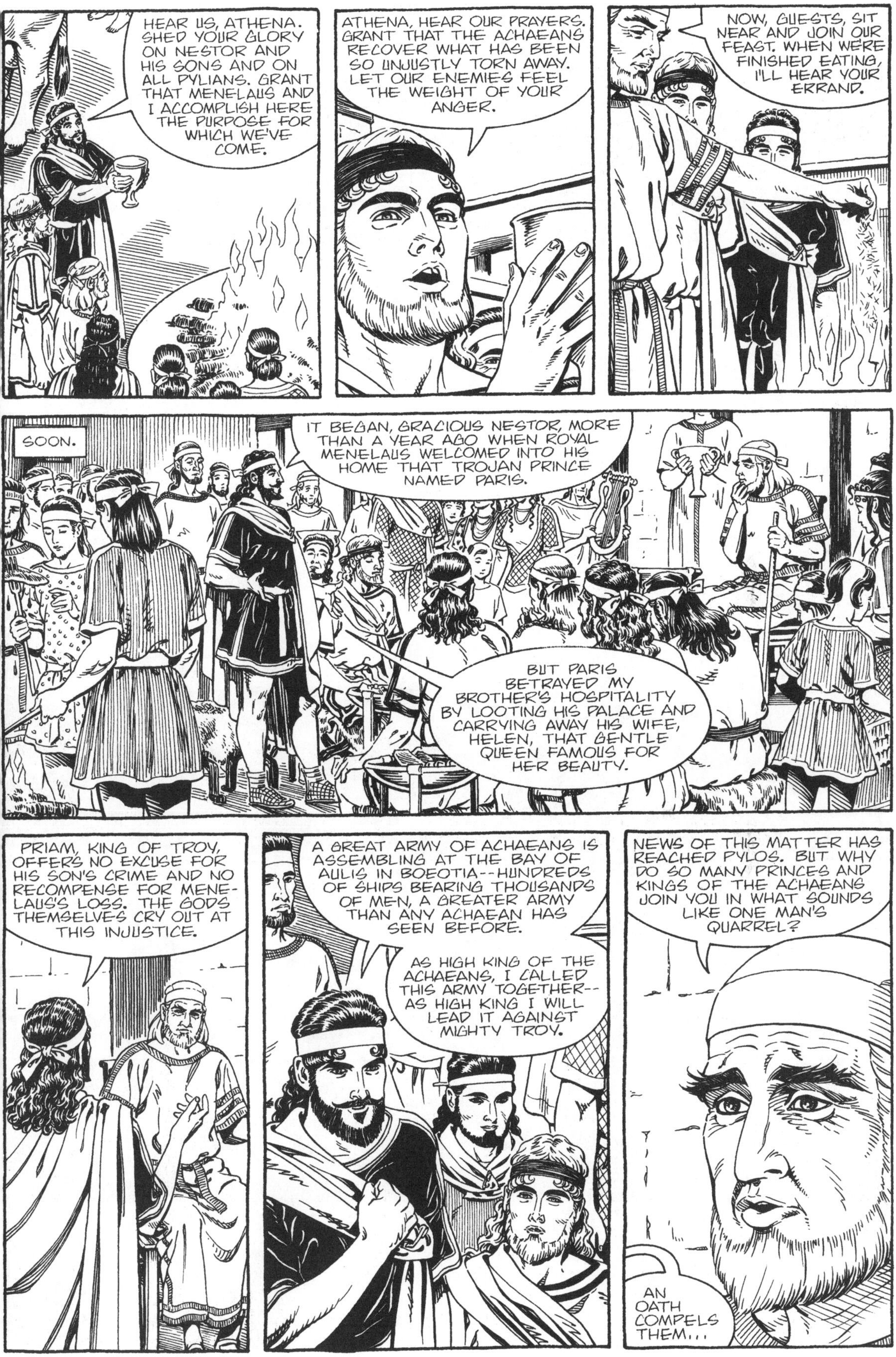
HEAR US, ATHENA. SHED YOUR GLORY ON NESTOR AND HIS SONS AND ON ALL PYLIANS. GRANT THAT MENELAUS AND I ACCOMPLISH HERE THE PURPOSE FOR WHICH WE'VE COME.
ATHENA, HEAR OUR PRAYERS. GRANT THAT THE ACHAEANS RECOVER WHAT HAS BEEN SO UNJUSTLY TORN AWAY. LET OUR ENEMIES FEEL THE WEIGHT OF YOUR ANGER.
NOW, GUESTS, SIT NEAR AND JOIN OUR FEAST. WHEN WE'RE FINISHED EATING, I'LL HEAR YOUR ERRAND.
SOON.
IT BEGAN, GRACIOUS NESTOR, MORE THAN A YEAR AGO WHEN ROYAL MENELAUS WELCOMED INTO HIS HOME THAT TROJAN PRINCE NAMED PARIS.
BUT PARIS BETRAYED MY BROTHER'S HOSPITALITY BY LOOTING HIS PALACE AND CARRYING AWAY HIS WIFE, HELEN, THAT GENTLE QUEEN FAMOUS FOR HER BEAUTY.
PRIAM, KING OF TROY, OFFERS NO EXCUSE FOR HIS SON'S CRIME AND NO RECOMPENSE FOR MENELAUS'S LOSS. THE GODS THEMSELVES CRY OUT AT THIS INJUSTICE.
A GREAT ARMY OF ACHAEANS IS ASSEMBLING AT THE BAY OF AULIS IN BOEOTIA--HUNDREDS OF SHIPS BEARING THOUSANDS OF MEN, A GREATER ARMY THAN ANY ACHAEAN HAS SEEN BEFORE.
AS HIGH KING OF THE ACHAEANS, I CALLED THIS ARMY TOGETHER-- AS HIGH KING I WILL LEAD IT AGAINST MIGHTY TROY.
NEWS OF THIS MATTER HAS REACHED PYLOS. BUT WHY DO SO MANY PRINCES AND KINGS OF THE ACHAEANS JOIN YOU IN WHAT SOUNDS LIKE ONE MAN'S QUARREL?
AN OATH COMPELS THEM...

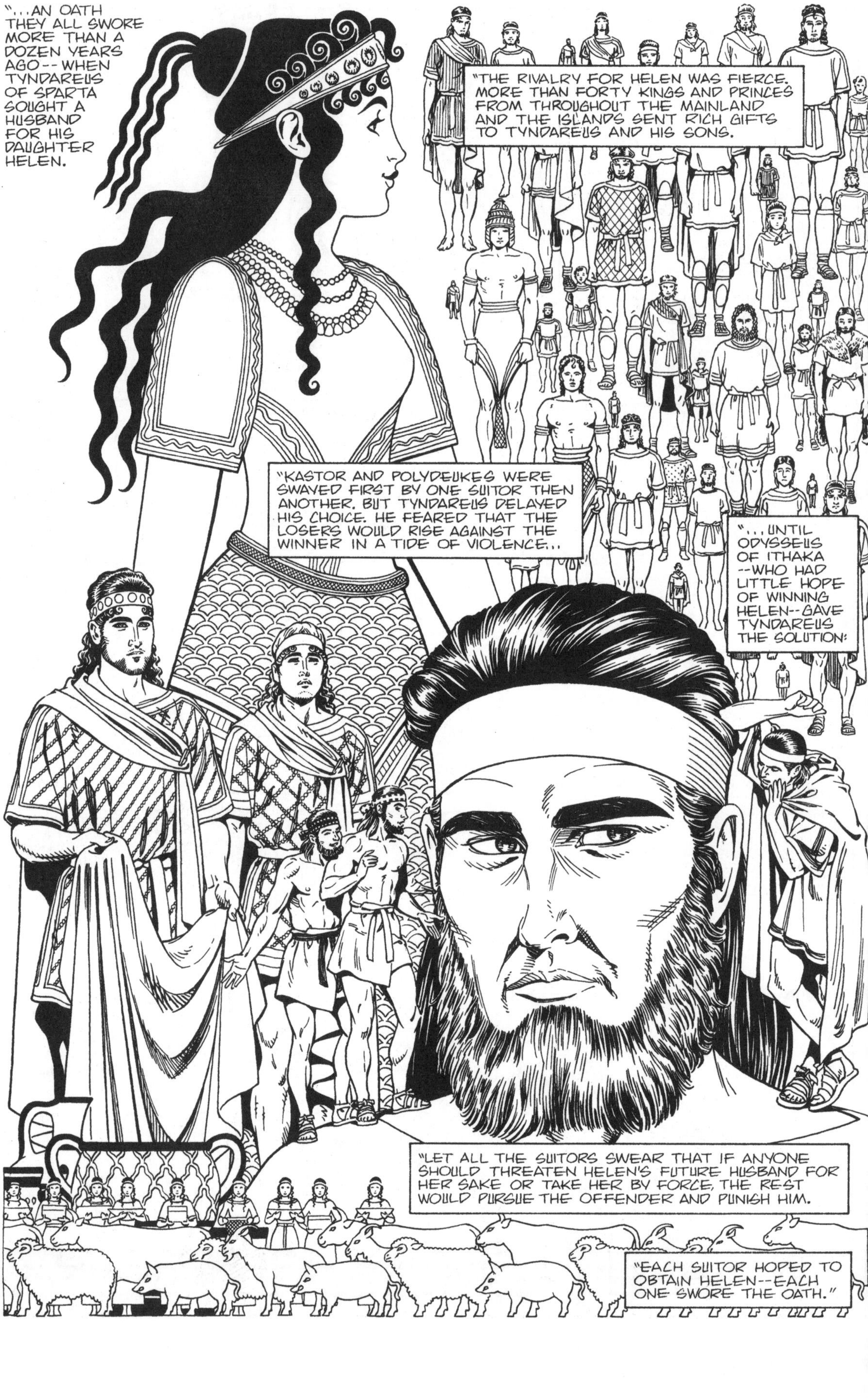
"...AN OATH THEY ALL SWORE MORE THAN A DOZEN YEARS AGO--WHEN TYNDAREUS OF SPARTA SOUGHT A HUSBAND FOR HIS DAUGHTER HELEN.
"THE RIVALRY FOR HELEN WAS FIERCE. MORE THAN FORTY KINGS AND PRINCES FROM THROUGHOUT THE MAINLAND AND THE ISLANDS SENT RICH GIFTS TO TYNDAREUS AND HIS SONS.
"KASTOR AND POLYDEUKES WERE SWAYED FIRST BY ONE SUITOR THEN ANOTHER. BUT TYNDAREUS DELAYED HIS CHOICE. HE FEARED THAT THE LOSERS WOULD RISE AGAINST THE WINNER IN A TIDE OF VIOLENCE...
"...UNTIL ODYSSEUS OF ITHAKA --WHO HAD LITTLE HOPE OF WINNING HELEN--GAVE TYNDAREUS THE SOLUTION:
"LET ALL THE SUITORS SWEAR THAT IF ANYONE SHOULD THREATEN HELEN'S FUTURE HUSBAND FOR HER SAKE OR TAKE HER BY FORCE, THE REST WOULD PURSUE THE OFFENDER AND PUNISH HIM.
"EACH SUITOR HOPED TO OBTAIN HELEN--EACH ONE SWORE THE OATH."

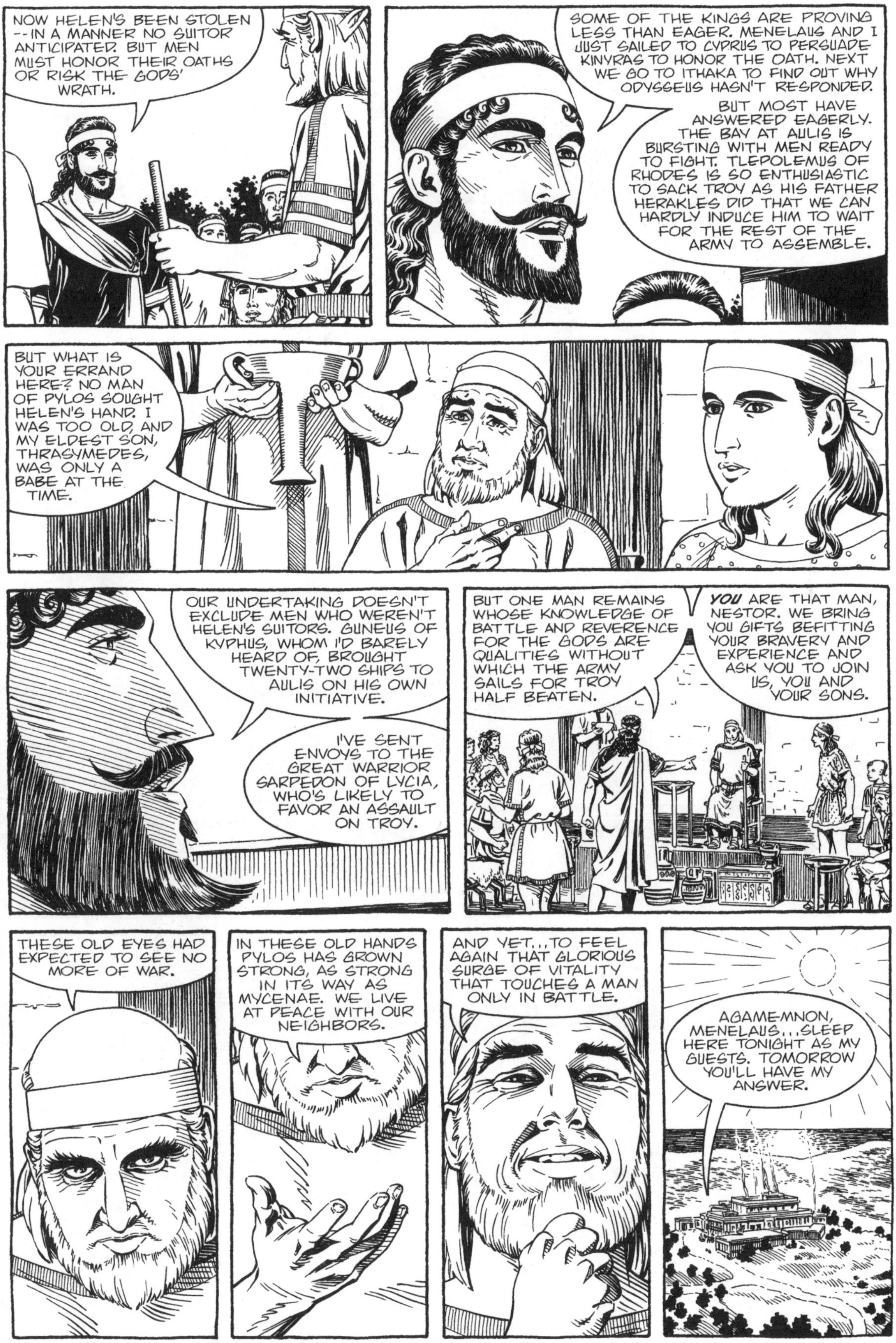
NOW HELEN'S BEEN STOLEN --IN A MANNER NO SUITOR ANTICIPATED. BUT MEN MUST HONOR THEIR OATHS OR RISK THE GODS' WRATH.
SOME OF THE KINGS ARE PROVING LESS THAN EAGER. MENELAUS AND I JUST SAILED TO CYPRUS TO PERSUADE KINYRAS TO HONOR THE OATH. NEXT WE GO TO ITHAKA TO FIND OUT WHY ODYSSEUS HASN'T RESPONDED.
BUT MOST HAVE ANSWERED EAGERLY. THE BAY AT AULIS IS BURSTING WITH MEN READY TO FIGHT. TLEPOLEMUS OF RHODES IS SO ENTHUSIASTIC TO SACK TROY AS HIS FATHER HERAKLES DID THAT WE CAN HARDLY INDUCE HIM TO WAIT FOR THE REST OF THE ARMY TO ASSEMBLE.
BUT WHAT IS YOUR ERRAND HERE? NO MAN OF PYLOS SOUGHT HELEN'S HAND. I WAS TOO OLD, AND MY ELDEST SON, THRASYMEDES, WAS ONLY A BABE AT THE TIME.
OUR UNDERTAKING DOESN'T EXCLUDE MEN WHO WEREN'T HELEN'S SUITORS. GUNEUS OF KYPHUS, WHOM I'D BARELY HEARD OF, BROUGHT TWENTY-TWO SHIPS TO AULIS ON HIS OWN INITIATIVE.
I'VE SENT ENVOYS TO THE GREAT WARRIOR SARPEDON OF LYCIA, WHO'S LIKELY TO FAVOR AN ASSAULT ON TROY.
BUT ONE MAN REMAINS WHOSE KNOWLEDGE OF BATTLE AND REVERENCE FOR THE GODS ARE QUALITIES WITHOUT WHICH THE ARMY SAILS FOR TROY HALF BEATEN.
YOU ARE THAT MAN, NESTOR. WE BRING YOU GIFTS BEFITTING YOUR BRAVERY AND EXPERIENCE AND ASK YOU TO JOIN US, YOU AND YOUR SONS.
THESE OLD EYES HAD EXPECTED TO SEE NO MORE OF WAR.
IN THESE OLD HANDS PYLOS HAS GROWN STRONG, AS STRONG IN ITS WAY AS MYCENAE. WE LIVE AT PEACE WITH OUR NEIGHBORS.
AND YET... TO FEEL AGAIN THAT GLORIOUS SURGE OF VITALITY THAT TOUCHES A MAN ONLY IN BATTLE.
AGAMEMNON, MENELAUS... SLEEP HERE TONIGHT AS MY GUESTS. TOMORROW YOU'LL HAVE MY ANSWER.

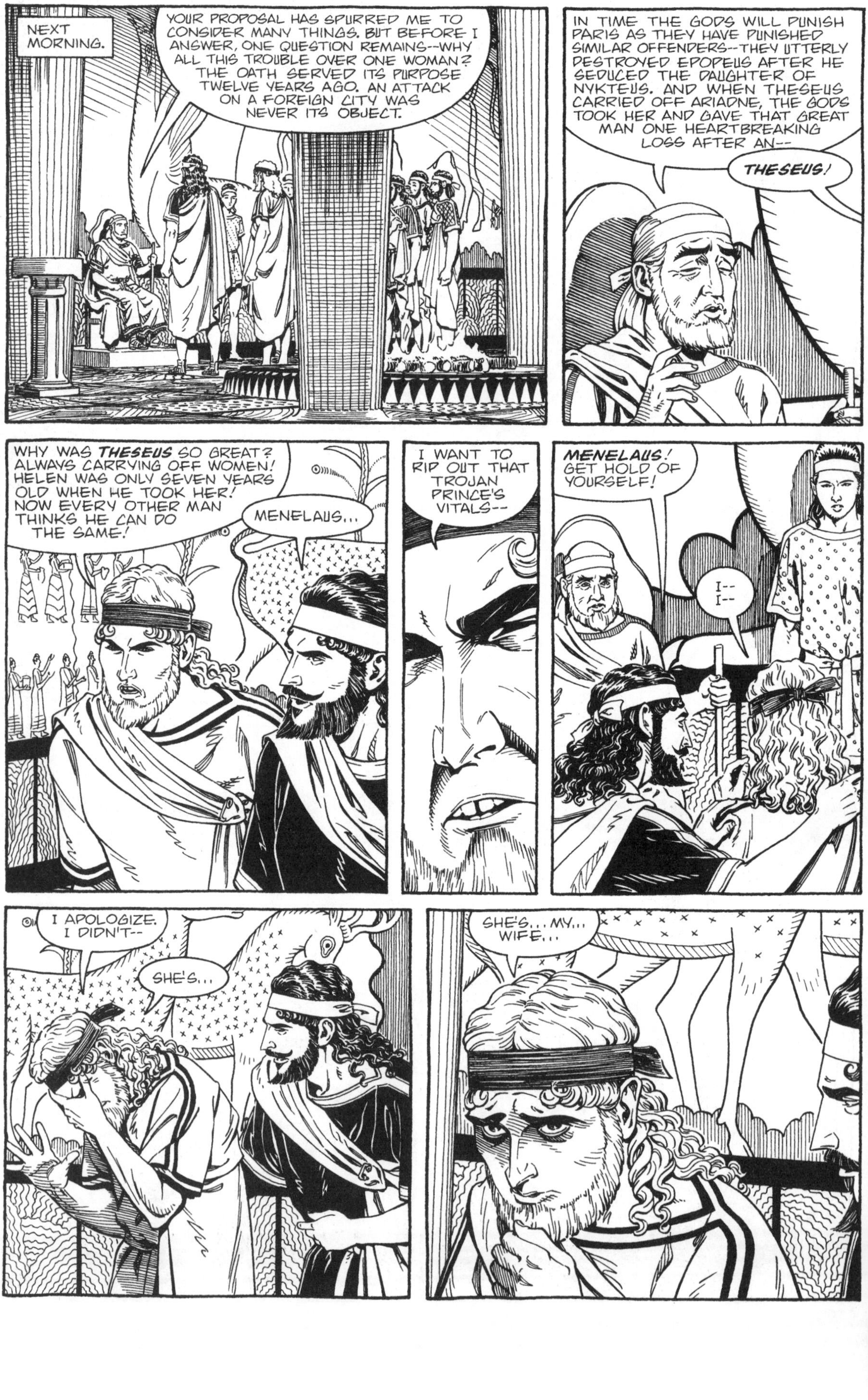
NEXT MORNING.
YOUR PROPOSAL HAS SPURRED ME TO CONSIDER MANY THINGS. BUT BEFORE I ANSWER, ONE QUESTION REMAINS--WHY ALL THIS TROUBLE OVER ONE WOMAN? THE OATH SERVED ITS PURPOSE TWELVE YEARS AGO. AN ATTACK ON A FOREIGN CITY WAS NEVER ITS OBJECT.
IN TIME THE GODS WILL PUNISH PARIS AS THEY HAVE PUNISHED SIMILAR OFFENDERS--THEY UTTERLY DESTROYED EPOPEUS AFTER HE SEDUCED THE DAUGHTER OF NYKTEUS. AND WHEN THESEUS CARRIED OFF ARIADNE, THE GODS TOOK HER AND GAVE THAT GREAT MAN ONE HEARTBREAKING LOSS AFTER AN--
THESEUS!
WHY WAS THESEUS SO GREAT? ALWAYS CARRYING OFF WOMEN! HELEN WAS ONLY SEVEN YEARS OLD WHEN HE TOOK HER! NOW EVERY OTHER MAN THINKS HE CAN DO THE SAME!
MENELAUS...
I WANT TO RIP OUT THAT TROJAN PRINCE'S VITALS--
MENELAUS! GET HOLD OF YOURSELF!
I-- I--
I APOLOGIZE. I DIDN'T--
SHE'S...
SHE'S... MY... WIFE...

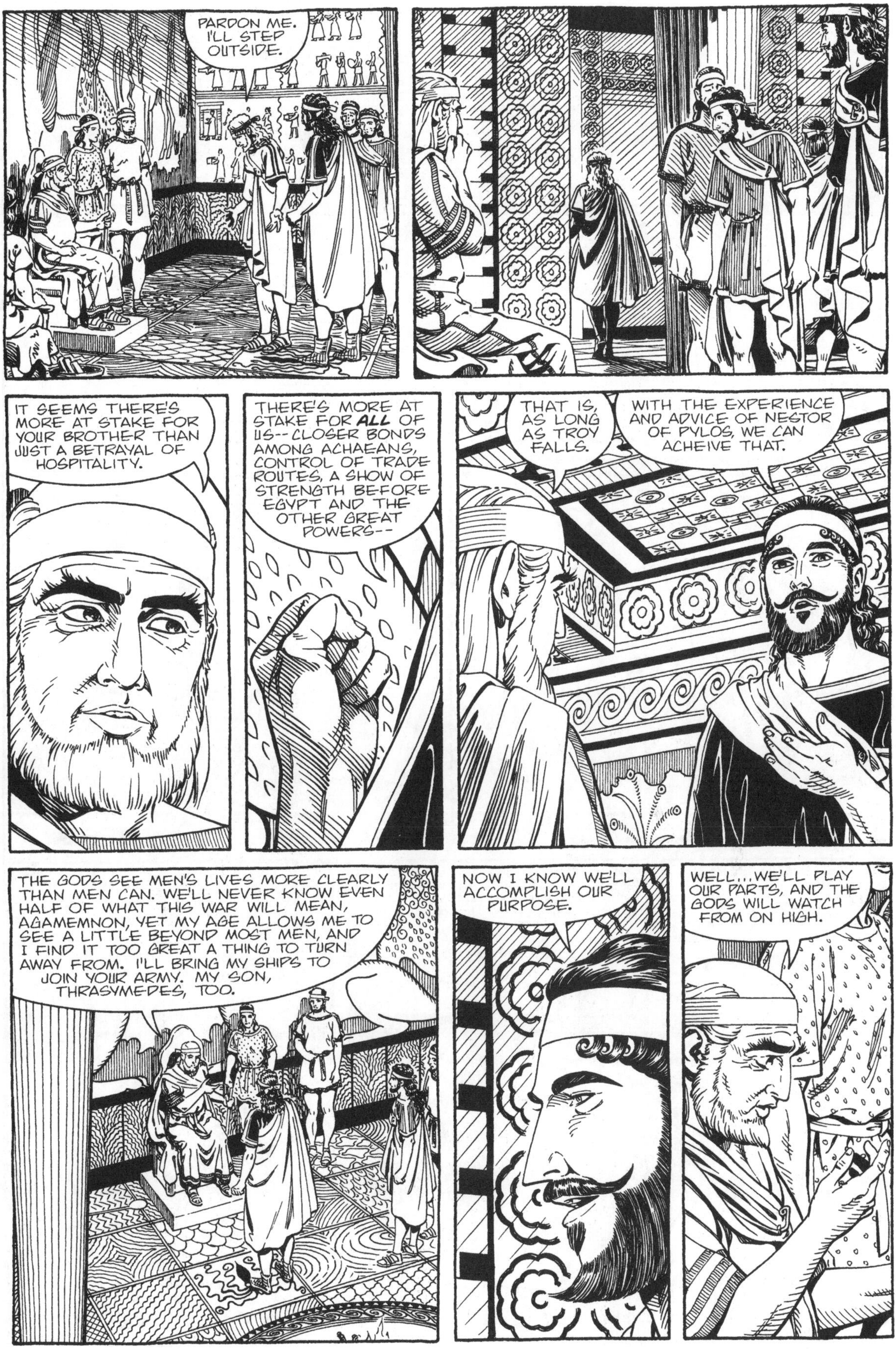
PARDON ME. I'LL STEP OUTSIDE.
IT SEEMS THERE'S MORE AT STAKE FOR YOUR BROTHER THAN JUST A BETRAYAL OF HOSPITALITY.
THERE'S MORE AT STAKE FOR ALL OF US--CLOSER BONDS AMONG ACHAEANS, CONTROL OF TRADE ROUTES, A SHOW OF STRENGTH BEFORE EGYPT AND THE OTHER GREAT POWERS--
WITH THE EXPERIENCE AND ADVICE OF NESTOR OF PYLOS, WE CAN ACHEIVE THAT.
THAT IS, AS LONG AS TROY FALLS.
THE GODS SEE MEN'S LIVES MORE CLEARLY THAN MEN CAN. WE'LL NEVER KNOW EVEN HALF OF WHAT THIS WAR WILL MEAN, AGAMEMNON, YET MY AGE ALLOWS ME TO SEE A LITTLE BEYOND MOST MEN, AND I FIND IT TOO GREAT A THING TO TURN AWAY FROM. I'LL BRING MY SHIPS TO JOIN YOUR ARMY. MY SON, THRASYMEDES, TOO.
NOW I KNOW WE'LL ACCOMPLISH OUR PURPOSE.
WELL...WE'LL PLAY OUR PARTS, AND THE GODS WILL WATCH FROM ON HIGH.

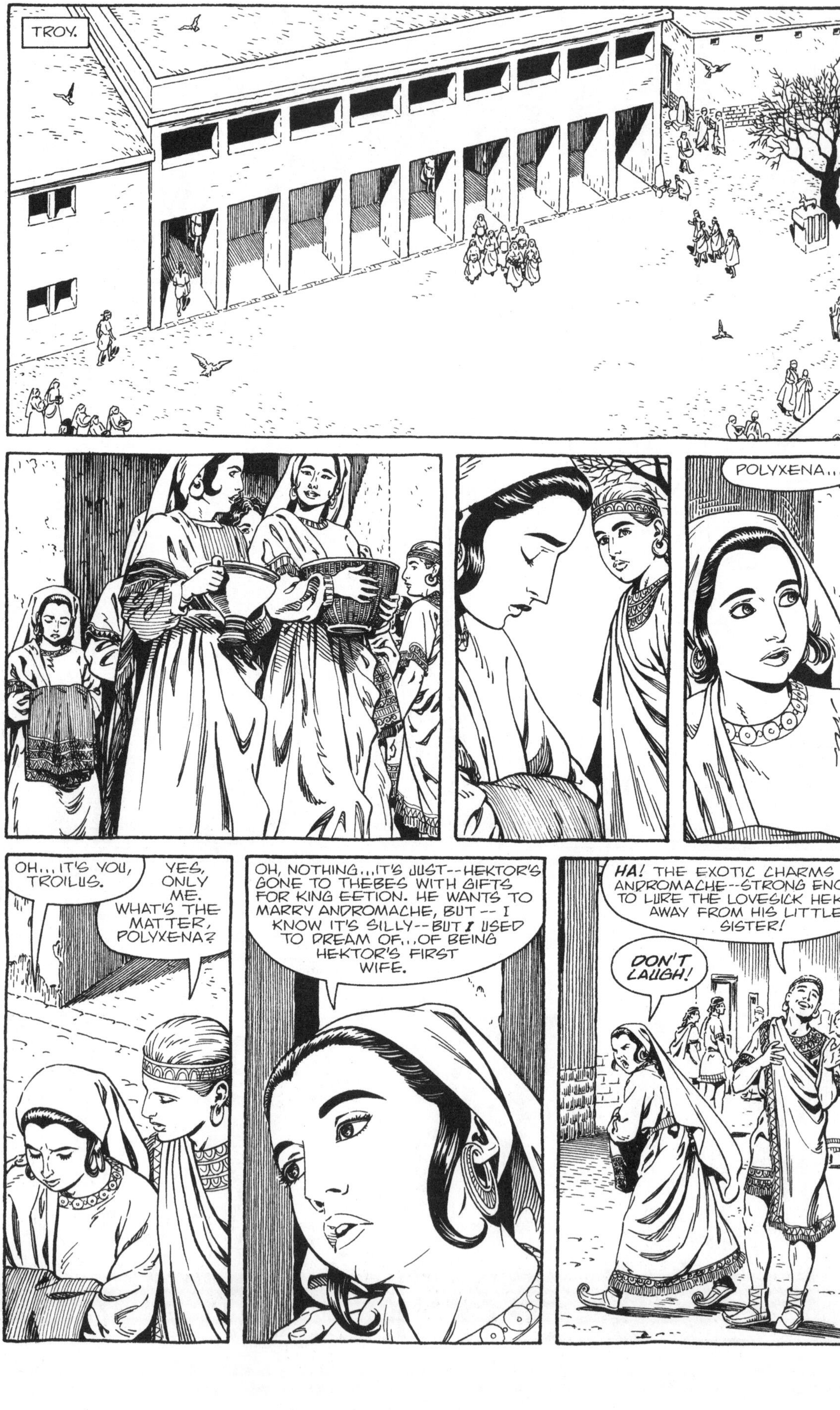
TROY.
POLYXENA...
OH... IT'S YOU, TROILUS.
YES, ONLY ME. WHAT'S THE MATTER, POLYXENA?
OH, NOTHING... IT'S JUST--HEKTOR'S GONE TO THEBES WITH GIFTS FOR KING EETION. HE WANTS TO MARRY ANDROMACHE, BUT -- I KNOW IT'S SILLY--BUT I USED TO DREAM OF... OF BEING HEKTOR'S FIRST WIFE.
HA! THE EXOTIC CHARMS OF ANDROMACHE--STRONG ENOUGH TO LURE THE LOVESICK HEKTOR AWAY FROM HIS LITTLE SISTER!
DON'T LAUGH!

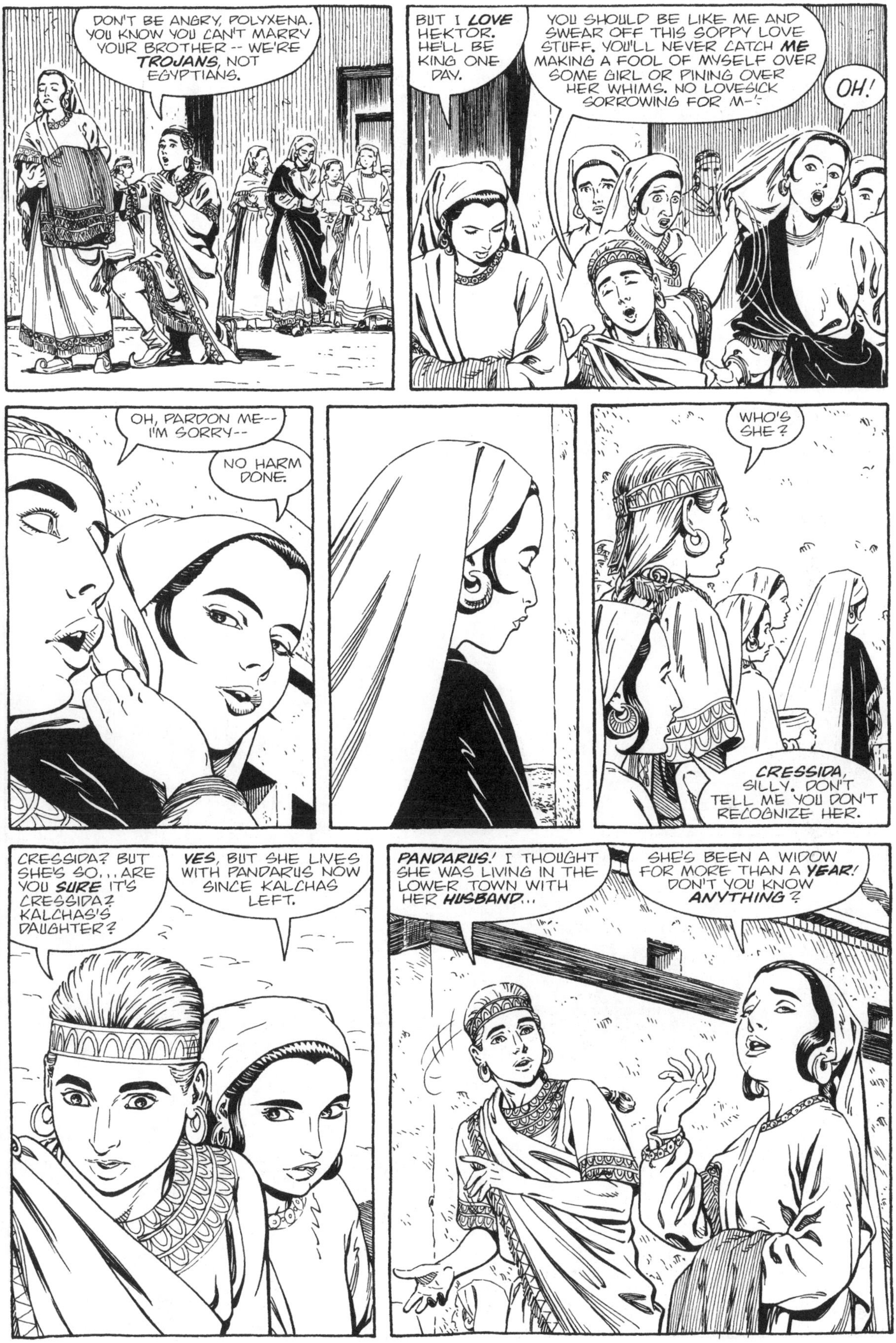

DON'T BE ANGRY, POLYXENA. YOU KNOW YOU CAN'T MARRY YOUR BROTHER -- WE'RE TROJANS, NOT EGYPTIANS.
BUT I LOVE HEKTOR. HE'LL BE KING ONE DAY.
YOU SHOULD BE LIKE ME AND SWEAR OFF THIS SOPPY LOVE STUFF. YOU'LL NEVER CATCH ME MAKING A FOOL OF MYSELF OVER SOME GIRL OR PINING OVER HER WHIMS. NO LOVESICK SORROWING FOR M-
OH!
OH, PARDON ME-- I'M SORRY--
NO HARM DONE.
WHO'S SHE?
CRESSIDA, SILLY. DON'T TELL ME YOU DON'T RECOGNIZE HER.
CRESSIDA? BUT SHE'S SO... ARE YOU SURE IT'S CRESSIDA? KALCHAS'S DAUGHTER?
YES, BUT SHE LIVES WITH PANDARUS NOW SINCE KALCHAS LEFT.
PANDARUS! I THOUGHT SHE WAS LIVING IN THE LOWER TOWN WITH HER HUSBAND...
SHE'S BEEN A WIDOW FOR MORE THAN A YEAR! DON'T YOU KNOW ANYTHING?

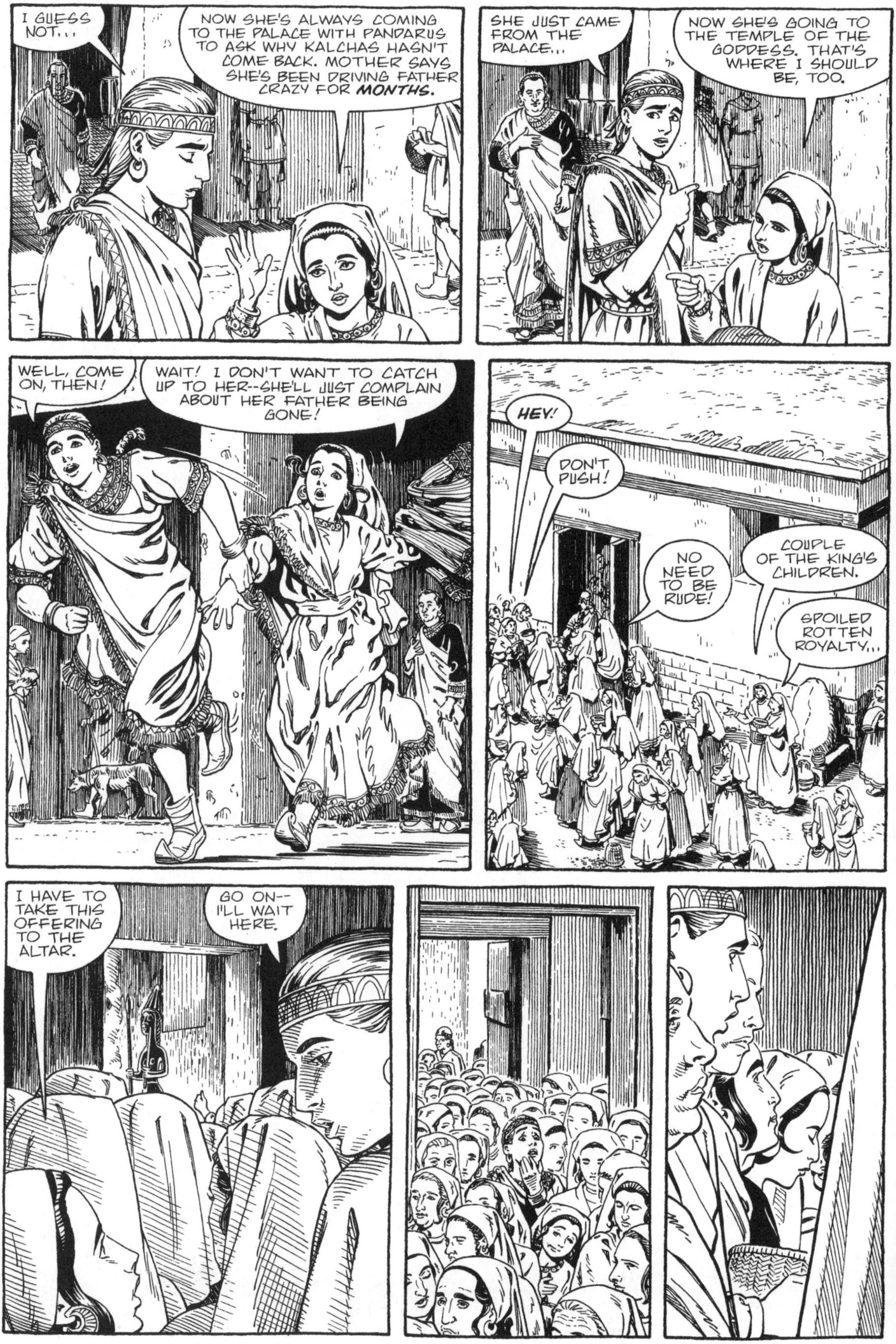
I GUESS NOT...
NOW SHE'S ALWAYS COMING TO THE PALACE WITH PANDARUS TO ASK WHY KALCHAS HASN'T COME BACK. MOTHER SAYS SHE'S BEEN DRIVING FATHER CRAZY FOR MONTHS.
SHE JUST CAME FROM THE PALACE...
NOW SHE'S GOING TO THE TEMPLE OF THE GODDESS. THAT'S WHERE I SHOULD BE, TOO.
WELL, COME ON, THEN!
WAIT! I DON'T WANT TO CATCH UP TO HER--SHE'LL JUST COMPLAIN ABOUT HER FATHER BEING GONE!
HEY!
DON'T PUSH!
NO NEED TO BE RUDE!
COUPLE OF THE KING'S CHILDREN.
SPOILED ROTTEN ROYALTY...
I HAVE TO TAKE THIS OFFERING TO THE ALTAR.
GO ON--I'LL WAIT HERE.

I HAD NO IDEA THE WOMEN'S RITUALS HELD SUCH INTEREST FOR YOU, SON OF PRIAM.

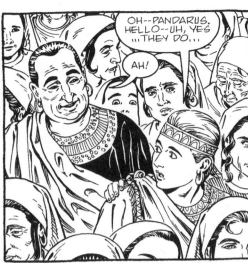
OH--PANDARUS. HELLO--UH, YES ...THEY DO...

AH!

OR COULD IT BE--JUST BY CHANCE--THAT ONE OF THESE LOVELY LADIES DRAWS YOU HERE? MY NEICE CRESSIDA, PERHAPS?

UH--NO --I...

WELL, YES.

DELIGHTED TO HEAR IT. LATELY, CRESSIDA'S HAD HER SHARE OF PRIVATE ADVERSITY--HER HUSBAND GONE, HER FATHER MISSING. NOW WITH PRIAM'S FEARS OF WAR WITH THE ACHAEANS--

WHAT?!

COME NOW, TROILUS, IT'S NO GREAT SECRET. NOW AS I WAS SAYING, WITH SUCH TROUBLE LOOMING OVER US ALL, MY NEICE MAY SOON NEED A TRUE FRIEND TO TURN TO, SOMEONE TO COMFORT HER AND PROTECT HER.

SOMEONE FULL OF YOUTH AND VIGOR... SOMEONE LIKE... YOU, PERHAPS? HMM?

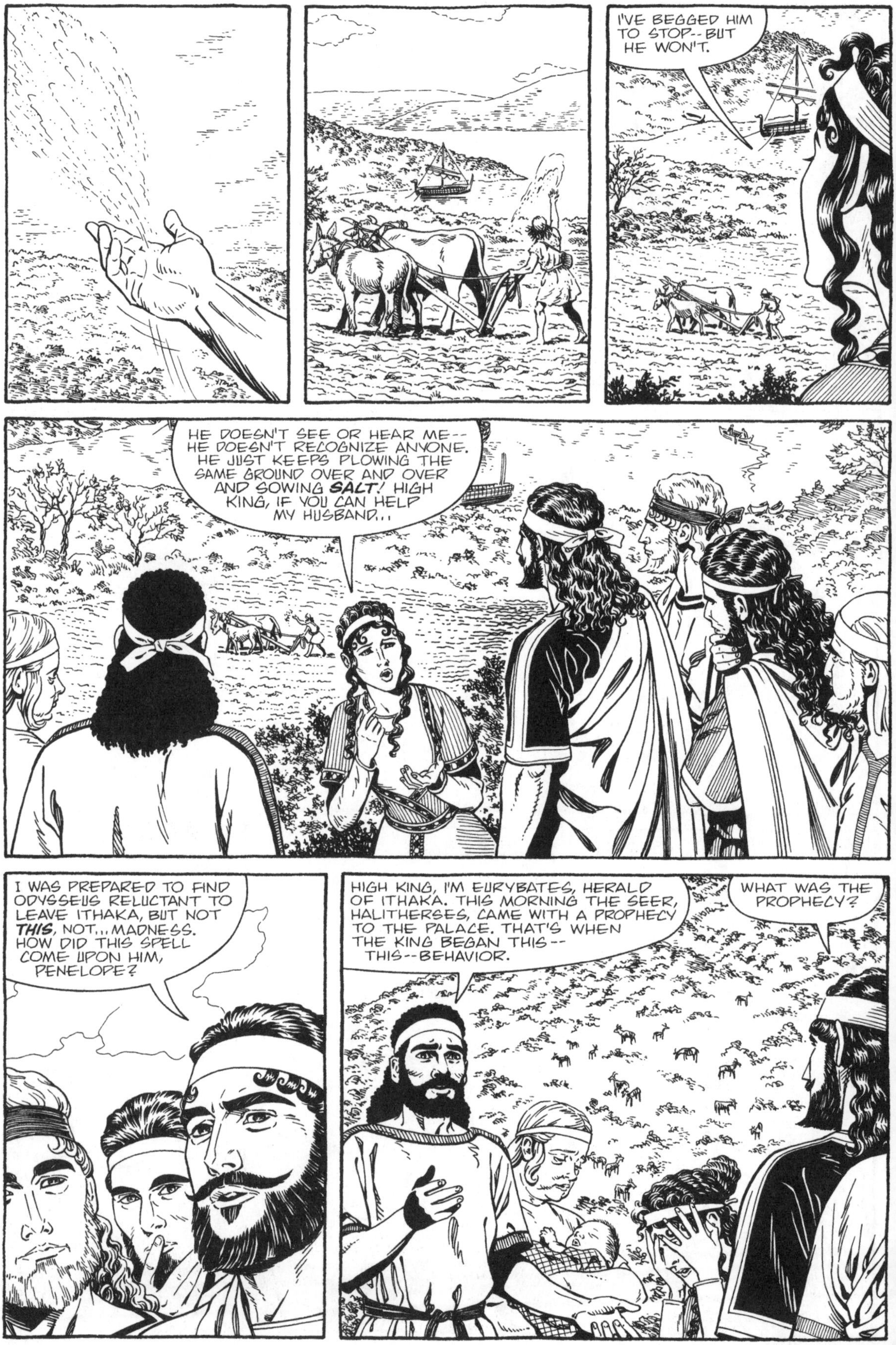
I'VE BEGGED HIM TO STOP-- BUT HE WON'T.
HE DOESN'T SEE OR HEAR ME-- HE DOESN'T RECOGNIZE ANYONE. HE JUST KEEPS PLOWING THE SAME GROUND OVER AND OVER AND SOWING **SALT**! HIGH KING, IF YOU CAN HELP MY HUSBAND...
I WAS PREPARED TO FIND ODYSSEUS RELUCTANT TO LEAVE ITHAKA, BUT NOT **THIS**, NOT... MADNESS. HOW DID THIS SPELL COME UPON HIM, PENELOPE?
HIGH KING, I'M EURYBATES, HERALD OF ITHAKA. THIS MORNING THE SEER, HALITHERSES, CAME WITH A PROPHECY TO THE PALACE. THAT'S WHEN THE KING BEGAN THIS-- THIS--BEHAVIOR.
WHAT WAS THE PROPHECY?

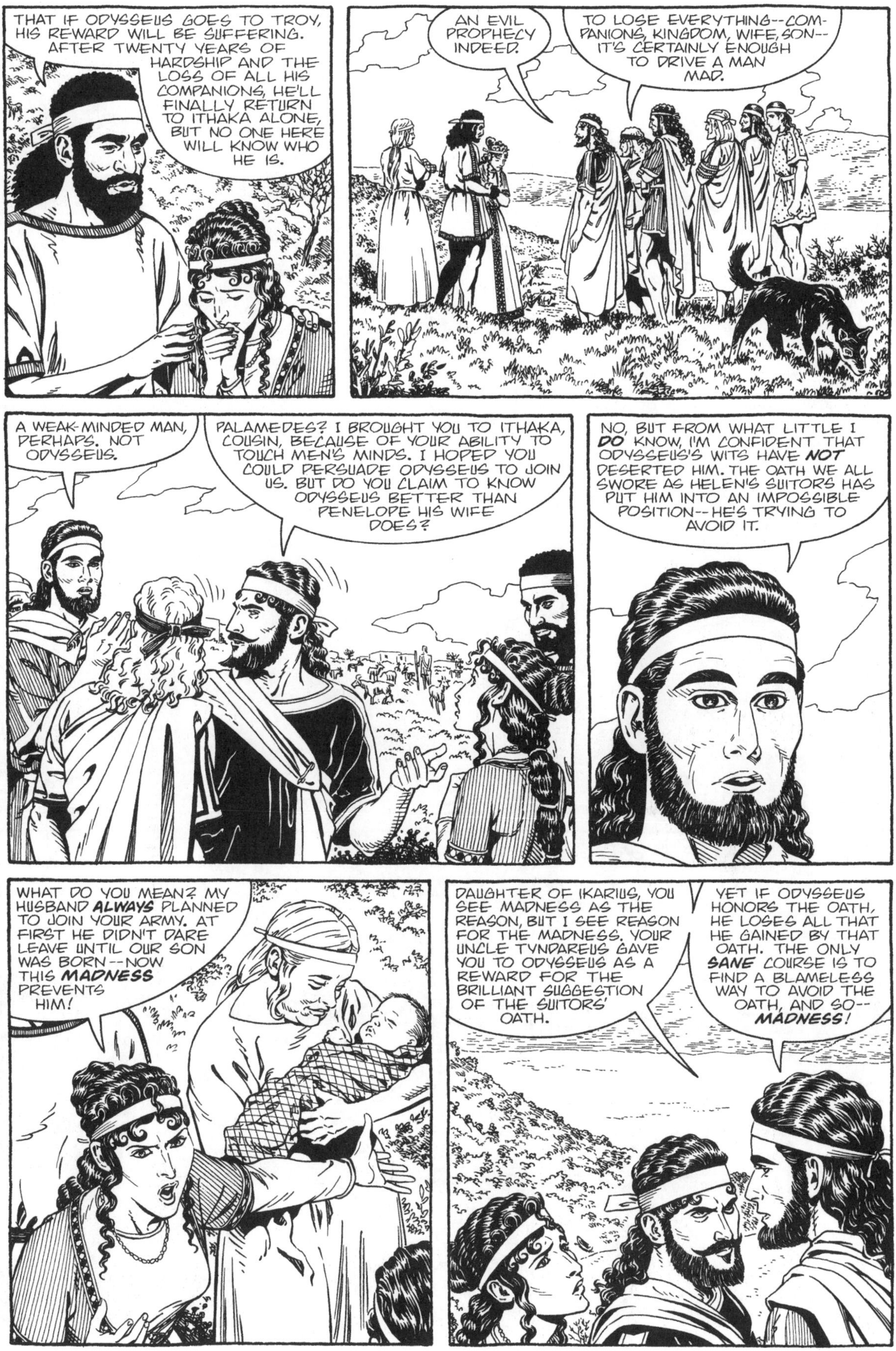
THAT IF ODYSSEUS GOES TO TROY, HIS REWARD WILL BE SUFFERING. AFTER TWENTY YEARS OF HARDSHIP AND THE LOSS OF ALL HIS COMPANIONS, HE'LL FINALLY RETURN TO ITHAKA ALONE, BUT NO ONE HERE WILL KNOW WHO HE IS.
AN EVIL PROPHECY INDEED.
TO LOSE EVERYTHING--COMPANIONS, KINGDOM, WIFE, SON--IT'S CERTAINLY ENOUGH TO DRIVE A MAN MAD.
A WEAK-MINDED MAN, PERHAPS. NOT ODYSSEUS.
PALAMEDES? I BROUGHT YOU TO ITHAKA, COUSIN, BECAUSE OF YOUR ABILITY TO TOUCH MEN'S MINDS. I HOPED YOU COULD PERSUADE ODYSSEUS TO JOIN US. BUT DO YOU CLAIM TO KNOW ODYSSEUS BETTER THAN PENELOPE HIS WIFE DOES?
NO, BUT FROM WHAT LITTLE I **DO** KNOW, I'M CONFIDENT THAT ODYSSEUS'S WITS HAVE **NOT** DESERTED HIM. THE OATH WE ALL SWORE AS HELEN'S SUITORS HAS PUT HIM INTO AN IMPOSSIBLE POSITION--HE'S TRYING TO AVOID IT.
WHAT DO YOU MEAN? MY HUSBAND **ALWAYS** PLANNED TO JOIN YOUR ARMY. AT FIRST HE DIDN'T DARE LEAVE UNTIL OUR SON WAS BORN--NOW THIS **MADNESS** PREVENTS HIM!
DAUGHTER OF IKARIUS, YOU SEE MADNESS AS THE REASON, BUT I SEE REASON FOR THE MADNESS. YOUR UNCLE TYNDAREUS GAVE YOU TO ODYSSEUS AS A REWARD FOR THE BRILLIANT SUGGESTION OF THE SUITORS' OATH.
YET IF ODYSSEUS HONORS THE OATH, HE LOSES ALL THAT HE GAINED BY THAT OATH. THE ONLY **SANE** COURSE IS TO FIND A BLAMELESS WAY TO AVOID THE OATH, AND SO--**MADNESS**!

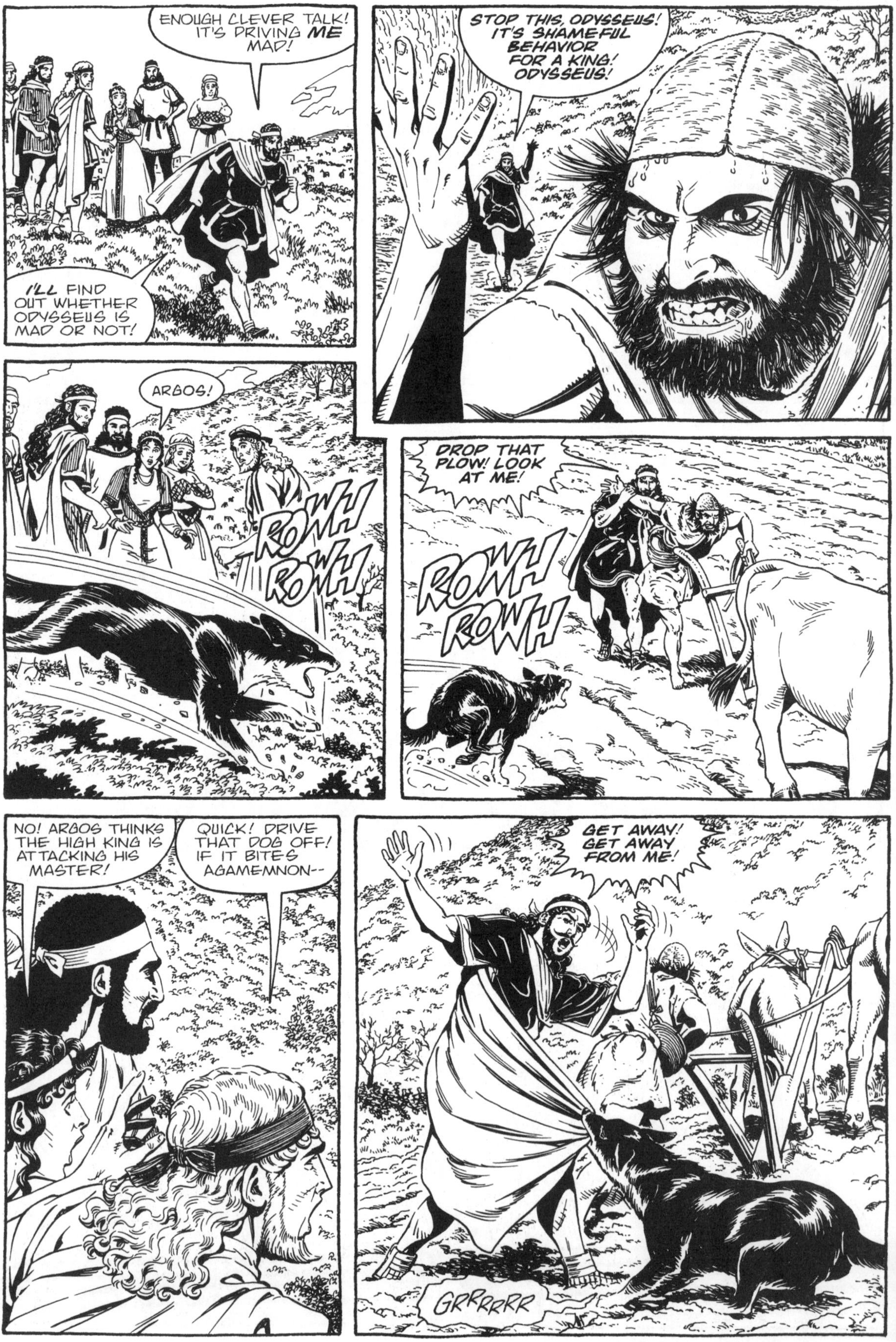
ENOUGH CLEVER TALK! IT'S DRIVING ME MAD!
I'LL FIND OUT WHETHER ODYSSEUS IS MAD OR NOT!
STOP THIS, ODYSSEUS! IT'S SHAMEFUL BEHAVIOR FOR A KING! ODYSSEUS!
ARGOS!
ROWH ROWH ROWH
DROP THAT PLOW! LOOK AT ME!
ROWH ROWH
NO! ARGOS THINKS THE HIGH KING IS ATTACKING HIS MASTER!
QUICK! DRIVE THAT DOG OFF! IF IT BITES AGAMEMNON--
GET AWAY! GET AWAY FROM ME!
GRRRRRR

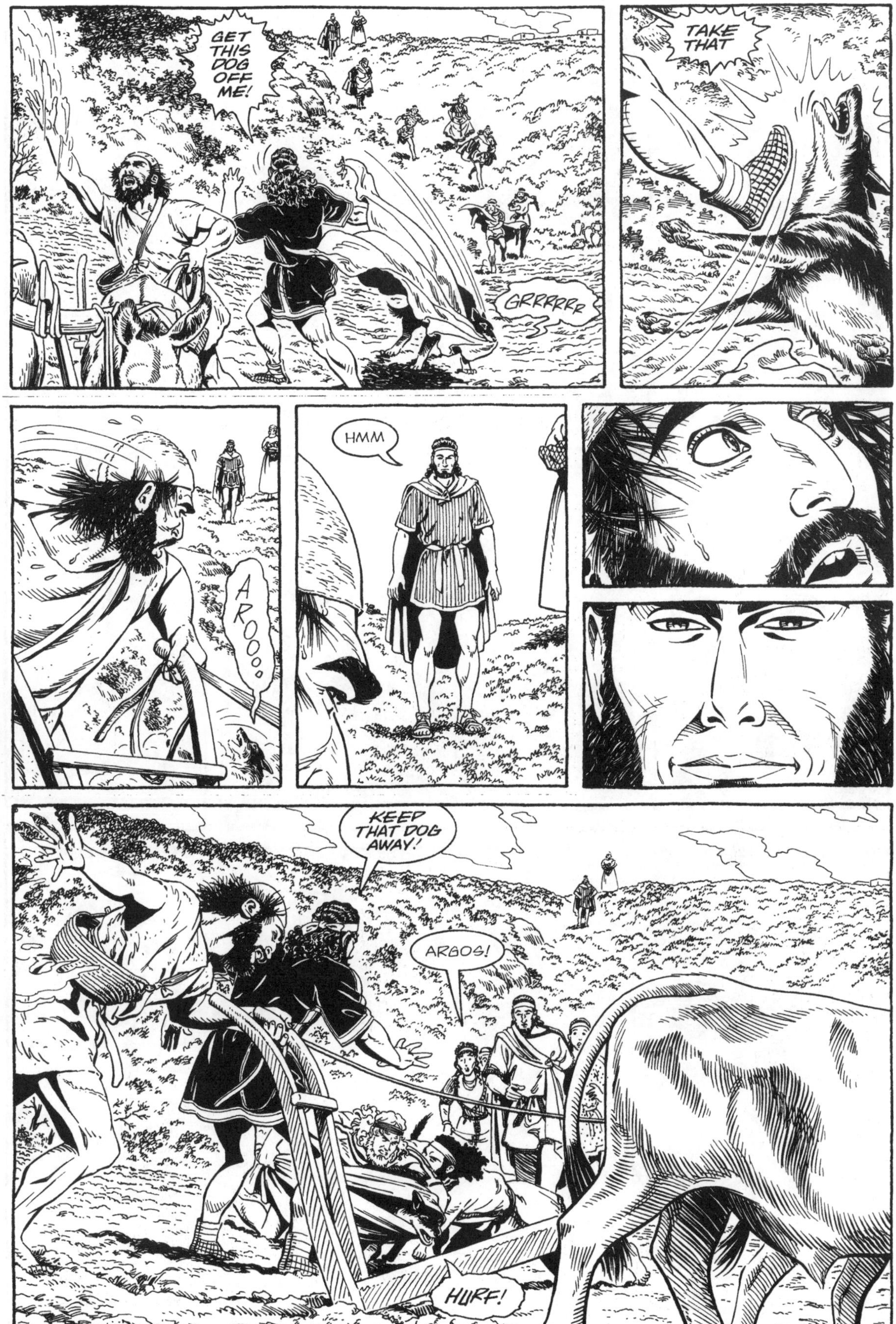
GET THIS DOG OFF ME!
GRRRRRR
TAKE THAT
AROOoo
HMM
KEEP THAT DOG AWAY!
ARGOS!
HURF!

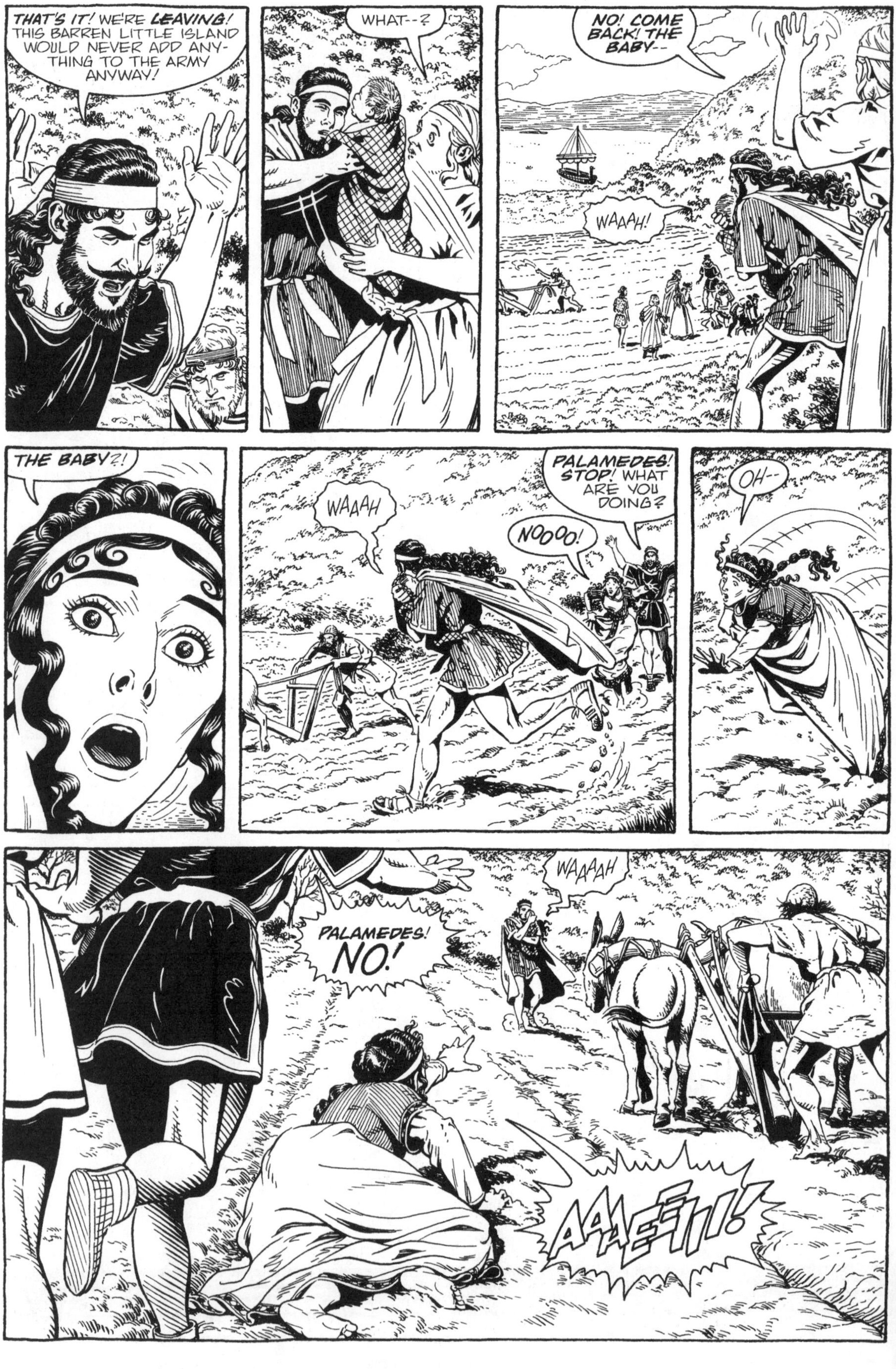
THAT'S IT! WE'RE LEAVING! THIS BARREN LITTLE ISLAND WOULD NEVER ADD ANYTHING TO THE ARMY ANYWAY!
WHAT--?
NO! COME BACK! THE BABY--
WAAAH!
THE BABY?!
WAAAH
PALAMEDES! STOP! WHAT ARE YOU DOING?
NOOOO!
OH--
WAAAAH
PALAMEDES! NO!
AAAEEIII!

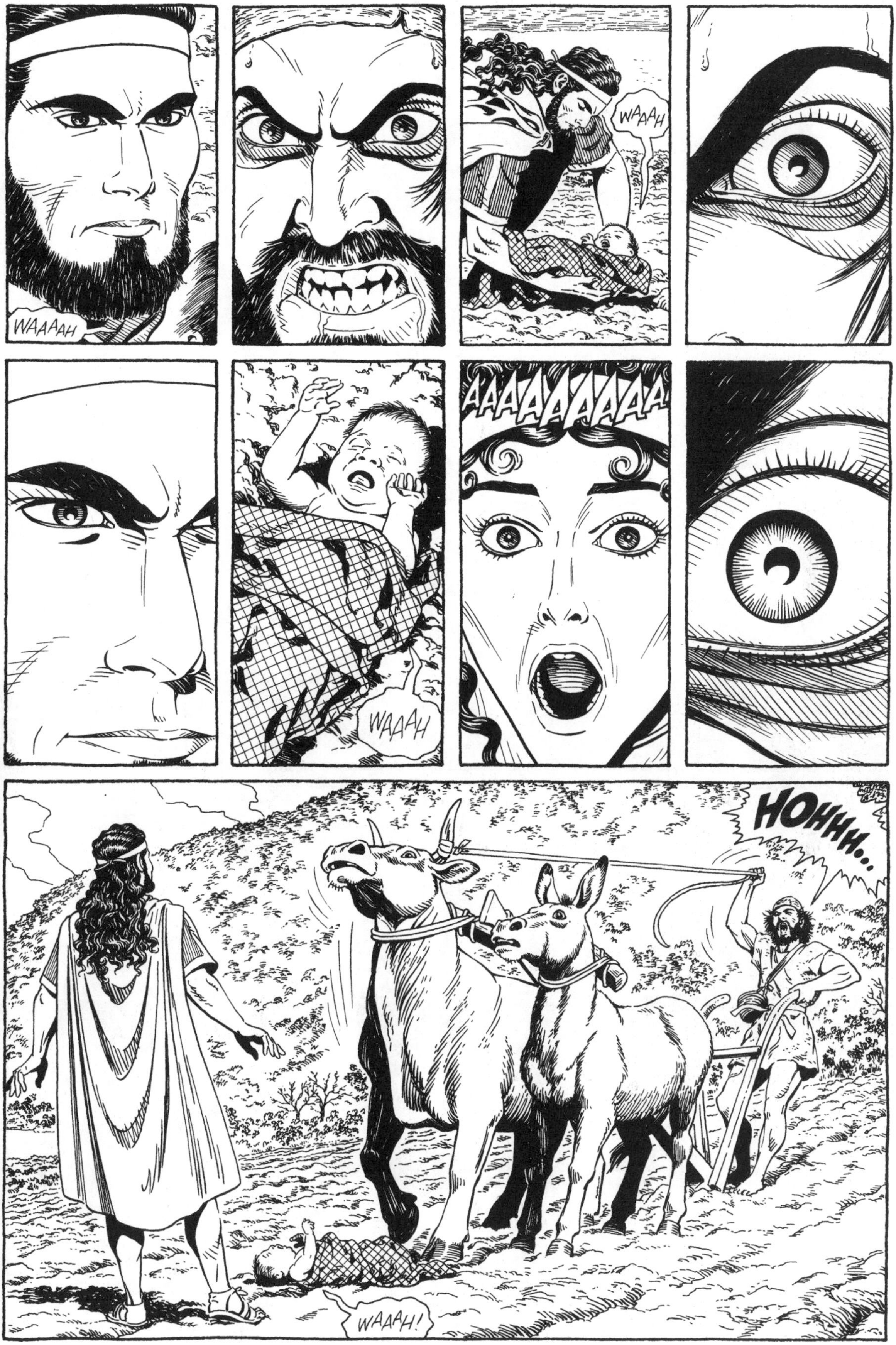
WAAAAH
WAAAH
AAAAAAAAAA
WAAAH
HOHHH...
WAAAH!

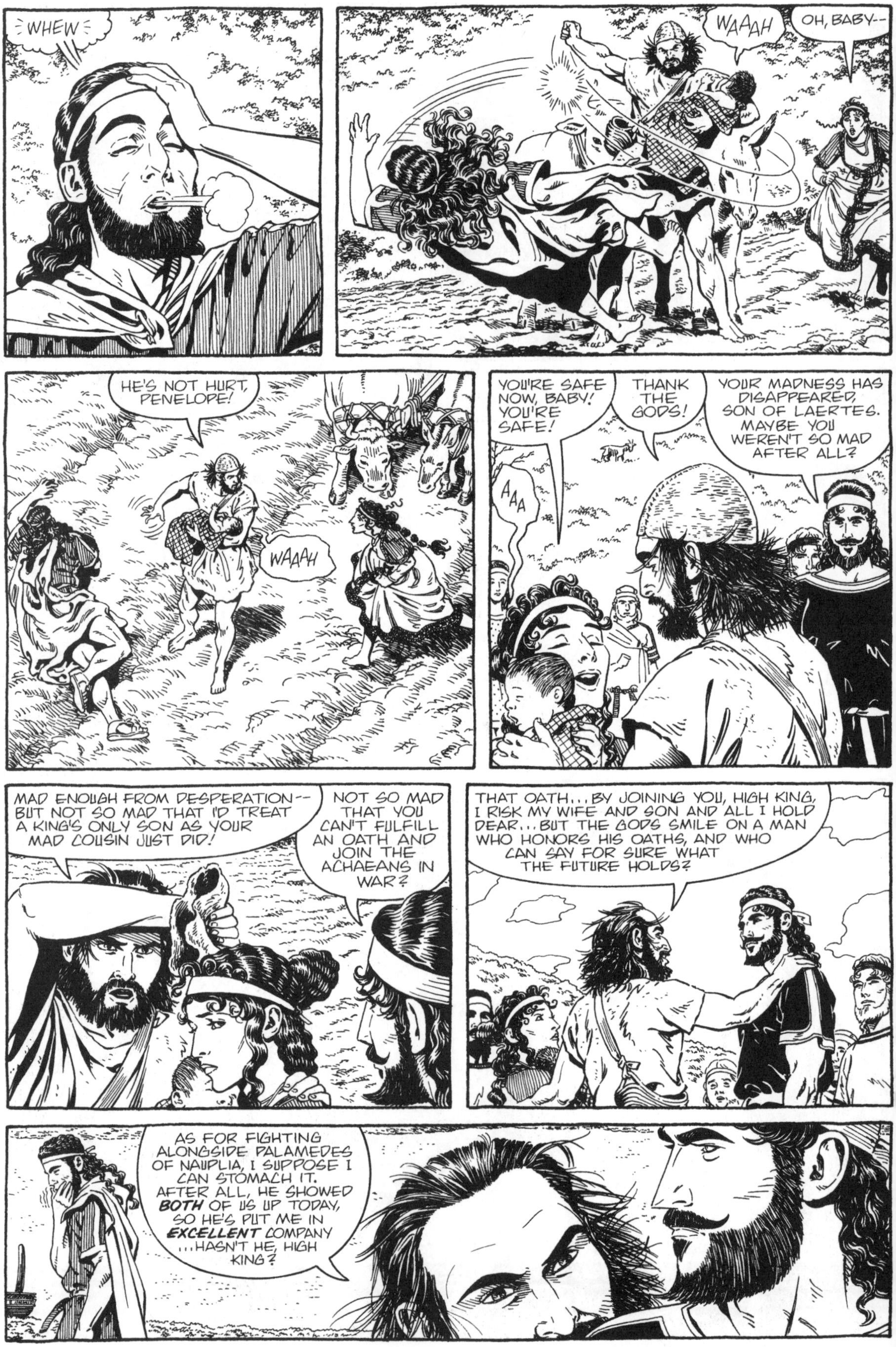
WHEW
WAAAH
OH, BABY--
HE'S NOT HURT, PENELOPE!
WAAAH
YOU'RE SAFE NOW, BABY! YOU'RE SAFE!
AAA
THANK THE GODS!
YOUR MADNESS HAS DISAPPEARED, SON OF LAERTES. MAYBE YOU WEREN'T SO MAD AFTER ALL?
MAD ENOUGH FROM DESPERATION-- BUT NOT SO MAD THAT I'D TREAT A KING'S ONLY SON AS YOUR MAD COUSIN JUST DID!
NOT SO MAD THAT YOU CAN'T FULFILL AN OATH AND JOIN THE ACHAEANS IN WAR?
THAT OATH... BY JOINING YOU, HIGH KING, I RISK MY WIFE AND SON AND ALL I HOLD DEAR... BUT THE GODS SMILE ON A MAN WHO HONORS HIS OATHS, AND WHO CAN SAY FOR SURE WHAT THE FUTURE HOLDS?
AS FOR FIGHTING ALONGSIDE PALAMEDES OF NAUPLIA, I SUPPOSE I CAN STOMACH IT. AFTER ALL, HE SHOWED BOTH OF US UP TODAY, SO HE'S PUT ME IN EXCELLENT COMPANY ...HASN'T HE, HIGH KING?

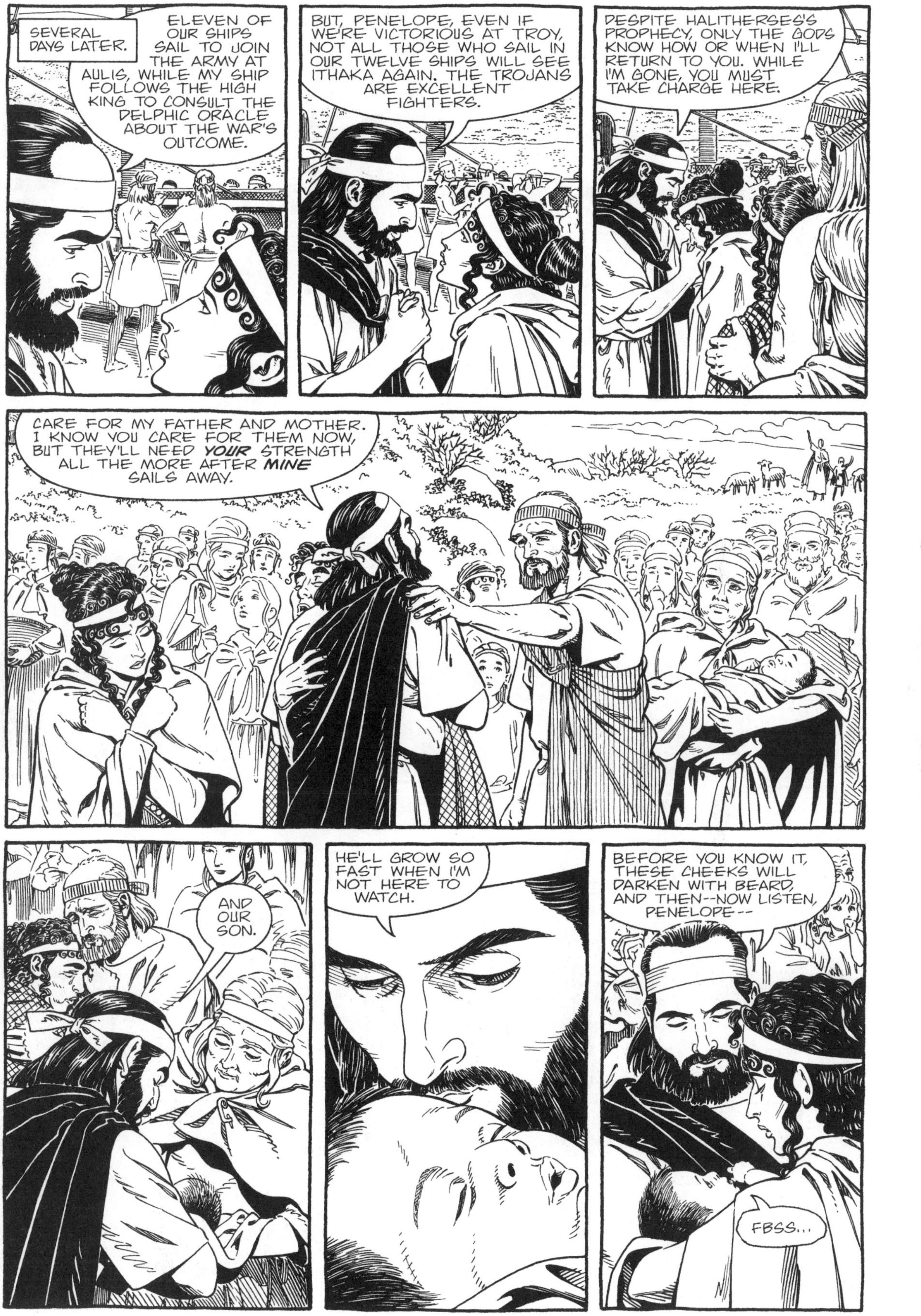
SEVERAL DAYS LATER.
ELEVEN OF OUR SHIPS SAIL TO JOIN THE ARMY AT AULIS, WHILE MY SHIP FOLLOWS THE HIGH KING TO CONSULT THE DELPHIC ORACLE ABOUT THE WAR'S OUTCOME.
BUT, PENELOPE, EVEN IF WE'RE VICTORIOUS AT TROY, NOT ALL THOSE WHO SAIL IN OUR TWELVE SHIPS WILL SEE ITHAKA AGAIN. THE TROJANS ARE EXCELLENT FIGHTERS.
DESPITE HALITHERSES'S PROPHECY, ONLY THE GODS KNOW HOW OR WHEN I'LL RETURN TO YOU. WHILE I'M GONE, YOU MUST TAKE CHARGE HERE.
CARE FOR MY FATHER AND MOTHER. I KNOW YOU CARE FOR THEM NOW, BUT THEY'LL NEED ***YOUR*** STRENGTH ALL THE MORE AFTER ***MINE*** SAILS AWAY.
AND OUR SON.
HE'LL GROW SO FAST WHEN I'M NOT HERE TO WATCH.
BEFORE YOU KNOW IT, THESE CHEEKS WILL DARKEN WITH BEARD, AND THEN--NOW LISTEN, PENELOPE--
FBSS...

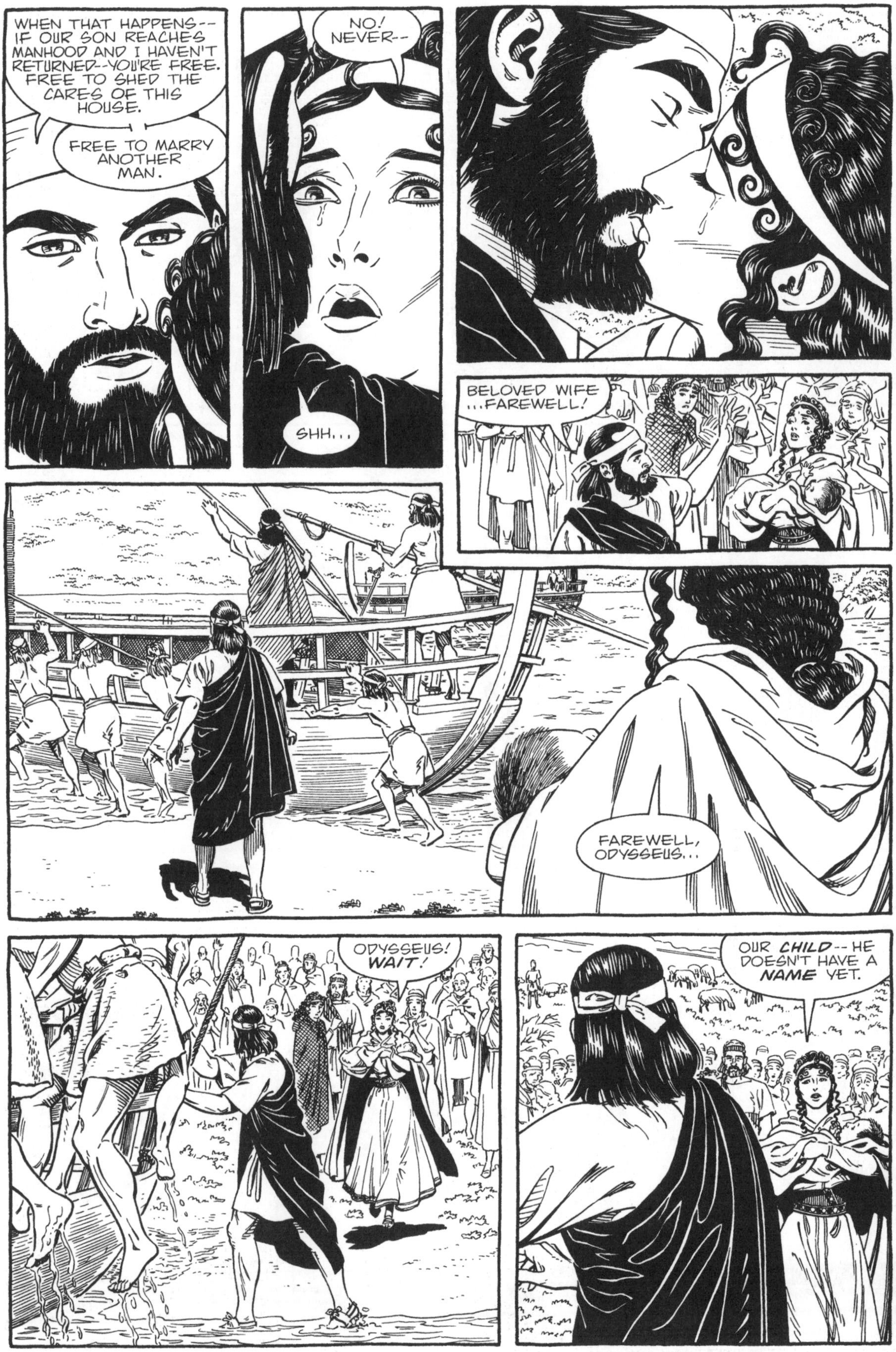
WHEN THAT HAPPENS--IF OUR SON REACHES MANHOOD AND I HAVEN'T RETURNED--YOU'RE FREE. FREE TO SHED THE CARES OF THIS HOUSE.
FREE TO MARRY ANOTHER MAN.
NO! NEVER--
SHH...
BELOVED WIFE ...FAREWELL!
FAREWELL, ODYSSEUS...
ODYSSEUS! WAIT!
OUR CHILD--HE DOESN'T HAVE A NAME YET.

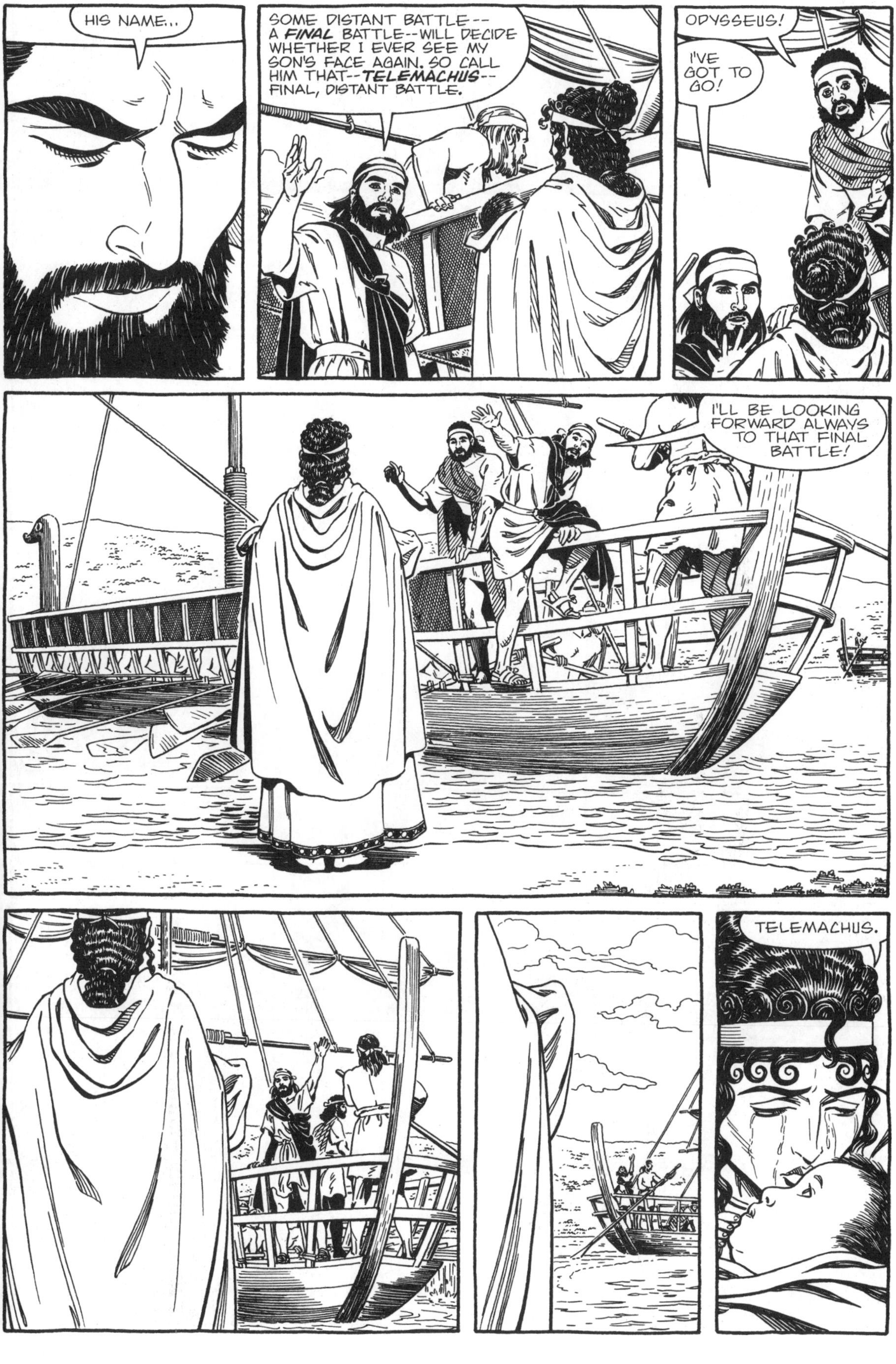
HIS NAME...
SOME DISTANT BATTLE-- A FINAL BATTLE--WILL DECIDE WHETHER I EVER SEE MY SON'S FACE AGAIN. SO CALL HIM THAT--TELEMACHUS-- FINAL, DISTANT BATTLE.
ODYSSEUS!
I'VE GOT TO GO!
I'LL BE LOOKING FORWARD ALWAYS TO THAT FINAL BATTLE!
TELEMACHUS.

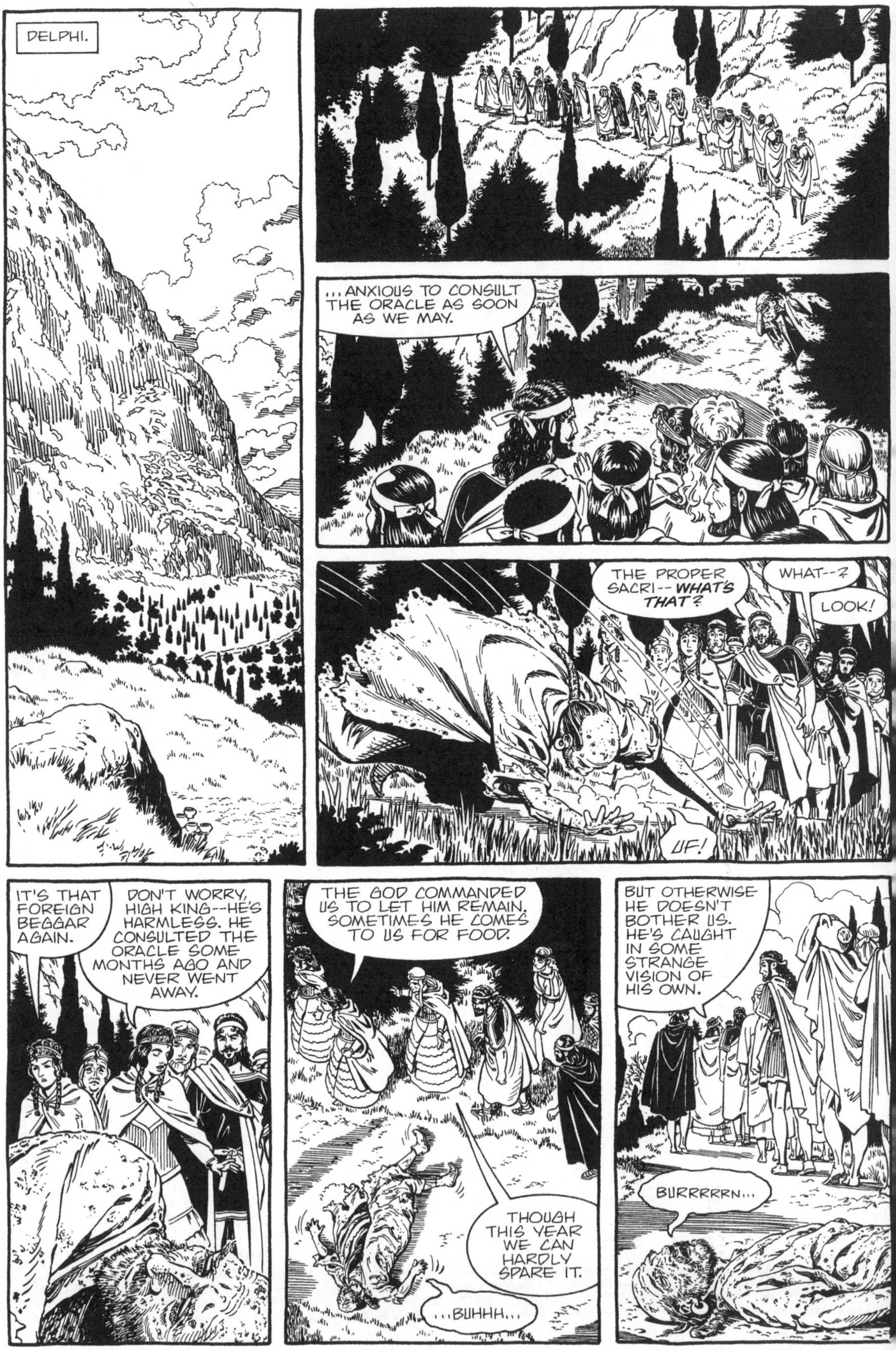
DELPHI.
...ANXIOUS TO CONSULT THE ORACLE AS SOON AS WE MAY.
THE PROPER SACRI-- WHAT'S THAT?
WHAT--?
LOOK!
UF!
IT'S THAT FOREIGN BEGGAR AGAIN.
DON'T WORRY, HIGH KING--HE'S HARMLESS. HE CONSULTED THE ORACLE SOME MONTHS AGO AND NEVER WENT AWAY.
THE GOD COMMANDED US TO LET HIM REMAIN. SOMETIMES HE COMES TO US FOR FOOD.
THOUGH THIS YEAR WE CAN HARDLY SPARE IT.
...BUHHH...
BUT OTHERWISE HE DOESN'T BOTHER US. HE'S CAUGHT IN SOME STRANGE VISION OF HIS OWN.
BURRRRRN...

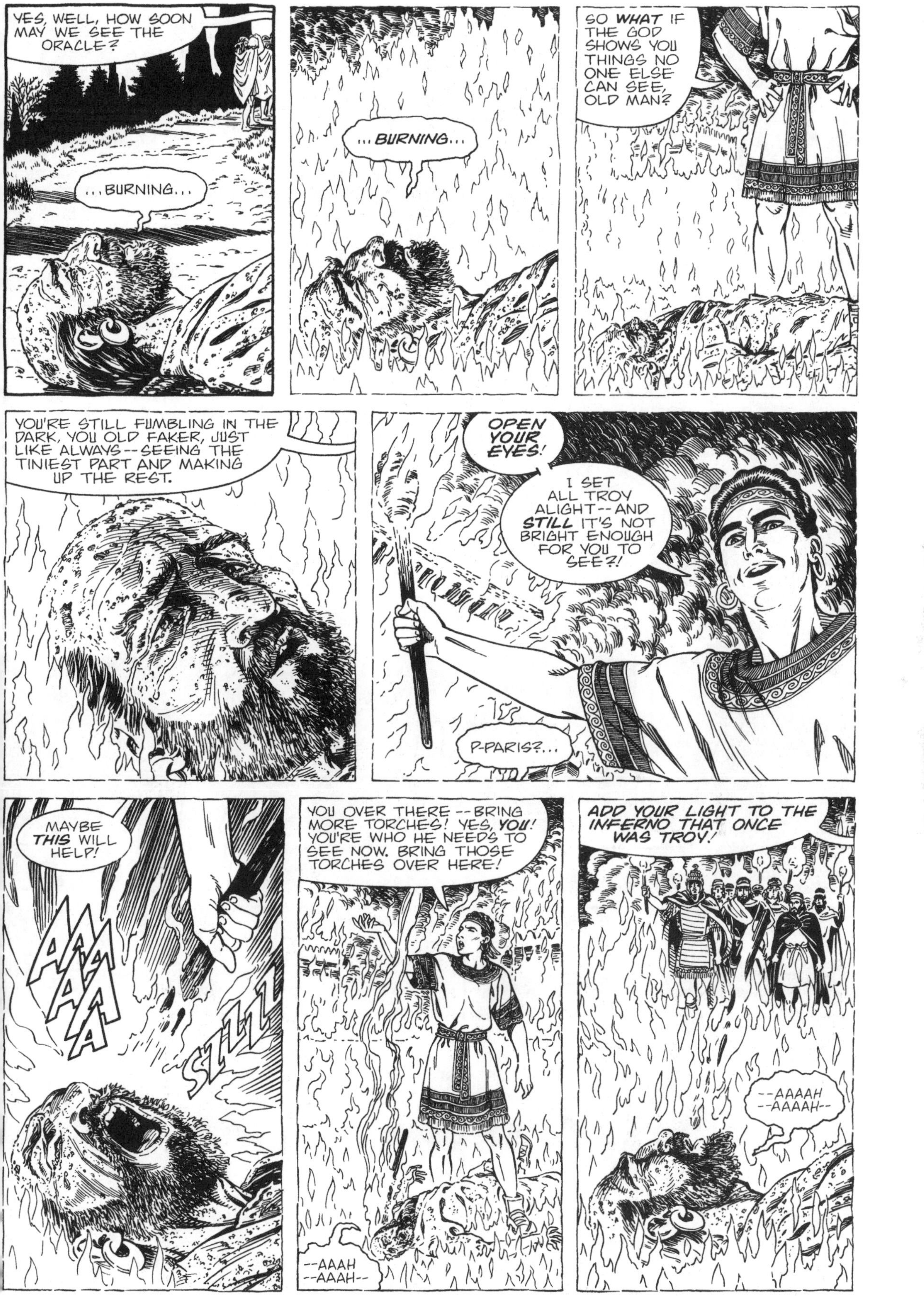
YES, WELL, HOW SOON MAY WE SEE THE ORACLE?
...BURNING...
...BURNING...
SO WHAT IF THE GOD SHOWS YOU THINGS NO ONE ELSE CAN SEE, OLD MAN?
YOU'RE STILL FUMBLING IN THE DARK, YOU OLD FAKER, JUST LIKE ALWAYS--SEEING THE TINIEST PART AND MAKING UP THE REST.
OPEN YOUR EYES!
I SET ALL TROY ALIGHT--AND STILL IT'S NOT BRIGHT ENOUGH FOR YOU TO SEE?!
P-PARIS?...
MAYBE THIS WILL HELP!
AAAAA
SZZZ
YOU OVER THERE--BRING MORE TORCHES! YES, YOU! YOU'RE WHO HE NEEDS TO SEE NOW. BRING THOSE TORCHES OVER HERE!
--AAAH --AAAH--
ADD YOUR LIGHT TO THE INFERNO THAT ONCE WAS TROY!
--AAAAH --AAAAH--

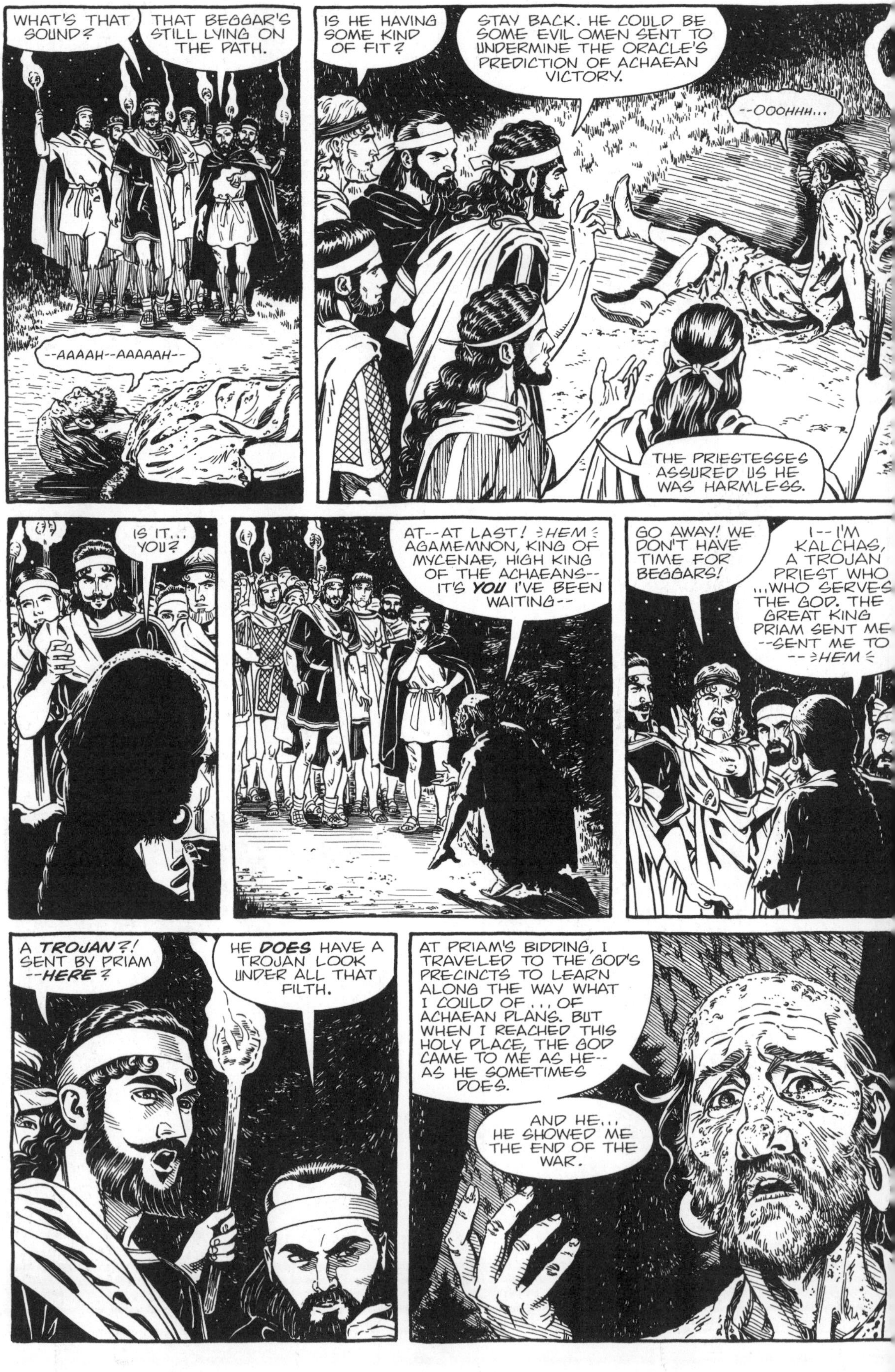
WHAT'S THAT SOUND?
THAT BEGGAR'S STILL LYING ON THE PATH.
--AAAAH--AAAAAH--
IS HE HAVING SOME KIND OF FIT?
STAY BACK. HE COULD BE SOME EVIL OMEN SENT TO UNDERMINE THE ORACLE'S PREDICTION OF ACHAEAN VICTORY.
--OOOHHH...
THE PRIESTESSES ASSURED US HE WAS HARMLESS.
IS IT... YOU?
AT--AT LAST! HEM AGAMEMNON, KING OF MYCENAE, HIGH KING OF THE ACHAEANS--IT'S YOU I'VE BEEN WAITING--
GO AWAY! WE DON'T HAVE TIME FOR BEGGARS!
I--I'M KALCHAS, A TROJAN PRIEST WHO ...WHO SERVES THE GOD. THE GREAT KING PRIAM SENT ME --SENT ME TO --HEM
A TROJAN?! SENT BY PRIAM --HERE?
HE DOES HAVE A TROJAN LOOK UNDER ALL THAT FILTH.
AT PRIAM'S BIDDING, I TRAVELED TO THE GOD'S PRECINCTS TO LEARN ALONG THE WAY WHAT I COULD OF... OF ACHAEAN PLANS. BUT WHEN I REACHED THIS HOLY PLACE, THE GOD CAME TO ME AS HE--AS HE SOMETIMES DOES.
AND HE... HE SHOWED ME THE END OF THE WAR.

I'VE **SEEN** IT--**FIRE**--A GREAT INFERNO CONSUMING TROY... AND THEN, WELL, HE TOLD ME NOT TO RETURN HOME. HE COMMANDED ME TO... TO WAIT FOR YOU... ≶HEM≶ ... TO JOIN YOU...

JOIN US?!

NEVER TRUST A TROJAN-- THAT'S WHAT **I'VE** LEARNED. **OBVIOUSLY** HE'S BEEN SENT TO **SPY** ON US!

PERHAPS...

...THOUGH IF THE GOD TRULY SPEAKS THROUGH HIM, WE CAN'T AFFORD TO TURN THIS MAN AWAY.

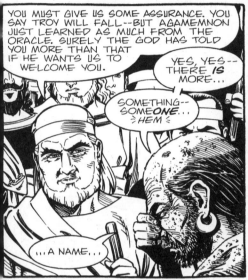

YOU MUST GIVE US SOME ASSURANCE. YOU SAY TROY WILL FALL--BUT AGAMEMNON JUST LEARNED AS MUCH FROM THE ORACLE. SURELY THE GOD HAS TOLD YOU MORE THAN THAT IF HE WANTS US TO WELCOME YOU.

YES, YES-- THERE **IS** MORE...

SOMETHING-- SOME**ONE**... ≶HEM≶

...A NAME...

ACHILLES.

WITHOUT ACHILLES, THE ACHAEANS CAN NEVER CLAIM VICTORY.

ACHILLES?!

THE SON OF **PELEUS**? HE'S STILL A **CHILD**!

NO, HE'S CERTAINLY ON THE VERGE OF MANHOOD BY NOW. AND HE'S A PUPIL OF CHEIRON-- THAT'S AN IM- PRESSIVE CRE- DENTIAL.

ACHILLES? YOU'RE SURE?

YES, YES! YOU'LL NEVER TAKE TROY WITHOUT **ACHILLES** ON YOUR SIDE. THAT'S ...≶HEM≶...THAT'S ALL...ALL I KNOW.

AGAMEMNON?

BRING HIM, BUT GUARD HIM CLOSELY. IF HE SPEAKS TRULY, THEN THE GOD FAVORS US. AND IF HE'S LYING, I DON'T WANT HIM BOLTING BACK TO PRIAM.

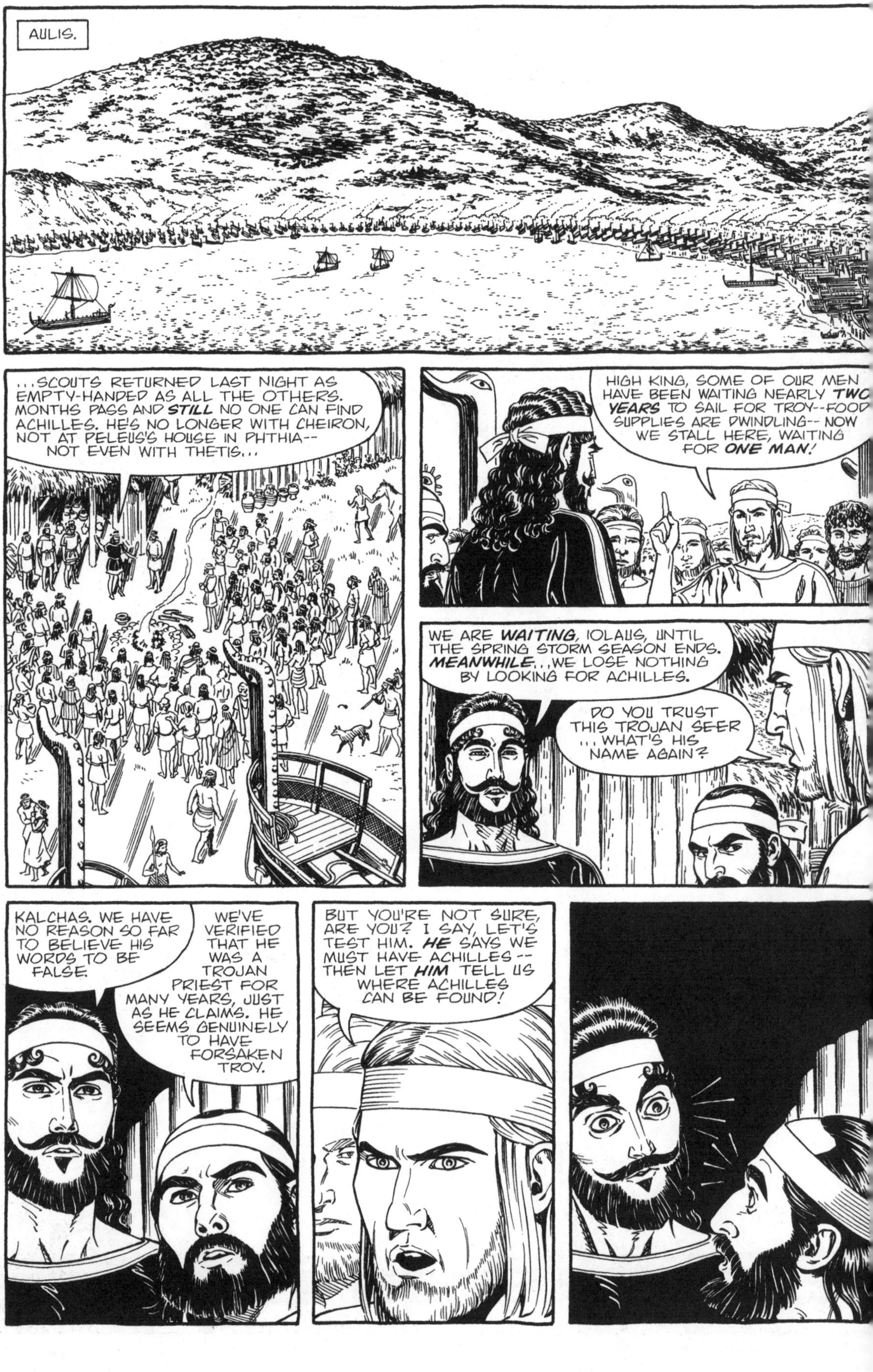

AULIS.
...SCOUTS RETURNED LAST NIGHT AS EMPTY-HANDED AS ALL THE OTHERS. MONTHS PASS AND **STILL** NO ONE CAN FIND ACHILLES. HE'S NO LONGER WITH CHEIRON, NOT AT PELEUS'S HOUSE IN PHTHIA-- NOT EVEN WITH THETIS...
HIGH KING, SOME OF OUR MEN HAVE BEEN WAITING NEARLY **TWO YEARS** TO SAIL FOR TROY--FOOD SUPPLIES ARE DWINDLING-- NOW WE STALL HERE, WAITING FOR **ONE MAN**!
WE ARE **WAITING**, IOLAUS, UNTIL THE SPRING STORM SEASON ENDS. **MEANWHILE**...WE LOSE NOTHING BY LOOKING FOR ACHILLES.
DO YOU TRUST THIS TROJAN SEER ...WHAT'S HIS NAME AGAIN?
KALCHAS. WE HAVE NO REASON SO FAR TO BELIEVE HIS WORDS TO BE FALSE.
WE'VE VERIFIED THAT HE WAS A TROJAN PRIEST FOR MANY YEARS, JUST AS HE CLAIMS. HE SEEMS GENUINELY TO HAVE FORSAKEN TROY.
BUT YOU'RE NOT SURE, ARE YOU? I SAY, LET'S TEST HIM. **HE** SAYS WE MUST HAVE ACHILLES -- THEN LET **HIM** TELL US WHERE ACHILLES CAN BE FOUND!

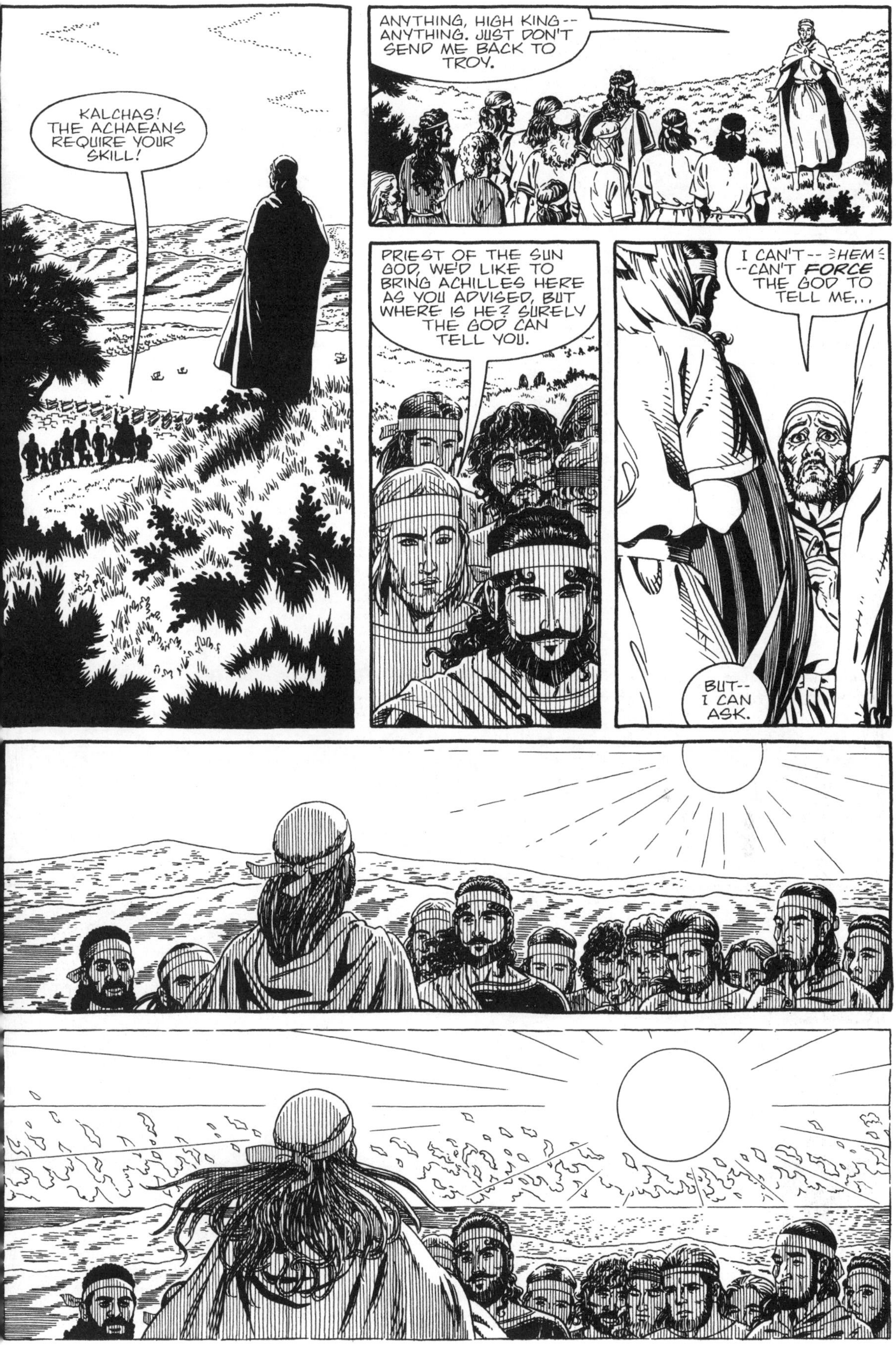
KALCHAS! THE ACHAEANS REQUIRE YOUR SKILL!
ANYTHING, HIGH KING-- ANYTHING. JUST DON'T SEND ME BACK TO TROY.
PRIEST OF THE SUN GOD, WE'D LIKE TO BRING ACHILLES HERE AS YOU ADVISED, BUT WHERE IS HE? SURELY THE GOD CAN TELL YOU.
I CAN'T-- HEM --CAN'T FORCE THE GOD TO TELL ME...
BUT-- I CAN ASK.

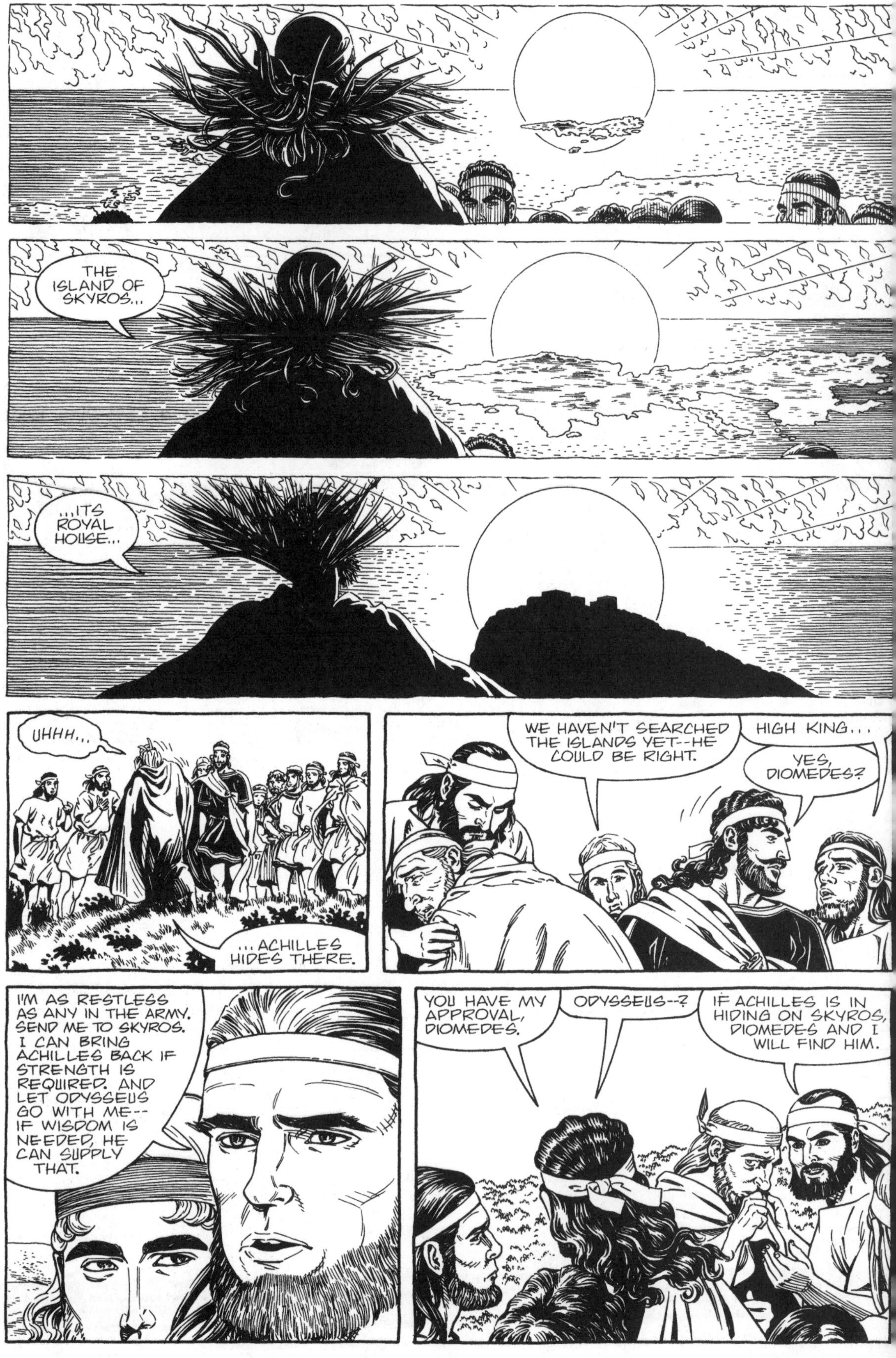
THE ISLAND OF SKYROS...
...ITS ROYAL HOUSE...
UHHH...
...ACHILLES HIDES THERE.
WE HAVEN'T SEARCHED THE ISLANDS YET--HE COULD BE RIGHT.
HIGH KING...
YES, DIOMEDES?
I'M AS RESTLESS AS ANY IN THE ARMY. SEND ME TO SKYROS. I CAN BRING ACHILLES BACK IF STRENGTH IS REQUIRED. AND LET ODYSSEUS GO WITH ME-- IF WISDOM IS NEEDED, HE CAN SUPPLY THAT.
YOU HAVE MY APPROVAL, DIOMEDES.
ODYSSEUS--?
IF ACHILLES IS IN HIDING ON SKYROS, DIOMEDES AND I WILL FIND HIM.

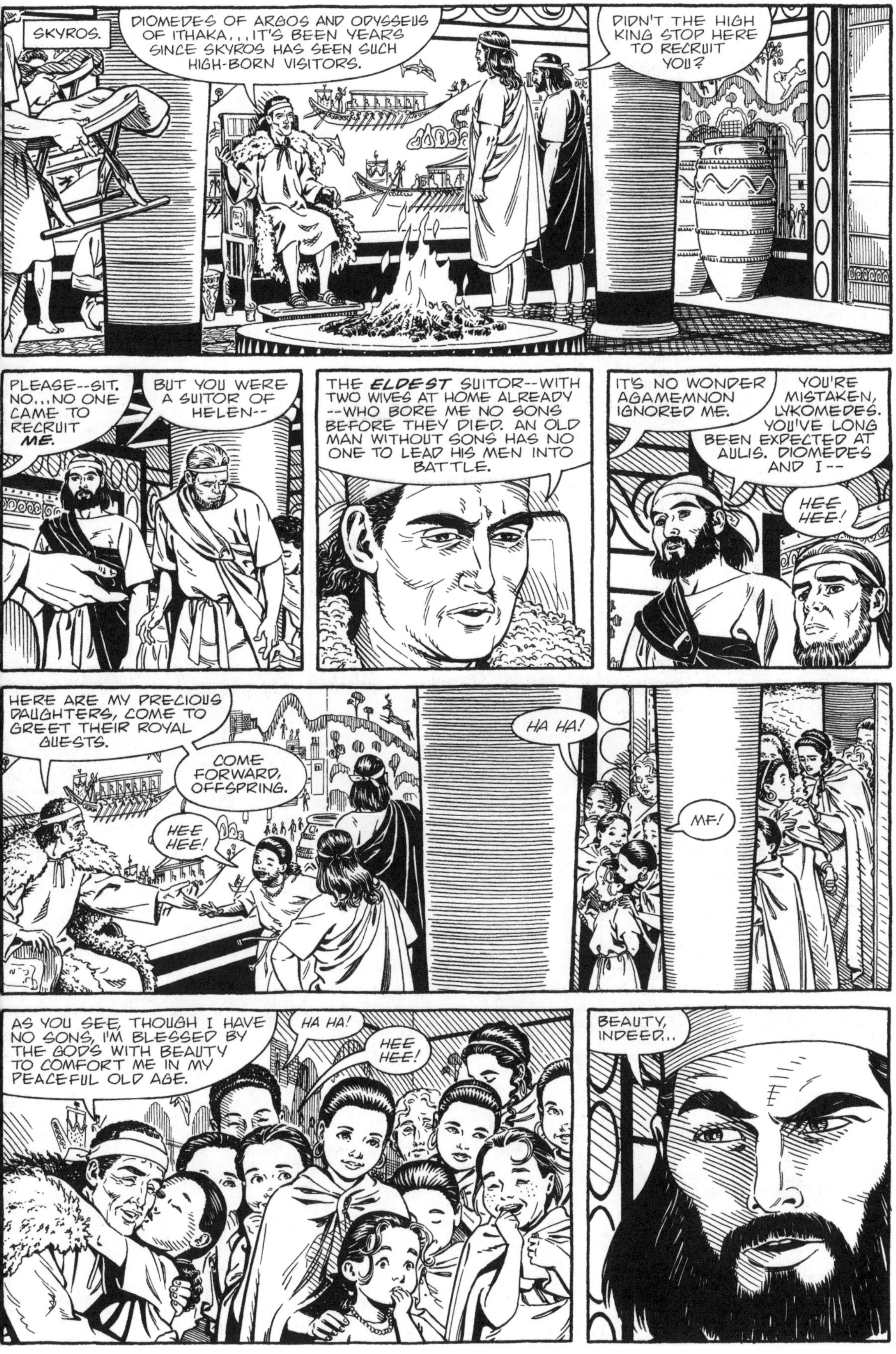
SKYROS.
DIOMEDES OF ARGOS AND ODYSSEUS OF ITHAKA... IT'S BEEN YEARS SINCE SKYROS HAS SEEN SUCH HIGH-BORN VISITORS.
DIDN'T THE HIGH KING STOP HERE TO RECRUIT YOU?
PLEASE--SIT. NO... NO ONE CAME TO RECRUIT ME.
BUT YOU WERE A SUITOR OF HELEN--
THE ELDEST SUITOR--WITH TWO WIVES AT HOME ALREADY --WHO BORE ME NO SONS BEFORE THEY DIED. AN OLD MAN WITHOUT SONS HAS NO ONE TO LEAD HIS MEN INTO BATTLE.
IT'S NO WONDER AGAMEMNON IGNORED ME.
YOU'RE MISTAKEN, LYKOMEDES. YOU'VE LONG BEEN EXPECTED AT AULIS. DIOMEDES AND I--
HEE HEE!
HERE ARE MY PRECIOUS DAUGHTERS, COME TO GREET THEIR ROYAL GUESTS.
COME FORWARD, OFFSPRING.
HEE HEE!
HA HA!
MF!
AS YOU SEE, THOUGH I HAVE NO SONS, I'M BLESSED BY THE GODS WITH BEAUTY TO COMFORT ME IN MY PEACEFUL OLD AGE.
HA HA!
HEE HEE!
BEAUTY, INDEED...

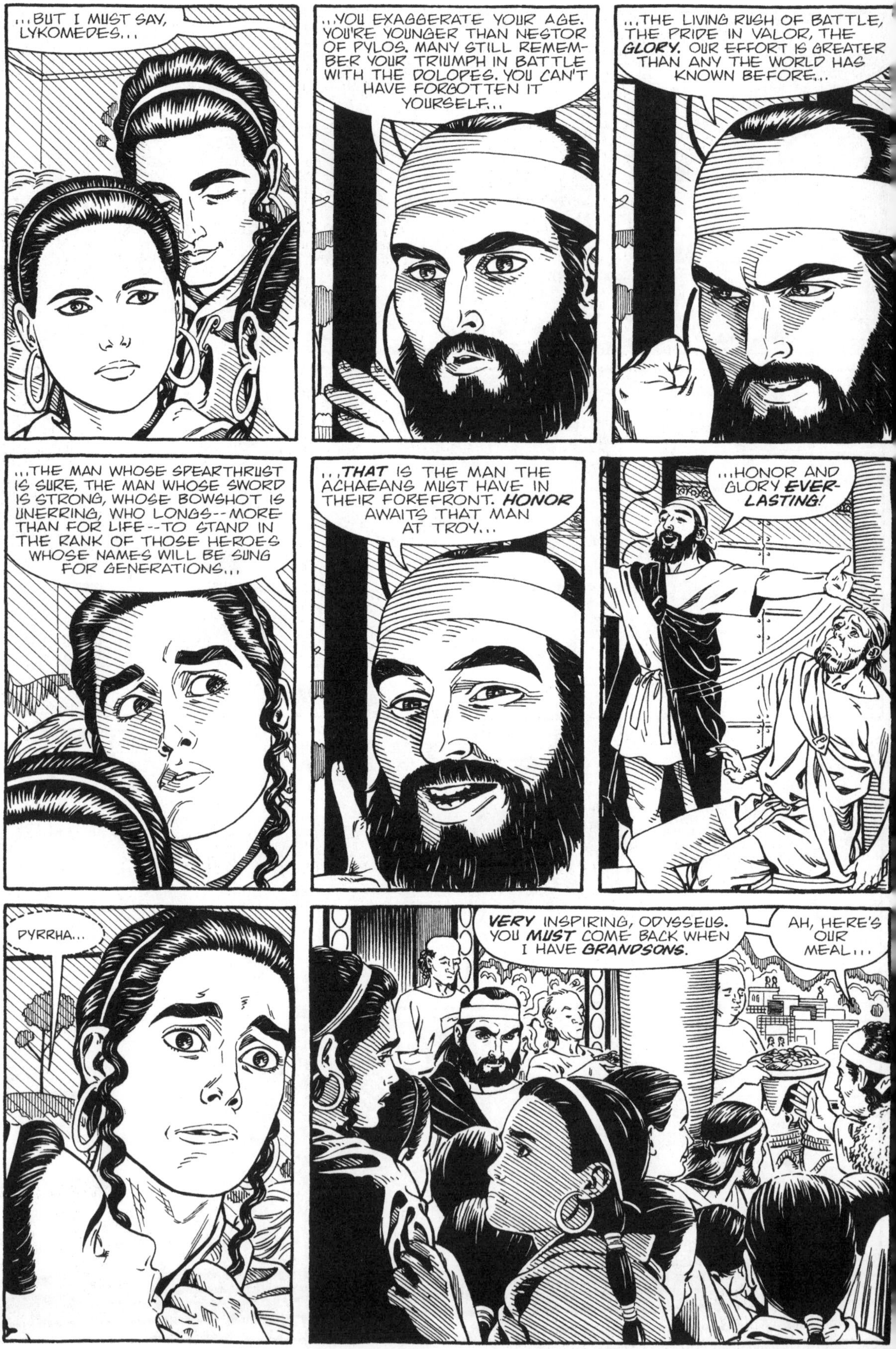
...BUT I MUST SAY, LYKOMEDES...
...YOU EXAGGERATE YOUR AGE. YOU'RE YOUNGER THAN NESTOR OF PYLOS. MANY STILL REMEMBER YOUR TRIUMPH IN BATTLE WITH THE DOLOPES. YOU CAN'T HAVE FORGOTTEN IT YOURSELF...
...THE LIVING RUSH OF BATTLE, THE PRIDE IN VALOR, THE GLORY. OUR EFFORT IS GREATER THAN ANY THE WORLD HAS KNOWN BEFORE...
...THE MAN WHOSE SPEARTHRUST IS SURE, THE MAN WHOSE SWORD IS STRONG, WHOSE BOWSHOT IS UNERRING, WHO LONGS--MORE THAN FOR LIFE--TO STAND IN THE RANK OF THOSE HEROES WHOSE NAMES WILL BE SUNG FOR GENERATIONS...
...THAT IS THE MAN THE ACHAEANS MUST HAVE IN THEIR FOREFRONT. HONOR AWAITS THAT MAN AT TROY...
...HONOR AND GLORY EVERLASTING!
PYRRHA...
VERY INSPIRING, ODYSSEUS. YOU MUST COME BACK WHEN I HAVE GRANDSONS.
AH, HERE'S OUR MEAL...

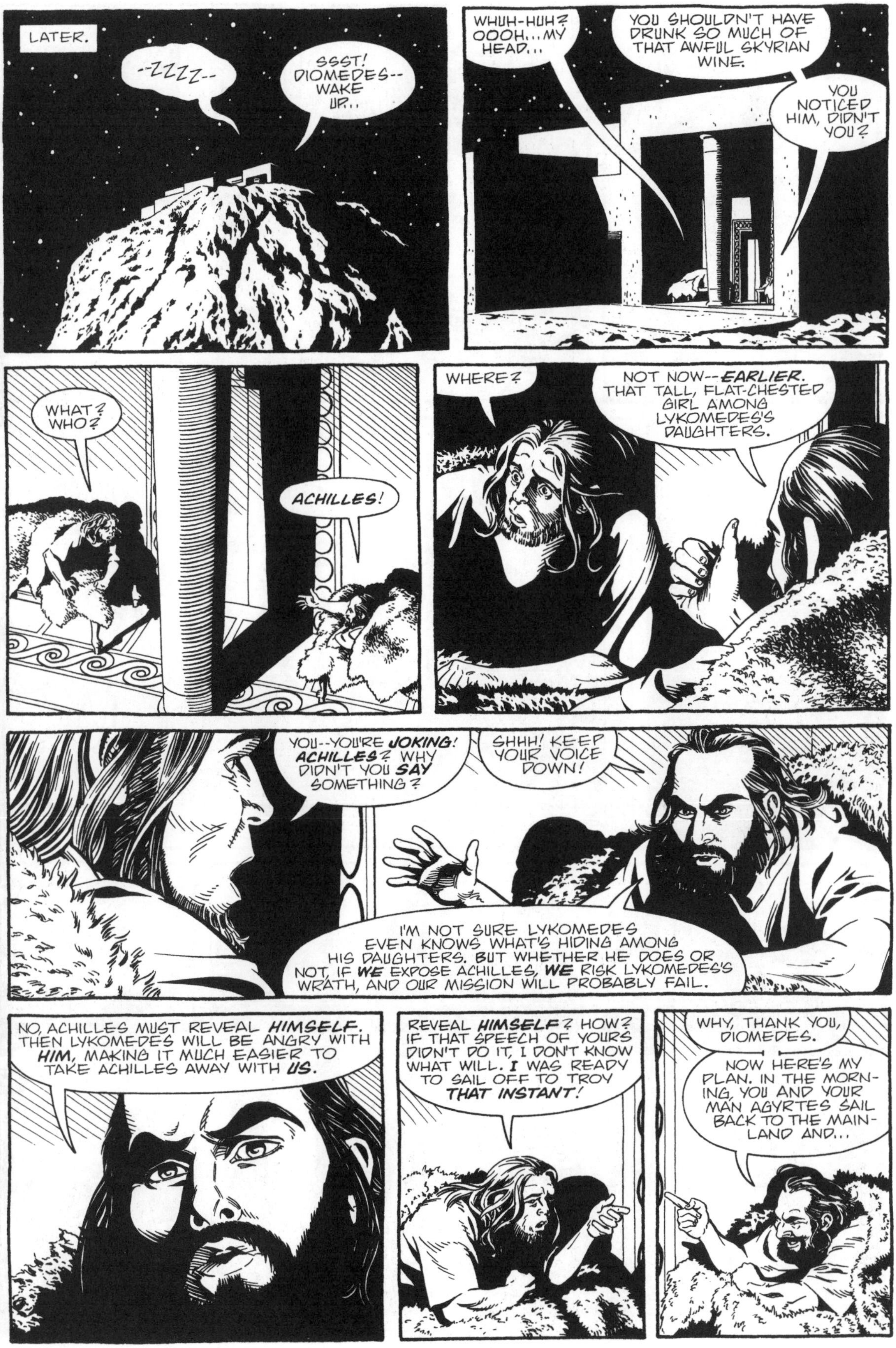
LATER.
--ZZZZ--
SSST! DIOMEDES-- WAKE UP...
WHUH-HUH? OOOH...MY HEAD...
YOU SHOULDN'T HAVE DRUNK SO MUCH OF THAT AWFUL SKYRIAN WINE.
YOU NOTICED HIM, DIDN'T YOU?
WHAT? WHO?
ACHILLES!
WHERE?
NOT NOW--EARLIER. THAT TALL, FLAT-CHESTED GIRL AMONG LYKOMEDES'S DAUGHTERS.
YOU--YOU'RE JOKING! ACHILLES? WHY DIDN'T YOU SAY SOMETHING?
SHHH! KEEP YOUR VOICE DOWN!
I'M NOT SURE LYKOMEDES EVEN KNOWS WHAT'S HIDING AMONG HIS DAUGHTERS. BUT WHETHER HE DOES OR NOT, IF WE EXPOSE ACHILLES, WE RISK LYKOMEDES'S WRATH, AND OUR MISSION WILL PROBABLY FAIL.
NO, ACHILLES MUST REVEAL HIMSELF. THEN LYKOMEDES WILL BE ANGRY WITH HIM, MAKING IT MUCH EASIER TO TAKE ACHILLES AWAY WITH US.
REVEAL HIMSELF? HOW? IF THAT SPEECH OF YOURS DIDN'T DO IT, I DON'T KNOW WHAT WILL. I WAS READY TO SAIL OFF TO TROY THAT INSTANT!
WHY, THANK YOU, DIOMEDES.
NOW HERE'S MY PLAN. IN THE MORNING, YOU AND YOUR MAN AGYRTES SAIL BACK TO THE MAINLAND AND...

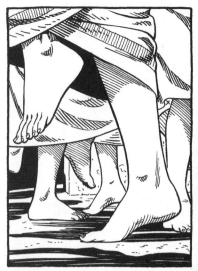

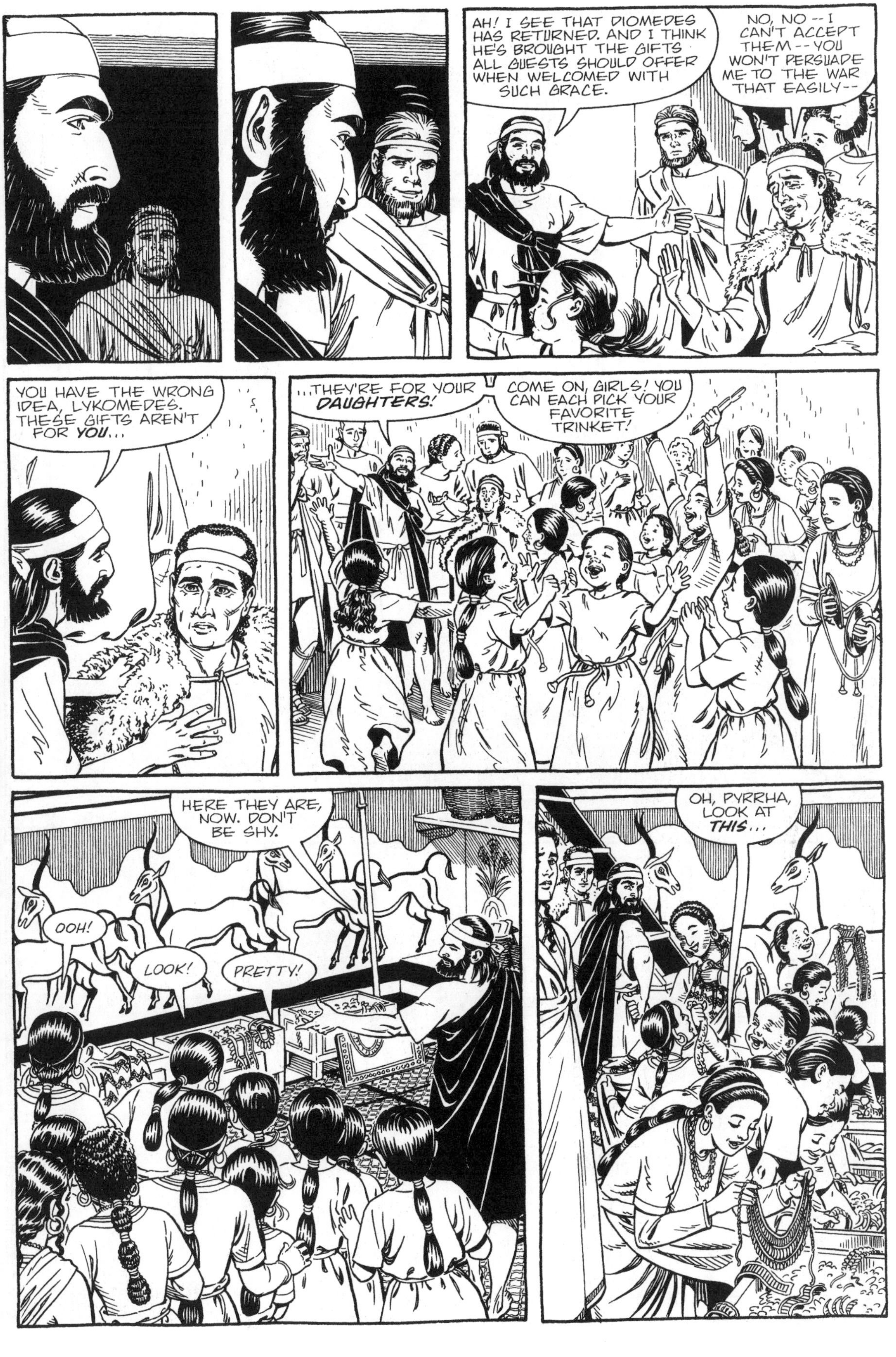
AH! I SEE THAT DIOMEDES HAS RETURNED. AND I THINK HE'S BROUGHT THE GIFTS ALL GUESTS SHOULD OFFER WHEN WELCOMED WITH SUCH GRACE.
NO, NO -- I CAN'T ACCEPT THEM -- YOU WON'T PERSUADE ME TO THE WAR THAT EASILY--
YOU HAVE THE WRONG IDEA, LYKOMEDES. THESE GIFTS AREN'T FOR *YOU*...
...THEY'RE FOR YOUR *DAUGHTERS!*
COME ON, GIRLS! YOU CAN EACH PICK YOUR FAVORITE TRINKET!
HERE THEY ARE, NOW. DON'T BE SHY.
OOH!
LOOK!
PRETTY!
OH, PYRRHA, LOOK AT *THIS*...

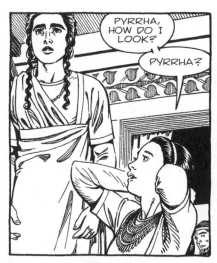
PYRRHA, HOW DO I LOOK?

PYRRHA?

PYRRHA, WHAT ARE YOU...?

SON OF PELEUS -- WHY ARE YOU HESITATING? TAKE THE GIFT YOU'VE CHOSEN. THE ACHAEANS ARE WAITING FOR YOU TO LEAD THEM. THE WALLS OF TROY TREMBLE IN ANTICIPATION OF YOUR SPEARTHRUST.

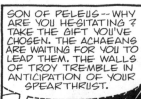

PYRRHA...?

PYRRHA, THAT MUST BE A GIFT FOR FATHER!

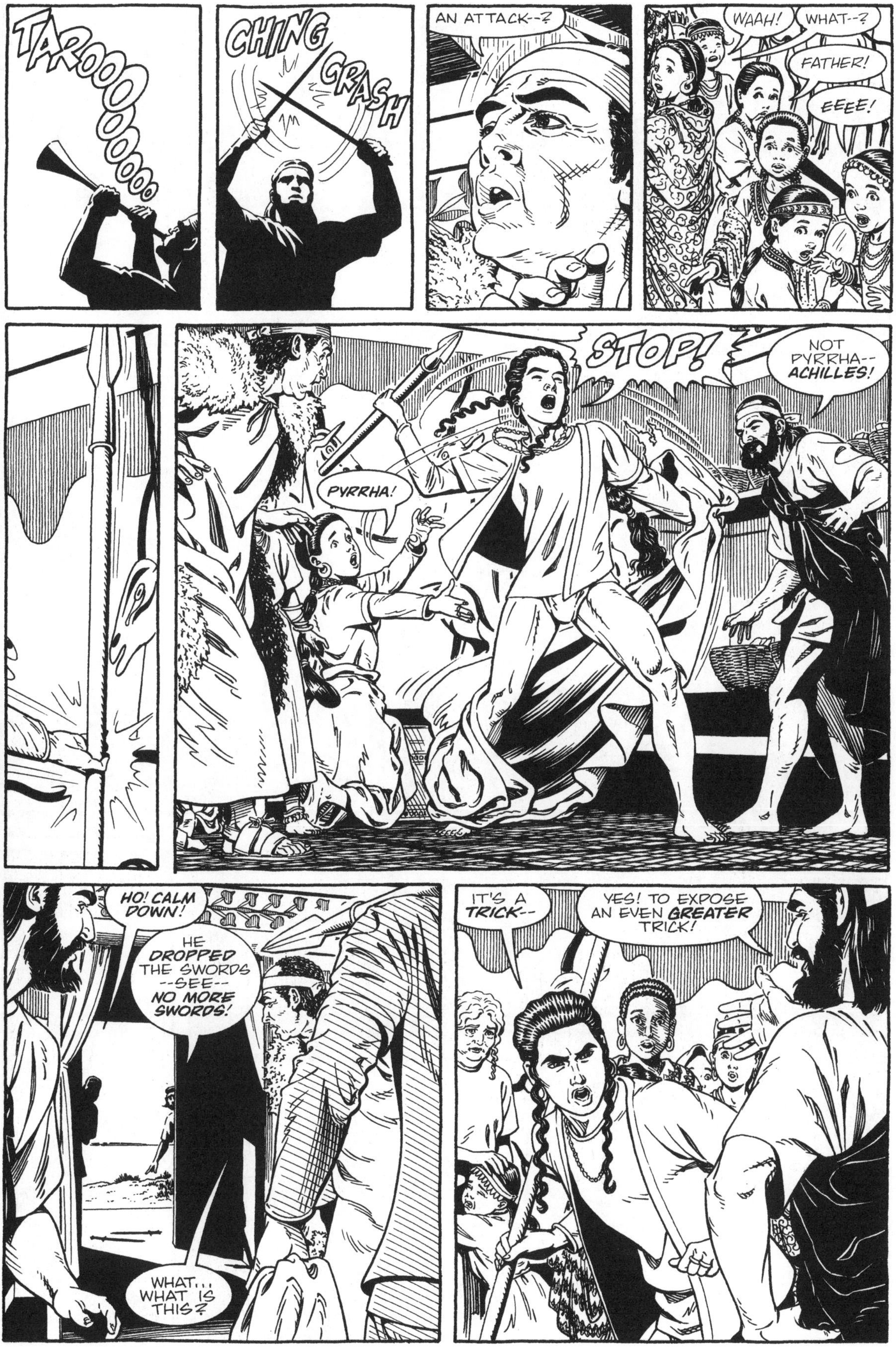

TAROOOOOOOOO
CHING
CRASH
AN ATTACK--?
WAAH!
WHAT--?
FATHER!
EEEE!
STOP!
NOT PYRRHA-- ACHILLES!
PYRRHA!
HO! CALM DOWN!
HE DROPPED THE SWORDS --SEE-- NO MORE SWORDS!
WHAT... WHAT IS THIS?
IT'S A TRICK--
YES! TO EXPOSE AN EVEN GREATER TRICK!

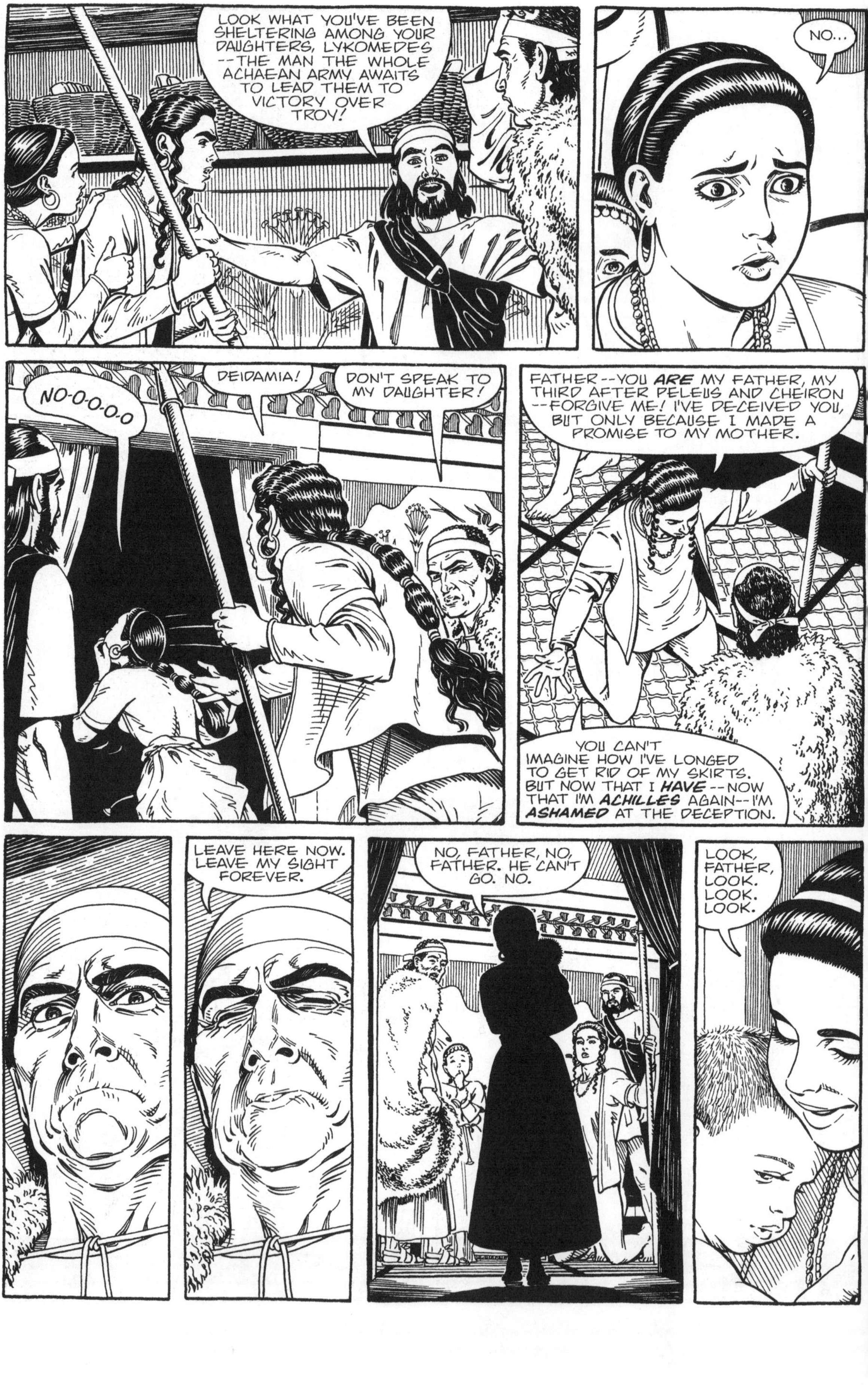
LOOK WHAT YOU'VE BEEN SHELTERING AMONG YOUR DAUGHTERS, LYKOMEDES --THE MAN THE WHOLE ACHAEAN ARMY AWAITS TO LEAD THEM TO VICTORY OVER TROY!
NO...
NO-O-O-O-O
DEIDAMIA!
DON'T SPEAK TO MY DAUGHTER!
FATHER--YOU **ARE** MY FATHER, MY THIRD AFTER PELEUS AND CHEIRON --FORGIVE ME! I'VE DECEIVED YOU, BUT ONLY BECAUSE I MADE A PROMISE TO MY MOTHER.
YOU CAN'T IMAGINE HOW I'VE LONGED TO GET RID OF MY SKIRTS. BUT NOW THAT I **HAVE**--NOW THAT I'M **ACHILLES** AGAIN--I'M **ASHAMED** AT THE DECEPTION.
LEAVE HERE NOW. LEAVE MY SIGHT FOREVER.
NO, FATHER, NO, FATHER. HE CAN'T GO. NO.
LOOK, FATHER, LOOK. LOOK. LOOK.

THIS IS OUR CHILD --YOU THOUGHT IT WAS NURSE'S, BUT IT'S OURS -- PYRRHA'S AND MINE.

HIS NAME IS PYRRHUS.

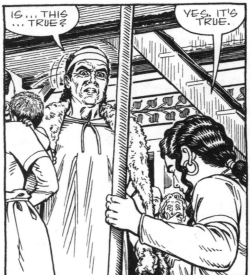

IS... THIS ...TRUE?

YES. IT'S TRUE.

FATHER, THIS IS A SHAME I CAN SET RIGHT--WITH YOUR CONSENT. PLEASE--JOIN MY HAND WITH DEIDAMIA'S--ACCEPT ME AS YOUR SON. I'M ALREADY PART OF YOUR FAMILY--RELATED TO YOU THROUGH MY SON, YOUR GRANDCHILD.

FATHER, FATHER, FATHER, SAY YES!

YES, YES!

YEEUH?

VERY WELL.

WAIT. THINK FIRST, LYKOMEDES. THE KINGS OF THE ACHAEANS REQUIRE ACHILLES TO INSURE VICTORY IN THE WAR. WILL YOU STAND IN THE WAY OF THE ENTIRE ARMY?

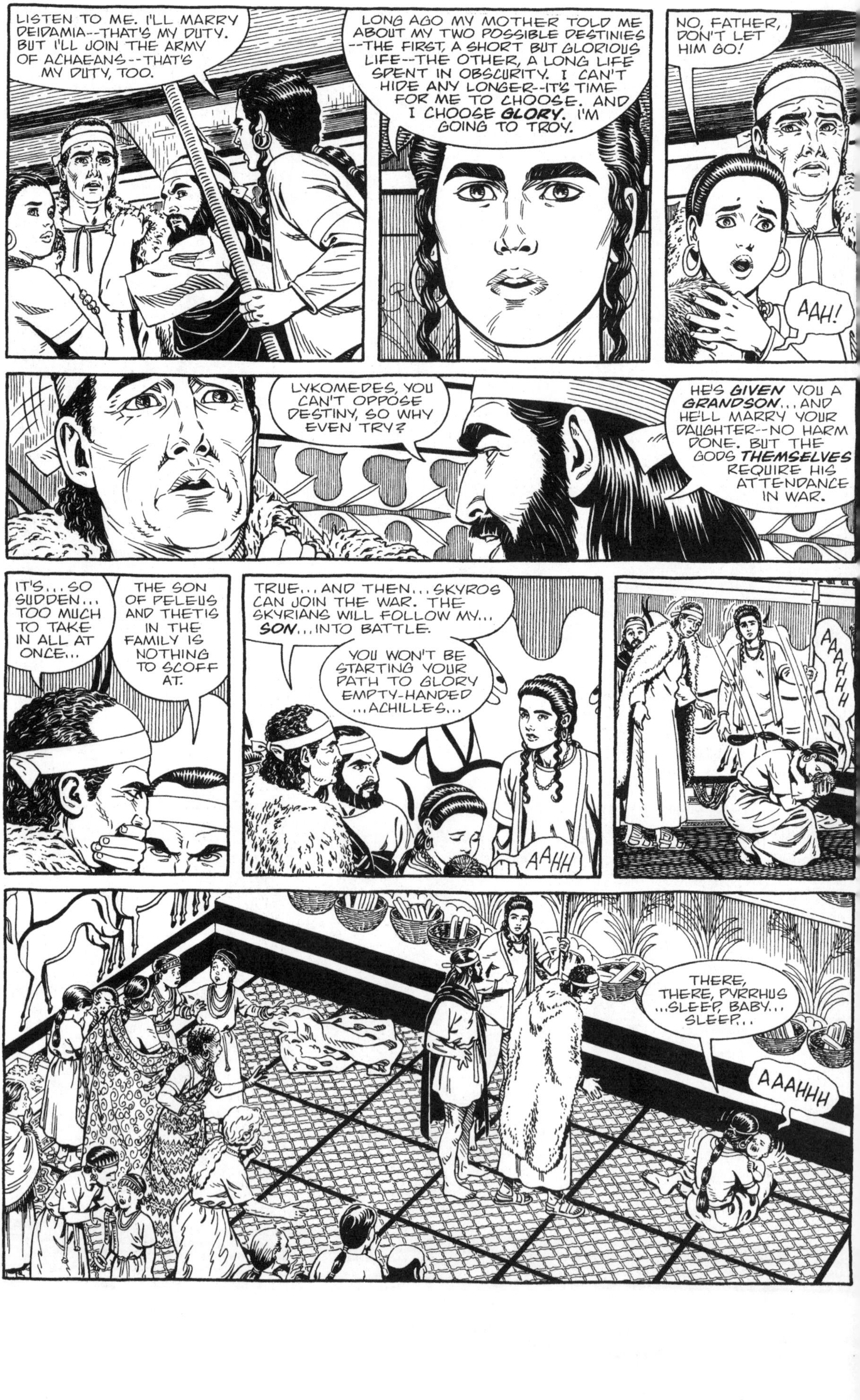
LISTEN TO ME. I'LL MARRY DEIDAMIA--THAT'S MY DUTY. BUT I'LL JOIN THE ARMY OF ACHAEANS--THAT'S MY DUTY, TOO.
LONG AGO MY MOTHER TOLD ME ABOUT MY TWO POSSIBLE DESTINIES --THE FIRST, A SHORT BUT GLORIOUS LIFE--THE OTHER, A LONG LIFE SPENT IN OBSCURITY. I CAN'T HIDE ANY LONGER--IT'S TIME FOR ME TO CHOOSE. AND I CHOOSE GLORY. I'M GOING TO TROY.
NO, FATHER, DON'T LET HIM GO!
AAH!
LYKOMEDES, YOU CAN'T OPPOSE DESTINY, SO WHY EVEN TRY?
HE'S GIVEN YOU A GRANDSON... AND HE'LL MARRY YOUR DAUGHTER--NO HARM DONE. BUT THE GODS THEMSELVES REQUIRE HIS ATTENDANCE IN WAR.
IT'S... SO SUDDEN... TOO MUCH TO TAKE IN ALL AT ONCE...
THE SON OF PELEUS AND THETIS IN THE FAMILY IS NOTHING TO SCOFF AT.
TRUE... AND THEN... SKYROS CAN JOIN THE WAR. THE SKYRIANS WILL FOLLOW MY... SON... INTO BATTLE.
YOU WON'T BE STARTING YOUR PATH TO GLORY EMPTY-HANDED ...ACHILLES...
AAHH
AAAHHHH
THERE, THERE, PYRRHUS ...SLEEP, BABY... SLEEP...
AAAHHH

...FOUR HUNDRED AND THIRTEEN CHARIOT BODIES, TWO HUNDRED AND FIFTY-SEVEN CHARIOT WHEELS...

...FIVE LAME HORSES, FIFTEEN INCOMPLETE LEATHER CORSELETS...

...FORTY THREE--

HIGH KING, I HAVE NEWS.

TALTHYBIUS, UNLESS A SHIPLOAD OF GRAIN HAS ARRIVED FROM THRACE, I DON'T WANT TO HEAR IT.

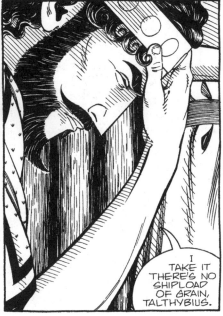

I TAKE IT THERE'S NO SHIPLOAD OF GRAIN, TALTHYBIUS.

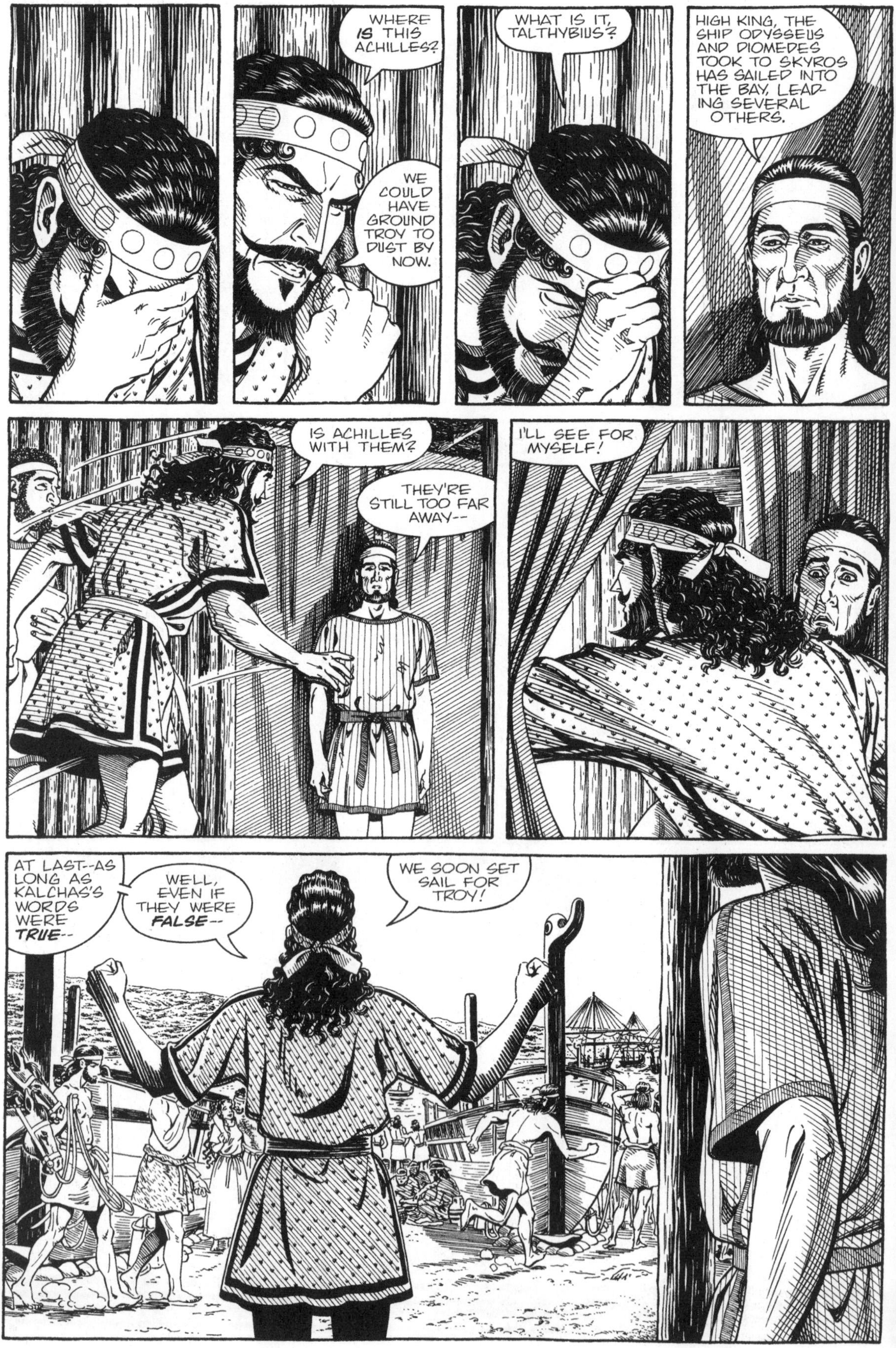
WHERE IS THIS ACHILLES?
WE COULD HAVE GROUND TROY TO DUST BY NOW.
WHAT IS IT, TALTHYBIUS?
HIGH KING, THE SHIP ODYSSEUS AND DIOMEDES TOOK TO SKYROS HAS SAILED INTO THE BAY, LEADING SEVERAL OTHERS.
IS ACHILLES WITH THEM?
THEY'RE STILL TOO FAR AWAY--
I'LL SEE FOR MYSELF!
AT LAST--AS LONG AS KALCHAS'S WORDS WERE TRUE--
WELL, EVEN IF THEY WERE FALSE--
WE SOON SET SAIL FOR TROY!

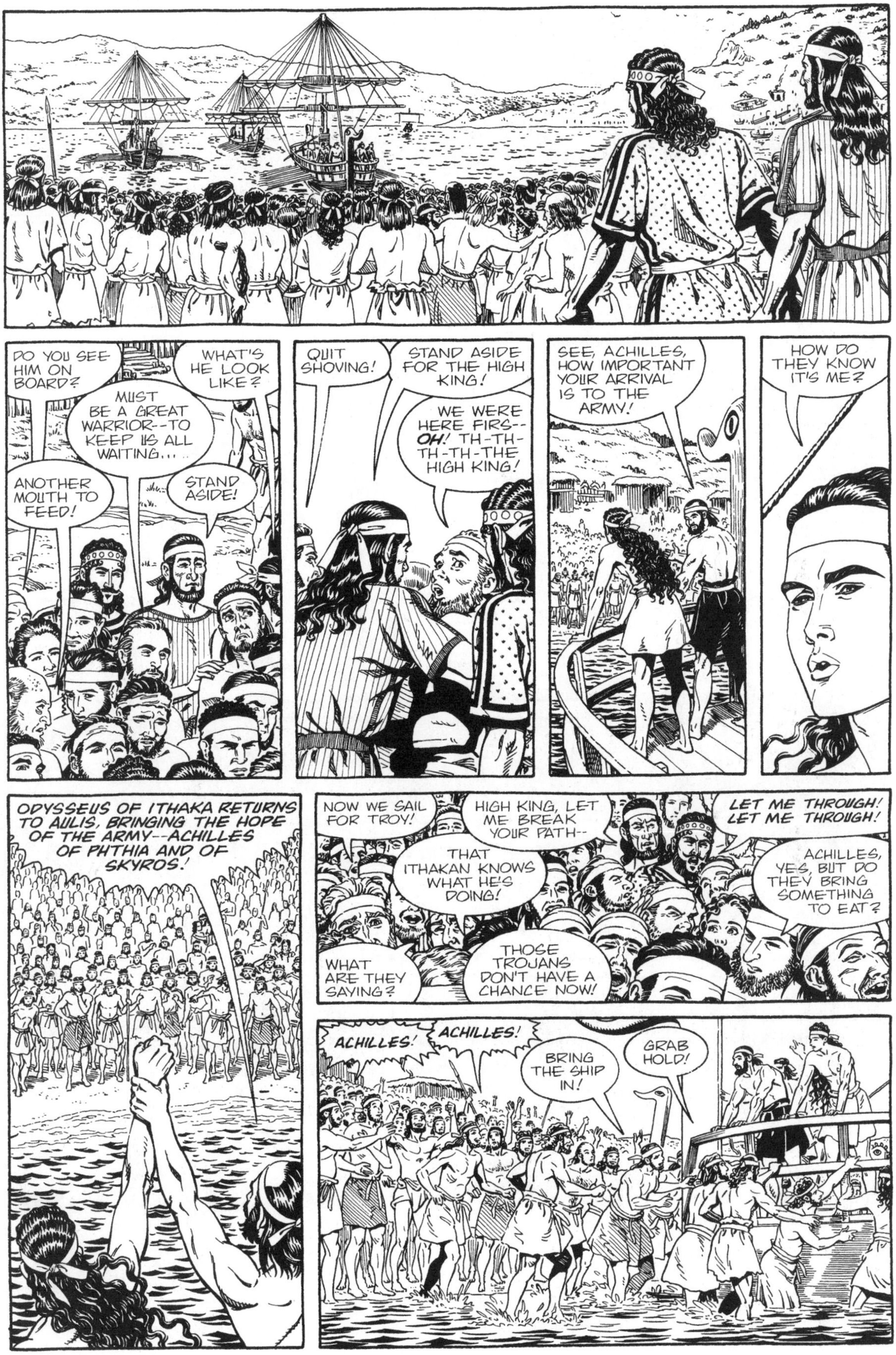
DO YOU SEE HIM ON BOARD?
WHAT'S HE LOOK LIKE?
MUST BE A GREAT WARRIOR--TO KEEP US ALL WAITING...
ANOTHER MOUTH TO FEED!
STAND ASIDE!
QUIT SHOVING!
STAND ASIDE FOR THE HIGH KING!
WE WERE HERE FIRS-- OH! TH-TH-TH-TH-THE HIGH KING!
SEE, ACHILLES, HOW IMPORTANT YOUR ARRIVAL IS TO THE ARMY!
HOW DO THEY KNOW IT'S ME?
ODYSSEUS OF ITHAKA RETURNS TO AULIS, BRINGING THE HOPE OF THE ARMY--ACHILLES OF PHTHIA AND OF SKYROS!
NOW WE SAIL FOR TROY!
HIGH KING, LET ME BREAK YOUR PATH--
LET ME THROUGH! LET ME THROUGH!
THAT ITHAKAN KNOWS WHAT HE'S DOING!
ACHILLES, YES, BUT DO THEY BRING SOMETHING TO EAT?
WHAT ARE THEY SAYING?
THOSE TROJANS DON'T HAVE A CHANCE NOW!
ACHILLES!
ACHILLES!
BRING THE SHIP IN!
GRAB HOLD!

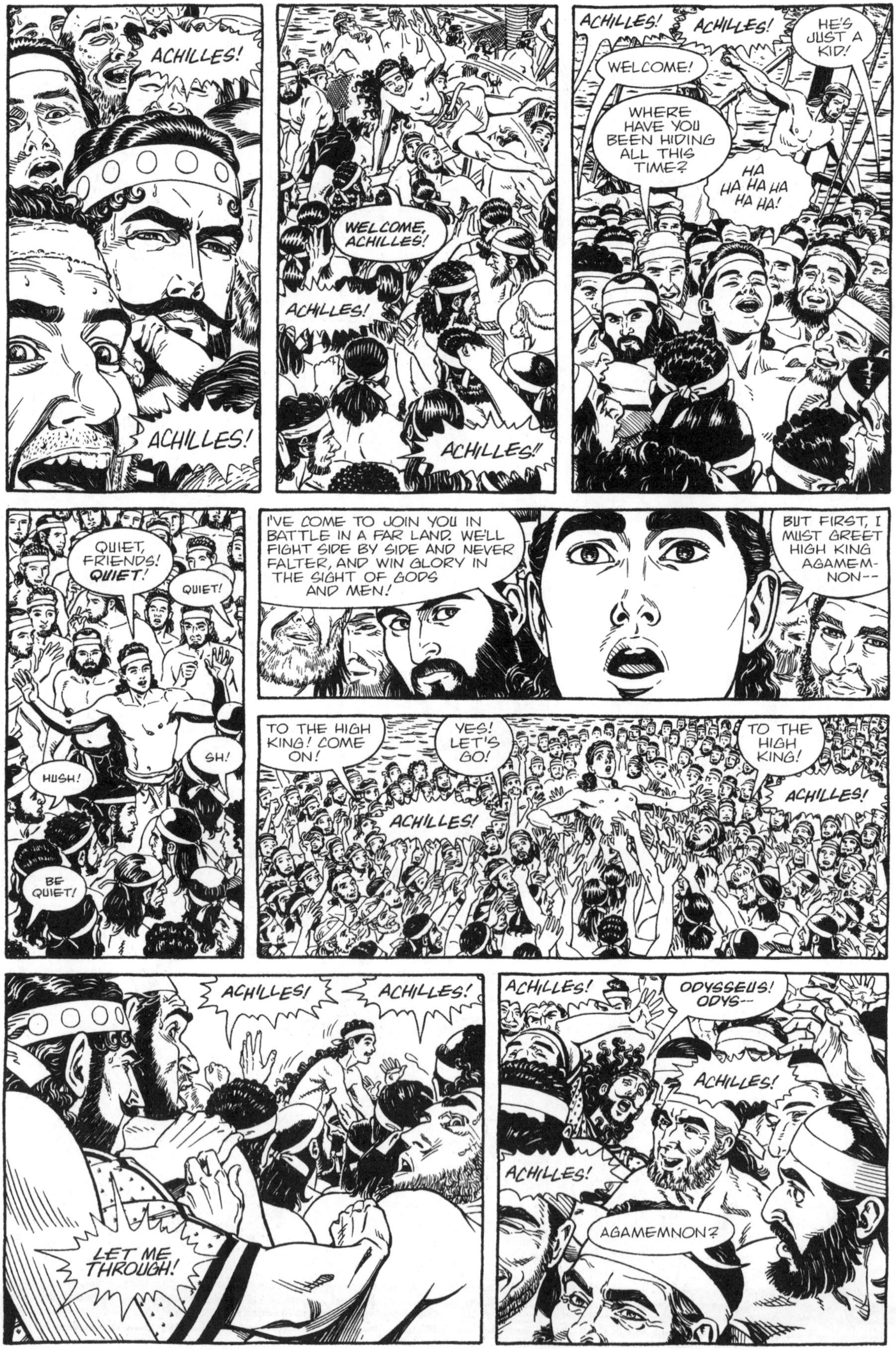
ACHILLES!
ACHILLES!
WELCOME, ACHILLES!
ACHILLES!
ACHILLES!!
ACHILLES!
ACHILLES!
HE'S JUST A KID!
WELCOME!
WHERE HAVE YOU BEEN HIDING ALL THIS TIME?
HA HA HA HA HA HA!
QUIET, FRIENDS! QUIET!
QUIET!
SH!
HUSH!
BE QUIET!
I'VE COME TO JOIN YOU IN BATTLE IN A FAR LAND. WE'LL FIGHT SIDE BY SIDE AND NEVER FALTER, AND WIN GLORY IN THE SIGHT OF GODS AND MEN!
BUT FIRST, I MUST GREET HIGH KING AGAMEMNON--
TO THE HIGH KING! COME ON!
YES! LET'S GO!
TO THE HIGH KING!
ACHILLES!
ACHILLES!
ACHILLES!
ACHILLES!
LET ME THROUGH!
ACHILLES!
ODYSSEUS! ODYS--
ACHILLES!
ACHILLES!
AGAMEMNON?

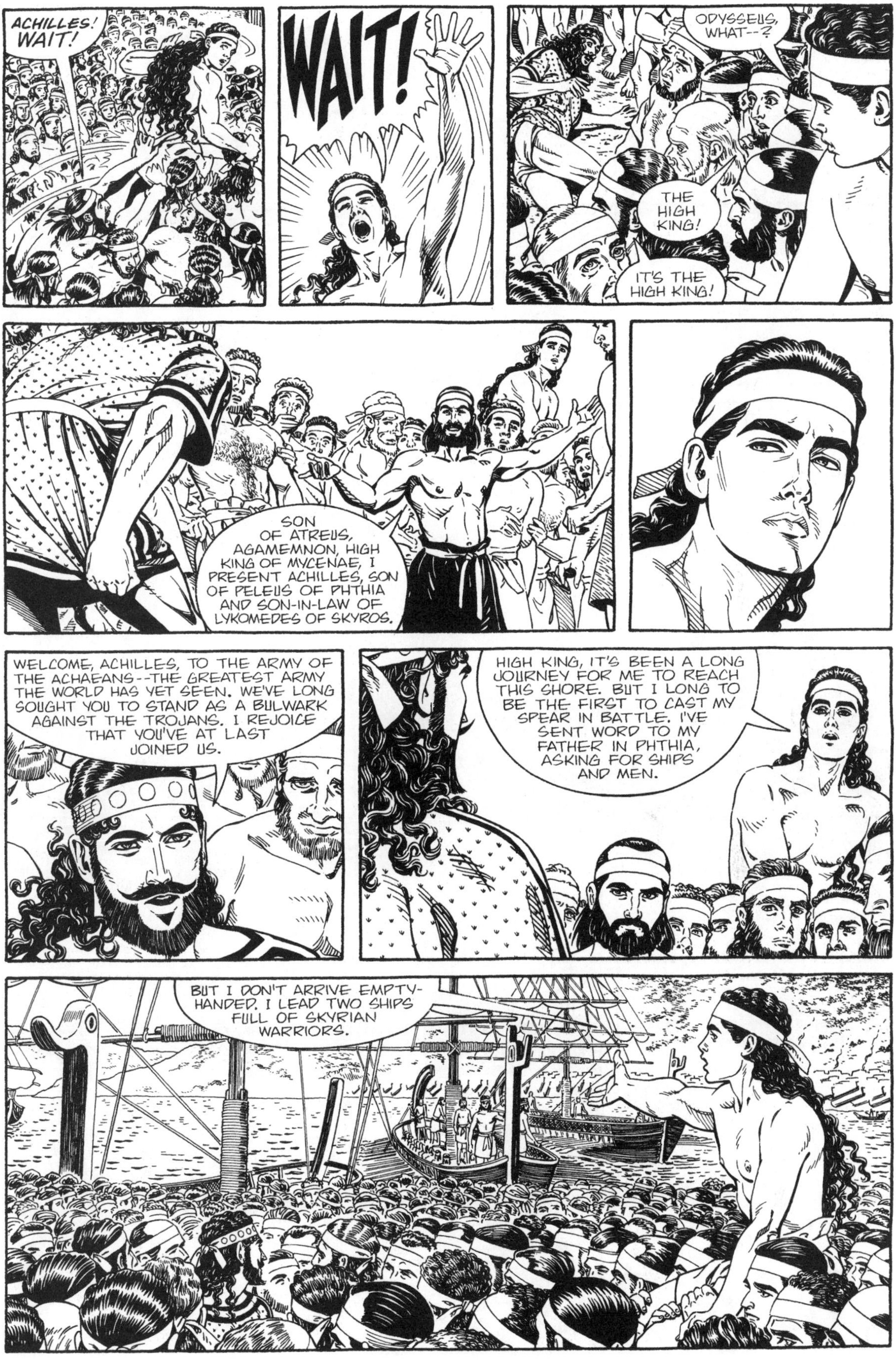
ACHILLES! WAIT!
WAIT!
ODYSSEUS, WHAT--?
THE HIGH KING!
IT'S THE HIGH KING!
SON OF ATREUS, AGAMEMNON, HIGH KING OF MYCENAE, I PRESENT ACHILLES, SON OF PELEUS OF PHTHIA AND SON-IN-LAW OF LYKOMEDES OF SKYROS.
WELCOME, ACHILLES, TO THE ARMY OF THE ACHAEANS--THE GREATEST ARMY THE WORLD HAS YET SEEN. WE'VE LONG SOUGHT YOU TO STAND AS A BULWARK AGAINST THE TROJANS. I REJOICE THAT YOU'VE AT LAST JOINED US.
HIGH KING, IT'S BEEN A LONG JOURNEY FOR ME TO REACH THIS SHORE. BUT I LONG TO BE THE FIRST TO CAST MY SPEAR IN BATTLE. I'VE SENT WORD TO MY FATHER IN PHTHIA, ASKING FOR SHIPS AND MEN.
BUT I DON'T ARRIVE EMPTY-HANDED. I LEAD TWO SHIPS FULL OF SKYRIAN WARRIORS.

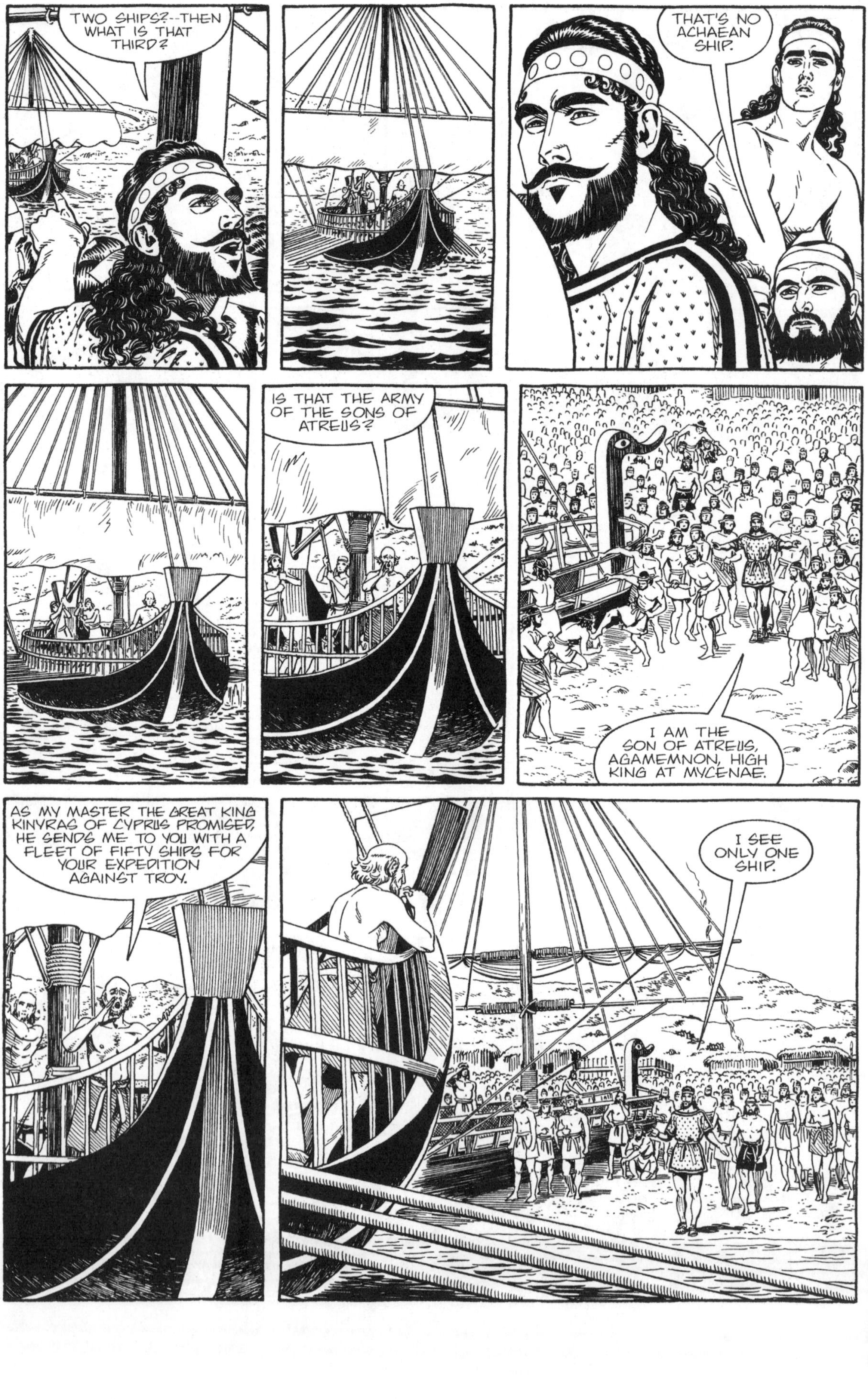
TWO SHIPS?--THEN WHAT IS THAT THIRD?
THAT'S NO ACHAEAN SHIP.
IS THAT THE ARMY OF THE SONS OF ATREUS?
I AM THE SON OF ATREUS, AGAMEMNON, HIGH KING AT MYCENAE.
AS MY MASTER THE GREAT KING KINYRAS OF CYPRUS PROMISED, HE SENDS ME TO YOU WITH A FLEET OF FIFTY SHIPS FOR YOUR EXPEDITION AGAINST TROY.
I SEE ONLY ONE SHIP.

WHAT ARE THOSE?

ODYSSEUS...

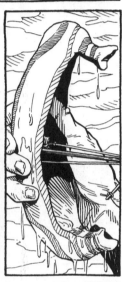

SHIPS! TERRA COTTA MODELS OF SHIPS!

FORTY-NINE OF THEM--VOTIVE OFFERINGS!

THIS IS HOW KINYRAS KEEPS HIS PROMISES?! I DON'T NEED OFFERINGS--I NEED *WARRIORS!* DOESN'T CYPRUS HAVE ENOUGH BRAVE MEN TO FILL FIFTY SHIPS?

THE *BRAVE* ONES ALL FOLLOWED PARIS OF TROY TO SIDON!

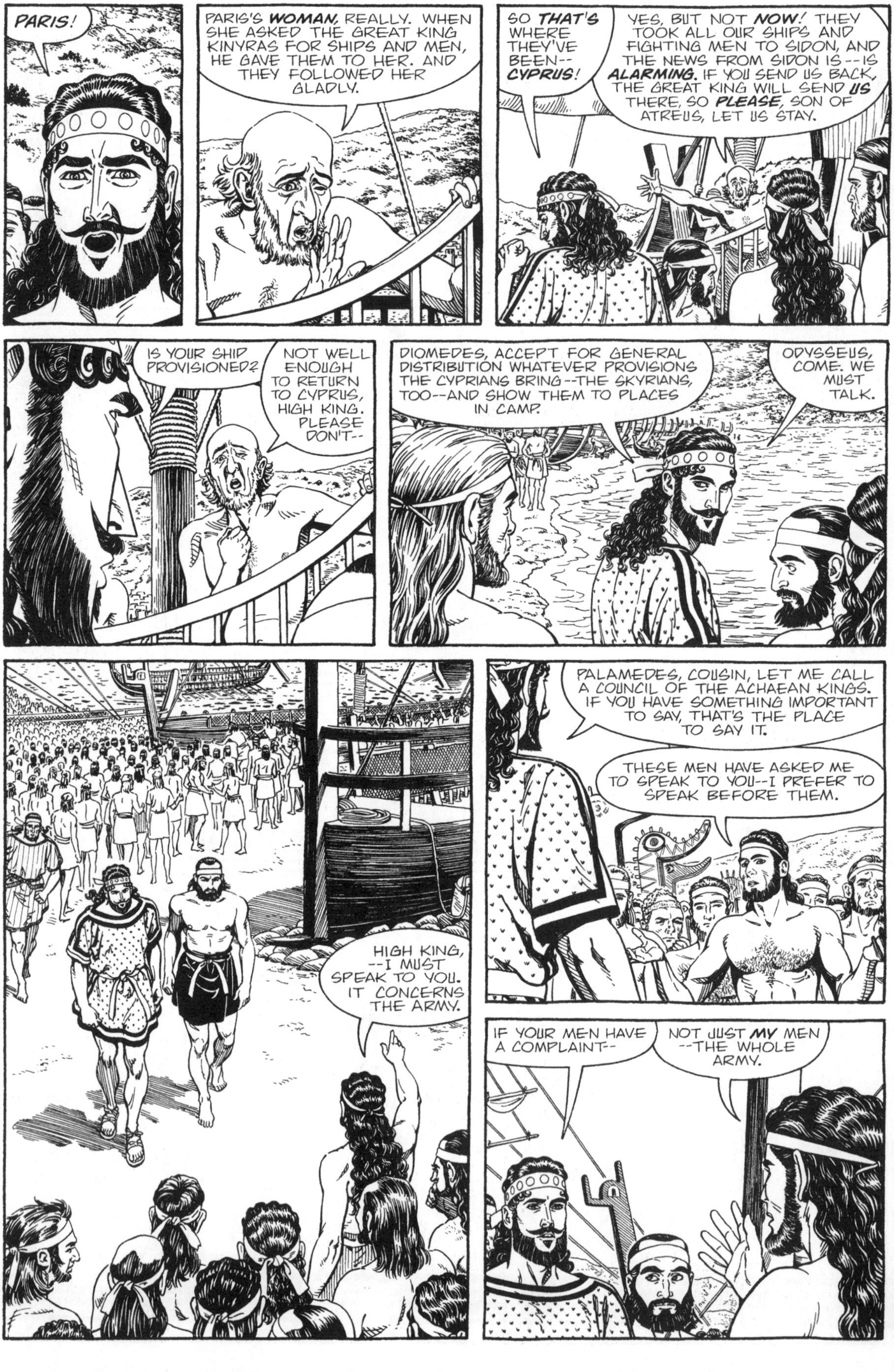
PARIS!
PARIS'S WOMAN, REALLY. WHEN SHE ASKED THE GREAT KING KINYRAS FOR SHIPS AND MEN, HE GAVE THEM TO HER. AND THEY FOLLOWED HER GLADLY.
SO THAT'S WHERE THEY'VE BEEN--CYPRUS!
YES, BUT NOT NOW! THEY TOOK ALL OUR SHIPS AND FIGHTING MEN TO SIDON, AND THE NEWS FROM SIDON IS--IS ALARMING. IF YOU SEND US BACK, THE GREAT KING WILL SEND US THERE, SO PLEASE, SON OF ATREUS, LET US STAY.
IS YOUR SHIP PROVISIONED?
NOT WELL ENOUGH TO RETURN TO CYPRUS, HIGH KING. PLEASE DON'T--
DIOMEDES, ACCEPT FOR GENERAL DISTRIBUTION WHATEVER PROVISIONS THE CYPRIANS BRING--THE SKYRIANS, TOO--AND SHOW THEM TO PLACES IN CAMP.
ODYSSEUS, COME. WE MUST TALK.
HIGH KING, --I MUST SPEAK TO YOU. IT CONCERNS THE ARMY.
PALAMEDES, COUSIN, LET ME CALL A COUNCIL OF THE ACHAEAN KINGS. IF YOU HAVE SOMETHING IMPORTANT TO SAY, THAT'S THE PLACE TO SAY IT.
THESE MEN HAVE ASKED ME TO SPEAK TO YOU--I PREFER TO SPEAK BEFORE THEM.
IF YOUR MEN HAVE A COMPLAINT--
NOT JUST MY MEN --THE WHOLE ARMY.

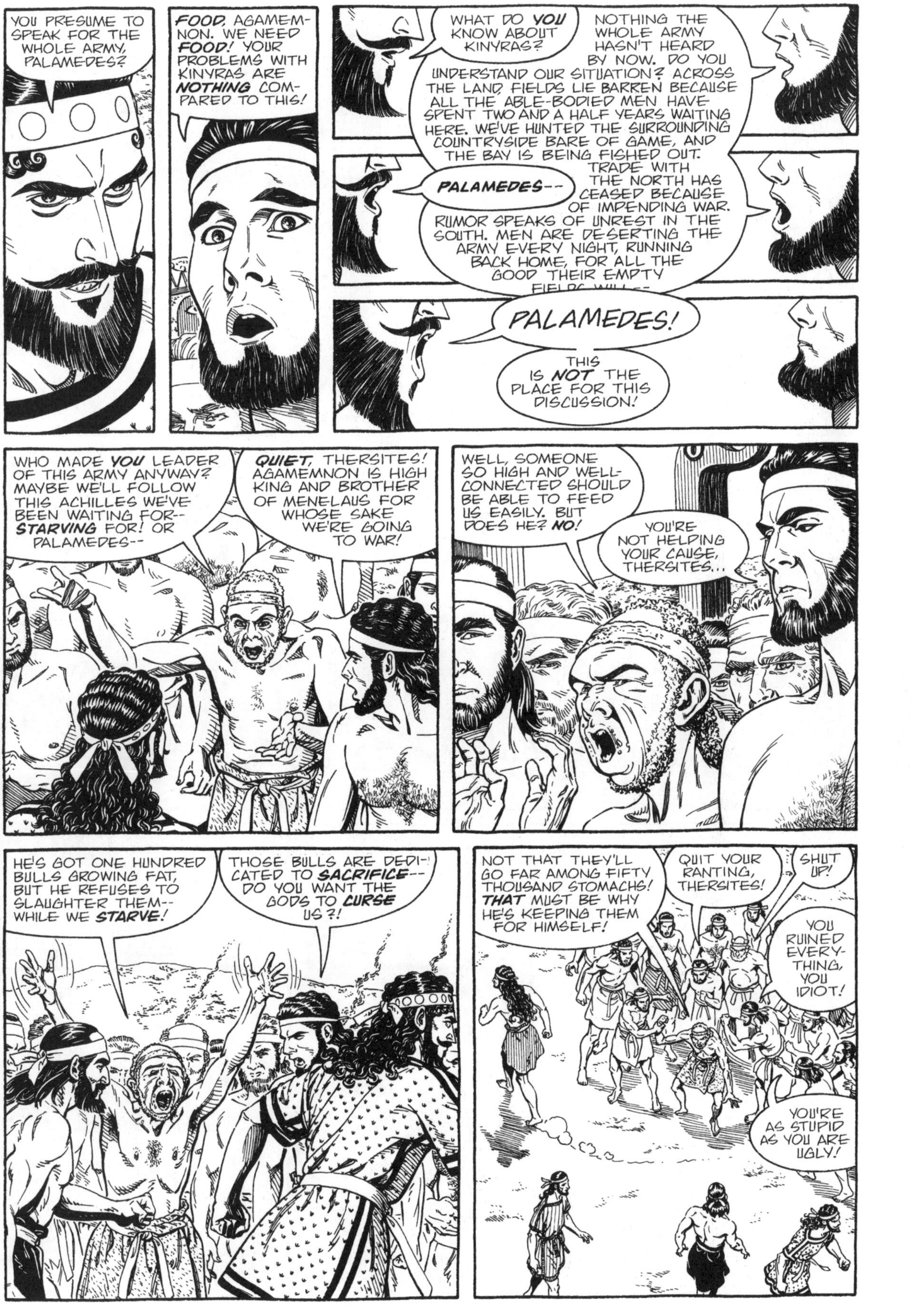
YOU PRESUME TO SPEAK FOR THE WHOLE ARMY, PALAMEDES?
FOOD, AGAMEMNON. WE NEED FOOD! YOUR PROBLEMS WITH KINYRAS ARE NOTHING COMPARED TO THIS!
WHAT DO YOU KNOW ABOUT KINYRAS?
NOTHING THE WHOLE ARMY HASN'T HEARD BY NOW. DO YOU UNDERSTAND OUR SITUATION? ACROSS THE LAND FIELDS LIE BARREN BECAUSE ALL THE ABLE-BODIED MEN HAVE SPENT TWO AND A HALF YEARS WAITING HERE. WE'VE HUNTED THE SURROUNDING COUNTRYSIDE BARE OF GAME, AND THE BAY IS BEING FISHED OUT.
PALAMEDES--
TRADE WITH THE NORTH HAS CEASED BECAUSE OF IMPENDING WAR. RUMOR SPEAKS OF UNREST IN THE SOUTH. MEN ARE DESERTING THE ARMY EVERY NIGHT, RUNNING BACK HOME, FOR ALL THE GOOD THEIR EMPTY
PALAMEDES!
THIS IS NOT THE PLACE FOR THIS DISCUSSION!
WHO MADE YOU LEADER OF THIS ARMY ANYWAY? MAYBE WE'LL FOLLOW THIS ACHILLES WE'VE BEEN WAITING FOR--STARVING FOR! OR PALAMEDES--
QUIET, THERSITES! AGAMEMNON IS HIGH KING AND BROTHER OF MENELAUS FOR WHOSE SAKE WE'RE GOING TO WAR!
WELL, SOMEONE SO HIGH AND WELL-CONNECTED SHOULD BE ABLE TO FEED US EASILY. BUT DOES HE? NO!
YOU'RE NOT HELPING YOUR CAUSE, THERSITES...
HE'S GOT ONE HUNDRED BULLS GROWING FAT, BUT HE REFUSES TO SLAUGHTER THEM--WHILE WE STARVE!
THOSE BULLS ARE DEDICATED TO SACRIFICE--DO YOU WANT THE GODS TO CURSE US?!
NOT THAT THEY'LL GO FAR AMONG FIFTY THOUSAND STOMACHS! THAT MUST BE WHY HE'S KEEPING THEM FOR HIMSELF!
QUIT YOUR RANTING, THERSITES!
SHUT UP!
YOU RUINED EVERYTHING, YOU IDIOT!
YOU'RE AS STUPID AS YOU ARE UGLY!

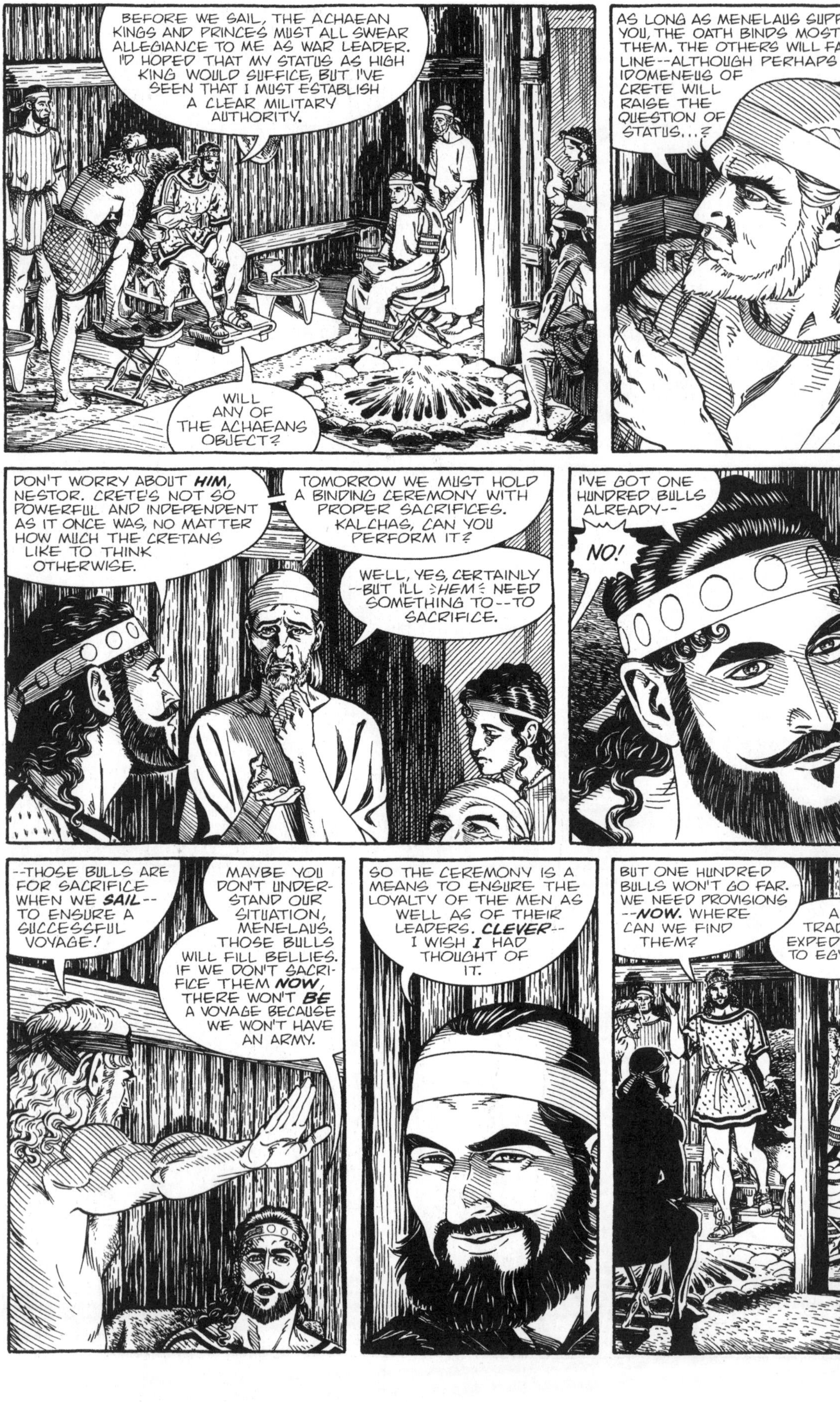
BEFORE WE SAIL, THE ACHAEAN KINGS AND PRINCES MUST ALL SWEAR ALLEGIANCE TO ME AS WAR LEADER. I'D HOPED THAT MY STATUS AS HIGH KING WOULD SUFFICE, BUT I'VE SEEN THAT I MUST ESTABLISH A CLEAR MILITARY AUTHORITY.
WILL ANY OF THE ACHAEANS OBJECT?
AS LONG AS MENELAUS SUPPORTS YOU, THE OATH BINDS MOST OF THEM. THE OTHERS WILL FALL IN LINE--ALTHOUGH PERHAPS IDOMENEUS OF CRETE WILL RAISE THE QUESTION OF STATUS...?
DON'T WORRY ABOUT HIM, NESTOR. CRETE'S NOT SO POWERFUL AND INDEPENDENT AS IT ONCE WAS, NO MATTER HOW MUCH THE CRETANS LIKE TO THINK OTHERWISE.
TOMORROW WE MUST HOLD A BINDING CEREMONY WITH PROPER SACRIFICES. KALCHAS, CAN YOU PERFORM IT?
WELL, YES, CERTAINLY --BUT I'LL HEM NEED SOMETHING TO--TO SACRIFICE.
I'VE GOT ONE HUNDRED BULLS ALREADY--
NO!
--THOSE BULLS ARE FOR SACRIFICE WHEN WE SAIL-- TO ENSURE A SUCCESSFUL VOYAGE!
MAYBE YOU DON'T UNDERSTAND OUR SITUATION, MENELAUS. THOSE BULLS WILL FILL BELLIES. IF WE DON'T SACRIFICE THEM NOW, THERE WON'T BE A VOYAGE BECAUSE WE WON'T HAVE AN ARMY.
SO THE CEREMONY IS A MEANS TO ENSURE THE LOYALTY OF THE MEN AS WELL AS OF THEIR LEADERS. CLEVER-- I WISH I HAD THOUGHT OF IT.
BUT ONE HUNDRED BULLS WON'T GO FAR. WE NEED PROVISIONS --NOW. WHERE CAN WE FIND THEM?
A TRADING EXPEDITION TO EGYPT?

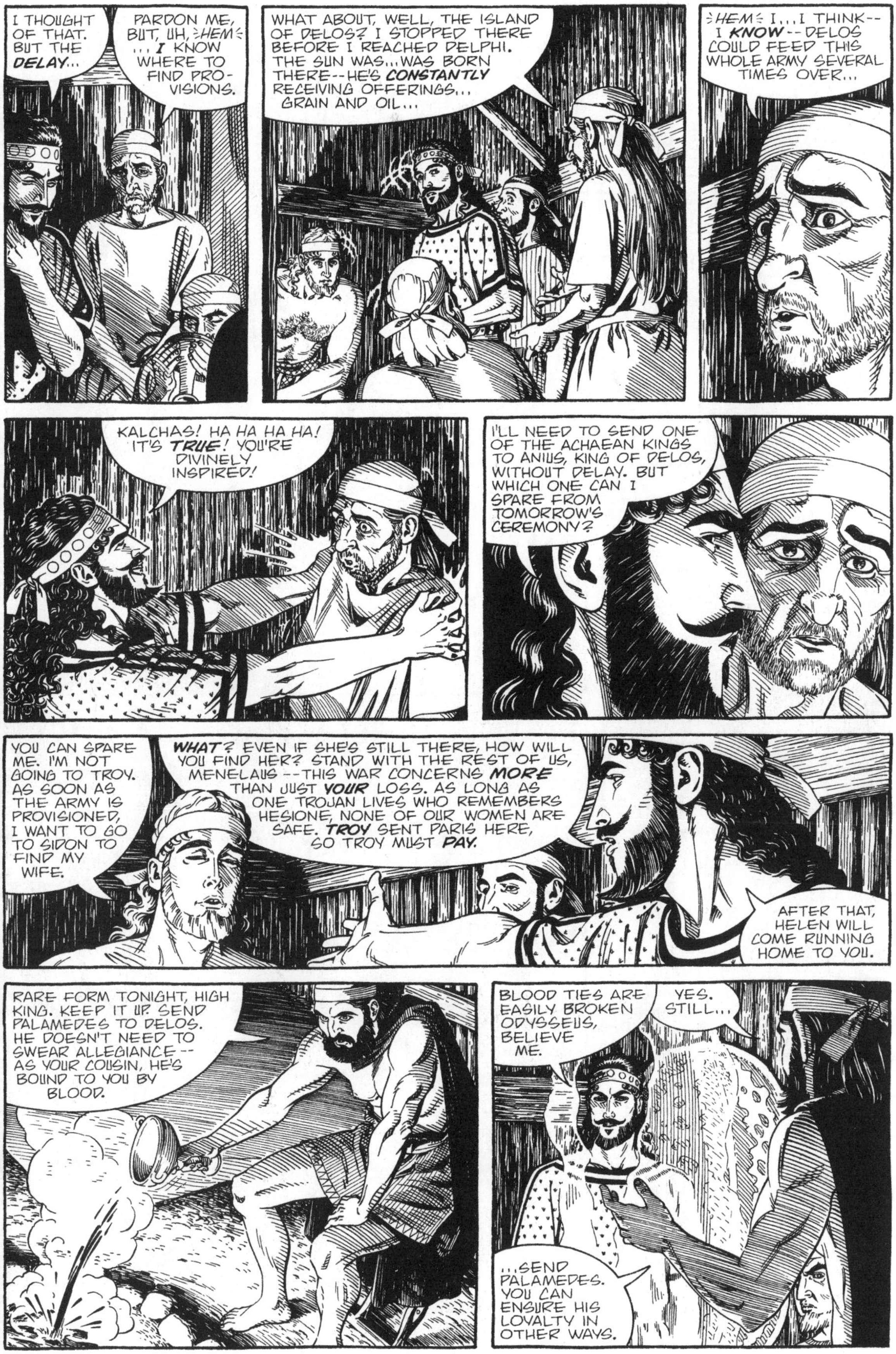
I THOUGHT OF THAT. BUT THE DELAY...
PARDON ME, BUT, UH, HEM ... I KNOW WHERE TO FIND PROVISIONS.
WHAT ABOUT, WELL, THE ISLAND OF DELOS? I STOPPED THERE BEFORE I REACHED DELPHI. THE SUN WAS...WAS BORN THERE--HE'S CONSTANTLY RECEIVING OFFERINGS... GRAIN AND OIL...
HEM I...I THINK-- I KNOW--DELOS COULD FEED THIS WHOLE ARMY SEVERAL TIMES OVER...
KALCHAS! HA HA HA HA! IT'S TRUE! YOU'RE DIVINELY INSPIRED!
I'LL NEED TO SEND ONE OF THE ACHAEAN KINGS TO ANIUS, KING OF DELOS, WITHOUT DELAY. BUT WHICH ONE CAN I SPARE FROM TOMORROW'S CEREMONY?
YOU CAN SPARE ME. I'M NOT GOING TO TROY. AS SOON AS THE ARMY IS PROVISIONED, I WANT TO GO TO SIDON TO FIND MY WIFE.
WHAT? EVEN IF SHE'S STILL THERE, HOW WILL YOU FIND HER? STAND WITH THE REST OF US, MENELAUS--THIS WAR CONCERNS MORE THAN JUST YOUR LOSS. AS LONG AS ONE TROJAN LIVES WHO REMEMBERS HESIONE, NONE OF OUR WOMEN ARE SAFE. TROY SENT PARIS HERE, SO TROY MUST PAY.
AFTER THAT, HELEN WILL COME RUNNING HOME TO YOU.
RARE FORM TONIGHT, HIGH KING. KEEP IT UP. SEND PALAMEDES TO DELOS. HE DOESN'T NEED TO SWEAR ALLEGIANCE-- AS YOUR COUSIN, HE'S BOUND TO YOU BY BLOOD.
BLOOD TIES ARE EASILY BROKEN ODYSSEUS, BELIEVE ME.
YES. STILL...
...SEND PALAMEDES. YOU CAN ENSURE HIS LOYALTY IN OTHER WAYS.

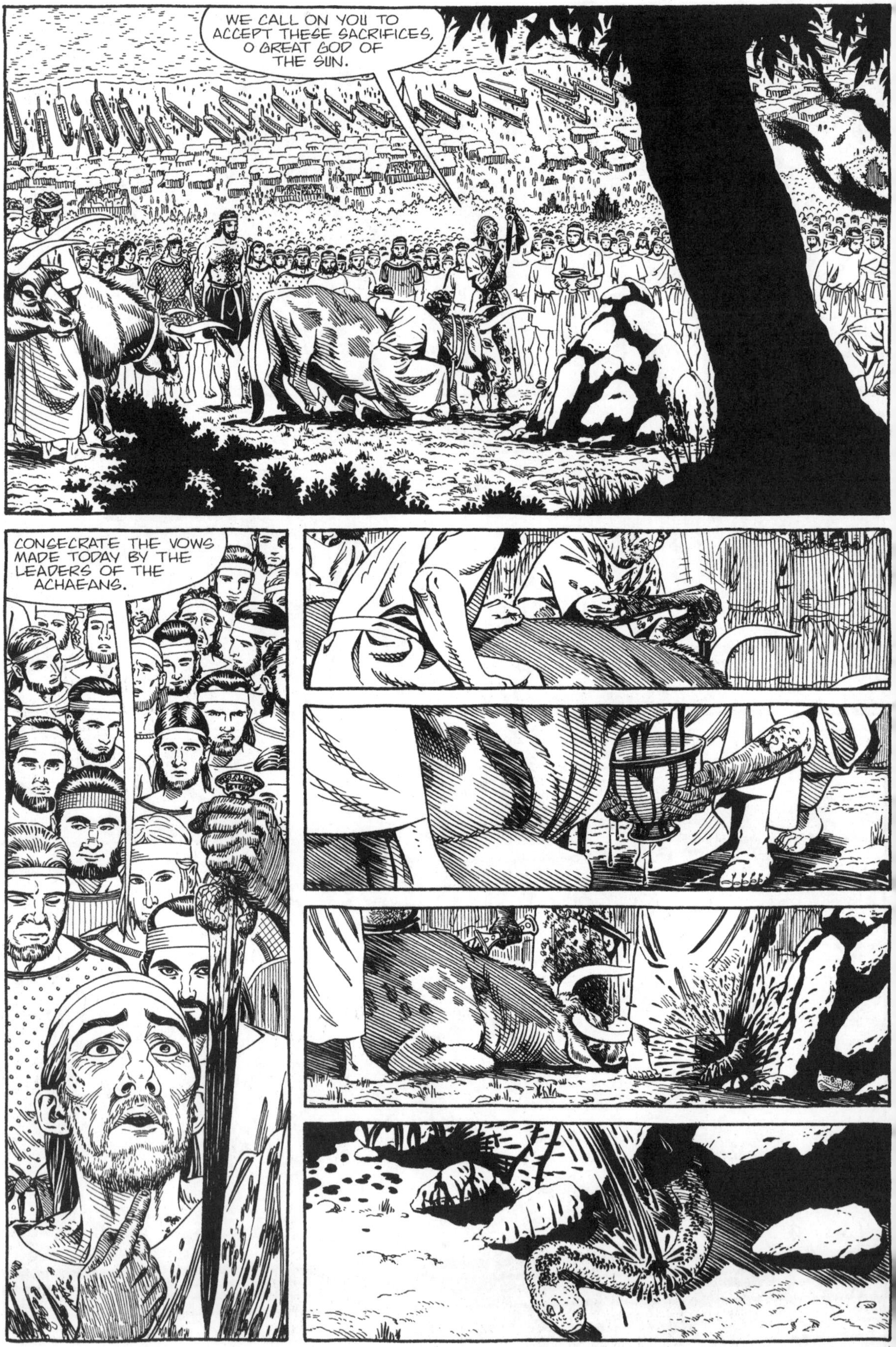
WE CALL ON YOU TO ACCEPT THESE SACRIFICES, O GREAT GOD OF THE SUN.
CONSECRATE THE VOWS MADE TODAY BY THE LEADERS OF THE ACHAEANS.

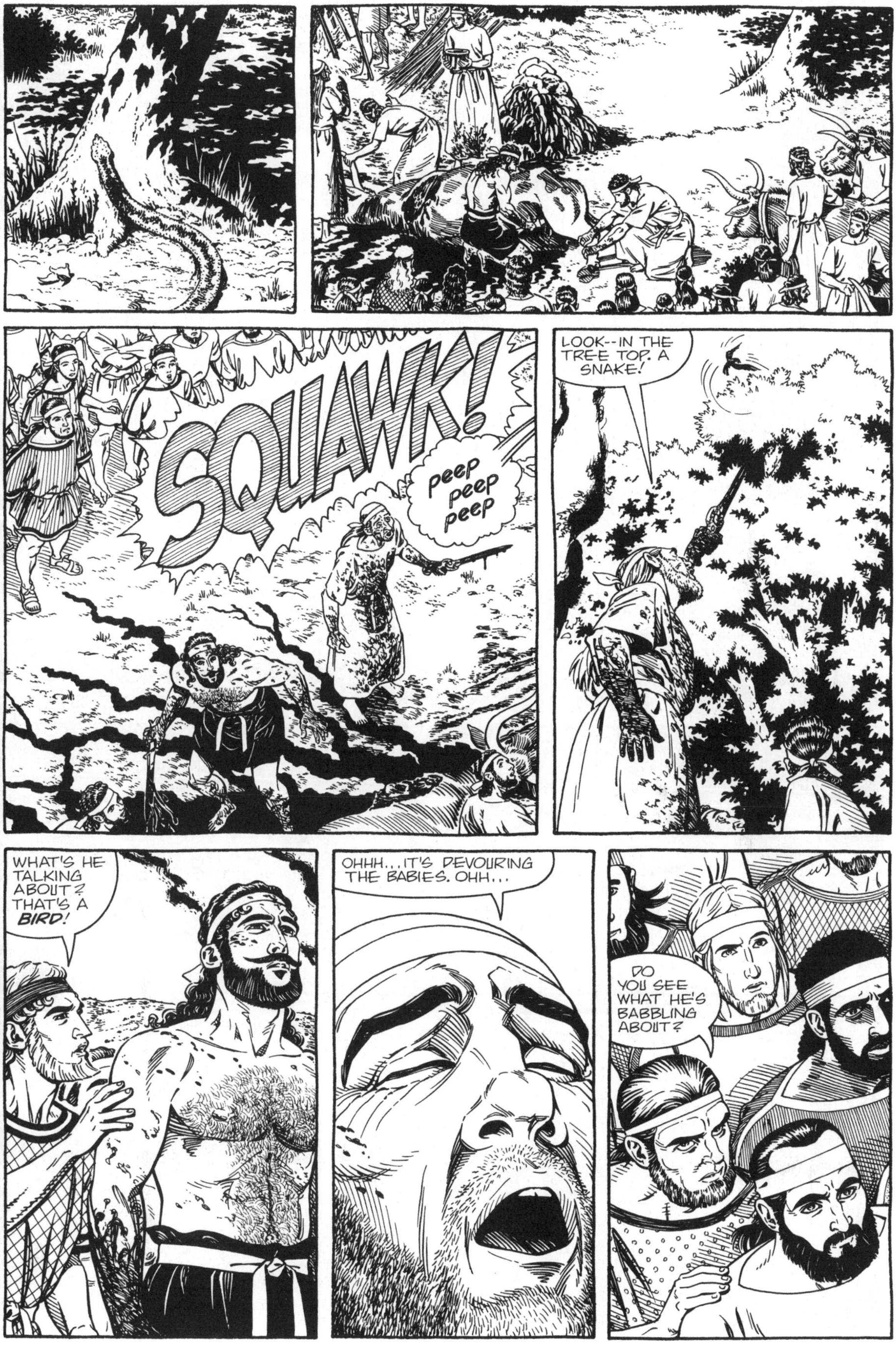
SQUAWK!
peep peep peep
LOOK--IN THE TREE TOP. A SNAKE!
WHAT'S HE TALKING ABOUT? THAT'S A BIRD!
OHHH...IT'S DEVOURING THE BABIES. OHH...
DO YOU SEE WHAT HE'S BABBLING ABOUT?

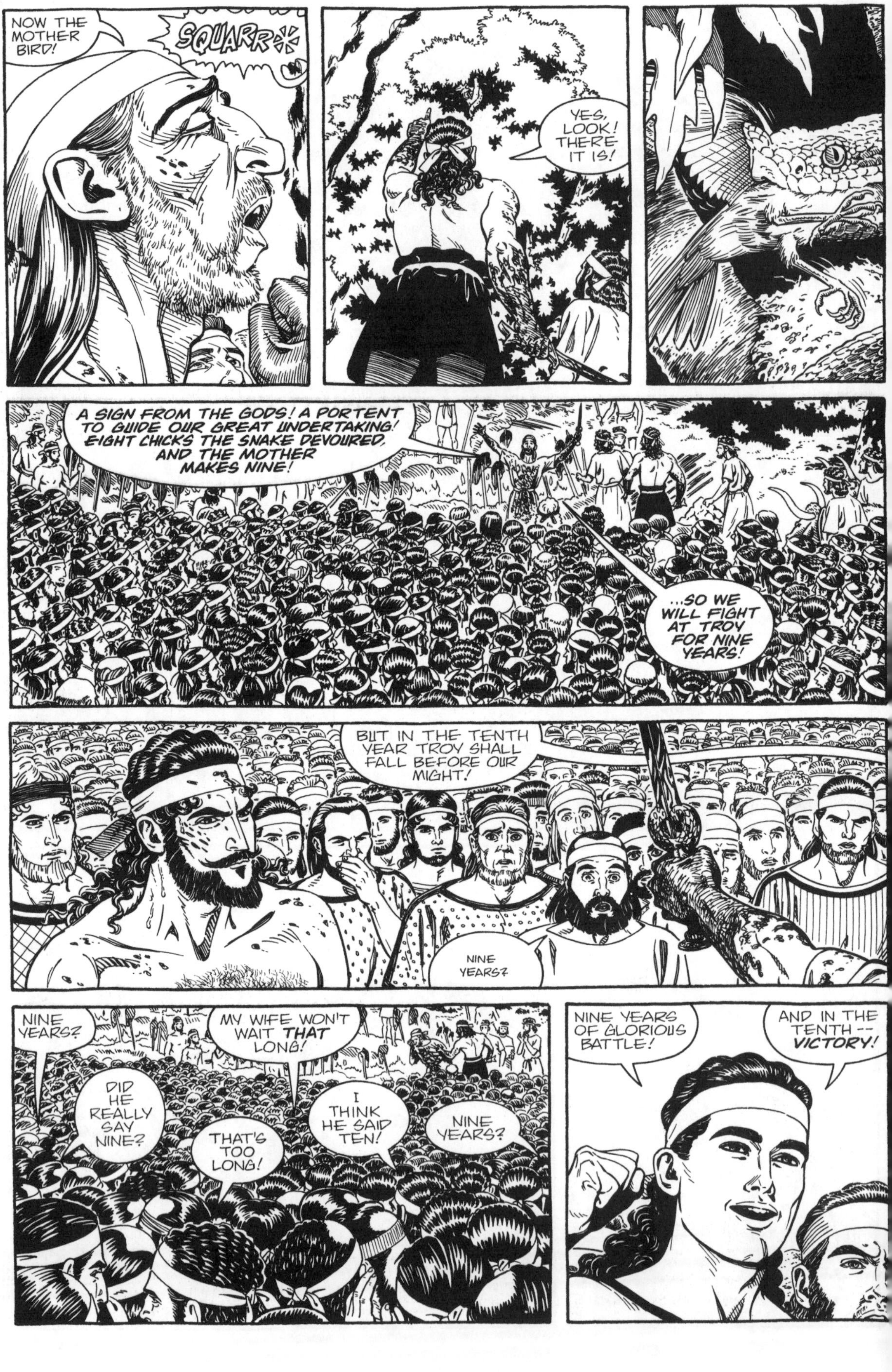
NOW THE MOTHER BIRD!
SQUARR
YES, LOOK! THERE IT IS!
A SIGN FROM THE GODS! A PORTENT TO GUIDE OUR GREAT UNDERTAKING! EIGHT CHICKS THE SNAKE DEVOURED, AND THE MOTHER MAKES NINE!
...SO WE WILL FIGHT AT TROY FOR NINE YEARS!
BUT IN THE TENTH YEAR TROY SHALL FALL BEFORE OUR MIGHT!
NINE YEARS?
NINE YEARS?
MY WIFE WON'T WAIT THAT LONG!
DID HE REALLY SAY NINE?
THAT'S TOO LONG!
I THINK HE SAID TEN!
NINE YEARS?
NINE YEARS OF GLORIOUS BATTLE!
AND IN THE TENTH -- VICTORY!

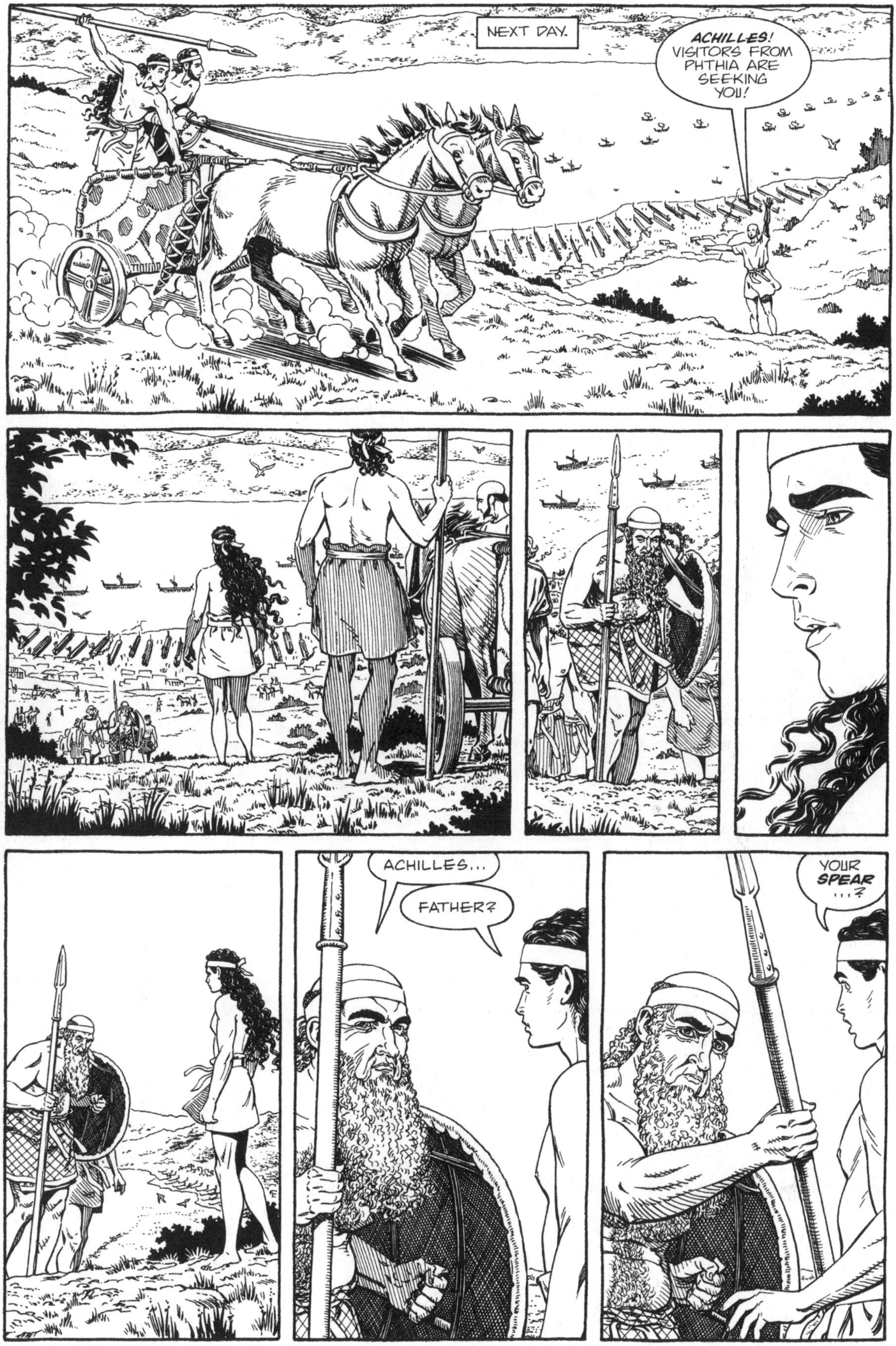
NEXT DAY.
ACHILLES! VISITORS FROM PHTHIA ARE SEEKING YOU!
ACHILLES...
FATHER?
YOUR SPEAR ...?

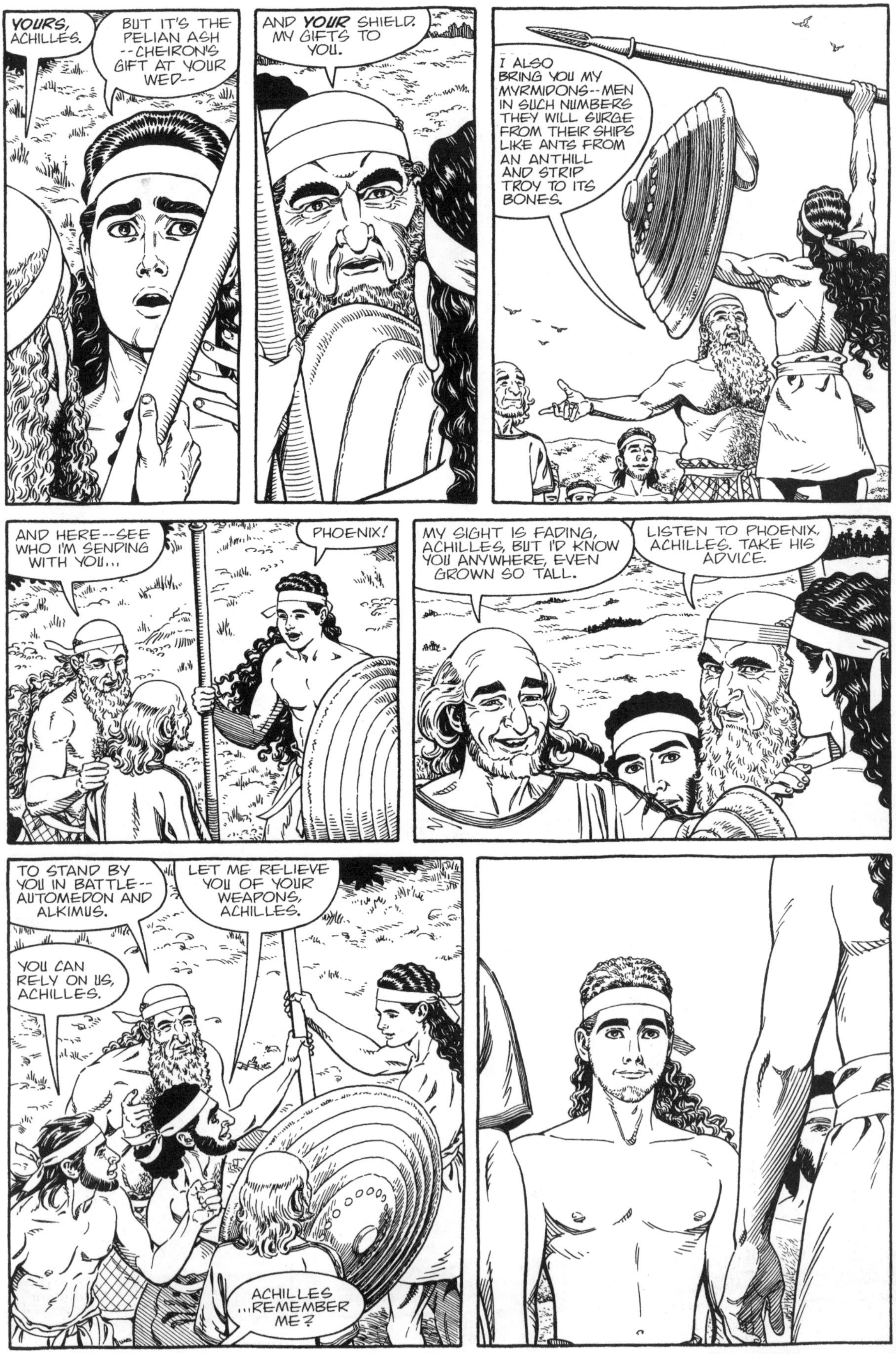
YOURS, ACHILLES.
BUT IT'S THE PELIAN ASH --CHEIRON'S GIFT AT YOUR WED--
AND YOUR SHIELD. MY GIFTS TO YOU.
I ALSO BRING YOU MY MYRMIDONS--MEN IN SUCH NUMBERS THEY WILL SURGE FROM THEIR SHIPS LIKE ANTS FROM AN ANTHILL AND STRIP TROY TO ITS BONES.
AND HERE--SEE WHO I'M SENDING WITH YOU...
PHOENIX!
MY SIGHT IS FADING, ACHILLES, BUT I'D KNOW YOU ANYWHERE, EVEN GROWN SO TALL.
LISTEN TO PHOENIX, ACHILLES. TAKE HIS ADVICE.
TO STAND BY YOU IN BATTLE-- AUTOMEDON AND ALKIMUS.
LET ME RELIEVE YOU OF YOUR WEAPONS, ACHILLES.
YOU CAN RELY ON US, ACHILLES.
ACHILLES ...REMEMBER ME?

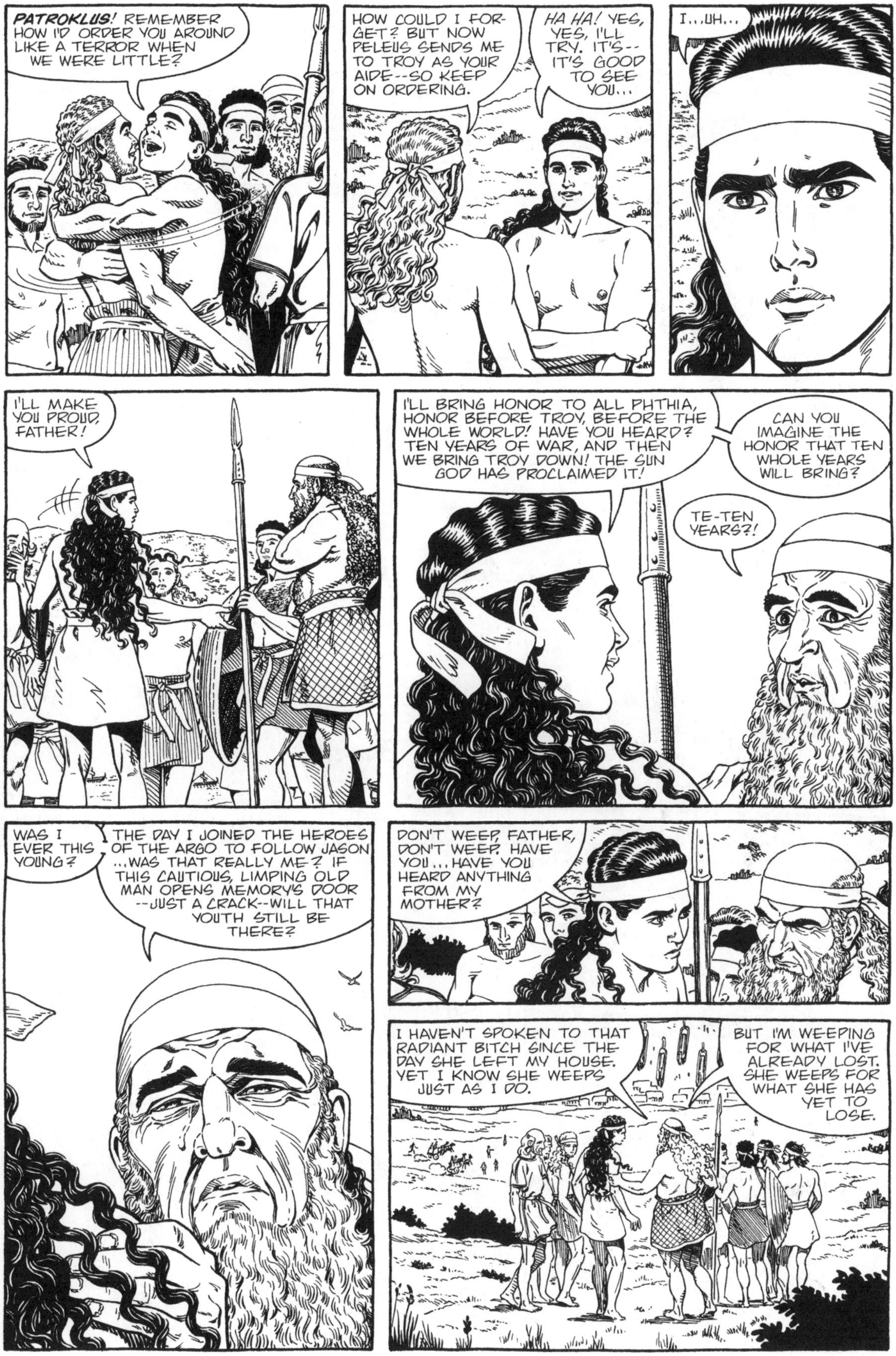
PATROKLUS! REMEMBER HOW I'D ORDER YOU AROUND LIKE A TERROR WHEN WE WERE LITTLE?
HOW COULD I FORGET? BUT NOW PELEUS SENDS ME TO TROY AS YOUR AIDE--SO KEEP ON ORDERING.
HA HA! YES, YES, I'LL TRY. IT'S--IT'S GOOD TO SEE YOU...
I...UH...
I'LL MAKE YOU PROUD, FATHER!
I'LL BRING HONOR TO ALL PHTHIA, HONOR BEFORE TROY, BEFORE THE WHOLE WORLD! HAVE YOU HEARD? TEN YEARS OF WAR, AND THEN WE BRING TROY DOWN! THE SUN GOD HAS PROCLAIMED IT!
CAN YOU IMAGINE THE HONOR THAT TEN WHOLE YEARS WILL BRING?
TE-TEN YEARS?!
WAS I EVER THIS YOUNG?
THE DAY I JOINED THE HEROES OF THE ARGO TO FOLLOW JASON ...WAS THAT REALLY ME? IF THIS CAUTIOUS, LIMPING OLD MAN OPENS MEMORY'S DOOR --JUST A CRACK--WILL THAT YOUTH STILL BE THERE?
DON'T WEEP, FATHER, DON'T WEEP. HAVE YOU...HAVE YOU HEARD ANYTHING FROM MY MOTHER?
I HAVEN'T SPOKEN TO THAT RADIANT BITCH SINCE THE DAY SHE LEFT MY HOUSE. YET I KNOW SHE WEEPS JUST AS I DO.
BUT I'M WEEPING FOR WHAT I'VE ALREADY LOST. SHE WEEPS FOR WHAT SHE HAS YET TO LOSE.

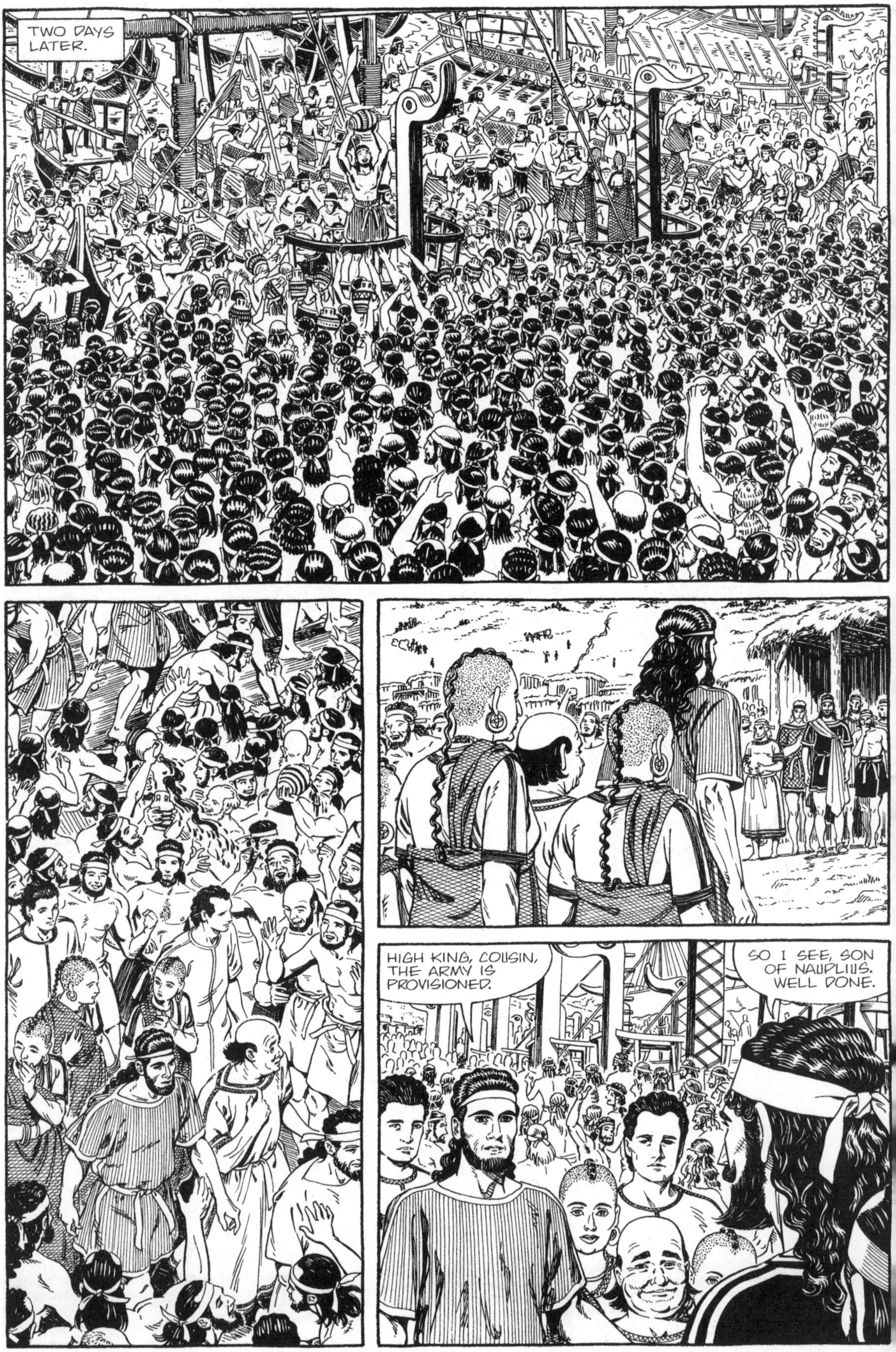
TWO DAYS LATER.
HIGH KING, COUSIN, THE ARMY IS PROVISIONED.
SO I SEE, SON OF NAUPLIUS. WELL DONE.

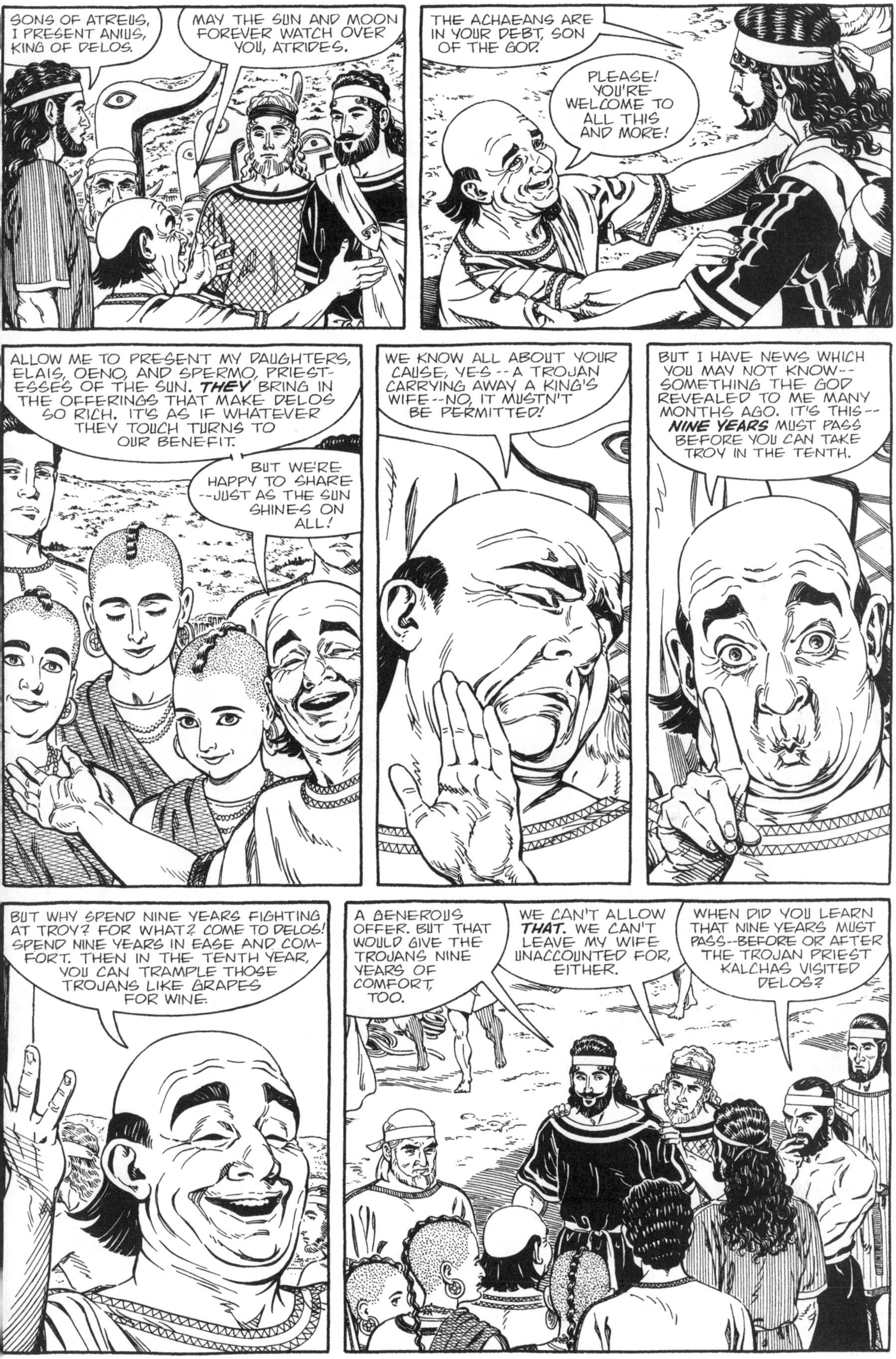
SONS OF ATREUS, I PRESENT ANIUS, KING OF DELOS.
MAY THE SUN AND MOON FOREVER WATCH OVER YOU, ATRIDES.
THE ACHAEANS ARE IN YOUR DEBT, SON OF THE GOD.
PLEASE! YOU'RE WELCOME TO ALL THIS AND MORE!
ALLOW ME TO PRESENT MY DAUGHTERS, ELAIS, OENO, AND SPERMO, PRIEST-ESSES OF THE SUN. THEY BRING IN THE OFFERINGS THAT MAKE DELOS SO RICH. IT'S AS IF WHATEVER THEY TOUCH TURNS TO OUR BENEFIT.
BUT WE'RE HAPPY TO SHARE --JUST AS THE SUN SHINES ON ALL!
WE KNOW ALL ABOUT YOUR CAUSE, YES --A TROJAN CARRYING AWAY A KING'S WIFE--NO, IT MUSTN'T BE PERMITTED!
BUT I HAVE NEWS WHICH YOU MAY NOT KNOW-- SOMETHING THE GOD REVEALED TO ME MANY MONTHS AGO. IT'S THIS-- NINE YEARS MUST PASS BEFORE YOU CAN TAKE TROY IN THE TENTH.
BUT WHY SPEND NINE YEARS FIGHTING AT TROY? FOR WHAT? COME TO DELOS! SPEND NINE YEARS IN EASE AND COMFORT. THEN IN THE TENTH YEAR, YOU CAN TRAMPLE THOSE TROJANS LIKE GRAPES FOR WINE.
A GENEROUS OFFER. BUT THAT WOULD GIVE THE TROJANS NINE YEARS OF COMFORT, TOO.
WE CAN'T ALLOW THAT. WE CAN'T LEAVE MY WIFE UNACCOUNTED FOR, EITHER.
WHEN DID YOU LEARN THAT NINE YEARS MUST PASS--BEFORE OR AFTER THE TROJAN PRIEST KALCHAS VISITED DELOS?

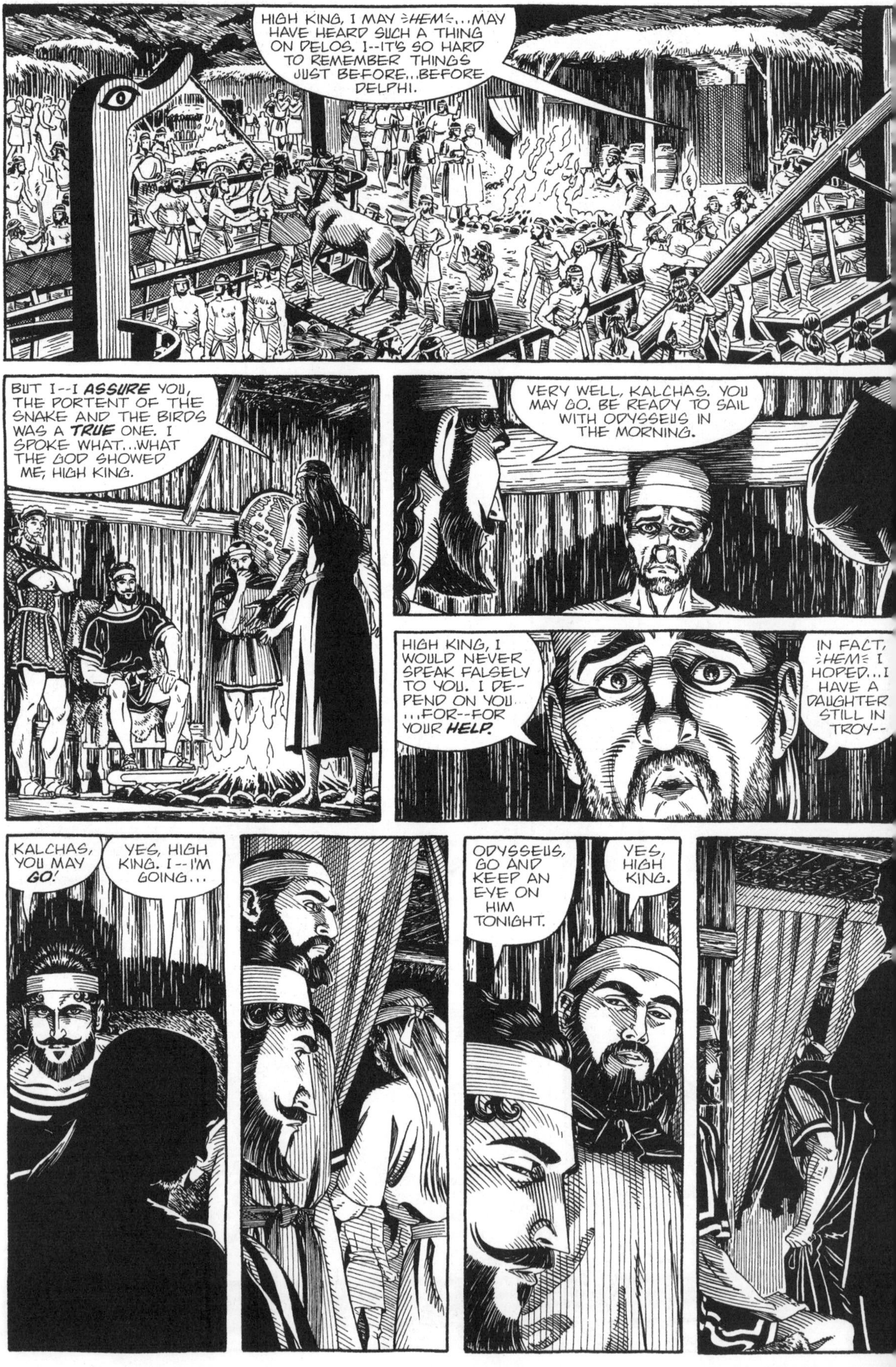
HIGH KING, I MAY ≡HEM≡... MAY HAVE HEARD SUCH A THING ON DELOS. I--IT'S SO HARD TO REMEMBER THINGS JUST BEFORE... BEFORE DELPHI.
BUT I--I ASSURE YOU, THE PORTENT OF THE SNAKE AND THE BIRDS WAS A TRUE ONE. I SPOKE WHAT... WHAT THE GOD SHOWED ME, HIGH KING.
VERY WELL, KALCHAS. YOU MAY GO. BE READY TO SAIL WITH ODYSSEUS IN THE MORNING.
HIGH KING, I WOULD NEVER SPEAK FALSELY TO YOU. I DEPEND ON YOU ...FOR--FOR YOUR HELP.
IN FACT, ≡HEM≡ I HOPED... I HAVE A DAUGHTER STILL IN TROY--
KALCHAS, YOU MAY GO!
YES, HIGH KING. I--I'M GOING...
ODYSSEUS, GO AND KEEP AN EYE ON HIM TONIGHT.
YES, HIGH KING.

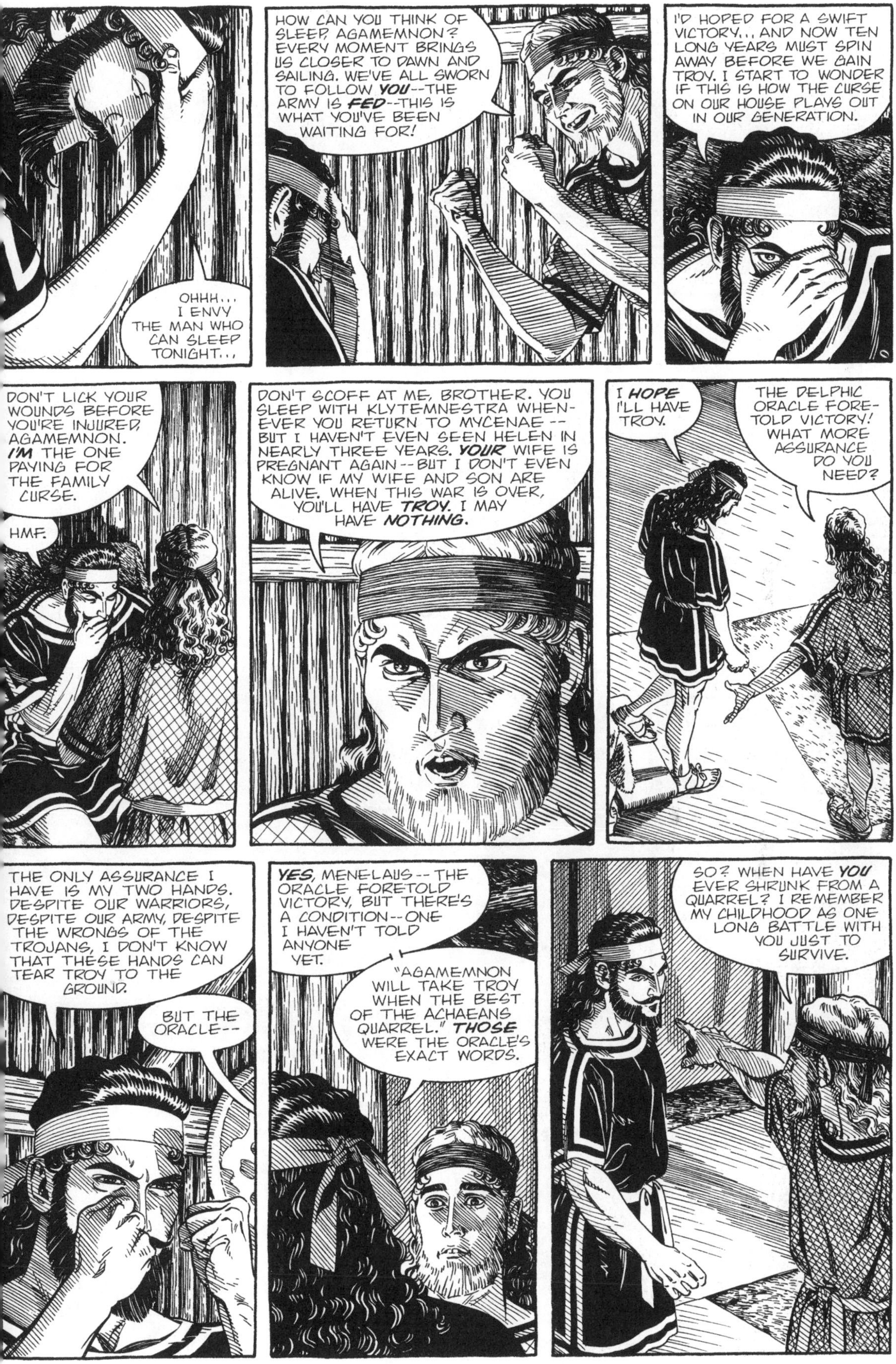
OHHH... I ENVY THE MAN WHO CAN SLEEP TONIGHT...
HOW CAN YOU THINK OF SLEEP, AGAMEMNON? EVERY MOMENT BRINGS US CLOSER TO DAWN AND SAILING. WE'VE ALL SWORN TO FOLLOW YOU--THE ARMY IS FED--THIS IS WHAT YOU'VE BEEN WAITING FOR!
I'D HOPED FOR A SWIFT VICTORY... AND NOW TEN LONG YEARS MUST SPIN AWAY BEFORE WE GAIN TROY. I START TO WONDER IF THIS IS HOW THE CURSE ON OUR HOUSE PLAYS OUT IN OUR GENERATION.
DON'T LICK YOUR WOUNDS BEFORE YOU'RE INJURED, AGAMEMNON. I'M THE ONE PAYING FOR THE FAMILY CURSE.
HMF.
DON'T SCOFF AT ME, BROTHER. YOU SLEEP WITH KLYTEMNESTRA WHENEVER YOU RETURN TO MYCENAE--BUT I HAVEN'T EVEN SEEN HELEN IN NEARLY THREE YEARS. YOUR WIFE IS PREGNANT AGAIN--BUT I DON'T EVEN KNOW IF MY WIFE AND SON ARE ALIVE. WHEN THIS WAR IS OVER, YOU'LL HAVE TROY. I MAY HAVE NOTHING.
I HOPE I'LL HAVE TROY.
THE DELPHIC ORACLE FORETOLD VICTORY! WHAT MORE ASSURANCE DO YOU NEED?
THE ONLY ASSURANCE I HAVE IS MY TWO HANDS. DESPITE OUR WARRIORS, DESPITE OUR ARMY, DESPITE THE WRONGS OF THE TROJANS, I DON'T KNOW THAT THESE HANDS CAN TEAR TROY TO THE GROUND.
BUT THE ORACLE--
YES, MENELAUS--THE ORACLE FORETOLD VICTORY, BUT THERE'S A CONDITION--ONE I HAVEN'T TOLD ANYONE YET.
"AGAMEMNON WILL TAKE TROY WHEN THE BEST OF THE ACHAEANS QUARREL." THOSE WERE THE ORACLE'S EXACT WORDS.
SO? WHEN HAVE YOU EVER SHRUNK FROM A QUARREL? I REMEMBER MY CHILDHOOD AS ONE LONG BATTLE WITH YOU JUST TO SURVIVE.

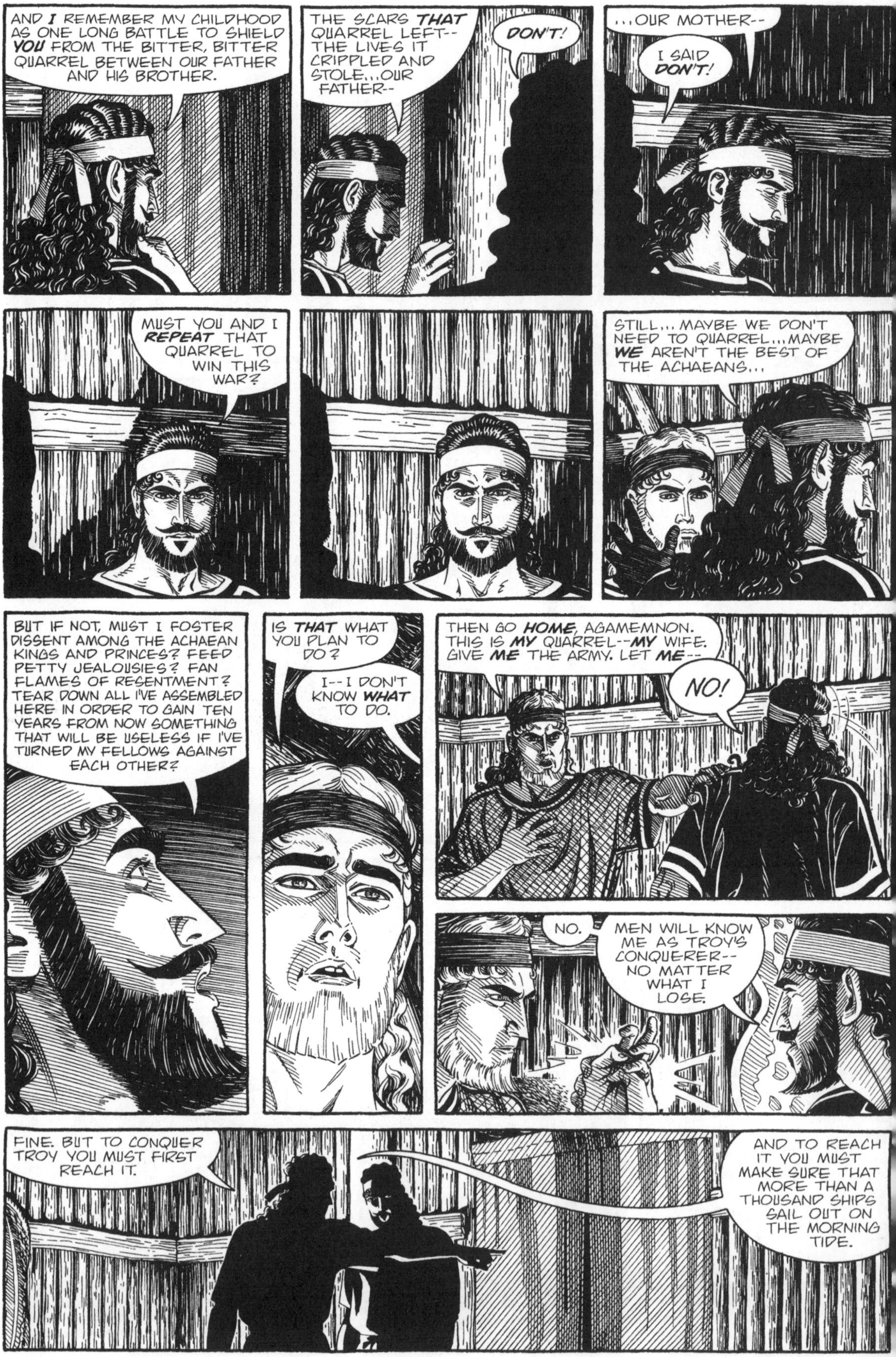
AND I REMEMBER MY CHILDHOOD AS ONE LONG BATTLE TO SHIELD YOU FROM THE BITTER, BITTER QUARREL BETWEEN OUR FATHER AND HIS BROTHER.
THE SCARS THAT QUARREL LEFT-- THE LIVES IT CRIPPLED AND STOLE...OUR FATHER--
DON'T!
...OUR MOTHER--
I SAID DON'T!
MUST YOU AND I REPEAT THAT QUARREL TO WIN THIS WAR?
STILL... MAYBE WE DON'T NEED TO QUARREL...MAYBE WE AREN'T THE BEST OF THE ACHAEANS...
BUT IF NOT, MUST I FOSTER DISSENT AMONG THE ACHAEAN KINGS AND PRINCES? FEED PETTY JEALOUSIES? FAN FLAMES OF RESENTMENT? TEAR DOWN ALL I'VE ASSEMBLED HERE IN ORDER TO GAIN TEN YEARS FROM NOW SOMETHING THAT WILL BE USELESS IF I'VE TURNED MY FELLOWS AGAINST EACH OTHER?
IS THAT WHAT YOU PLAN TO DO?
I--I DON'T KNOW WHAT TO DO.
THEN GO HOME, AGAMEMNON. THIS IS MY QUARREL--MY WIFE. GIVE ME THE ARMY. LET ME--
NO!
NO.
MEN WILL KNOW ME AS TROY'S CONQUERER-- NO MATTER WHAT I LOSE.
FINE. BUT TO CONQUER TROY YOU MUST FIRST REACH IT.
AND TO REACH IT YOU MUST MAKE SURE THAT MORE THAN A THOUSAND SHIPS SAIL OUT ON THE MORNING TIDE.

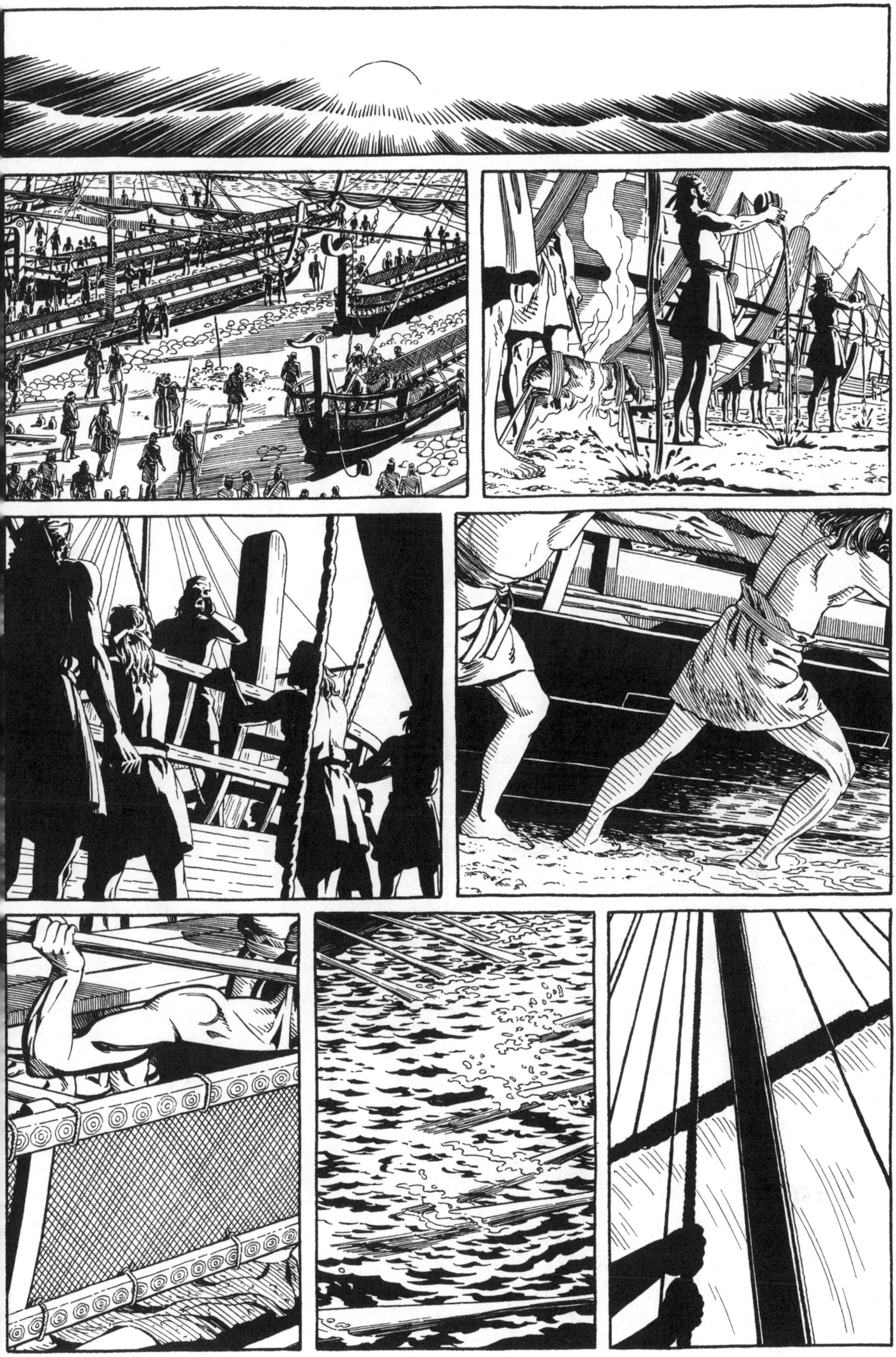

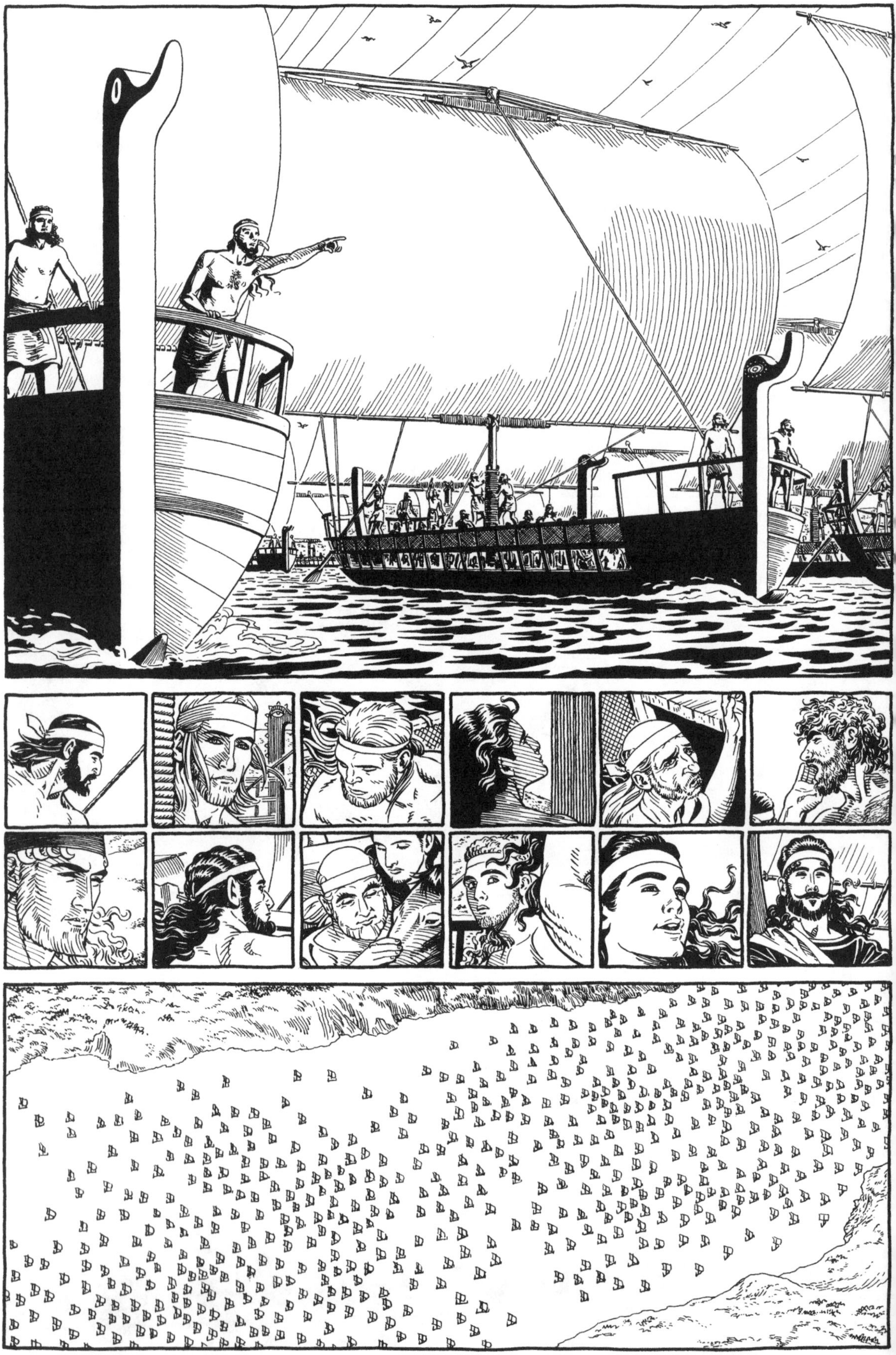

AFTERWORD

A Thousand Ships is the first in a projected seven volume series titled *Age of Bronze* which will tell the complete story of the Trojan War—from Paris's days herding cattle on the slopes of Mount Ida, through the end of the war as the heroes depart for home.

HOW IT BEGAN

The Trojan War snuck up on me.

I usually listen to audio books while I am inking or painting. In February 1991, I listened to *The March of Folly: From Troy to Vietnam* by Barbara W. Tuchman and was drawn in by her chapter on the Trojan War. While that chapter seems shockingly brief to me now, at that time it opened a door to a fascinating world.

Not quite a new world. Although I had never read Homer's *Iliad* (and once I did, I was surprised to learn that instead of the story of the entire Trojan War, *The Iliad* tells only a brief portion of the story, never even mentioning the most famous episode, the Trojan Horse!), as a child I had read children's versions of the story of Troy. I recall one which I read as a sixth grader more vividly than others—Olivia Coolidge's book *The Trojan War,* probably because of its striking cover art. But the Trojan War had never seemed to me anything particularly special. It was an interesting Greek myth, a legend, an exciting adventure story, no more or less engaging than a thousand other stories. But Tuchman's book made me suddenly realize that the story of the Trojan War could make a fascinating comic book.

Maybe someday I'll get around to it, I thought, but first I'll have to finish this, accomplish that. . . . I jotted down a couple notes about the Trojan War onto a scrap of paper, shoved the notes into my idea file, and promptly went back to the projects at hand.

But the Trojan War didn't let me go. Even while I was burying my nose in book after book on Ancient Egypt for a since-aborted comics project, the Trojan War kept poking its head out from around corners and signaling me, tapping me on the shoulder to say, "Hey, pay attention over here." By fall of 1991 I gave up on Ancient Egypt and began research on the Trojan War.

THE STORY

One thing that drew me so strongly to the Trojan War was the story's development over the millennia. So many writers, poets, artists, and playwrights—both great and not so great—have added to, refined, revealed, or otherwise made their marks on the story, until the permutations and divergences seem endless. The challenge of forging all these disparate versions into one continuous, coherent storyline fascinated me—and I continue to find this the most interesting part of working on *Age of Bronze*.

I'd like to relate a couple examples of the sort of thing I deal with while plotting and writing the script.

One of the most famous Greek myths is the story of the Golden Fleece. In it, the hero Jason and his companions the Argonauts sail to Kolchis to find the fleece. Medea, daughter of the King of Kolchis, falls for Jason and runs away with him.

Theseus, the great Athenian hero, would have accompanied the Argonauts if he hadn't been trapped in Hades, the land of the dead, at the time. But the strange thing is that he'd met Medea years before, when he was a young man. Theseus's father, the King of Athens, had an old crone as an advisor. Her name was Medea, and she'd been brought from Kolchis many years before by Jason and the Argonauts.

Do you see the paradox? How could Theseus as a young man have met Medea at his father's court if she wasn't even to arrive until years later? But what, you ask, has this all got to do with the Trojan War?

Well, Greek myth is all interconnected.

In *A Thousand Ships,* Priam tells the story of Herakles's sack of Troy. Somewhat late in his career, the great Achaean hero Herakles accompanied Jason and the Argonauts part way on their quest for the Golden Fleece. He stopped at Troy along the way and rescued the king's daughter from a monster in exchange for a reward. But the King of Troy withheld the reward, so Herakles sacked Troy with a small army. The sack occurred when Priam was still a boy. Since Priam is an old man during the Trojan War, we know that Herakles's sack of Troy took place several decades previously.

But Theseus, before becoming trapped in Hades while the Argonauts were questing, carried off Helen while she was still a girl. That makes Helen a girl while Priam was a boy, yet Helen is not an old woman during the Trojan War.

Confused? I don't blame you. And it goes on. Greek mythology is hopelessly convoluted and contradictory. I get a kick trying to untangle it. Sometimes it's just flat out impossible to solve—I make a decision and skirt the irreconcilable. In *A Thousand Ships,* I've had to decide upon ages for the characters—Helen, Priam, and so on—and simply avoid a fixed date for the Argonautic expedition to Kolchis.

Here's another challenge to forging this story: Troilus and Cressida. The ancient *written* sources are silent about Troilus, except for one instance, the passing mention of his name in Homer's *Iliad.* But the ancient *artistic* sources—mostly painted vases—reveal a rich and detailed episode—possibly elaborated from the single mention in *The Iliad,* or possibly predating *The Iliad* and actually a part of the story which Homer expected everyone to know. Cressida is never mentioned in ancient sources. She is, as far as anyone knows, a twelfth century CE invention, first appearing in Benoit de Sainte-Maure's *Roman de Troie.*

Later writers developed a completely new story for Troilus, culminating in Shakespeare's play *Troilus and Cressida.* This line of development has very little to do with Greek myth and much to do with the concept of courtly love developed

in the Middle Ages. The themes and treatment are alien to Homer and other ancient tellers of the story. Yet the Troilus and Cressida story is a well-known and vital part of the Trojan War tradition. I just can't see how my version could avoid it. I wouldn't want to avoid it anyway.

See the problems I've got to deal with here? It's wonderful.

WHERE ARE THE GREEK GODS?

Every era tells the Trojan War legend a little differently. That's only natural. Homer's *Iliad* features the gods directly influencing the action—even joining in some of the battles. I've gone so far as to shove the gods offstage—not an original move on my part in retelling this story, it's been in and out of fashion for centuries—but a decision which I think is relevant to this twenty-first century world where so many are quick to look beyond themselves for answers or to assign blame.

I've chosen to downplay the supernatural element in order to emphasize the human element. The only fantastic details I've retained are dreams and visions. And when you think about it, these aren't necessarily as supernatural as they might first appear. Everyone dreams. Many people have hallucinations. Others are convinced they've had visions. People the world over believe they communicate with gods—it's called prayer. So I've let dreams and visions remain—they're pretty human after all.

But no gods in the flesh.

Because of this, I've had to interpret the story in ways which those readers only familiar with the traditional versions may find odd. For instance, consider the well-known episode commonly called the Judgement of Paris, in which Paris is called upon to choose the fairest of three goddesses. I needed a way to present this episode without introducing the goddesses as characters. I didn't have to search far. Sometime during the second or third century CE, Dares of Phrygia wrote his *Excidio Troiae Historia (History of the Destruction of Troy)* in which Paris dreams the judgement. This version of events colored most of the Medieval versions of the Troy legend and provided me with a source to have Paris call this episode a dream.

NEW IDEAS FROM OLD

Another decision that a reader might question was my making Paris a cowherd during his pastoral period, rather than a shepherd as he is often represented. There are a few sources—for example, Ovid's *Heroides XVI* and *The Rape of Helen* by Colluthus—that present Paris as tending cattle, and these are solid sources for my representation, but there's more to my decision. One of my reasons to use cows instead of sheep concerns the very first panel of *A Thousand Ships*. Originally I planned to have Paris wake from his dream of the Judgement at that moment. His dream-vision of the goddess Aphrodite would have faded into the face of the cow—a cow rather than a sheep because a cow's eyes were seen

as a symbol of beauty in past ages and Paris in his dream would have just judged Aphrodite the most beautiful goddess. The idea of the Judgement as a dream developed differently in execution. But the cow stayed to show that Paris is comfortable with cattle in order to reinforce the credibility of the actions Paris takes to recover his bull.

I had to make similar decisions at every step of the way in retelling the story. My purpose in *A Thousand Ships* isn't to invent, but to tell anew, so I have done my best to base everything on existing sources.

Sometimes I've had to really stretch to let the story unfold. At first, the episode of the Madness of Odysseus refused to move. It's a prominent and exciting episode, but it seems rather bizarre and senseless in all of the older versions. I had to look beyond the episode to find a way to give it life. My answer was to introduce the dog, Argos. But don't misunderstand—I didn't invent Argos. He's firmly established in Homer's *Odyssey*, Book 19, as a faithful companion to the Ithakan king prior to his leaving for Troy. Readers may disagree over whether Argos's unprecedented presence in the Madness episode constitutes a revision of the story, but since the pieces were already there for me to put together, I'll defend the dog's appearance as more than reasonable.

THE ARCHAEOLOGY

Although the story is the most important aspect of *Age of Bronze,* it's only one aspect. Next most important is the drawings. I knew from the start that I wanted my retelling of the Trojan War to look as historically accurate as possible.

So I researched the archaeology of Late Bronze Age Troy and Greece. While nowhere near as daunting as the archaeology of Ancient Egypt, there's still a lot of material to cover. My enthusiasm refused to flag, however, and early on I realized that I had enough commitment to a comic book retelling of the Trojan War to see such a massive undertaking through to the end.

I wanted my version of the story to look different than the stereotypical presentation of Greek myth. I didn't want my characters parading around—as has been pictured time after time—in romantic versions of Classical Greek armor and lounging around the Corinthian capitalled columns of Classical Greek temples. My versions of the characters would be down to earth, clad in the garb and inhabiting the environment of the Late Bronze Age Aegean—less familiar than the anachronistic stereotype, but I hope, more interesting because of its unfamiliarity.

For many decades, archaeologists have been digging into the earth to find remains from the Late Bronze Age. Some of the story's locations still exist. Every year thousands of people visit the city of Troy in present-day Turkey where they can view walls from the excavation level Troy VI, generally accepted as dating from the time of the Trojan War (although some scholars argue for Troy VII).

Mycenae still sits proudly on its hill and has given its name to the culture that lived in Bronze Age Greece—Mycenaean. You can still see Agamemnon's great hall (the portion, at least, that hasn't slid down the hill). Nestor's Pylos is probably

the best-preserved of all the Mycenaean palaces, yielding the remains of walls, paintings, pottery, and written records. These locations have found their way into *A Thousand Ships,* though my reconstructions of the lost portions is merely conjecture.

For other locations, I've had fewer archaeological sources to draw from. There are Mycenaean remains on a hill near Sparta, but who can say if these were ever the palace of a king named Menelaus? And if Lykomedes ever had a palace on top of the Chora of Skyros, it's long disappeared. I've drawn inspiration for it largely from remains at Akrotiri on the Greek island of Thera, modern Santorini.

But what did the people look like who once lived in these palaces? Determining the appearance of the Greeks—or as Homer calls them, the Achaeans—wasn't a problem. Surviving paintings, carvings, and sculptures show the costumes and hairstyles of the people who inhabited Greece in the Late Bronze Age, and I've done my best to incorporate them. No one can say for certain what Agamemnon looked like—if the man ever really existed—but I hope that the face I've given him—based on the most famous of the gold masks from Mycenae's royal shaft graves—is at least plausible, if not probable.

But what did the Trojans look like? The remains of Troy's citadel still exist—just as remains of many of the great Mycenaean centers still do. But we have no depictions of humans that can specifically be labeled Trojan. Homer and later writers seem to present the Trojans similarly to the Achaeans. I could have followed Homer's lead and drawn my Trojans as a Mycenaean culture.

But that just didn't seem right. In a story with such a large cast, I wanted as much visual differentiation between the characters as possible. The Trojans had to look different from the Achaeans. But how? I cast about for an answer without much result. I began to study the Bronze Age culture in Thrace north of Greece and Troy, but the Thracians didn't seem right, either. Here and there in my research I had run across references to the great empire of the Hittites which flourished in Turkey at roughly the same time the Mycenaean civilization flourished in Greece. Should I make the Trojans look like Hittites, I asked myself. I must admit I was reluctant to open an entirely new branch of research. Then—almost unlooked for—came an opportunity to ask the one man who might give me a final answer to my question about the Trojans' appearance.

THE EXCAVATORS

That man is Manfred Korfmann, excavator of Troy. But Prof. Korfmann wasn't the first person to dig at Troy.

The first excavator of Troy—the man popularly known as its discoverer—was Heinrich Schliemann, called the father of modern archaeology, who revealed to the rapt world the many successive levels of Troy at the hill of Hissarlik in northwestern Turkey in 1870 and who later excavated Mycenae and elsewhere. The second excavator of Troy was Wilhelm Dorpfeld, who assisted Schliemann and continued the Troy excavations after Schliemann's death. In the 1930s Carl W.

Blegen excavated at Troy, but when he moved on to dig at Pylos, excavation at Troy stopped for decades. Then in 1988 an international team of archaeologists began new excavations at Troy. Prof. Manfred Korfmann of the University of Tubingen in Germany led—and continues to lead—these excavations, supported by many other archaeologists and scientists. He oversees the Bronze Age excavations while C. Brian Rose oversees the later period and Roman excavations.

PROFESSOR MANFRED KORFMANN

In February 1997, Prof. Korfmann took part in the World of Troy symposium at the Smithsonian Institution in Washington, DC. I made sure to be there, determined to come home with answers to several specific questions, the most important being what the Trojans looked like. During his fascinating slide show on the architecture of Troy VI and Troy VII—which zipped by much, much too quickly for my taste—Prof. Korfmann suggested that the Bronze Age Trojans were a Luwian culture within the sphere of the Hittite empire. After the slide show, I approached him—nervously. And a bit self-consciously since I had a hulking, gray, metal-and-foam brace encasing most of my left leg—still recovering from a broken kneecap a couple months before.

Now, Manfred Korfmann is a serious scientist. He has stated again and again that his excavation at Troy is not driven by some romantic vision of the Trojan War. He is at Troy not to find support for the legends, but to study what is actually there.

So there I was, hugely intimidated to be face to face with the great man—the man following in the footsteps of legends—of Schliemann, Dorpfeld, and Blegen—in order to ask what would surely seem a fanciful question. But I had to know his opinion. So without explaining *why* I wanted to know, *certainly* without mentioning that I was preparing a comic book version of the Trojan War story, I asked Prof. Korfmann what the Trojan people of the Late Bronze Age would have looked like. He suggested that I look at the remains of the Hittite culture as a model. Thank you from the bottom of my cartoonist soul, Prof. Korfmann. That's why the Trojans in *A Thousand Ships* are based on the Hittites. (And if I've misinterpreted or misrepresented anything—the Trojans, the Hittites, or Prof. Korfmann himself—it's my fault, not his.)

WHAT'S ALL THE FUSS?

There are three great questions surrounding the subject of the Trojan War. They are:
1) Who—or what—was Homer?
2) Was Heinrich Schliemann a charlatan?
3) How much, if any, of the Trojan War story is historically accurate?

These questions have been debated by many people for many years, and they continue to be debated—hotly. And none of these questions really matters to *A Thousand Ships,* as far as I can see.

A Thousand Ships

Question one is really many questions. Was Homer one man, many men, a woman? Did Homer create his works in a burst of divine inspiration, or was he merely a compiler? Did Homer compose orally, or was Homer a writer? Me, I don't care. We have Homer's *Iliad* and *Odyssey*. That's what matters.

Question two, about Heinrich Schliemann, I have no desire to address. Very controversial nowadays. Thank goodness it lies beyond the scope of *A Thousand Ships*.

That leaves us with question three.

Did the Trojan War really happen?

I care more about this question than the first two. I believe there were armed conflicts in the eastern Mediterranean during the Late Bronze Age. I believe that the site of Hissarlik in Turkey is Troy. But was there a Trojan War? Did a massive army from the area now known to the rest of the world as Greece attack a city on the south shore of what we now call the Dardanelles? We'll probably never know for sure. But it doesn't really affect *A Thousand Ships* any more than the first two questions.

What really matters, and what isn't addressed by the three great questions, is how much of the Trojan War story is *humanly* accurate. I think the answer to that has been proven by the story's longevity—twenty-eight centuries long. The story speaks to our basic humanity, dealing as it does with questions not so much great as eternal, questions of love, lust, death, sense of self, and the individual's relationship to the world. How else has this story fascinated so many people for so many centuries? How else has it been continually renewed from one era to the next, told over and over, details refined, old episodes embellished, new episodes grafted on?

Call it what you will—myth, legend, fantasy, historical fiction, soap opera, revision—here's the story again. A new version for a new century.

Eric Shanower
San Diego
March 2001
eric@hungrytigerpress.com

Prior to book publication, the next volume of the story—*Sacrifice*—is serialized in Eric Shanower's continuing comic book *Age of Bronze*, available at finer comic stores everywhere. To locate the comic store nearest you, call toll-free 1-888-COMIC-BOOK.

GLOSSARY OF NAMES

Anyone seeking consistency among the forms of character and place names in *A Thousand Ships* should look elsewhere.

Pronunciation of names varies widely—and wildly—with time and geography. Many names have undergone radical changes from one period to another—from Archaic to Classical to Medieval to Renaissance and beyond. For instance, Priam is also known as Priamos, Priamus, and Pryant, depending on the source. What I present here is merely a guide and needn't be considered definitive.

In general, the better-known characters use the more familiar Roman forms — Achilles instead of Akhilleos, Helen instead of Helena, etc. Lesser-known and minor characters use a more Greek form—Teukros instead of Teucer, Polydeukes instead of Pollux. I've preferred the letter "k" over the letter "c"—Kassandra instead of Cassandra—except when "h" follows "c"—Andromache—and in place names still current—Crete—and for the name Cressida which is a Renaissance form of Criseyde derived from Briseida, in turn derived from Briseis.

a as in lap	ee as in see	i as in sit	oo as in wool	u as in us
ay as in say	eye as in hike	o as in not	s as in less	uh as in duh
e as in bed	g as in get	oh as in note	th as in thick	

Listed alphabetically   Stress italicized syllable

Achaea a-*kee*-uh, in general, the area now known as Greece
Achaean a-*kee*-uhn, of the area now known as Greece
Achilles a-*kil*-eez, son of Peleus and Thetis, prince of Phthia
Aeneas ee-*nee*-as, prince of Dardania, cousin to Hektor
Aesakus *ee*-sa-kus, a seer, son of Priam and Arisbe
Agamemnon a-ga-*mem*-non, king of Mycenae, High King of the Achaeans
Agathon a-ga-thon, prince of Troy, youngest son of Priam and Hekuba
Agelaus a-je-*lay*-us, a cattleherd
Agyrtes a-*jir*-teez, steward of Diomedes
Aithra *ay*-thra, servant of Helen, mother of Theseus
Ajax (Great) *ay*-jax, son of Telamon, prince of Salamis
Alkimus *al*-ki-mus, companion of Achilles
Amurru a-*moo*-roo, country south of Troy, roughly modern Syria
Andromache an-*dro*-ma-kee, princess of Thebes
Anius *ay*-nee-us, king of Delos
Antenor an-*tee*-nor, Trojan elder
Antimachus an-*ti*-ma-kus, Trojan elder
Argo *ar*-goh, ship of Jason and the Argonauts
Argos *ar*-gos, (1) dog of Odysseus, (2) area ruled by Diomedes
Ariadne a-ree-*ad*-nee, Cretan princess carried away by Theseus
Arisbe a-*riz*-bee, Priam's first wife
Arzawa ar-*za*-wa, a country south of Troy

Asphalion as-*fay*-lee-on, palace servant of Menelaus
Assyria a-*sir*-ee-uh, empire southeast of Troy
Athena a-*thee*-na, goddess of wisdom and war
Athens a-thenz, city formerly ruled by Theseus
Atreus *ay*-tryoos, father of Agamemnon and Menelaus
Atrides a-*treye*-deez, Agamemnon and Menelaus, the sons of Atreus
Attica a-ti-ka, area of Achaea which includes Athens
Aulis *aw*-lis, bay where army assembles
Automedon o-*to*-me-don, charioteer of Achilles
Babylon *ba*-bi-lon, country southeast of Troy, roughly modern Iraq
Boeotia bee-*o*-shuh, area where Aulis is located
Cheiron *keye*-ron, Kentaur teacher of young Achilles
Chromius *kro*-mee-us, son of Priam and Hekuba
Cressida *kres*-i-duh, daughter of Kalchas
Crete kreet, island ruled by Idomeneus
Cyprus *seye*-prus, island ruled by Kinyras
Dardania dar-*day*-nee-uh, kingdom of Anchises
Deidamia dee-i-da-*meye*-uh, eldest daughter of Lykomedes of Skyros
Deiphobus de-*if*-oh-bus, prince of Troy, son of Priam and Hekuba
Delos *dee*-los, island sacred to the Sun God
Delphi *del*-feye, location of the chief Achaean oracle
Delphic *del*-fik, of the oracle at Delphi
Diomedes deye-o-*mee*-deez, king of Argos
Dolopes *do*-lo-peez, an Achaean tribe
Eetion ee-*et*-ee-on, king of Hypoplacian Thebes
Egypt *ee*-jipt, country of the Nile, across the sea south of Troy and Achaea
Elais ee-*lay*-is, daughter of Anius of Delos
Epopeus ee-*poh*-pyoos, son of Poseidon, a king of Sikyon
Eupompe yoo-*pom*-pee, "sister" of Thetis
Europa yoo-*roh*-puh, Phoenician princess carried off by Zeus
Eurybates yoo-*rib*-a-teez, comrade of Odysseus
Guneus *goon*-yoos, king of Kyphus
Halitherses ha-li-*ther*-seez, seer of Ithaka
Hatti *ha*-tee, empire of the Hittites east of Troy
Hektor *hek*-tor, prince of Troy, eldest son of Priam and Hekuba
Hekuba *hek*-yoo-buh, Priam's chief wife
Helen *he*-len, wife of Menelaus
Helenus *he*-le-nus, prince of Troy, son of Priam and Hekuba, twin of Kassandra
Hellespont *he*-le-spont, body of water leading northeast from the Aegean Sea
Herakles *her*-a-kleez, greatest of Achaean heroes
Hermione hur-*meye*-o-nee, daughter of Menelaus and Helen
Hesione he-*seye*-uh-nee, sister of Priam, wife of Telamon, mother of Teukros
Hiketaon hi-ke-*tay*-on, Trojan elder

Ida *eye*-duh, mountain south of Troy

Idomeneus eye-*do*-men-yoos, king of Crete

Ikarius eye-*kar*-ee-us, father of Penelope, brother of Tyndareus

Iliona i-lee-*oh*-na, daughter of Priam and Hekuba

Iolaus eye-oh-*lay*-us, king of Phylake

Ithaka *i*-tha-ka, island ruled by Odysseus

Jason *jay*-son, leader of the Argonauts

Kalchas *kal*-kas, Trojan priest

Kallisto ka-*lis*-to, woman seduced by Zeus

Kassandra ka-*san*-druh, daughter of Priam and Hekuba, a seer, twin of Helenus

Kastor *kas*-tor, brother of Helen, twin of Polydeukes

Katreus *ka*-tryoos, maternal grandfather of Agamemnon, former king of Crete

Kinyras *ki*-ni-ras, king of Cyprus

Klytemnestra kleye-tem-*nes*-tra, wife of Agamemnon, sister of Helen

Klytius *kli*-tee-us, Trojan elder

Kolchis *kol*-kis, rich land in the east

Kreusa kree-*oo*-suh, eldest daughter of Priam and Hekuba

Kyphus *ky*-fus, area ruled by Guneus

Laertes lay-*ur*-teez, father of Odysseus

Lakedaemon la-ke-*dee*-mon, area including Sparta and ruled by Menelaus

Lakedaemonian lak-e-dee-*mon*-ee-an, of the area known as Lakedaemon

Lampus *lam*-pus, Trojan elder

Laodike lay-*o*-di-kee, daughter of Priam and Hekuba

Laomedon lay-*o*-me-don, former king of Troy, father of Priam

Lycia *li*-sha, area ruled by Sarpedon

Lykomedes leye-ko-*mee*-deez, king of Skyros

Medea me-*dee*-uh, princess of Kolchis, lover of Jason

Menelaus me-ne-*lay*-us, king of Lakedaemon, brother of Agamemnon

Mycenae meye-*see*-nee, city of Agamemnon

Myrmidons *mur*-mi-donz, followers of Achilles, subjects of Peleus

Nauplia *naw*-plee-uh, area ruled by Nauplius the father of Palamedes

Neleus *neel*-yoos, father of Nestor

Neoptolemus nee-op-*to*-le-mus, son of Achilles and Deidamia

Nereids *nee*-ree-idz, nymphs of the sea, "sisters" of Thetis

Nestor *nes*-tor, elderly king of Pylos

Nykteus *nik*-tyoos, a king of Thebes, father of Antiope

Odysseus o-*dis*-yoos, king of Ithaka

Oeno *ee*-noh, daughter of Anius of Delos

Oenone ee-*noh*-nee, first lover of Paris

Omphale *om*-fa-lee, queen of Lydia and lover of Herakles

Palamedes pa-la-*mee*-deez, prince of Nauplia, cousin of Agamemnon

Pandarus *pan*-da-rus, brother of Kalchas, uncle of Cressida

Panthous *pan*-thoh-us, Trojan elder, father of Polydamas

~~~~~~

Paris *pa*-ris, a poor cattleherd

Patroklus pa-*trok*-lus, friend of Achilles

Peleus *peel*-yoos, king of Phthia, father of Achilles

Pelion *pee*-lee-on, mountain abode of Cheiron

Penelope pe-*nel*-oh-pee, wife of Odysseus

Periboea pe-ri-*bee*-uh, wife of Telamon, mother of Great Ajax

Philomela fi-loh-*mee*-luh, daughter of Priam and Hekuba

Phisadie fi-sa-*deye*-ee, servant of Helen, sister of Peirithoos

Phoenix *fee*-niks, tutor and companion of Achilles

Phthia *ftheye*-a, area ruled by Peleus

Pleisthenes plee-*is*-the-neez, son of Helen and Menelaus

Podarkes po-*dar*-keez, original name of Priam

Polites po-*leye*-teez, prince of Troy, son of Priam and Hekuba

Polydeukes po-li-*dyoo*-keez, brother of Helen, twin of Kastor

Polyxena poh-*liks*-ee-nuh, daughter of Priam and Hekuba

Poseidon po-*seye*-don, god of ocean and earthquake

Priam *preye*-am, king of Troy

Pylos *peye*-los, area ruled by Nestor

Pyrrha *peer*-uh, Achilles's name in female disguise

Pyrrhus *peer*-us, original name of son of Achilles and Deidamia

Salamis *sa*-la-mis, area ruled by Telamon

Sarpedon sar-*pee*-don, king of Lycia

Sidon *seye*-don, city on the coast of the levant

Skyros *skeye*-ros, island ruled by Lykomedes

Sparta *spar*-tuh, city ruled by Menelaus

Spermo *sper*-moh, daughter of Anius of Delos

Talthybius tal-*thi*-bee-us, herald of Agamemnon

Telamon *tel*-a-mon, king of Salamis, father of Great Ajax

Telemachus te-*le*-ma-kus, son of Odysseus and Penelope

Teukros *tyoo*-kros, half-brother of Great Ajax, son of Telamon and Hesione

Theano thee-*ay*-no, Trojan priestess, wife of Antenor

Thebes theebz, city ruled by Eetion

Thersites ther-*seye*-teez, ill-tempered cousin of Diomedes

Theseus *thees*-yoos, an Achaean hero, former king of Athens

Thetis *thee*-tis, influential Achaean priestess, mother of Achilles

Thrace thrays, area northwest of Troy

Thrasymedes thras-i-*mee*-deez, son of Nestor

Thymoetes theye-*mee*-teez, Trojan elder

Tlepolemus tle-*po*-le-mus, king of Rhodes, son of Herakles

Troilus *troy*-lus, prince of Troy, son of Priam and Hekuba

Tyndareus tin-*dar*-yoos, father of Helen

Ukalegon yoo-*kal*-e-gon, Trojan elder

Zeus zyoos, god of thunder and sky

ACKNOWLEDGMENTS

Many people have offered help, advice, encouragement, and support during the years I've been working on this project. I offer my thanks and appreciation to you all. In particular I thank:

Wendy Roth for taking photographs at the site of Troy.

Bruce Conklin for nearly publishing the comic book series.

Erik Larsen for publishing the comic book series.

Everyone in the Image Central office past and present who has supported this project, particularly Brent Braun, Jim Valentino, Anthony Bozzi, and Larry Marder.

The archaeologists Shelley Wachsmann of the Nautical Archaeology Program at Texas A&M University; Getzel Cohen of the Institute for Mediterranean Studies at the University of Cincinnati; David Moyer; Louise A. Hitchcock of the Cotsen Institute at the University of California, Los Angeles; and Eric Cline of the Department of Classics and Semitics at George Washington University for generously taking time from their busy schedules to help me in my busy schedule.

Stephen Kent Jusick, Ed Brubaker, Michael O. Riley, Michael Lovitz, Sharon Cho, Colleen Doran, Axel Alonso, Maggie Thompson, Edward Einhorn, Anina Bennett, Paul Guinan, Larry Gonick, Ron Randall, Ernie Daw, Will Shetterly, Megan Kelso, Marc Biagi, Matt Blumberg, Susan Hueck Allen, Lothar Jungeblut, Shane Amaya, Gareth Hinds, Katherine Keller, Jim Ottaviani, Mark Badger, Martha Breen, Bernice Jones, Sellers Lawrence, Kenneth J. Reckford, Marc Lewis, Johanna Draper Carlson, Marc Bryant, Scott Dunbier, Laura Gjovaag, Willis Maxine, Eloise Jarvis McGraw, Rachel Cosgrove Payes, Rory Root, Peter David, Aubrey Stallings, Diane Thompson, J. V. Luce, Susan Riddle, Larry Young, Kathy Bottarini, Marilyn Goodman, John Younger and the subscribers of the e-mail list AEGEANET.

Mossy Pike; Adolfo J. Dominguez, Prof. of Ancient History; Anastasia Tsaliki, Doctoral Researcher; Anne Lou Robkin; Carole Gillis; Don Dupont; Louise Bashford, University of Birmingham; David Kelly, Department of Classics, Montclair State University; E.S. Van Ness; Connie Rodriguez; Anne Stewart; Mike Shupp; Stuart O'Steen; and Dr. Judith Maitland, Department of Classics and Ancient History, the University of Western Australia for their comments on early issues of the comic book.

The current excavators of Troy, Manfred Korfmann of the University of Tubingen and C. Brian Rose of the University of Cincinnati.

My parents, James and Karen Shanower, for more than I can adequately say.

Most of all to my partner, David Maxine, who has been with me all along the way.

ERIC SHANOWER

Genealogical Chart: The Achaeans

Characters in bold appear and are named in *A Thousand Ships*.

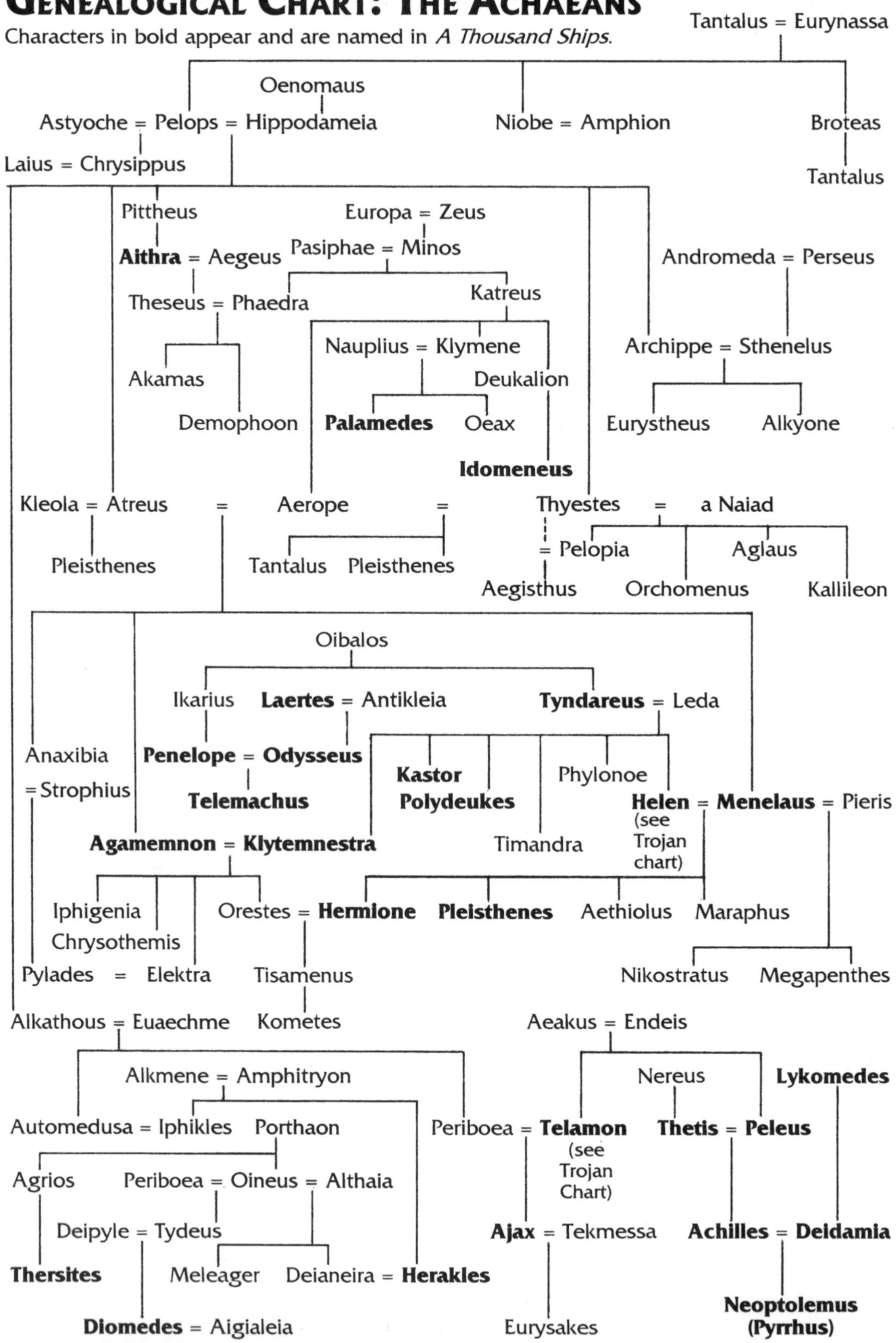

Tantalus = Eurynassa
Oenomaus
Astyoche = Pelops = Hippodameia
Niobe = Amphion
Broteas
Laius = Chrysippus
Tantalus
Pittheus
Europa = Zeus
Aithra = Aegeus
Pasiphae = Minos
Andromeda = Perseus
Theseus = Phaedra
Katreus
Nauplius = Klymene
Archippe = Sthenelus
Akamas
Deukalion
Demophoon
Palamedes
Oeax
Eurystheus
Alkyone
Idomeneus
Kleola = Atreus
=
Aerope
=
Thyestes
=
a Naiad
= Pelopia
Aglaus
Pleisthenes
Tantalus
Pleisthenes
Aegisthus
Orchomenus
Kallileon
Oibalos
Ikarius
Laertes = Antikleia
Tyndareus = Leda
Anaxibia
Penelope = **Odysseus**
= Strophius
Kastor
Phylonoe
Telemachus
Polydeukes
Helen = **Menelaus** = Pieris
(see Trojan chart)
Agamemnon = **Klytemnestra**
Timandra
Iphigenia
Orestes = **Hermione**
Pleisthenes
Aethiolus
Maraphus
Chrysothemis
Pylades = Elektra
Tisamenus
Nikostratus
Megapenthes
Alkathous = Euaechme
Kometes
Aeakus = Endeis
Alkmene = Amphitryon
Nereus
Lykomedes
Automedusa = Iphikles
Porthaon
Periboea = **Telamon**
(see Trojan Chart)
Thetis = **Peleus**
Agrios
Periboea = Oineus = Althaia
Deipyle = Tydeus
Ajax = Tekmessa
Achilles = **Deidamia**
Thersites
Meleager
Deianeira = **Herakles**
Neoptolemus (Pyrrhus)
Diomedes = Aigialeia
Eurysakes

GENEALOGICAL CHART: THE TROJAN ROYAL FAMILY

Characters in bold appear and are named in *A Thousand Ships*.

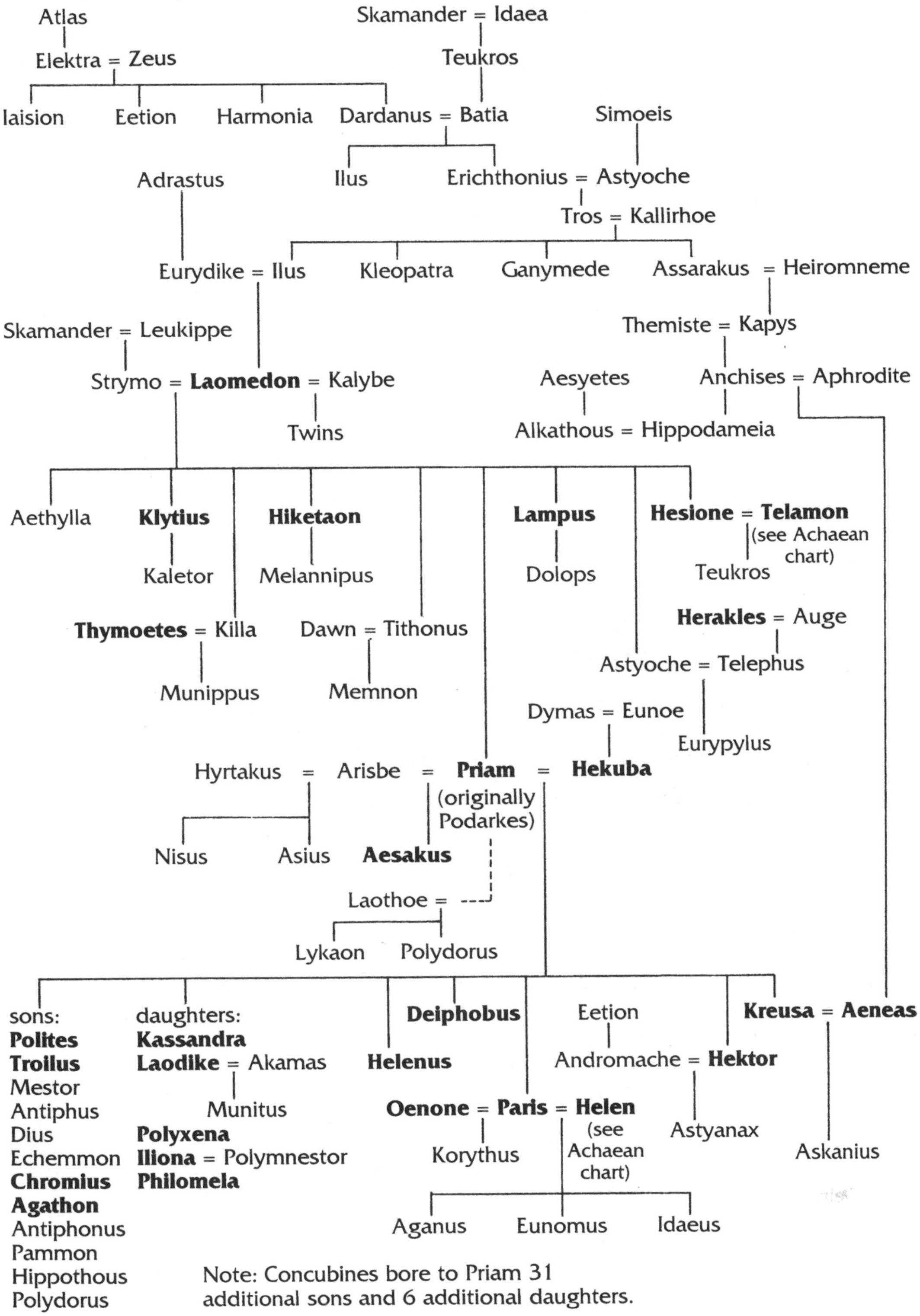

Atlas
Skamander = Idaea
Elektra = Zeus
Teukros
Iaision
Eetion
Harmonia
Dardanus = Batia
Simoeis
Adrastus
Ilus
Erichthonius = Astyoche
Tros = Kallirhoe
Eurydike = Ilus
Kleopatra
Ganymede
Assarakus = Heiromneme
Skamander = Leukippe
Themiste = Kapys
Strymo = **Laomedon** = Kalybe
Aesyetes
Anchises = Aphrodite
Twins
Alkathous = Hippodameia
Aethylla
Klytius
Hiketaon
Lampus
Hesione = **Telamon**
(see Achaean chart)
Kaletor
Melannipus
Dolops
Teukros
Thymoetes = Killa
Dawn = Tithonus
Herakles = Auge
Astyoche = Telephus
Munippus
Memnon
Dymas = Eunoe
Eurypylus
Hyrtakus = Arisbe = **Priam** = **Hekuba**
(originally Podarkes)
Nisus
Asius
Aesakus
Laothoe =
Lykaon
Polydorus
sons:
Polites
Troilus
Mestor
Antiphus
Dius
Echemmon
Chromius
Agathon
Antiphonus
Pammon
Hippothous
Polydorus
daughters:
Kassandra
Laodike = Akamas
Munitus
Polyxena
Iliona = Polymnestor
Philomela
Deiphobus
Helenus
Eetion
Andromache = **Hektor**
Kreusa = **Aeneas**
Oenone = **Paris** = **Helen**
(see Achaean chart)
Korythus
Astyanax
Askanius
Aganus
Eunomus
Idaeus
Note: Concubines bore to Priam 31 additional sons and 6 additional daughters.

JOIN THE DEFENSE OF TROY

Every summer since 1988 an international team of archaeologists and other scientists has undertaken the most extensive excavation yet conducted of the hill of Hissarlik in northwestern Turkey, the site identified by Heinrich Schliemann (and Frank Calvert) in the late nineteenth century as the location of the city of Troy. The digging continues, and publication of the finds will follow for years as the evidence is studied and understood. And what finds they are! A previously unsuspected Bronze Age defensive ditch surrounding the city—a magnificent statue of the Roman Emperor Hadrian—as well as finds less spectacular but no less valuable to our understanding of the architecture, culture, and religion of the Trojan people for a period spanning more than 2000 years.

Be part of it by joining the Friends of Troy, a group of people from all over the world with one thing in common—an interest in this most legendary of archaeological sites. All it takes to join each year is a donation—*any amount is welcome.* Your money will help support the current Troy excavation and publication of the results. And it's tax deductible since Friends of Troy is a non-profit organization.

Send your check or money order to:

Friends of Troy
Institute for Mediterranean Studies
7086 Aracoma Drive
Cincinnati, OH 45237
USA

As one of the Friends of Troy you'll receive updates on the excavations and notices of events of interest to Troy enthusiasts. For more information, contact the Institute for Mediterranean Studies:

Phone: 513/631-8049
Fax: 513/631-1715
E-mail: studies@usa.net
Website: www.studies.org

BIBLIOGRAPHY

I've included sources consulted for the story and the archaeology in this and future volumes. Not included are sources on general subjects—such as weaving, childbirth, animals, and the geography of Greece, Turkey, and the Aegean islands not specific to the Late Bronze Age.

I've divided the sources into broad categories to assist readers interested in seeking further information on specific aspects of *A Thousand Ships*.

THE STORY

Accius. *Tragedies* and *Unassigned Fragments of Plays*. In *Remains of Old Latin,* vol. II, 326. Trans. E.H. Warmington (Loeb Classical Library). Cambridge: Harvard University Press, 1935.

Aeschylus. *Aeschylus 1: Oresteia*. Trans. Richmond Lattimore. Chicago: The University of Chicago Press, 1953.

—. *The Oresteia*. Trans. Robert Fagles. New York: Bantam Books, 1977.

—. *The Plays of Aeschylus (Agamemnon, Choephoroe, and Eumenides)*. In *Aeschylus, Sophocles, Euripides, Aristophanes*. Trans. G.M. Cookson (Great Books of the Western World series). Chicago: Encyclopaedia Britannica, 1952.

Alcaeus. *Sappho and Alcaeus*. In *Greek Lyric,* vol. 1, 256-261, 333, 338-341. Trans. David A. Campbell (Loeb Classical Library). Cambridge: Harvard University Press, 1982.

Anderson, Michael J. *The Fall of Troy in Early Greek Poetry and Art*. Oxford: Clarendon Press, 1997.

[Apollodorus.] *Gods and Heroes of the Greeks: The Library of Apollodorus*. Trans. Michael Simpson. Amherst: University of Massachusetts Press, 1976.

—. *The Library of Greek Mythology*. Trans. Robin Hard. Oxford: Oxford University Press, 1997.

Apollonius of Rhodes. *The Voyage of Argo*. Trans. E.V. Rieu. Harmondsworth: Penguin Books, 1959.

Apollonius Rhodius. *Argonautica*. Trans. R.C. Seaton (Loeb Classical Library). Cambridge: Harvard University Press, 1912.

Arnold, Matthew. "Palladium." In *The Norton Anthology of Poetry*, 394. New York: W.W. Norton & Company, 1975.

Athenaeus. *The Deipnosophists,* vol. I. Trans. Charles Burton Gulick (Loeb Classical Library). Cambridge: Harvard University Press, 1927

Auden, W.H. "The Shield of Achilles." In *The Norton Anthology of Poetry*, 552-53. New York: W.W. Norton & Company, 1975.

Baldwin, James. "A Cause of War." In *Hero Tales from Many Lands,* selected by Alice I. Hazeltine, 13-25. New York and Nashville: Abingdon Press, 1961.

Bate, Alan Keith. *Excidium Troie*. Frankfurt am Main: Verlag Peter Lang, 1986.

Berlioz, Hector. *Les Troyens*. Produced by The Metropolitan Opera. 4 hours 13 min. Metropolitan Opera, 1984. Videocassette.

Brooke, Rupert. "Menelaus and Helen." In *The Collected Poems*. New York: Dodd, Mead & Company, 1943.

Brooks, Dr. Edward. *The Story of the Iliad*. Philadelphia: Penn Publishing Company, 1924.

Thompson, Ann. *Shakespeare's Chaucer: A Study in Literary Origins*. New York: Barnes & Noble Books, 1978.

Bulfinch, Thomas. *The Age of Fable; or, Stories of Gods and Heroes*. Chicago: Donohue Brothers, n.d.

Carden, Richard. *The Papyrus Fragments of Sophocles: An Edition with Prolegomena and Commentary*. Hawthorne, NY: Walter de Gruyter, 1974.

Carpenter, Thomas H. *Art and Myth in Ancient Greece: A Handbook*. London: Thames & Hudson, 1991.

Chaucer, Geoffrey. *The Poetical Works*. ed. F. N. Robinson. Boston: Houghton Mifflin Company, 1933.

—. *Troilus and Criseyde*. Trans. George Philip Krapp. New York: Literary Guild, 1932.

—. *Troilus and Criseyde*. Trans. Nevill Coghill. Harmondsworth: Penguin, 1971.

Christodorus of Thebes in Egypt. *Book II: Christodorus of Thebes in Egypt*. In *Greek Anthology*, vol. 1. Trans. W.R. Paton (Loeb Classical Library). Cambridge: Harvard University Press, 1916.

Church, (Rev.) Alfred J. *The Iliad of Homer*. New York: Macmillan Company, 1935.

—. *The Odyssey for Boys and Girls: Told from Homer*. New York: Macmillan, 1925.

Colluthus. *The Rape of Helen*. In *Oppian. Colluthus. Tryphiodorus*. Trans. A.W. Mair (Loeb Classical Library). Cambridge: Harvard University Press, 1928.

Coolidge, Olivia (E.). *The King of Men*. Boston: Houghton Mifflin Company, 1966.

—. *The Trojan War*. Boston: Houghton Mifflin Company, 1952.

Cox, Miriam. *The Magic and the Sword: The Greek Myths Retold*. Evanston and White Plains: Row, Peterson and Company, 1956.

Creeley, Robert. "Heroes." In *The Norton Anthology of Poetry*, 599. New York: W.W. Norton & Company, 1975.

d'Aulaire, Ingri, and Parin d'Aulaire. *Book of Greek Myths*. New York: Dell Publishing, 1992.

Griffin, Jasper. "Reading Homer after 2,800 Years." *Archaeology Odyssey* 1 (Premiere Issue 1998): 34-39.

De Columnis, Guido. *Historia Destructionis Troiae*. Cambridge: Harvard University Press, 1936.

Dictys of Crete and Dares the Phrygian. *The Trojan War: The Chronicles of Dictys of Crete and Dares the Phrygian*. Trans. R.M. Frazer, Jr. Bloomington and London: Indiana University Press, 1966.

Dio Chrysostom. *Discourses*, vol. I. Trans. J. W. Cohoon (Loeb Classical Library). Cambridge: Harvard University Press, 1932.

Diodorus Siculus. *Library of History*, vol. I. Trans. C.H. Oldfather (Loeb Classical Library). Cambridge: Harvard University Press, 1933.

Dionysus of Halicarnassus. *Roman Antiquities*, vol. I. Trans. Earnest Cary (Loeb Classical Library). Cambridge: Harvard University Press, 1937.

Dreyfus, Renee, and Ellen Schraudolph. *Pergamon: The Telephos Frieze from the Great Altar*, 2 volumes. San Francisco: Fine Arts Museums of San Francisco, 1996.

Dryden, John. "Song from Troilus and Cressida." In *The Norton Anthology of Poetry*, 160. New York: W.W. Norton & Company, 1975.

Eneas: A Twelfth Century Romance. Trans. John A. Yunck. New York and London: Columbia University Press, 1974.

Ennius. *Tragedies*. In *Remains of Old Latin*, vol. I, 218. Trans. E.H. Warmington (Loeb Classical Library). Cambridge: Harvard University Press, 1935.

Erskine, John. *The Private Life of Helen of Troy*. Indianapolis: The Bobbs-Merrill Company, 1925.

Euripides. *Hecuba*. Trans. Janet Lembke and Kenneth J. Reckford. New York and Oxford: Oxford University Press, 1991.

—. *The Plays of Euripides (Rhesus, The Trojan Women, Helen, Andromache, Electra, Hecuba, Orestes, and Iphigenia at Aulis)*. In *Aeschylus, Sophocles, Euripides, Aristophanes*. Trans. Edward P. Coleridge (Great Books of the Western World series). Chicago: Encyclopaedia Britannica, 1952.

—. *The Trojan Women*. Trans. Edith Hamilton. Including the screenplay by Michael Cacoyannis. New York: Bantam Books, 1971.

—. *The Trojan Women*. Adapted by Marianne McDonald. Old Globe Theatre, San Diego, October 2000.

—. *The Women of Troy and Helen*. In *The Bacchae and Other Plays*. Trans. by Philip Vellacott. Harmondsworth: Penguin, 1954.

Evslin, Bernard. *The Trojan War*. New York: Scholastic Book Services, 1971.

Fontenrose, Joseph. *The Delphic Oracle: Its Responses and Operations*. Berkeley: University of California Press, 1978.

Gantz, Timothy. *Early Greek Myth*. Baltimore: Johns Hopkins University Press, 1993.

Goodrich, Norma Lorre. *Ancient Myths.* New York and Scarborough, Ontario: A Mentor Book, 1960.

Gordon, R.K. *The Story of Troilus as told by Benoit de Sainte-Maure, Giovanni Boccaccio (translated into English Prose), Geoffrey Chaucer and Robert Henryson.* London: J.M. Dent & Sons, 1934.

Graves, Robert. *The Greek Myths,* 2 volumes. Harmondsworth: Penguin, 1960.

—. *The Siege and Fall of Troy.* New York: Dell Publishing Company, 1965.

Green, Roger Lancelyn. *The Tale of Troy.* Harmondsworth: Puffin Books, 1958.

Haaren, John H. *Famous Men of Greece.* New York: American Book Company, 1904.

H.D. (Hilda Doolittle). "Helen." In *The Norton Anthology of Poetry,* 502. New York: W.W. Norton & Company, 1975.

Helen of Troy (Four Color No. 684). New York: Dell Publishing Co., 1956.

Helen of Troy. Produced by Warner Bros. Directed by Robert Wise. 141 min. Warner Bros. Classics, 1996. Videocassette.

Herodotus. *The Persian Wars,* vol. 3. Trans. A.D. Godley (Loeb Classical Library). Cambridge: Harvard University Press, 1922.

Hesiod. *Theogony.* Trans. Norman O. Brown. New York: Macmillan, 1953.

Heywood, Thomas. *The Iron Age.* In *The Dramatic Works of Thomas Heywood,* vol. 3. N.P.: Pearson, 1874.

—. *Oenone and Paris.* In *Elizabethan Minor Epics,* ed. Elizabeth Story Donno, 127-54. New York: Columbia University Press, 1963.

Homer. *The Iliad.* Trans. Samuel Butler. Roslyn, NY: Walter J. Black, 1942.

—. *The Iliad.* Trans. William Cowper (abridged). Produced by Nicolas Soames. 3 hours 56 min. Naxos Audiobooks, 1995. Compact Disc.

—. *The Iliad.* Trans. Robert Fagles. Harmondsworth: Penguin, 1991.

—. *The Iliad.* Trans. Robert Fitzgerald. Recorded Books, 1994. Audio Cassette.

—. *The Iliad.* Trans. Andrew Lang, Walter Leaf, and Ernest Meyers. New York: Modern Library, 1950.

—. *The Iliad.* Trans. Alexander Pope. New York: W. Borradaile, 1825.

—. *The Iliad.* Trans. W.H.D. Rouse. Produced by Blackstone Audiobooks. Blackstone Audiobooks, 1991. Audio Cassette.

—. *The Odyssey.* Trans. Robert Fitzgerald. Garden City, NY: Anchor Books, 1963.

—. *The Odyssey.* Trans. Richmond Lattimore. New York: Harper & Row, Publishers, 1967.

—. *The Toils and Travels of Odysseus.* Trans. Cyril A. Pease. Boston: Allyn and Bacon, 1926.

[Homerica.] *Hesiod and the Homeric Hymns. Epic Cycle. Homerica.* Trans. H.G. Evelyn-White (Loeb Classical Library). Cambridge: Harvard University Press, 1914.

Hyginus. *The Myths.* Trans. Mary Grant. Lawrence: University of Kansas Press, 1960.

Kerenyi, C. *The Heroes of the Greeks.* Trans. H.J. Rose. N.P.: Thames & Hudson, 1974.

Landor, Walter Savage. "Past Ruined Ilion Helen Lives." In *The Norton Anthology of Poetry,* 272-73. New York: W.W. Norton & Company, 1975.

Lang, Andrew. *Helen of Troy.* Portland, Maine: Thomas B. Mosher, 1897.

Lefevre, Raoul. *Recuyell of the Historyes of Troye,* as translated and printed by William Caxton. London: David Nuttin, 1894.

Livius Andronicus. *Tragedies.* In *Remains of Old Latin,* vol. II, 2. Trans. E.H. Warmington (Loeb Classical Library). Cambridge: Harvard University Press, 1935.

Livy. *History of Rome,* vol. I. Trans. B.O. Foster (Loeb Classical Library). Cambridge: Harvard University Press, 1919.

Lucian. *Selected Satires.* Trans. Lionel Casson. New York: Norton Library, 1962.

Lucian. Volume VII. *Dialogues of the Dead. Dialogues of the Sea-Gods. Dialogues of the Gods. Dialogues of the Courtesans.* Trans. M.D. Macleod (Loeb Classical Library). Cambridge: Harvard University Press, 1961.

Lycophron. *Alexandra.* In *Callimachus and Lycophron.* Trans. A.W. Mair. New York: G.P. Putnam's Sons, 1921.

Malalas, John. *The Chronicle*. Trans. E. Jeffreys, M. Jeffreys, and Roger Scott. Melbourne: Australian Association for Byzantine Studies, 1986.

Marlowe, Christopher. *Dido, Queen of Carthage and The Tragical History of Doctor Faustus*. In *The Complete Plays*. Harmondsworth: Penguin, 1980.

—. *Doctor Faustus*. New York: Appleton-Century-Crofts, 1950.

Masefield, John. Excerpt from "The Taking of Helen." In *A Book of Prose Selections*, 88-97. New York: Macmillan, 1950.

—. *A Tale of Troy*. New York: Macmillan, 1932.

McLaughlin, Ellen. *Iphigenia and Other Daughters*. Chautauqua Conservatory Theater Company, Chautauqua, NY, August 1995 (reading), July 1996 (performance).

Meredith, Owen. *The Poetical Works*. New York: Thomas Y. Crowell & Co., n.d.

Morley, Christopher. *The Trojan Horse*. N.P.: J.B. Lippincott Company, 1957.

Naevius. *Tragedies*. In *Remains of Old Latin*, vol. II, 110-19. Trans. E.H. Warmington (Loeb Classical Library). Cambridge: Harvard University Press, 1935.

Nashe, Thomas. "A Litany in Time of Plague." In *The Norton Anthology of Poetry*, 87-88. New York: W.W. Norton & Company, 1975.

Ovid. *Volume V. Fasti*. Trans. Sir James George Frazer (Loeb Classical Library). Cambridge: Harvard University Press, 1931.

—. *Volume I. Heroides, Amores*. Trans. Grant Showerman (Loeb Classical Library). Cambridge: Harvard University Press, 1914.

—. *Metamorphoses*. Trans. Rolfe Humphries. Bloomington: Indiana University Press, 1955.

Parthenius. *The Love Romances*. In *Longus. Parthenius*. Trans. Stephen Gaselee (Loeb Classical Library). Cambridge: Harvard University Press, 1916.

Philostratus the Elder. *Imagines*. In *Philostratus the Elder. Philostratus the Younger. Callistratus*. Trans. Arthur Fairbanks (Loeb Classical Library). Cambridge: Harvard University Press, 1931.

Philostratus the Younger. *Imagines*. In *Philostratus the Elder. Philostratus the Younger. Callistratus*. Trans. Arthur Fairbanks (Loeb Classical Library). Cambridge: Harvard University Press, 1931.

Pindar. *Pindar's Victory Songs*. Trans. Frank J. Nisetich. Baltimore and London: Johns Hopkins University Press, 1980.

Pliny. *Natural History*, vol. IV. Trans. H. Rackham (Loeb Classical Library). Cambridge: Harvard University Press, 1945.

Plutarch. *Lives*. Trans. John Dryden. New York: Modern Library, n.d.

—. *Moralia*, vol. IV. Trans. Frank Cole Babbitt (Loeb Classical Library). Cambridge: Harvard University Press, 1936.

Poe, Edgar Allen. "To Helen." In *The Norton Anthology of Poetry*, 337. New York: W.W. Norton & Company, 1975.

Presson, Robert K. *Shakespeare's Troilus and Cressida & the Legends of Troy*. Madison: University of Wisconsin Press, 1953.

Quintus of Smyrna. *The War at Troy: What Homer Didn't Tell*. Trans. Frederick M. Combellack. Norman: University of Oklahoma Press, 1968.

Racine, Jean. *Andromache*. In *Andromache and Other Plays*. Trans. John Cairncross. Baltimore: Penguin, 1967.

—. *Iphigenia*. In *Iphigenia, Phaedra, Athaliah*. Trans. John Cairncross. Harmondsworth: Penguin, 1970.

Renault, Mary. *The Bull from the Sea*. New York: Pantheon Books, 1962.

Rose, H.J. *A Handbook of Greek Mythology*. New York: E.P. Dutton & Co., 1959.

Sappho. *Sappho and Alcaeus*. In *Greek Lyric*, vol. 1, 67, 88-91. Trans. David A. Campbell (Loeb Classical Library). Cambridge: Harvard University Press, 1982.

Scherer, Margaret R. *The Legends of Troy in Art and Literature*. New York and London: Phaidon Press, 1964.

Schwab, Gustav. *Gods and Heroes.* Trans. Olga Marx and Ernst Morwitz. New York: Pantheon, 1946.

Scodel, Ruth. "The Trojan Trilogy of Euripides." In *Hypomnemata, Untersuchungen zur Antike und zu Ihrem Nachleben,* Heft 60, 20-63. Gottingen: Vandenhoeck & Ruprecht, 1980.

Seneca. *Agamemnon.* Trans. John Studley. In *Seneca's Tragedies,* ed. Eric C. Baade. New York: Macmillan, 1969.

—. *The Daughters of Troy.* In *Two Tragedies.* Trans. Ella Isabel Harris. Boston and New York: Houghton, Mifflin and Company, 1899.

—. *Thyestes.* Trans. E.F. Watling. Baltimore: Penguin, 1966.

—. *The Trojan Women.* Trans. E.F. Watling. In *Seneca. Thyestes, Phaedra, The Trojan Women, Oedipus; with Octavia.* New York: Penguin Classics, 1966.

Shakespeare, William. *The Tragedy of Troilus and Cressida.* New Haven: Yale University Press, 1956.

—. *Troilus and Cressida.* Produced by the BBC and Time-Life Films. The Complete Dramatic Works of William Shakespeare, 1981. Videocassette.

—. *Troilus and Cressida.* Delacorte Theatre, New York, August 1995.

Shelley, Percy Bysshe. "From Hellas: Two Choruses." In *The Norton Anthology of Poetry,* 298-300. New York: W.W. Norton & Company, 1975.

Sophocles. *Ajax* and *Philoctetes.* In *The Complete Greek Tragedies: Sophocles II,* ed. David Grene and Richmond Lattimore. Trans. various. New York: Washington Square Press, 1967.

—. *Ajax, Philoctetes,* and *Electra.* In *The Complete Plays.* Trans. Sir Richard Claverhouse Jebb, ed. Moses Hadas. New York: Bantam Books, 1967.

—. *Electra.* New Jersey Shakespeare Festival, Madison, NJ, June 1994.

—. *Sophocles: Tragedies and Fragments.* London: Isbister, 1902.

—. *The Plays of Sophocles (Ajax, Electra,* and *Philoctetes).* In *Aeschylus, Sophocles, Euripides, Aristophanes.* Trans. G.M. Cookson (Great Books of the Western World series). Chicago: Encyclopaedia Britannica, 1952.

Stanford, W.B., and J. V. Luce. *The Quest for Ulysses.* New York: Praeger Publishers, 1974.

Stansbury-O'Donnell. "Polygnotos's Iliupersis: A New Reconstruction." *American Journal of Archaeology,* 93:2 (1989): 203-15.

Statius. *Achilleid.* Trans. J.H. Mozley (Loeb Classical Library). Cambridge: Harvard University Press, 1928.

Steiner, George, ed. *Homer in English.* Harmondsworth: Penguin, 1996.

Stuart, Kelly. *Furious Blood.* Sledgehammer Theatre, San Diego, February 2000.

Sutcliffe, Rosemary. *Black Ships Before Troy: The Story of The Iliad.* New York: Delacorte Press, 1993.

"Tale CLVI. Of the Subversion of Troy." In *Gesta Romanorum: or, Entertaining Moral Tales.* Trans. the Rev. Charles Swan, revised Wynnard Hooper. New York: Dover Publications, 1959.

Taylor, N.B. *The Aeneid of Virgil.* New York: Henry Z. Walck, 1961.

Teasdale, Sara. "Helen of Troy." In *The Collected Poems.* New York: Macmillan, 1937.

Tennyson, Alfred, Lord. "Oenone," "The Lotos-Eaters," "A Dream of Fair Women," "Ulysses," and "Tithonus." In *The Complete Poetical Works.* Boston: Houghton Mifflin Company, 1898.

Tryphiodorus. *The Destruction of Troy: Being the Sequel of the Iliad.* Trans. J. Merrick. Printed at the Theatre, 1739.

—. *The Taking of Ilios.* In *Oppian, Colluthus, Tryphiodorus.* Trans. A.W. Mair (Loeb Classical Library). Cambridge: Harvard University Press, 1928.

Tuchman, Barbara W. *The March of Folly: From Troy to Vietnam.* New York: Alfred A. Knopf, 1984.

Virgil. *The Aeneid.* Trans. Robert Fitzgerald. New York: Vintage Books, 1984.

—. *Aeneid.* Trans. Levi Hart and V.R. Osborn. Eastchester, NY: Translation Publishing Company, 1961.

—. *The Aeneid.* Trans. C. Day Lewis. Garden City, New York: Doubleday Anchor Books, 1953.

—. *The Aeneid.* Trans. Allen Mandelbaum. New York: Bantam Books, 1972.

Von Kliest, Heinrich. *Penthesilea.* Trans. Joel Agee. N.P.: Michael di Capua Books, 1998.

Wager, C.H.A., ed. *The Seege of Troye,* edited from Manuscript Harl. 525. New York: Macmillan, 1899.

Walton, Sir William. *Troilus and Cressida*. Produced by Christopher Bishop. 67.37 min. EMI Classics, 1995. Compact disc with libretto.

Woodford, Susan. *The Trojan War in Ancient Art*. London: Gerald Duckworth & Co., 1993.

Yeats, William Butler. "Leda and the Swan." In *The Norton Anthology of Poetry*, 443. New York: W.W. Norton & Company, 1975.

THE CHARACTERS

Mackie, C.J. *The Characterization of Aeneas*. Edinburgh: Scottish Academic Press, 1988.

Meagher, Robert Emmet. *Helen: Myth, Legend, and the Culture of Misogyny*. New York: Continuum, 1995.

Sergent, Bernard. *Homosexuality in Greek Myth*. Trans. Arthur Goldhammer. Boston: Beacon Press, 1986.

Van Nortwick, Thomas. *Somewhere I Have Never Travelled: The Hero's Journey*. New York and Oxford: Oxford University Press, 1996.

Zanker, Graham. *The Heart of Achilles: Characterization and Personal Ethics in the Iliad*. Ann Arbor: University of Michigan Press, 1994.

THE SETTINGS IN GENERAL

Alexander, Caroline. "Echoes of the Heroic Age: Ancient Greece Part 1." *National Geographic* (December 1999): 54-79.

Baines, John, and Jaromir Malek. *Atlas of Ancient Egypt*. New York and Oxford: Facts on File, 1980.

Barbarian Tides (TimeFrame 1500-600 BC series). Alexandria, VA: Time-Life Books, 1987.

Baumann, Hans. *Lion Gate and Labyrinth*. Trans. Stella Humphries. New York: Pantheon Books, 1967.

Biers, William R. *The Archaeology of Greece: An Introduction*. Ithaca, NY: Cornell University Press, 1980.

Catling, Hector. "Sub-Minoan Burials from Crete." In *The Ages of Homer*, ed. Jane B. Carter and Sarah P. Morris, 131-136. Austin: University of Texas, 1995.

Cline, Eric H. "Achilles in Anatolia: Myth, History, and the Assuwa Rebellion." In *Crossing Boundaries and Linking Horizons*, ed. Gordon D. Young, 189-99. Bethesda, MD: CDL Press, 1997.

—. "Assuwa and the Achaeans: The Mycenaean Sword at Hattusas and its Possible Implications." *The Annual of the British School at Athens* 91 (1996): 137-51.

—. "Littoral Truths: The Perils of Seafaring in the Bronze Age." *Archaeology Odyssey* 2 (November/December 1999): 52-57, 61.

—, and Martin J. Cline. "Of Shoes and Ships and Sealing Wax." *Expedition* 33, 3 (1991): 46-54.

—. "A Possible Hittite Embargo Against the Mycenaeans." *Historia*, Band XL, Heft 1 (1991): 1-9.

—. *Sailing the Wine-Dark Sea: International Trade and the Late Bronze Age Aegean* (British Archaeological Reports series). Oxford: Tempus Reparatum, 1994

Cottrell, Leonard. *The Bull of Minos: The Discoveries of Schliemann and Evans*. New York: Facts on File, 1953.

Denham, H.M. *The Aegean: A Sea-Guide to its Coasts and Islands*. New York: W.W. Norton & Company, 1975.

—. *The Ionian Islands to Rhodes: A Sea-Guide*. New York: W.W. Norton & Company, 1976.

Dickinson, Oliver. *The Aegean Bronze Age*. Cambridge: Cambridge University Press, 1994.

Thomas, Carol G. "Searching for the Historical Homer." *Archaeology Odyssey* 1 (Premiere Issue 1998): 26-33.

Drews, Robert. *The End of the Bronze Age: Changes in Warfare and the Catastrophe ca. 1200 B.C.* Princeton, Princeton University Press, 1993.

Duruy, Victor. *The World of Legendary Greece*. New York and Paris: Leon Amiel, 1975.

Edmonds, I.G. *The Mysteries of Homer's Greeks*. New York: Elsevier/Nelson Books, 1981.

Gilbert, Katharine Stoddert, Joan K. Holt and Sara Hudson. *Treasures of Tutankhamun*. N.P.: Metropolitan Museum of Art, 1976.

Greece '84. N.P.: Greek National Tourist Organization, n.d.

Greece 1974. N.P.: National Tourist Organisation of Greece, 1973.

Hart, George. *Ancient Egypt* (Eyewitness Books series). New York: Alfred A. Knopf, 1990.

Hawkes, Jacquetta. *Dawn of the Gods*. New York: Random House, 1968.

Jones, Bernice R. "Revealing Minoan Fashions." *Archaeology* 53 (May/June 2000): 36-41.

Leacroft, Helen, and Richard Leacroft. *The Buildings of Ancient Greece*. New York: William R. Scott, 1966.

Logiadou-Platanos, Mrs. Sosso. *Knossos: The Palace of Minos*. Athens: no publisher, 1979.

Lorimer, H.L. Homer and the Monuments. London: Macmillan, 1950.

Luce, J.V. *Celebrating Homer's Landscapes: Troy and Ithaca Revisited*. New Haven and London: Yale University Press, 1998.

—. *Homer and the Heroic Age*. New York: Harper & Row, Publishers, 1975.

MacKendrick, Paul. *The Greek Stones Speak*. New York and Toronto: A Mentor Book, 1966.

McDonald, William A. *Progress Into the Past*. Bloomington and London: Indiana University Press, 1969.

Mellink, Machteld J., ed. *Troy and the Trojan War: A Symposium Held at Bryn Mawr College, October 1984*. Bryn Mawr: Bryn Mawr College, 1986.

Myres, Sir John L. *Homer and His Critics*, ed. Dorothea Gray. London: Routledge & Kegan Paul, 1958.

Nur, Amos, and Eric H. Cline. "Poseidon's Horses: Plate Tectonics and Earthquake Storms in the Late Bronze Age Aegean and Eastern Mediterranean." *Journal of Archaeological Science*. [Publication data missing] 1999.

Preziosi, Donald, and Louise A. Hitchcock. *Aegean Art and Architecture*. Oxford and New York: Oxford University Press, 1999.

Quennell, Marjorie, and C.B.H. Quennell. *Everyday Things in Homeric Greece*. London: B.T. Batsford, 1929.

Pluckrose, Henry, ed. *Ancient Greeks*. New York and Toronto: Gloucester Press, 1982.

Reeves, Nicholas. *The Complete Tutankhamun: The King, The Tomb, The Treasure*. New York: Thames & Hudson, 1990.

Saggs, H.W.F. *Civilization Before Greece and Rome*. New Haven and London: Yale University Press, 1989.

Sakellarakis, J.A. *Herakleion Museum: Illustrated Guide to the Museum*. Athens: Ekdotike Athenon S.A., 1982.

Schliemann, Heinrich. *Troja*. New York: Arno Press, 1976.

Severin, Tim. *The Jason Voyage: The Quest for the Golden Fleece*. New York: Simon and Schuster, 1985.

Stead, Miriam. *Egyptian Life*. Cambridge: Harvard University Press, 1986.

Stewart, Desmond. *Turkey*. New York: Time, 1965.

Taylour, Lord William. *The Mycenaeans*. London: Thames and Hudson, 1983.

Ventura, Piero, and Gian Paolo Ceserani. *In Search of Troy*. Morristown, NJ: Silver Burdett Company, 1985.

Vermeule, Emily. *Greece in the Bronze Age*. Chicago: University of Chicago Press, 1972.

Venardis, Yiannis. *The Photographer of Skyros*. Athens: Edition: Society of Traditional Aegean Studies, 1984.

Wachsmann, Shelley. *Seagoing Ships & Seamanship in the Bronze Age Levant*. London: Chatham Publishing, 1998.

Warren, Peter. *The Making of the Past: The Aegean Civilizations*. New York: Peter Bedrick Books, 1989.

Webster, T.B.L. *From Mycenae to Homer*. New York: Norton Library, 1964.

221

~~~

Wilkinson, Charles K., and Marsha Hill. *Egyptian Wall Paintings: The Metropolitan Museum of Art's Collection of Facsimiles.* New York: Metropolitan Museum of Art, 1983.

Wondrous Realms of the Aegean (Lost Civilizations series). Alexandria, VA: Time-Life Books, 1993.

Wood, Michael. *In Search of the Trojan War.* New York and Oxford: Facts on File, 1985. Revised edition: Berkeley and Los Angeles: University of California Press, 1998.

—. *In Search of the Trojan War.* Produced by BBC. 6 hours. Privately recorded, 1984. Videocassette.

Troy

Alexander, Caroline. "Troy's Prodigious Ruin." *Natural History* 105 (April 1996): 42-51.

Brandau, Birgit. "Can Archaeology Discover Homer's Troy?" *Archaeology Odyssey* 1 (Premiere Issue 1998): 14-25.

Blegen, Carl W. *Troy and the Trojans.* New York: Frederick A. Praeger, 1963.

Duchene, Herve. *Golden Treasures of Troy: The Dream of Heinrich Schliemann.* Trans. Jeremy Leggatt. New York: Harry N. Abrams, 1996.

Dupont, Donald A. *Troy.* Albany, CA: Donald A. Dupont, 1977. Game.

Eberl, Ulrich. "Behind the Myth of Troy." *DaimlerBenz HighTechReport* (1/1995): 16-22.

Fleischman, John. "The Riddle of Troy." *The Sciences* (March/April 1994): 32-37.

—, and Coskun Aral. "Digging Deeper into the Mysteries of Troy." *Smithsonian* 22 (1992): 29-38.

Korfmann, Manfred, and Brian Rose. *Friends of Troy Newsletter.* Cincinnati: The Institute for Mediterranean Studies, November 1996.

—, and Brian Rose. *Friends of Troy Newsletter, 1997.* Cincinnati: The Institute for Mediterranean Studies, September 1997.

—, and Brian Rose. *Friends of Troy Newsletter 1998.* Cincinnati: The Institute for Mediterranean Studies, October 1998.

—, and Brian Rose. *Friends of Troy Newsletter 1999.* Cincinnati: The Institute for Mediterranean Studies, October 1999.

Ottaway, James H., Jr. "New Assault on Troy." *Archaeology* 44 (September/October 1991): 54-59.

Riorden, Elizabeth. "Visions of Troy." *Archaeology* 53 (January/February 2000): 52-59.

"Troy's Legend Grows." *Time* (March 1993): 22.

Studia Troica. Band 1. Mainz am Rhein: Verlag Philipp Von Zabern, 1991.

Studia Troica. Band 2. Mainz am Rhein: Verlag Philipp Von Zabern, 1992.

Studia Troica. Band 3. Mainz am Rhein: Verlag Philipp Von Zabern, 1993.

Studia Troica. Band 4. Mainz am Rhein: Verlag Philipp Von Zabern, 1994.

Studia Troica. Band 5. Mainz am Rhein: Verlag Philipp Von Zabern, 1995.

Studia Troica. Band 6. Mainz am Rhein: Verlag Philipp Von Zabern, 1996.

Studia Troica. Band 7. Mainz am Rhein: Verlag Philipp Von Zabern, 1997.

Studia Troica. Band 8. Mainz am Rhein: Verlag Philipp Von Zabern, 1998.

Troy: Results of the 1993 & 1994 Excavations. Narrated by C. Brian Rose. Produced by University of Cincinnati. Videocassette.

The Mycenaeans

Blegen, Carl W., and Marion Rawson. *The Palace of Nestor at Pylos in Western Messenia: Excavations conducted by the University of Cincinnati, 1939, 1952-1965,* vol. 1, 1-2, The Buildings and Their Contents. Princeton: Princeton University Press, 1966.

Chadwick, John. *The Mycenaean World.* Cambridge: Cambridge University Press, 1976.

Galaty, Michael L., and William A. Parkinson, eds. *Rethinking Mycenaean Palaces: New Interpretations of an Old Idea.* Los Angeles: Cotsen Institute of Archaeology at University of California, Los Angeles, 1999.

Hirsch, Ethel S. "Another Look at Minoan and Mycenaean Interrelationships in Floor Decoration." *American Journal of Archaeology* 84 (1980): 453-62.

The Illustrated Atlas of Archaeology. New York: Warwick Press, 1982.

Mabel Lang. *The Palace of Nestor at Pylos in Western Messenia: Excavations conducted by the University of Cincinnati, 1939, 1952-1965*, vol. 2, The Frescoes. Princeton: Princeton University Press, 1969.

Lenas, Peter M. *A Historical Guide: Old Corinth, Mycenae, Epidauros, Argos, Nauplia, Byzantine Churches*. Athens, P. Patsilinakos, n.d.

Mylonas, George E. *Mycenae and the Mycenaean Age*. Princeton: Princeton University Press, 1966.

Powell, Anton. *The Greek World*. New York: Warwick Press, 1987.

Prag, John, and Richard Neave. *Making Faces*. London: British Museum Press, 1999.

Robkin, Anne Lou. "The Agricultural Year, the Commodity *SA* and the Linen Industry of Mycenaean Pylos." *American Journal of Archaeology* 83 (1979): 469-74.

Tarsouli, Georgia. *Argolis: Mycenae, Tiryns, Nauplia, Epidaurus*. Athens: M. Pechlivanides & Co. S.A., n.d.

THE TROJANS (BASED UPON THE HITTITES)

Akurgal, Ekrem. *The Art of the Hittites*. London: Thames & Hudson, 1962.

Bryce, Trevor. *The Kingdom of the Hittites*. Oxford: Clarendon Press, 1998.

Burney, Charles. *The Ancient Near East*. Ithaca, NY: Cornell University Press, 1977.

Buttery, Alan. *Armies and Enemies of Ancient Egypt and Assyria, 3200 B.C. to 612 B.C.* (Ancients series). Sussex: Wargames Research Group, 1975.

Ceram, C.W. *The Secret of the Hittites: The Discovery of an Ancient Empire*. New York: Alfred A. Knopf, 1958.

Editors of Time-Life Books. *Anatolia: Cauldron of Cultures* (Lost Civilizations series). Alexandria, VA: Time-Life Books, 1995.

Gurney, O.R. *The Hittites*. Harmondsworth: Penguin, 1990.

Guterbock, H.G., and Timothy Kendall. "A Hittite Silver Vessel in the Form of a Fist." In *The Ages of Homer*, ed. Jane B. Carter and Sarah P. Morris, 131-136. Austin: University of Texas, 1995.

Healy, Mark. *Qadesh 1300 BC: Clash of the Warrior Kings* (Campaign Series). London: Osprey Publishing, 1993.

Hicks, Jim, and the editors of Time-Life Books. *The Empire Builders* (The Emergence of Man series). New York: Time-Life Books, 1974.

Lehmann, Johannes. *The Hittites: People of a Thousand Gods*. Trans. J. Maxwell Brownjohn. New York: Viking Press, 1977.

Lloyd, Seton. *Ancient Turkey: A Traveller's History of Anatolia*. N.P.: University of California Press, 1989.

MacQueen, J.G. *The Hittites and Their Contemporaries in Asia Minor*. Boulder, CO: Westview Press, 1975. Revised edition, London: Thames & Hudson, 1986.

Mikasa, Prince Takahito, ed. *Essays on Ancient Anatolia and Its Surrounding Civilizations*. Wiesbaden: Harrassowitz Verlag, 1995.

Morrison, Sean. *Armor*. New York, Thomas Y. Crowell Company, 1963.

Ozguc, Tahsin. "Excavations at the Hittite Site, Masat Hoyuk: Palace, Archives, Mycenaean Pottery." *American Journal of Archaeology* 84 (1980): 305-09.

Pritchard, James B. ed. *The Ancient Near East, Volume 1: An Anthology of Text and Pictures*. Princeton: Princeton University Press, 1958.

Vieyra, Maurice. *Hittite Art 2300-750 B.C.* London: Alec Tiranti, 1955.

223

MORE GREAT BOOKS FROM IMAGE COMICS

40 OZ. COLLECTED TP
ISBN# 1582403298
$9.95

AGE OF BRONZE
VOL. 1: A THOUSAND SHIPS TP
issues 1-9
ISBN# 1582402000
$19.95
VOL. 2: SACRIFICE HC
issues 10-19
ISBN# 1582403600
$29.95

THE BLACK FOREST GN
ISBN# 1582403503
$9.95

CITY OF SILENCE TP
ISBN# 1582403678
$9.95

CLASSIC 40 OZ.:
TALES FROM THE BROWN BAG TP
ISBN# 1582404380
$14.95

CREASED GN
ISBN# 1582404216
$9.95

DEEP SLEEPER TP
ISBN# 1582404933
$12.95

DIORAMAS, A LOVE STORY GN
ISBN# 1582403597
$12.95

EARTHBOY JACOBUS GN
ISBN# 1582404925
$17.95

FLIGHT, VOL. 1 GN
ISBN# 1582403816
$19.95

FLIGHT, VOL. 2 GN
ISBN# 1582404771
$24.95

FOUR-LETTER WORLDS GN
ISBN# 1582404399
$12.95

GRRL SCOUTS
VOL. 1 TP
ISBN# 1582403163
$12.95
VOL. 2: WORK SUCKS TP
ISBN# 1582403430
$12.95

HAWAIIAN DICK, VOL. 1:
BYRD OF PARADISE TP
ISBN# 1582403171
$14.95

HEAVEN, LLC. GN
ISBN# 1582403511
$12.95

KANE
VOL. 1: GREETINGS FROM NEW EDEN TP
issues 1-4
ISBN# 1582403406
$11.95
VOL. 2: RABBIT HUNT TP
issues 5-8
ISBN# 1582403554
$12.95
VOL. 3: HISTORIES TP
issues 9-12
ISBN# 1582403821
$12.95
VOL. 4: THIRTY NINTH TP
issues 13-18
ISBN# 1582404682
$16.95

LAZARUS CHURCHYARD
THE FINAL CUT GN
ISBN# 1582401802
$14.95

LIBERTY MEADOWS
VOL. 1:
EDEN LANDSCAPE ED TP
issues 1-9
ISBN# 1582402604
$19.95
VOL. 2:
CREATURE COMFORTS HC
issues 10-18
ISBN# 1582403333
$24.95

PUTTIN' THE BACKBONE BACK TP
(MR)
ISBN# 158240402X
$9.95

PvP
THE DORK AGES TP
original miniseries 1-6
ISBN# 1582403457
$11.95
VOL.1: PVP AT LARGE TP
issues 1-6
ISBN# 1582403740
$11.95
VOL. 2: PVP RELOADED TP
issues 7-12
ISBN# 158240433X
$11.95

REX MUNDI
VOL. 1:
THE GUARDIAN OF THE TEMPLE TP
issues 0-5
ISBN# 158240268X
$14.95
VOL. 2:
THE RIVER UNDERGROUND TP
issues 6-11
ISBN# 1582404798
$14.95

SMALL GODS, VOL. 1:
KILLING GRIN TP
issues 1-4
ISBN# 1582404577
$9.95

TOMMYSAURUS REX GN
ISBN# 1582403953
$11.95

ULTRA: SEVEN DAYS TP
ISBN# 1582404836
$17.95

THE WALKING DEAD
VOL. 1: DAYS GONE BYE TP
issues 1-6
ISBN# 1582403589
$12.95
VOL. 2: MILES BEHIND US TP
issues 7-12
ISBN# 1582404135
$12.95
VOL. 3: SAFETY BEHIND BARS TP
issues 13-18
ISBN# 1582404879
$12.95

THE WICKED WEST GN
ISBN# 1582404143
$9.95

For a comic shop near you carrying graphic novels from Image Comics, please call toll free: 1-888-COMIC-BOOK